APPROACHING THE DISCIPLINE OF

INTERNATIONAL RELATIONS

COMPETING PARADIGMS AND CONTRASTING EPISTEMES

APPROACHING THE DISCIPLINE OF INTERNATIONAL RELATIONS

COMPETING PARADIGMS AND CONTRASTING EPISTEMES

NADIA MOSTAFA

Edited by AMIRA ABOU SAMRA (ACADEMIC REVISOR AND EDITOR) *and* MOHAMMAD ABDERRAZZAQ

Translated from the Arabic by GAMAL ELGEZEERY *and* ALIAA WAGDY

INTERNATIONAL INSTITUTE OF ISLAMIC THOUGHT

LONDON · WASHINGTON

IIIT, P.O. Box 669, Herndon, VA 20172, USA • www.iiit.org
P.O. Box 126, Richmond, Surrey TW9 2UD, UK • www.iiituk.com

ISBN 978-1-64205-608-2 PAPERBACK
ISBN 978-1-64205-607-5 HARDBACK
ISBN 978-1-64205-606-8 EBOOK

Layout and Design by Shiraz Khan

Printed in USA

TO ALL THOSE WHO BELIEVE IN
DIVERSITY, ACQUAINTANCE, AND DIALOGUE

*

TO MY STUDENTS
WHOM I HAVE LEARNED WITH AND FROM

CONTENT

Acknowledgments XI
Publisher's Note XIII
Foreword XV
Author's Preface XXIII

PART I: INTRODUCTION: THEORIZING INTERNATIONAL RELATIONS 1

1. PATTERNS OF THEORIZING AND REASONS FOR THEORETICAL DIVERSITY AND PLURALITY 3
   1.1 The Essence and Significance of Theorizing 5
   1.2 Paradigms and The Paradigm Debates as an Approach to the Study of IR Theory 8

2. CONTRASTING EPISTEMES AND THEIR IMPACT ON THEORIZING 14
   2.1 The Essence of Contrasting Epistemes 15
   2.2 The Impact of Epistemological Differences on Theorizing 21

PART II: THE PARADIGM DEBATES: FROM DOMINANT PARADIGMS TO THE CRISIS OF THE DISCIPLINE 31

3. THE THREE GREAT DEBATES: FROM DOMINANT PARADIGMS TO COMPETING PARADIGMS 35
   3.1 The First Debate: Idealism versus Traditional Realism 36
   3.2 The Second Debate: Traditionalism versus Behavioralism 38
   3.3 The Third Debate: Realism versus Liberalism 40

4. THE END OF THE COLD WAR: TOWARDS A CRISIS IN THE DISCIPLINE OF IR 49
   4.1 The Characteristics of Post-Cold War International Relations 51
   4.2 Globalization: The Concept and its Impacts from the Perspective of Competing Paradigms 55

5. DEBATES BETWEEN COMPETING PARADIGMS: A DIVIDED DISCIPLINE 70
5.1 The Chaotic Designation of Paradigms 70
5.2 The Multiplicity of Schools and Strands 71
5.3 The Erosion of Boundaries between Paradigms 71
5.4 Can Paradigm Debates be Settled? 72
5.5 The Approach of Successive Competing Paradigms and the Perpetual Movement of Science 73
5.6 The General Pattern of the Evolution of Paradigm Debates 74
5.7 The Impact of Western-Centrism on the Discipline of IR: Claims of Universality in Question 76

PART III: THE CRISIS OF THE DISCIPLINE AND THE RISE OF CRITICAL APPROACHES: AN EPISTEMOLOGICAL TURN IN WESTERN THEORISING 81

6. THE GROUNDS FOR THE CRITICISM OF POSITIVISM AND WESTERN-CENTRISM AND THE MAP OF CRITICAL THEORETICAL APPROACHES 90
6.1 The Grounds for the Criticism of Positivism and Western-Centrism 90
6.2 The Map of Critical Theoretical Approaches: Assumptions and Hypotheses, and the Rationalist Positivist Counter-Criticism 94

7. THE DEFINING FEATURES OF CRITICAL THEORETICAL APPROACHES 108
7.1 Renewed and Rising Interest in Values 114
7.2 The Rise of Interest in Religious, Cultural, and Civilizational Dimensions 118
7.3 The Western-Centrism of the International Relations Discipline: The Criticism of Claims of Universality 126
7.4 Interdisciplinarity: The Engagement with Thought and History in International Theorizing as an Example 129
7.5 Global Change: The Relationship between Power and Knowledge and the Growing Significance of Normative Dimensions 133

PART IV: A COMPARATIVE ISLAMIC CIVILIZATIONAL PARADIGM OF INTERNATIONAL RELATIONS: THE MAP OF PROBLEMATICS AND CHARACTERISTICS 157

8. THE CHARACTERISTICS AND SOURCES OF AN ISLAMIC CIVILIZATIONAL PARADIGM 168
8.1 The Relationship between the Constant and the Variable Sources of the Paradigm 169
8.2 The Problematics of the Relationship between Values and Reality From an Islamic Perspective 190

9. THE ASSUMPTIONS OF AN ISLAMIC CIVILIZATIONAL PARADIGM: A COMPARATIVE MAP 208

9.1 Mapping the Assumptions of the Paradigms: A Horizontal Comparison 210
9.2 Mapping the Assumptions of the Islamic Civilizational Paradigm 214
9.3 Da'wah, Power, and Jihad 217
9.4 Actors and Units and Levels of Analysis 222
9.5 International Processes, Interactions, and Tools 228
9.6 The System of Interrelated and Concerted Issues 229

10. APPLYING THE ISLAMIC PERSPECTIVE TO CONTEMPORARY INTERNATIONAL RELATIONS ISSUES: MOTIVES AND CRITICISM 245

10.1 Areas and Objectives of Application 250
10.2 The Islamic Civilizational Paradigm: Questioned, Refuted, and Criticized 256
10.3 The Islamic Civilizational Paradigm: Academic Reactions 262

CONCLUSION 275

Bibliography 277

About the Author 312

ACKNOWLEDGMENTS

I am indebted to many throughout my career who have been instrumental in bringing this work to fruition, *alhamdulillah*. First and foremost my family, especially my late husband Dr. Hussein Saad, who generously provided me with the essential moral and material support I needed.

My deep and sincere thanks to my home department and institution, the Faculty of Economics and Political Science, Cairo University, for providing the rich and pluralist academic setting and thereby diverse opportunities for intellectual and academic interaction, of which this book is largely a product. Central to this interaction have been my esteemed colleagues and students, especially my graduate students, who have learned with me and whom I have learned from.

I extend my immense gratitude to the International Institute of Islamic Thought (IIIT) for sponsoring my "collective" research experience since 1986; an experience that was initiated in search of an Islamic Civilizational Paradigm of International Relations and which has continued contributing to its construction and development ever since. The Civilization Center – also established by IIIT- has played a central role in this research process since 1997.

My deep appreciation goes to the various Western IR paradigms, whose diversified production, rigorous debates, and critical self-reflection have enriched my knowledge and understanding of the field. In the process I have come to appreciate how the differing Western schools of IR construct maps of the field and academically engage with each other to produce accumulative and novel knowledge. I have also seen the fissures, including how claims to universality and superiority upheld by certain of these paradigms, have been challenged by other paradigms. Realizing as a corollary that nothing about IR theories is absolute or universal, and that IR theory is rather predominantly Western-centric, I was led to question the suitability of IR theories to non-Western civilizational contexts.

I would also like to acknowledge the great value added to my research through acquaintance with the world's various cultures, civilizations, and religions which became perfect arenas for testing and generating ideas and theories. What I became deeply aware of was the fact of multiple crises afflicting societies world widely, in particular the crisis of moral values, and the need for unbiased and informed solutions to effectively deal with and eliminate them.

Last but not least, special thanks go to all those involved in the publication of the English version of this study, including Dr. Ahmed Alwani, Vice President of IIIT, for initiating the idea, Gamal Elgezeery and Aliaa Wagdy for their superb translation, Dr. Haggag Ali for his important edits, and Dr. Mohammad Abderrazzaq for his invaluable editing and management of the publication process. My deep thanks to Dr. Amira Abou Samra, Associate Professor of Political Science at the Faculty of Economics and Political Science, who also happens to be a former distinguished student of mine whilst doing her Master's and Doctoral studies and who has taken part in many of my research projects. I thank her for her support in the academic revision and editing of the translated text of this study. It was a difficult task that only she was uniquely qualified to do being deeply engaged with Western schools of IR and strongly interested in developing an Islamic Civilizational Paradigm in the discipline. Finally, my sincere thanks and appreciation to Professor Bahgat Korany for his insightful Foreword to this book.

PUBLISHER'S NOTE

THE INTERNATIONAL INSTITUTE OF ISLAMIC THOUGHT is pleased to present this important work on *Approaching the Discipline of International Relations: Competing Paradigms and Contrasting Epistemes.* The study attempts to present an Islamic paradigm of International Relations, exploring historical developments and dominant paradigms intrinsic to the discipline of IR as studied from a Euro-centric, Western perspective, and to question their efficacy in relation to the socio-economic-religious realities and context of the Muslim world which are in dire need of change. Terminologies and concepts such as Ummah are developed as integral aspects of an Islamic Paradigm of International Relations theory, with premises rooted in the foundational sources of the Qur'an and the Sunnah.

In constructing an Islamic Paradigm of International Relations theory the author simultaneously challenges the place that Islam broadly occupies within secular paradigms currently dominating IR theory in academia and explores the type of research questions and analysis that need to be addressed for an Islamic paradigm to have a viable future.

Written in a clear and lucid style, the book will benefit both general and specialist readers alike, increasing their awareness of the issue of International Relations as a discipline and the cultural-specific values inherent in paradigms taken from a Western perspective.

Since its establishment in 1981, the IIIT has served as a major center to facilitate serious scholarly efforts. Towards this end it has, over the decades, conducted numerous programs of research, seminars, and conferences as well as published scholarly works specializing in the social sciences and areas of theology, which to date number more than seven hundred titles in English and Arabic, many of which have been translated into other major languages.

We would like to thank Professor Nadia Mahmoud Mostafa for her cooperation throughout the various stages of the book's production. We also thank Dr. Haggag Ali for overseeing the translation process, the translators, Gamal Elgezeery and Aliaa Wagdy for the quality of their work, as well as Dr. Amira Abou Samra and Dr. Mohammad Abderrazzaq for their invaluable revision and editorial work on the translation. Finally, our gratitude to all those who were directly or indirectly involved in the completion of this book. May God reward them for their efforts.

IIIT

MARCH 2022

FOREWORD

Professor Nadia Mahmoud Mostafa's *Approaching the Discipline of International Relations: Competing Paradigms and Contrasting Epistemes* is an important contribution to the growing body of knowledge in the field of IR. This volume forms the culmination of several works of a school of thought at Cairo University's Faculty of Economics and Political Science under the leadership of Mostafa, a prolific author in Arabic and an award-winning scholar. Mostafa's approach, continuing the inter-paradigm debate in international relations theory, has been to focus on providing an "Islamic perspective" to the study and analysis of IR, that is an identifiable school of thought with an emphasis on the "civilizational" component. Mostafa's work comprises a series of publications mainly in Arabic associated with this perspective, and a series of graduate studies which include some distinguished doctoral dissertations. Basically, it presents an Islam-based epistemological approach, in the sense of, as Mostafa tells us in the introduction to Part IV, an "Islamic *civilizational* paradigm," not merely an "Islamic paradigm" [emphasis mine].

The work is rich and informative tracing the evolution and fundamental premises of this school of thought from its origins almost forty years ago. And I am fortunate to have witnessed its development through conferences and workshops organized in Cairo which I was invited to attend, as well as to have been a thesis committee member for some of the School's numerous doctoral students. Given the critical nature of the questions Mostafa and her research team have examined and continue to address, as well as their significance, I have often suggested, even insisted, that these contributions should not be limited to their local sphere or published in Arabic alone, but rather be more widely known, with the objective of informing an English-speaking readership of the contribution and findings of Mostafa and her team, as well as acquainting them with the School's publications. The translation of this work from Arabic into English in my opinion adds significantly to current literature on IR as well as to the inter-paradigm debate in international relations theory.

Mostafa's book is an essential component of critical International Relations Theory (IRT), as developed by such notable authorities as my former professor Robert Cox. Though Cox is not mentioned in the references, Mostafa's book is indeed a confirmation and development of his contribution and the general thrust of critical IRT.[1] Interestingly, Chapter 11 in Cox's intellectual autobiography (2013) is entitled "Civilizations and World Order."[2] But differently from Cox's focus on political economy, Mostafa emphasizes the significance of a "cultural perspective." Differently also from Edward Said's classic *Orientalism*,[3] Mostafa situates her emphasis on a cultural perspective within a wider interest in non-material factors of IR and the importance of components such as values and identity. But whatever differences with other (critical) contributions, epistemological issues are shared and conceptual/methodological concerns respected. For instance, Mostafa does not avoid the nagging dialectical relation between the "constant" and the "changing" in Islamic principles and practice. Instead, she insists on the analytical link among the three basic components of Islam's episteme, history/practice, and evolving thought. As she tells us in Chapter 8, "In fact, we cannot separate the foundational sources (the sources of the worldview and episteme, i.e., the Quran and Sunnah) from history (practical experience), and thought (systems of values, priorities of interest, and responses to international changes)."

This delving into such Islamic specifics does not distract, however, from the book's main objective: the link to the wider IR discipline. Given its cultural emphasis, the book indeed reflects the rise of interest in values and identity, and joins IRT works associated with Social Constructivism. For as employed in the book, the "Islamic perspective" is not reduced to a narrow religious one but used in the sense of a wider "civilizational" approach. This is indeed the name of the Research Center where she and her team meet and dialogue. Chapters 8, 9, and 10 are very explicit and detailed in this respect. Specifically in relation to IRT, these chapters insist on two cardinal aspects: (1) the primacy of a normative approach and the significance of non-material factors in IR; and (2) in terms of international actors, the book emphasizes the importance of transnationalism based on the Ummah or global Muslim community rather than a state-centric approach.

Moreover, contrary to the view expressed in many explicit critical perspectives, this book's "civilizational" approach is not a monologue. On the contrary, it details standard IRT approaches and inter-paradigm debates. In fact, no less than half this book – chapters two to seven – is a presentation of these various debates and a discussion of their general propositions as well as their epistemological premises, as evidenced by its over 340 notes. And many of these notes are not limited to mentioning references but also offer detailed comments. Nadia Mostafa has indeed done her homework. As a result, and differently from some critical publications, this book promotes inter-school debate, to counter IR bias/partiality.

As the book's basic premise and its *raison d'etre*, how real is this partiality in contemporary IRT – supposedly universal by definition? Does this IR field continue to be – as Stanley Hoffmann asserted more than forty years ago – an "American Social Science," with all that this characterization implies? What do more recent findings tell us?

Even before seeing Mostafa's present book, I wanted to explore if Hoffmann's characterization of the field still persists.[4] Consequently, I embarked on my own content analysis of two influential handbooks by major publishers: the *Oxford Handbook of International Relations* and Sage's *Handbook of International Relations.*[5] As we know, such handbooks are both influential syntheses of knowledge in the field and also visible signposts mapping the field's future, even directing it. In relation to what Mostafa tells us, what do these major overviews/syntheses tell us about the current state of IR?

These two handbooks are composed of 77 chapters, totaling 1649 pages, by 91 authors, heavyweight in the field. Their research is truly impressive, at least quantitatively, being based on 7762 references. *Qualitatively*, however, these references tell a different story. Scratching beyond the surface shows that the field has not evolved beyond Hoffmann's characterization of IR more than 40 years ago as an "American Social Science." Content analysis data of both handbooks show some modest evolution in IRT, but the discipline is still very much American-based – epistemologically, conceptually, and methodologically. Here are some examples:

1. Many authors still speak in the first person: essentially, Americans addressing Americans (e.g., "our" foreign policy). If the author's name was to be anonymous, there would be no difficulty for any reader to know where the author is from and who their primary audience is.
2. IR is represented as a discipline which primarily Americans – or Anglo-Saxons – contribute to. The discipline is shown as revolving around the US, whereas the world outside there is beyond the water's edge – as Hoffmann's 1977 article says, "a relative zone of darkness."
3. Despite the large number of sources used, they are usually unilingual and mostly American sources. If "foreigners" are cited, they are usually those who have published in American journals or collaborated with American institutions. IR speaks English, and principally with an American accent.
4. The discipline is not only American-centric, but, even worse, verges on being incestuous. For instance, as even some North American scholars have lamented, authors dealing with similar topics but publishing in different U.S. Journals (e.g., *Journal of Conflict Resolution* vs. *International Security*) rarely quote each other. Thus, American academic tribes and cartels and their mutual neglect/narrow debate are brought in this supposedly universal field. Any potential breadth of vision is sacrificed.

No wonder that the cold war was described as the period of the "long peace," when the longest war in the post-1945 period, the Iran-Iraq one 1980-1988, had taken place. Moreover, IRT was busy splitting hairs between Neo-Realism/Neo-Liberalism and their different branches when the Berlin Wall was falling and the USSR was collapsing.

The required methodological replication supports Mostafa's basic premise about this partial aspect of IRT, confirming past and present analyses: dominant IR Theory still suffers from such high realm of narrowness/parochialism in relation to contemporary global complexity, and consequently fails in its mission as a universal discipline. One can go further and state that IRT is still partial in the double sense of the word: incomplete and biased. As a result, the unavoidable question is, as Lenin put it in a different context: what is to be done? A mandatory prerequisite step is to work for IRT universalization by bringing in other perspectives, especially from the marginalized Global South. After all, this Global South constitutes a "core" not only in global resources but also in central IR issues such as governance and state-formation/deformation.

This is why this book is important, as it contributes to the furthering of this objective, starting with Mostafa's commitment to a "scientific" approach, in terms of respect for rigor and openness. This commitment is explicit all along, right to her discussion of this Islamic/civilizational perspective. Interestingly, this scientific commitment reminds me of one of my classes in primary school where the religion teacher insistently attracted our attention to Islam's absolute respect of science and science-based knowledge. He used to quote one of the early admonitions by the archangel Gabriel to Prophet Muhammad, *iqrā'* (read), which eventually became the title of Surah 96 in the Qur'an. Similarly, the French surgeon Maurice Bucaille also thought it important to remind us of the Qur'an's respect for science by documenting Islam's great progress in astronomy.[6] Mostafa's scientific commitment is the more needed in the present context, a context too often dominated by both the hijacking of Islamic slogans by some violent groups and the prevalence of Islamophobia. In presenting the "civilizational perspective" to widen and deepen the debate on IRT, Mostafa's book thus offers some clarification about the relationship between Islam and science.

This "scientific" approach is also based – as scientific canons require – on openness. As Mostafa explicitly states in the introduction to Part IV:

> ... I do not claim that my conception of the Islamic civilizational paradigm is the only one available, nor the most original one. Rather, this conception

> only reflects my personal experience with the construction of an Islamic paradigm in IR. The proposed paradigm represents an open and interactive system, whose supporters neither consider it to be perfect, nor absolute.

The main objective of this civilizational paradigm then is an open and inclusionary IR discipline. An early contributor to this perspective, the late Mona Abul-Fadl, expressed it well: an IR discipline as an open ground where East meets West. This objective is not yet attained. Though IR schools have multiplied, this was not translated into multiplicity of basic paradigms. We are still dominated at best by a Western-centric paradigm, frequently an American-based one.

Whether we accept all or only part of this book's contribution, we can still agree that this is an important publication, indeed a milestone on the inter-paradigm debate in IR. It adds to the critical approach and joins such specific fields as Critical Security Studies and Foreign Policy Analysis.[7] The book really widens/deepens the overall debate on the required globalization of IRT and offers operational guidelines.[8] It thus suggests enlarging the IRT agenda by inviting us to bring back universal history. Specifically, it advises us to research what we can learn from examining patterns of Islamic history, including: characteristics of Islamic empires, original Islamic capitalism, impact of early trade diffusion and transnational interconnectedness, potentially distinct modes of Islamic sovereignty, and socialization and governance.

While pondering this agenda and even adding to it, this book will already encourage many of us to reconsider their epistemological penchant and conceptual lenses. In this respect, the IR discipline and its "inter-paradigm debates" will not be the same after reading Mostafa's *Approaching the Discipline of International Relations: Competing Paradigms and Contrasting Epistemes*.

BAHGAT KORANY

Professor of International Relations and Political Economy at the American University of Cairo (AUC) and Honorary Professor at the University of Montreal

JUNE 2020

NOTES

1. See: Robert W. Cox, *Production, Power, and World Order: Social Forces in the Making of History* (New York: Columbia University Press, 1987); Robert W. Cox and Timothy J. Sinclair, *Approaches to World Order* (Cambridge: Cambridge University Press, 1996).
2. Robert W. Cox, *Universal Foreigner: The Individual and the World* (Toh Tuck Link: World Scientific, 2013).
3. Edward W. Said, *Orientalism* (New York: Pantheon Books, 1978).
4. See: Bahgat Korany, "A Universal International Relations Discipline?" (Distinguished Global South Award speech, International Studies Association Convention, New Orleans, LA, 2015).
5. See: Christian Reus-Smit and Duncan Snidal, *The Oxford Handbook of International Relations* (New York: Oxford University Press, 2010); Walter Carlsnaes, Thomas Risse, and Beth A. Simmons, *Handbook of International Relations* (Thousand Oaks: SAGE, 2012).
6. See: Maurice Bucaille, *La Bible, le Coran et la science* (Paris: Seghers, 1976).
7. See: Keith Krause and Michael C. Williams, *Critical Security Studies: Concepts and Cases* (London: UCL Press, 1997); Klaus Brummer and Valerie M. Hudson, *Foreign Policy Analysis Beyond North America* (Boulder, CO: L. Rienner Publishers, 2015).
8. See: Amitav Acharya and Barry Buzan, *The Making of Global International Relations: Origins and Evolution of IR at its Centenary* (Cambridge: Cambridge University Press, 2019).

AUTHOR'S PREFACE

This study aims to introduce my own account of International Relations Theory. By no means do I claim to give *the* definitive account of the field. Rather, I give an account that reflects my own biases, and collective as well as individual experiences, which have been gathered over a four decade long journey involving comparative critical theorizing in the field of international relations (IR).[1]

That journey initially started from the mainstream domains of IR, i.e., from the Anglo-Saxon and Euro-Latin (especially French) literature in the field, which I was introduced to mainly while preparing for my Master's and PhD theses (1972-1981)[2] and during the early stages of individual research conducted into the theoretical aspects of the discipline (1981-1986).[3] Then a crucial transitional second stage set in as I participated in the "Project of International Relations in Islam" (1986-1996), which was to articulate a perspective that for me was formative. The Project was a collective and multidisciplinary endeavor that engaged with "Western theories and paradigms," explored the need for the construction of a comparative Islamic paradigm in the field of IR, reflected on the nature of that paradigm, including concepts and main assumptions, eventually contributing to the early stages of that paradigm's construction.[4]

The journey continued and its third stage (1996-2016) saw me gain experience in teaching and theoretical research, as well as supervising graduate theses. This culminated in the maturation of my hitherto developing critical perspective of the positivist paradigms and theories dominating (to deliberately avoid calling them "Western") academia, as well as crystallization of a notion and construction of an IR paradigm from a comparative Islamic civilizational perspective. The teaching and supervising role as well as its resulting valuable experience created a space for further examination, granting me a broad overview of the state of the discipline and its developments, whilst allowing comparison in relation to the "Islamic Civilizational Paradigm of International Relations"[5] and new critical theoretical approaches that have been on the rise particularly since the late 1990s.[6]

As the Islamic Civilizational Paradigm was clearly at this point moving beyond the foundational stage associated with the "Project of International Relations in Islam," I had to face the next and doubly complex challenge of developing it further, keeping abreast of emerging critical approaches in the field whilst maintaining a comparative outlook in relation to these and the Islamic paradigm. A major task was to critique and challenge the dominant positivist paradigms, a highly taboo subject because of the near universal acceptance of their validity and central tenets, especially the realist paradigm. Seminars as well as annual conferences, hosted by the Department of Political Science, were an outlet allowing the paradigm to engage with and challenge existing dominant paradigms, with the Islamic paradigm always receiving its share of debate and criticism – published records of the conferences and seminars attest to that.

As much as this study captures the historical development of International Relations as a discipline from its embryonic to its present state, it also attempts to critically engage with it from within. Analysis and inquiry focuses on matters pertaining to the pedagogy, content, and learning methods in the discipline, raising, thereby, multiple questions: How is IR being taught? What is being taught in IR? How can IR be studied? What is the content of IR that needs to be studied? Put differently, the study attempts to inductively reveal the theoretical diversity and multiplicity which is prevalent in the field of IR. By unraveling relevant aspects as well as examining the depth of the revision process which the dominant IR Theory has undergone, the study sets the stage for the introduction and the experience of a (non-Western) civilizational paradigm in IR. Thus, the overarching purpose and aim of this study justifies its approach to the state of the field, which analysis is pursued in four main parts.

Part 1 provides a methodological introduction to theorizing; its essence, its importance, and the reasons behind the plurality and diversity of theories. Chapter 1 attempts to explain the meaning and importance of theorizing, whereas Chapter 2 explores the differences between theoretical frameworks and the importance of approaching IR by calling upon paradigms and paradigm debates, as well as epistemological differences and their impact on theorizing.

Part II explores the first three great debates of the IR discipline, reflecting on the development of IR Theory from the stage of a dominant paradigm, through the stage of competing paradigms, to the stage of the crisis of a "divided discipline." Here, analysis covers three major points, corresponding to the following three chapters: Chapter 3 addresses particular features of the three great debates, from the dominant paradigm to competing paradigms; Chapter 4 treats the relationship between IR Theory and the end of the Cold War, from the stage of fluidity to the stage of a discipline in crisis; and Chapter 5 looks into the particular features of competing paradigms' debates, mainly the divide within the discipline.

Part III examines the crisis of a post-dominant paradigms-IR discipline and the rise of critical theoretical approaches, reflecting, thereby, on the prospects of an epistemological turn in Western theorizing. Chapter 5 maps these critical theoretical approaches, while looking at the criticisms they direct at positivism and Western centrism in the field. The common defining features of critical theoretical approaches are the focus of Chapter 7.

Finally, Part IV maps the problematics raised by a comparative Islamic Civilizational Paradigm of International Relations and its various aspects in three chapters. Chapter 8 defines the characteristics and sources of an Islamic Civilizational Paradigm. Chapter 9 examines the different assumptions of an Islamic Civilizational Paradigm compared to those of Western paradigms. Lastly, Chapter 10 identifies the agenda and maps the issues addressed by an Islamic Civilizational Paradigm in IR. The chapter also highlights aspects of criticism directed at the paradigm and at the prospects of its application.

NOTES

1. An elaborate account of the story behind my approach to International Relations theory can be found in *Al-ʿAlāqāt al-Dawliyyah fī ʿĀlim Mutaghayyir: Manẓūrāt wa Madākhil Muqāranah* [International Relations in a Changing World: Comparative Paradigms and Approaches], ed. Nadia Mahmoud Mostafa (Cairo: Hadara Center for Political Studies, 2016). The introduction (in volume one) to this three-volume work explains how it came about and what it aims to achieve. The three-volume work is comprised of seventeen studies taken from master's and doctoral theses authored by students of mine with research interest in international comparative theorization. These studies pertain to one of six main themes, of which extend a number of issues and topics, including: concepts (power, elites, civilizational change, civilizational relations), actors (states, alliances, peoples, and transnational and religious movements), international processes (wars, integration, international change, and rivalry), interdisciplinary areas and approaches (international political economy and international political thought), new theoretical trends, post-positivist and post-realist (globalism, cultural dimensions, normative dimensions, and new levels of analysis), and theoretical and practical issues (revolution, international public opinion institutions, American strategy toward the Arab world, and the formation of civilizational consciousness). The three-volume work was originally intended for Arab academia. It aims to explain the necessity of participating in a critical review of the state of the IR discipline, while also providing Arab academia an Islamic civilizational perspective on IR. This present work is a translation of the introduction (found in volume one) of the three-volume work. Its issuance is meant to fulfill a pivotal goal, that of providing Western academic circles exposure to an Islamic perspective of the IR discipline (especially those in Western academic circles who, over the past two decades, have been critical of Western-centric bias in the IR discipline and who have called for the participation of non-Western and Islamic perspectives). I should note that the lack of Western academic exposure to non-Western theories on IR has not been because of the nonexistence

of such theories; rather, it is due to several factors, including language barriers. The current work will thus enhance such exposure and fulfill several mutual academic objectives.

2. See the theoretical introductions in: Nadia Mostafa, "Al-Siyāsah al-Khārijiyyah li-Charles De Gaulle fī dhul al-Jumhūriyyah al-Khāmisah" [The Foreign Policy of Charles De Gaulle During the Fifth Republic] (master's thesis, Cairo University, 1976); "Siyāsah Faransiyyah Tijāha Azmat al-Sharq al-Awsaṭ (1967-1977)" [French Policy Towards the Middle East Crisis (1967-1977)] (PhD diss., Cairo University, 1981) (specifically, the dissertation chapter entitled, "Dawr al-Quwā al-Thānawiyyah Tijāha Ṣirāʿāt al-ʿĀlim al-Thālith" [The Role of Minor Powers Towards Third World Conflicts]).

3. The author's writings in this area include: "Muqadimah fī Dirāsat al-ʿAlaqāt al-Dawliyyah" [An Introduction to the Study of International Relations], (unpublished manuscript, 1981); "Naẓariyat al-Naẓm wa Dirāsat al-ʿAlaqāt al-Dawliyyah" [Systems Theory and the Study of International Relations], (unpublished manuscript, 1983); "Naẓariyat al-ʿAlaqāt al-Dawliyyah: Bayn al-Manẓūr al-Wāqiʿī wa al-Daʿwah ilā Manẓūr Jadīd" [International Relations Theory: Between the Realist Paradigm and the Call for a New One], *Al-Siyāsah Al-Dawliyyah*, no. 82 (1985): pp. 54-82; "Ḥawl Tajadud al-Ihtimām bi al-Iqtiṣād al-Siyāsī al-Dawlī" [On the Renewed Interest in International Political Economy], *Majalat al-ʿUlūm al-Ijtimāʿiyyah* 14, no. 3 (1986): pp. 15-42; "Muqadimah fī Naẓariyat al-ʿAlaqāt al-Dawliyyah" [An Introduction on International Relation's Theory] (unpublished manuscript, 1992).

4. The studies produced during this project were published as a twelve-part series. See Nadia Mostafa et al., *ʿAmāl Mashrūʿ al-ʿAlaqāt al-Dawliyyah* [The Project on International Relations in Islam] (Cairo: International Institute of Islamic Thought, 1996). The studies in this series include: Nadia M. Mostafa, *Al-Muqadimah al-ʿĀmah li al-Mashrūʿ* [An Introduction to the Project on International Relations in Islam], vol. 1 (Cairo: International Institute of Islamic Thought, 1996); Saif AbdelFattah, *Madkhal al-Qiyam Iṭār Marjaʿī li Dirāsat al-ʿAlaqāt al-Dawliyyah fī al-Islām* [Introduction to Values: A Referential Framework for the Study of International Relations in Islam], vol. 2 (Cairo: International Institute of Islamic Thought, 1996); Ahmad Abdelwanees et al., *Al-Madākhil al-Manhājiyyah li al-Baḥth fī al-*

ʿAlaqāt al-Dawliyyah fī al-Islām [Methodological Introductions for the Study of International Relations in Islam], vol. 3 (Cairo: International Institute of Islamic Thought, 1996); Mostafa Manjoud, *Al-Dawlah fī al-Islām: Waḥdat al-Taʿāmul al-Khārijī* [The State in Islam: The Unity of Foreign Action], vol. 4 (Cairo: International Institute of Islamic Thought, 1996); Ahmad Abdelwanees, *Al-Uṣūl al-ʿĀmah li al-ʿAlaqāt al-Dawliyyah fī al-Islām fī Waqt al-Silm* [General Foundations of International Relations in Islam in the Time of Peace], vol. 5 (Cairo: International Institute of Islamic Thought, 1996); A. Sakr, *Al-ʿAlaqāt al-Dawliyyah fī al-Islām fī Waqt al-Ḥarb: Dirāsat li al-Qawāʿid al-Munaẓamah li Sīr al-Qitāl* [International Relations in Islam in the Time of War: A Study of Rules of Engagement], vol. 6 (Cairo: International Institute of Islamic Thought, 1996); Nadia M. Mostafa, *Madkhal Minhājī li Dirāsat Taṭawur Waḍʿ wa Dawr al-ʿĀlim al-Islāmī fī al-Niẓām al-Dawlī* [Methodological Introduction for the Study of the Position and Role of the Islamic World in the World Order], vol. 7 (Cairo: International Institute of Islamic Thought, 1996); Ola Abou-Zeid, *Al-Dawlah al-Umawiyyah: Dawlat al-Futūḥāt* [The Umayyad Caliphate: The Age of Conquest (661-750 CE)], vol. 8 (Cairo: International Institute of Islamic Thought, 1996); Ola Abou-Zeid, *Al-Dawlah al-ʿAbāsiyyah: Min al-Takhallī ʿan Siyāsāt al-Fatḥ ilā al-Suqūṭ* [The Abbasid Caliphate: From Abandoning Policies of Conquest to its Downfall (750-1258 CE)], vol. 9 (Cairo: International Institute of Islamic Thought, 1996); Nadia M. Mostafa, *Al-ʿAṣr al-Mamlūkī: Min Taṣfiyat al-Wujūd al-Ṣalībī ilā Bidāyat al-Hajmah al-Awrūbiyyah al-Thāniyyah* [The Age of the Mamluks: From the End of the Crusaders Presence to the Beginning of the Second European Assault (1258-1517 CE), vol. 10 (Cairo: International Institute of Islamic Thought, 1996); Nadia Mostafa, *Al-ʿAṣr al-ʿUthmānī: Min al-Quwah wa al-Haymanah ilā Bidāyat al-Mas'alah al-Sharqiyyah* [The Ottoman Caliphate: From Power and Dominance to the Start of the Eastern Question], vol.11 (Cairo: International Institute of Islamic Thought, 1996); Wadoudah Badran, *Waḍʿ al-Duwal al-Islāmiyyah fi al-Niẓām al-Dawlī fī Aʿqāb Suqūṭ al-Khilāfah* [The Position of Islamic States in the International Order after the Fall of the Caliphate (1924-1991)], vol. 12 (Cairo: International Institute of Islamic Thought, 1996). A seminar was later held to discuss the project in 1997. Its studies were published in two volumes in N. Mostafa and S. Abdelfattah, eds., *Mashrūʿ al-ʿAlaqāt al-Dawliyyah fī al-Islām: Bayn al-Uṣūl al-Islāmiyyah wa Khibrat al-Tārīkh al-Islāmī* [The Project of International Relations in Islam: Between Islamic Fundamentals and Historic Experience] (Cairo: Cairo University Center of Political Research and Studies, 2000).

5. The "Islamic Civilizational Paradigm of International Relations," also referred to as "the Egyptian School of an Islamic Civilizational Paradigm" (written in capital letters), is the name given to the academic effort exerted by the Egyptian political science scholars working on constructing and developing an Islamic Paradigm of International Relations (IR). This is to distinguish these efforts from other efforts in the field that work on developing an Islamic perspective, theory, or paradigm, which will be referred to in small letters.

6. This study represents a culmination and further development of three previous studies I had presented during consecutive stages of comparing between Western paradigms and an Islamic paradigm in light of the state of the art. See: Nadia M. Mostafa, "ʿAmaliyat Bināʾ Manẓūr Islāmī li Dirāsat al-ʿAlaqāt al-Dawliyyah: Ishkāliyyāt Khibrat al-Baḥth wa al-Tadrīs" [The Process of Building an Islamic Paradigm for the Study of International Relations: Problems of Research and Teaching Experience], in *Al-Manhājiyyah al-Islāmiyyah fī al-ʿUlūm: Ḥaql al-ʿUlūm al-Siyāsiyyah Namūdhaj* [Islamic Methodology in the Social Sciences: The Case of Political Science], eds. Nadia M. Mostafa and Saif AbdelFattah (Cairo: Al-Hadara Center for Studies and Research and the International Institute of Islamic Thought, 2002); "Ishkāliyyāt al-Baḥth wa al-Tadrīs fī ʿIlm al-ʿAlaqāt al-Dawliyyah min Mandhūr Ḥaḍārī Muqāran" [The Problems of Research and Teaching International Relations from a Comparative Civilizational Paradigm], in *Fiqh al-Taḥayuz: Ruʾyah Maʿrifiyyah wa Daʿwah li al-Ijtihād* [Fiqh of Bias: An Epistemological Perspective and a Call for Ijtihād] (Cairo: International Institute of Islamic Thought and Dar Al-Salam, 2016), pp. 319-394; "Ishkāliyyāt al-Baḥth wa al-Tadrīs fī ʿIlm al-ʿAlaqāt al-Dawliyyah min Manẓūr Ḥaḍārī Muqāran" [The Problems of Research and Teaching International Relations from a Comparative Civilizational Paradigm], in A. Basha et al., *Al-Manhājiyyah al-Islāmiyyah* [The Islamic Methodology] (Cairo: Markaz al-Dirāsāt al-Maʿrifiyyah wa Dār al-Islām, 2010), 2:817-914. Other theoretical studies with an essentially

comparative critical character have preceded this study and branched from it. We will refer to them in their places in the study consecutively. These studies include: "Globalization and the Study of International Relations," "Redefining the Political," "The Debate on the Dialogue among Civilizations and the Relations between Them," "International Change and Global Democracy," and "The History and the Study of International Order and International Political Thought." These studies also concurred with other studies in both theoretical and applied dimensions, activating and implementing comparative theoretical frameworks in the study of current international issues.

PART I

INTRODUCTION: THEORIZING INTERNATIONAL RELATIONS

1
PATTERNS OF THEORIZING AND REASONS FOR THEORETICAL DIVERSITY AND PLURALITY

During the pinnacle period of the behavioralist school in the 1960s and 1970s, IR literature focused on defining theories according to their patterns, types, and criteria of classification.[1] As for post-behavioralist literature, it paid attention to the importance of theorizing and the distinction between theories and paradigms, using, in the process, paradigms (or the distinction between grand and small theories) as an approach to depict the evolution of the discipline.[2] By the end of the twentieth century, a state of methodological and theoretical fluidity dominated in the field of IR, as a consequence of a sharp increase in the number of writings and publications on theory.[3]

The evolution of the discipline of International Relations over more than fifty years has been deeply attached to the changes and transformations at the international and global levels. Theory can, therefore, be regarded as a product, and theorizing as a multi-level process that produces diverse theoretical products, which differ in their epistemological, ontological, and methodological aspects—aspects that lie at the heart of the philosophy of science and the theory of knowledge (the nature, origin, and scope of knowledge).

Hence, there are multiple approaches to the study of IR Theory and various ways to comprehend the conception and significance of theorizing. Therefore, I argue that a good starting point when teaching – or conducting research in – IR Theory, and IR in general, is to raise at least two fundamental questions: What is the essence and significance of "theory"? How is theory related to reality?

These questions serve different important goals: first, to introduce the essence of theorizing as an ongoing process and, secondly, to discuss the development of the discipline and reasons behind that development. One important conclusion out of this should be that science is not rigid. That is why a "methodological introduction" to the study at hand seeks to provide answers to these questions and to explain why it is important to raise these questions to begin with. Suggested here is that all theoretical courses should address these or similar questions.

Considering my teaching experience over the past two decades, I believe that the need for raising these questions is mainly justifiable by what can be described as students' "weak and confused methodological awareness"; one which is clearly manifest in the following:

- A dominant belief among Arab and Muslim students that science is a Western universal achievement, and that we, Arabs and Muslims, are mere consumers of this science, because we did not, and cannot, produce scientific knowledge.
- A weak general awareness of the significance of theoretical study, whether from Western or non-Western perspectives, thus undermining the role of theory in depicting, understanding, explaining, and coping with the changing realities of the world.
- A lack of comparative critical sensibility, which results in the failure to raise questions such as: Why do theories differ? What is meant by objectivity or bias? Are academic perspectives necessarily unbiased? When does a certain paradigm or theory become dominant? Is it possible to introduce theoretical contributions from non-Western perspectives? What kind of contributions can these be?
- An inability to relate "theories" to real "issues" of IR; that is, the lack of awareness that science serves "a function or several functions" and that non-Western civilizational circles can also produce useful knowledge.

This impression about the students' lack of methodological awareness has been stimulated, shaped, and consolidated over many years of teaching and interaction with graduate and postgraduate students at Cairo University, a conclusion usually arrived at after asking them a set of inductive questions.[4]

The purpose behind raising these questions at the beginning of each theoretical course that I teach has been to draw the students' attention to some crucial points:

- Theoretical study is not an abstract or philosophical study that is detached from reality. Rather, it aspires to a profound understanding of reality and to the serving of common good and human interests. Hence, theoretical study is neither an unbearable burden, nor a useless luxury.
- Theoretical study is an evolutionary and multi-approach process. It involves different paradigms and epistemes that produce various theories, which address different aspects (actors, concepts, processes, and issues).
- There is neither a single general theory of IR, nor are the various theories of IR universal in nature. These theories are the products of the "Western" civilizational experience and, hence, reflect the particular historical experience of the victorious powers of the two world wars, since the foundation of IR as an independent, modern social science. As Scott Burchill, Andrew Linklater,[5] and Steve Smith[6] indicate, the political circumstances surrounding the early days of the discipline had their impact on its content, evolution, aims, and objectives, both in application and in theory. Later, this fact became a subject of criticism from within Western academia, that is why the Western academic body cannot be considered as a unitary whole.

In the study at hand, four fundamental methodological steps are suggested to answer the aforementioned questions in a way that allows for the promotion of the theoretical awareness prerequired for a systematic, critical, and pluralist academic study of IR from comparative civilizational paradigms. These four steps will be addressed in the following four major points, throughout chapters 1 and 2: first, the essence and significance of theorizing; second, the differences between theoretical frameworks and the significance of the paradigm debates approach; third, the essence of contrasting epistemes; and fourth, the impact of epistemological differences on theorizing.

1.1 THE ESSENCE AND SIGNIFICANCE OF THEORIZING

When I ask my students how they see and describe ongoing global events, I do so driven by a belief that an inductive approach allows them to understand the meaning and significance of theorizing and how it is conducted. Students provide different definitions of international relations and describe the state of the world in variant ways. Their answers draw attention to aspects that need to be highlighted while teaching. Here, I draw on James Rosenau who made a distinct contribution in this regard.[7] According to Rosenau, world affairs are complex, and they change at a rapid pace, especially during periods of transformation. This makes it difficult, and even impossible, to comprehend all that is going on in the world, especially as it involves multiple actors and various patterns of cooperative and conflictual relations and interactions, let alone a plethora of global issues with infinite details (military, economic, cultural, etc.). This makes change the sole invariable truth in our world, and the only way to overcome the difficulties associated with this fact is through theorizing and theory-making. Literally, everyone engages in a theorizing process, once one observes world affairs. One finds oneself forced to make choices and to select the most important details to be observed (according to one's own preferences), while eliminating others. According to Rosenau, the selection process associated with observation is the first stage of theorizing, because selections are not made randomly, but are based on the observer's perception of what is meaningful. Yet, mere observation is insufficient for theorizing. Explanation is an essential second stage of theorizing and it requires two further subsequent steps to be taken: (1) Asking oneself, what does the observed signify?; and (2) Contemplation and verification that help upgrade the product of theorizing in such a way so as to give it an explanatory capacity. These two steps lead, hence, to more abstraction.

The transition from observation to conclusion and explanation means that historical facts and current events remain void of any inherent meaning, until we give them meaning. This is, according to Rosenau, what theorizing is all about; to reach broad meanings, generalizations, and rules by focusing on specific events. It is, therefore, important that scholars reveal their theoretical background. This makes it possible for them to identify sources of error, in case later developments in reality invalidate their findings or explanations.[8]

Rosenau's major argument is that theorizing is a reflection of reality, and that there is no such thing as unbiased theorizing. Observers of the same events make different assumptions and arrive at different conclusions. Each of them has their own experience that affects their choices, preferences, definitions and, accordingly, the explanations one suggests. Rosenau argues also that the highest level of abstraction in the theorizing process is the level at which an all-inclusive paradigm emerges; one that integrates various theories and offers a general explanation of causes and effects. For example, many theories are derived from the realist or the pluralist paradigms, they all share the main givens, hypotheses, and assumptions adopted by their corresponding paradigms. These paradigms are closed intellectual systems that do not come to ruin just whenever a few examples contradict their basic logical assumptions.

In short, Rosenau argues that adopting a certain paradigm helps researchers give a meaning to ongoing world developments. Hence, debates between the proponents of different paradigms, when explaining the same phenomenon, become inevitable. Rosenau believes that paradigms guide scholars through the processes of asking questions and finding answers. If a researcher is not aware of the necessity of abiding by a paradigm, they will be the victim of endless confusion and distraction. By giving attention to everything, the researcher becomes incapable of extracting any meaning from a permanently chaotic international scene.

Although advocating the essentiality of paradigms, Rosenau concludes, in defense of a pluralist perspective, that no single paradigm is true, while others are false, and that no paradigm is better than others. Rather, in some cases, some paradigms merely seem to be more useful than others, depending on the hypotheses that need to be tested.

Besides, different ways of understanding and explaining reveal differences between theoretical frameworks. One of the main teaching approaches to explaining theoretical diversity and the relationship between theory and reality is to ask students questions about the possible explanations of specific historical or current events, such as: How can the end of the Cold War and the collapse of the Soviet Union be explained? How can the Second Gulf War (the Iraqi invasion of

Kuwait) be explained? How can the war in the Balkans be explained? How can the 9/11 events be explained? How can the American aggression on Iraq in 2003 be explained? How can the impact of the growing Chinese influence on the world order be explained? Listening to different answers to these questions, along with being introduced to readings explaining different findings with reference to various theoretical frameworks,[9] can lead students to – inductively – uncover the meaning and essence of theoretical diversity and how it leads to different (sometimes competing and contradictory) explanations of the same reality. Here, Rosenau and Durfee argue that facing the challenges and difficulties of teaching abstract IR Theory requires rethinking theory beyond mere sophisticated abstract articulations of the world.[10] In other words, theories are better understood when applied to specific issues, and when specific incidents are explained differently from various theoretical perspectives.

It is useful to note that critical theorists – as will be further elaborated on in Part III – offer a totally different understanding of theorizing. On the one hand, they consider reality to be a reflection of the researcher's ideas, perspectives, and values. Hence, to them, developing different perspectives on "reality" is not a matter of paying attention to different aspects of a complex phenomenon or emphasizing certain details, while leaving out others. Rather, different perspectives on reality are the product of a disagreement on the existence of this reality, both in its entirety and in all its details. On the other hand, they consider dominant thought and theory to be a direct derivative of authority and power balances. Therefore, theorizing is not only a matter of finding better ways to understand reality and to solve its problems with the help of a theoretical framework, nor is it a matter of distinguishing between correct or false paradigms. Rather, it is a matter of understanding how theorizing reflects the practical goals of the centers of power and authority and serves their interests.[11]

1.2 PARADIGMS AND THE PARADIGM DEBATES AS AN APPROACH TO THE STUDY OF IR THEORY

"Paradigm," "school of thought," "perspective," and "image" are all vocabulary used interchangeably when addressing pre-theory, or what is also sometimes referred to as grand theories. Ever since the establishment of the discipline, the history of theorizing in IR has been approached in different ways, and one of them is the approach of "paradigms" and the paradigms' great debates.[12]

A paradigm is a dominant perspective on the nature of international phenomena as perceived and described by most theorists during each of the phases of the development of IR. It indicates a common stance on the main characteristics and aspects of international phenomena, on the questions to be raised, and the ways in which international phenomena need to be addressed. Some scholars, like Rosenau, consider paradigms as lens, through which we look at the universe around us.[13] They also argue that theorizing is the way to organize our comprehension and perception of the complex and overlapping issues of the international arena.

To other scholars, including Mona Abul-Fadl, approaching a discipline without having a paradigm is just like starting a tour without a guide or a map, because paradigms, according to her, serve different functions: they determine what belongs to the discipline and what falls outside its scope, identify the most crucial issues that deserve to be subjected to analysis, determine the units of analysis, and set the relationship between values and reality.[14] "Paradigms" have been used as tools to classify theorizing efforts in IR according to two criteria: (1) their fundamental ontological assumptions about the way in which the world is structured, and (2) their methodological assumptions, including the research methods and tools.

At different phases of the history of international politics, different major paradigms dominated the discipline of IR, before losing ground to some newly emerging paradigm that had directed its criticisms towards them. This succession has given rise to heated (great) debates between the proponents of the major successive paradigms. That is because, due to their different epistemological, philosophical, and ontological foundations, paradigms come up with different answers to the questions on the nature and methodology of IR. While some IR theorists emphasize the significance of the paradigm debates approach for teaching or explaining the evolution of the discipline, others express reservations about this approach.[15] Arguments of the advocates of a paradigm debates approach to IR can be summed up as follows:

- The paradigm debates approach is a tool for comparatively mapping perspectives and discussions; hence, it allows researchers to take stances and to select their own paradigm. This is something totally consistent with one of the main goals of postgraduate studies.
- Approaching the paradigm debates from a more holistic perspective, by reflecting on the similarities between apparently different paradigms, opens room for the introduction of new alternative paradigms, whether they belong to the same or to a different episteme. This applies to my own experience, in which the identification of epistemological similarities between the different Western paradigms justified, at least partially, the introduction of a comparative Islamic Civilizational Paradigm of IR.
- Emphasizing differences among paradigms explains the existence of different and multiple theories that tackle the same subject. There is no single theory of power, conflict, integration, or state; nor is there a single theory on the relationship between economics and politics, culture and politics, etc.
- In addition, this approach can help us answer important questions: What is the difference between theories of national interest, interest as derived from Shariʿah (Islamic moral and legal teachings), and global interest? What is the difference between theories of jihad (broadly defined as striving – whether morally, spiritually, or physically – toward that which is good or of benefit and with the aim of pleasing God), theories of holy war, and theories of national wars as distinct theories in IR? What is the difference between hegemony, balance of power, and smart power? What is the relationship between power, wealth, and knowledge?

The paradigm debates approach helps scholars to link international transformations to changes in theorizing; hence, it bridges the gap between theory and reality. That is why Rosenau and Smith believe that paradigms are not merely different perspectives on different worlds. To both, paradigms are different perspectives on specific aspects of the same world. These perspectives vary in importance and degree of endurance depending on the current global developments, which are also sophisticated, complex, and rapidly changing.

NOTES

1. See for example: Stanley Hoffmann, ed., *Contemporary Theory in International Relations* (Englewood Cliffs, N.J., Prentice-Hall, 1960); Philippe Braillard, *Theories de Relations Internationales* (Paris: Presses Universitaires de France, 1977); Ismail S. Maqlad, *Naẓariyyāt al-Siyāsah al-Dawliyyah: Dirāsāh fī al-Uṣūl wa al-Naẓariyyāt* [Theories of International Politics: Fundamentals and Theories] (Cairo: Al-Maktabah Al-Akadimiyyah, 1991); Paul R. Viotti and Mark V. Kauppi, *International Relations Theory: Realism, Pluralism, Globalism and Beyond*, 2nd ed. (USA Upper Saddle River: Prentice-Hall, 1998), pp. 1-14.
2. See for example: Paul R. Viotti and Mark V. Kauppi, *International Relations Theory*, 5th ed. (Boston: Longman, 2012), pp. 275-360; J. Dougherty and R. Pfaltzgraff, *Contending Theories of International Relations*, 5th ed. (New York: Longman, 2001).
3. See for example: Steve Smith, "Introduction: Diversity and Disciplinarity in International Relations Theories," in *International Relations Theories: Discipline and Diversity*, ed. Timothy Dunne et al. (Oxford: Oxford University Press, 2007).
4. For a detailed analysis of these manifestations in students' answers and feedbacks, see: Nadia M. Mostafa, "Ishkāliyyāt al-Baḥth wa al-Tadrīs fī ʿIlm al-ʿAlaqāt al-Dawliyyah min Manẓūr Ḥaḍārī Muqāran" [Problematics of Research and Teaching International Relations from a Comparative Civilizational Paradigm], in *Al-Manhajiyyah al-Islāmiyyah* [Islamic Methodology], ed. Ahmad-Fouad Basha et al. (Cairo: Markaz al-Dirāsāt al-Maʿrifiyyah wa Dār al-Islām, 2010), pp. 852-857.
5. Scott Burchill and Andrew Linklater, "Introduction," in *Theories of International Relations*, trans. Mohammed Soffar (Cairo: National Center for Translation, 2014), pp. 7-50.
6. Smith, "Diversity," pp. 1-14.

7. James Rosenau, "The Need of Theory," in *Thinking Theory Thoroughly: Coherent Approaches to an Incoherent World*, eds. James Rosenau and Mary Durfee (New York: West View Press, 1997), pp. 1-8 (see also 2nd ed., 2000, pp. 1-10).
8. The example used by Rosenau in the first and second editions of the book to explain this process is the failed coup d'état attempt in the Soviet Union in 1991.
9. For detailed analyses of the raised respective questions, see: Nadia M. Mostafa, "Review of 'Les temps de la guerre froide' by Pierre Grosser," *Al-Mustaqbal Al-Arabi*, vol. 8, 1999; "Nāqashāt: Li-Mādhā Inhār al-Ittiḥād al-Sūfīyitī" [Discussions: Why did the Soviet Union Collapse?], in *Inhiyār al-Ittiḥād al-Sūfīyitī wa Ta'thīrātuhu ʿalā al-Waṭan al-ʿArabī* [The Collapse of the Soviet Union and its Impact on the Arab World], ed. Taha Abdel-Aleem (Cairo: Al-Ahram Center for Political and Strategic Studies, 1993), pp. 93-107; Fred Halliday, *Islam and the Myth of Confrontation: Religion and Politics in the Middle East*, (Cairo: Madbouli Bookshop, 1996), pp. 91-114; Nadia M. Mostafa, "Al-Būsnah wa al-Harsak: Min Iʿlān al-Istiqlāl wa Ḥattā Farḍ al-Taqsīm: Najāḥ al-ʿUdwān al-Musliḥ fī Farḍ al-Amr al-Wāqiʿ Amām al-Niẓār wa al-Niẓām al-ʿĀlamī al-Jadīd" [Bosnia and Herzegovina from Declaration of Independence to Forced Division (March 1992 – July 1993): A De Facto Situation Imposed Successfully by Armed Aggression in Front of the New World Order] (Cairo: Center for Civilization Studies, 1994); Steve Walt, "IR: One World, Many Theories," in *Foreign Policy* (Spring 1998); Jack Snyder, "One World, Rival Theories," in *Foreign Policy* (November/December 2004).
10. James Rosenau and Mary Durfee, eds., *Thinking Theory Thoroughly*, 2nd ed. (Boulder: Taylor and Francis Group, 1999), pp. 1-10. Through the chapters of this book, they use three comparative paradigms (Realism, Liberalism, and Post Internationalism) to address some international issues.
11. For a comparison with a counter non-Western perspective, see: Abdelwahab Elmessiri, "Fiqh al-Taḥayuz" [The Fiqh of Bias], in *Ishkāliyyāt al-Taḥayuz* [The Problematic of Bias], ed. Abdelwahab Elmessiri, vol. 1 (Cairo: International Institute of Islamic Thought, 1995).

12. For a comparative study on approaches in IR Theory, see Steve Smith, "Ten Self-Images of a Discipline: A Genealogy of International Relations Theory," in *International Relations Theory Today*, eds. Ken Booth and Steve Smith (University Park: Pennsylvania State University Press, 1995), pp. 16-71.
13. Rosenau, "Thinking Theory Thoroughly," pp. 1-10.
14. Mona Abul-Fadl, "Paradigms in Political Science Revisited," *The American Journal of Islamic Social Sciences* 6, no. 1 (September 1989): pp. 1-15.
15. For more details, see: Steve Smith, "Ten Self-images of a Discipline: A Genealogy of International Relations Theory," in Ken Booth and Steve Smith, eds., *International Relations Theory Today* (Cambridge: Polity Press, 1995), pp. 16-71; Paul Viotti and Mark Kauppi, *International Relations Theory* (UK: Pearson, 2013), pp. 1-14; Ray Maghroori and Bennett Ramberg, eds., *Globalism versus Realism: International Third Debate* (Boulder: Westview Press, 1982).

2

CONTRASTING EPISTEMES AND THEIR IMPACT ON THEORIZING

Why do paradigms differ? Is it because they constitute different perspectives on the same world? Or, rather, is it because they constitute different perspectives on different worlds, as "*the* world" is not "out there" (i.e., it does not have a separate existence from those who seek to understand it)? The answer to the first question is in the affirmative, because of the ontological and methodological differences between the paradigms. The answer to the second question is also in the affirmative, because of the epistemological differences between the paradigms.

Of special significance is a comparison between the (Western) positivist episteme and the normative value-based episteme (including the Islamic episteme). Therefore, introducing "the model of contrasting or comparative epistemes" to IR Theory responds to an interest in the impact of the theory and philosophy of science on knowledge production; an interest that has developed from inside, as well as outside, Western academic circles.

Whereas reflecting on the state of the field pre-necessitates introducing the concept of "paradigm," speaking of schools that are critical of positivism in general and introducing a comparative Islamic Civilizational Paradigm in particular should go hand in hand with uncovering the impact of epistemes on IR. Students receive knowledge about political science in an academic milieu dominated by the positivist-realist paradigm. Their intellectual formation treats critical and Islamic knowledge, on the one hand, and positivist knowledge, on the other, as separate domains. This may explain their bewilderment and sense of alienation that I observe once I mention an Islamic Civilizational Paradigm of IR to them. In addition to that, there is a general weakness in the students' consciousness of the significance of theoretical study in general, not to mention the lack of awareness of the importance of epistemes and how they are related to the philosophy of science and sources of knowledge and how they impact social and political theorizing (both positivist and critical) within the Western circles. This is because the philosophy of science and sources of knowledge do not only explain the differences between the contrasting civilizational paradigms (Western and Islamic), but they also initially explain the epistemological and methodological differences within the Western circle (secular positivist, non-positivist, and non-secular as well), as will be further elaborated on in the third part of this study. Put differently, one cannot grasp the evolution of the discipline through the paradigms' great debates approach (the three great debates, the competing paradigms debate, or the debate between Western versus non-Western paradigms) without understanding the fundamental causes and manifestations of epistemological differences, and not only the ontological and methodological differences between paradigms.

What is the meaning of "episteme"? What are the most important types of epistemes in political science (comparative or contrasting, competitive or alternative epistemes)? What are the main characteristics of each one of them? How do their differences influence the paradigms and theories of political science? I do not intend to dig deep into these epistemological aspects, as my purpose here is just to draw attention to their impact on theoretical plurality and diversity in IR.

In this regard, it is useful to refer to some studies that have clearly addressed the general methodological problematics arising from the impact of different epistemes on comparative paradigms (Western and Islamic) in social sciences and humanities in general, and in IR in particular. These studies also reflect on some theoretical implications of these differences.[1] They also underline the epistemological differences among the Western paradigms; positivist and critical, as the latter criticizes Western epistemological and theoretical centrism.[2]

2.1 THE ESSENCE OF CONTRASTING EPISTEMES

Here, I limit my analysis to the contributions of three Muslim scholars who directed their criticism to positivist Western thought and its implications for the nature, concepts, and paradigms of the discipline. While departing from an Islamic background, early Muslim scholars' criticism of positivism preceded that of the growing critical Western approaches in political theory and IR Theory, and even in social sciences and humanities in general. As for the political science community of the Faculty of Economics and Political Science at Cairo University, it became attentive to the Western revisionist movement thanks to the early efforts of both Hamed Rabei and Mona Abul-Fadl, then to the "Project of International Relations in Islam," which was launched in the mid-1980s.

First, I will introduce Abul-Fadl's perspective on the significance of the comparative study of Western paradigms and the debates among them, in which she reflected on the impact of different epistemes on theorizing, and paved, thereby, the road for the establishment of an Islamic paradigm. Then, I will refer to the most important comparative aspects of both epistemes, mainly their characteristics and sources.

Abul-Fadl defines an episteme as the basic values and beliefs on knowledge, existence, and their sources. She also defines a paradigm as the structure of dominant discourse regarding the cognitive and normative system that regulates the process of thinking in a specific field, thus setting the scope, boundaries, concepts, worldviews, beliefs, values, and theories of that specific field.

Abul-Fadl asserts the nexus between epistemic differences and paradigm debates. She stresses that revisiting the field of political science by calling upon the paradigm debates is a tedious and challenging form of study, yet it is the most capable of revealing the meaning of diversity and difference in the field. To her, this approach is quite useful as it paves the way to introducing a contribution from within our Muslim circle; a paradigm expressive of our intellectual heritage and experience. It is time for Muslim scholars to take part in the debate over the state of the discipline, and they are expected to identify the opportunities opened up by the field's evolution that make it possible for alternative paradigms to emerge. This is because those who pursue an alternative world view should thoroughly comprehend the essence and content of the dominant view. They should critically observe the contributions of the "Other" with an eye on introducing their own alternative contribution. Considering paradigm debates leads, in fact, to the identification of the elements of homogeneity in a certain discipline and determines the prevalent degree of consensus on its scope, themes, values, and rules.[3]

Regarding the characteristics and sources of the two epistemes, I refer to Abdelwahab Elmessiri, Mona Abul-Fadl, and Ahmet Davutoğlu. In "The Fiqh of Bias," Elmessiri perceives episteme as a set of implicit and explicit values embedded in the means of thinking and research.[4] These values indicate human biases and personal inclinations and are, in turn, the result of a conscious (or unconscious) selection process where some values are embraced and others are excluded. Elmessiri believes that epistemes influence individual behavior, societal attitudes, and knowledge production. He uses an inductive and comparative methodology to gradually convey this definition to scholars and students so as to uncover "biases of science," or the subjectivity of theorizing. By discussing three sets of everyday life scenes from different parts of the world, he draws the attention to three important aspects of the impact of epistemic differences: the influence of civilizational values on individual behavior; the dominance of the Western civilizational societal patterns; and the bias in favor of a materialist episteme against a normative non-positivist, non-materialist one.[5] In a materialist episteme, the whole universe (including man and nature) turns into material objects, with no sanctity or sacredness, as interests and utility become the ultimate goals. The materialist episteme stands in stark contrast to an alternative value driven, non-positivist, non-materialist episteme.

Elmessiri defines the characteristics of the Western episteme as follows: It is a rationalist, materialist, and utilitarian episteme. It upholds the materialist monism doctrine, which started by advocating that man is the center of the universe and then moved on to claim that man and nature are identical, as both are subject to a linear evolution process that pursues equilibrium and moves constantly forward on a non-reversible track.[6] Elmessiri notes that this materialist episteme declared the death of God in the name of man, then the death of man in the name of the unity of nature. This episteme knows no sacred and no absolute, it knows no telos but pleasure and utility. It glorifies the material to the detriment of man. It favors the public over the private, the tangible and quantitatively measurable over the qualitative, and the rationalist/objective over the subjective.

When Elmessiri's work on "The Fiqh of Bias" was published in 1992, he utilized the depiction "Western" episteme. At that time, the dominant episteme in the West was the positivist, secular, and materialist episteme indeed. However, since the late 1980s, a critical perspective had been gradually making its way to social theory, political science, and international relations (as will be discussed later on).[7] By calling the materialist, positivist episteme "Western," Elmessiri seemed to be ignoring the outcomes of the revisionist attempts that had originated from within the West itself. It is worth noting that although these attempts have generated a non-materialist normative tendency critical of positivism, they remain in fact confined to a secular world view, and it is only over the last two decades that they have begun to become influential.[8] Elmessiri's conception of bias was criticized for neglecting the Western revisions of the subjectivity/objectivity problematic. It was also criticized for not offering an alternative perspective. However, his later contributions, reflecting on the concept of "the human," would provide the missing alternative from an Islamic perspective.[9]

Therefore, one might argue that Mona Abul-Fadl's preoccupation with contrasting epistemes (almost coinciding with Elmessiri's preoccupation with bias in the early 1990s) was a more balanced and integrated contribution. Abul-Fadl's attempt at "contrasting epistemics" – without labelling one as Western and the other as Islamic – had its significance for political analysis as follows: Abul-Fadl's approach of contrasting epistemes mainly focused on re-identifying the detailed characteristics of contemporary social theory in search of alternative perspectives to the dominant discourse. To Abul-Fadl, the contrasting epistemes refer to the Islamic *tawḥīdī*[10] episteme and the abstract secularist or "humanistic/naturalistic" episteme, where *tawḥīd* refers to the assertion of the oneness of God. The components of both epistemes constitute, in turn, a ground for two historically adjacent cultural types. *The median-culture type* represents a type where contrasts meet around a balance that regulates the relations between the whole and the part, the absolute and the relative, the static and the dynamic. *The oscillating culture type* dominates social theory, oscillating between spirit and matter, without having objective guiding principles or being able to reach a point of equilibrium.[11]

In her approach, Abul-Fadl attempts to overcome the typical stereotype that advocates a complete dichotomy and an inevitable confrontation between a superior classical Evangelical West (Greek – Roman and Jewish – Christian) and an inferior Muslim East. Therefore, Abul-Fadl stresses the complex relationship between normative cultural systems and historical civilizational groups or types. She considers the twinning between the historical West and the oscillating culture type to be temporary and accidental, neither necessary nor authentic. This explains why Abul-Fadl abstains from using the term "Western" to describe the secularist, humanistic episteme. By the same token, societies that happen to exist within the Islamic civilizational basin and to have historically belonged to the median culture type, have been formed according to fundamental principles that can be understood and adopted by other societies as well. Hence, a correlation between the median culture type and the historical Islamic society endures only as long as this organic bond between the fundamental principles of the episteme and the society remains intact, and vice versa.

Understanding this flexible relationship between the original ideal model and the historical real-life model makes the overriding of historical dichotomies and stereotyped polarization possible. Dichotomies and polarization are serving nothing but deepening disputes, confiscating history, and limiting the chances and potentials of liberty and responsibility.

Ahmet Davutoğlu, while sharing the same epistemological stance of Mona Abul-Fadl, adopts also a critical attitude towards political science. His work provides a comparative analysis of Islamic and Western epistemes, revealing, thereby, the different influences that these two epistemes have on the construction of concepts and comparative theories in social sciences in general, and in political science in particular.[12] He compares the two epistemes in terms of sources and characteristics. According to Davutoğlu, the positivist epistemology is based on the basic assumption that man is the master of the universe and its most important element. This epistemology stimulated the emergence of philosophies advocating the centrality of man in the universe and the centrality of nature; philosophies that were influenced by the ideas of Aristotle, Locke, and Kant on knowledge and reason leading to the outbreak of another epistemological-normative-social revolution in social and political theories. The outcome has been a comprehensive secularization of knowledge, life, thought, and science, and the dominance of the philosophy of individualism; a philosophy that upholds the hegemony of human will over the universe. This philosophy denies the existence of a transcendental will; a belief that is core to the Islamic sources of knowledge.

Davutoğlu believes that, unlike the Islamic episteme, secularization stimulates inner conflicts and contradictions that ruin man's inner equilibrium. In the Islamic episteme, there is only one God and, hence, one truth and one life. This belief promotes solid inner consistency supported by the coherence between the theory of knowledge and the Hereafter, on the one hand, and between values, sociology, and political science, on the other. Therefore, the Islamic perspective's refusal of the separation between ontology, epistemology, and axiology achieves inner consistency that rejects secularized thought, life, and science.

Davutoğlu's main hypothesis maintains that conflict and discrepancies between the Islamic and Western thought are not a result of mere historical differences. They are mainly the outcome of their different philosophical, methodological, and theoretical backgrounds, attributable to their different worldviews with their various ontological, epistemological, and axiological aspects.

Considering this view, the epistemological foundation of social sciences explains how Western academic production is neither objective nor universal; that is because it reflects a set of epistemological biases. Academic production departing from any other episteme is no exception and the Islamic paradigm is indeed not an exception either. Hence, Western and Islamic academic production differ because their epistemological backgrounds differ. Scholarly interest in the epistemological aspects of social and political sciences began in the early 1980s in Western and Islamic academic circles, however, it has not been until the fourth great debate that it started to become visible within the Western academic circles of IR.[13]

Since the early 1980s, the "Islamization of Knowledge" project has focused on contrasting epistemes, because criticizing Western thought in its entirely and its epistemological foundations was a basic step towards the foundation of Islamic social sciences.[14] Mona Abul-Fadl built on these efforts to introduce an Islamic Civilizational Paradigm in political science.[15]

The purpose of this methodological introduction is not the mere acknowledgement of the existence of contrasting epistemes or the recognition of their general impact. Rather, intended is also to reflect on the possibilities of theorizing from comparative paradigms that have different epistemological backgrounds, and to consider where to place these paradigms in the discipline of IR, which is currently witnessing its fourth debate that is distinguished, among other things, by an epistemological debate between positivist and critical schools of IR (as will be further elaborated on in the third part of this study).[16]

2.2 THE IMPACT OF EPISTEMOLOGICAL DIFFERENCES ON THEORIZING

The impact of epistemological differences on the theoretical study of political science and IR can be summarized as follows:

a) Epistemological differences have an impact on the very concept of science, and its sources, methods, and tools. They also have an impact on the concepts of objectivity, neutrality, and the role of values in science and the boundaries of the word "scientific." This impact shows clearly in two of the four great debates of IR: the debate of behavioralism versus traditionalism, and the debate of positivism versus reflectivism. It also manifests itself in the rise of a comparative Islamic Civilizational Paradigm.
b) Epistemological differences explain differences between paradigms, or between "analytical models," as designated by Elmessiri.[17] They also explain the rise of new critical post-positivist theoretical approaches that counter the dominant positivist paradigms.[18] Positivists and post-positivists disagree over epistemological points of departure, the dialectic of power and knowledge, and the purpose and role of science.

c) Comparative or contrasting concepts are key manifestations of the difference between the Western positivist, partial, reductionist, and materialist episteme, on the one hand, and the normative, comprehensive, and ethical episteme (including an Islamic one), on the other hand. Concepts are basic elements in the construction of theoretical and intellectual paradigms, acting as reservoirs of values and means of intellectual exchange. It is precisely for this reason that the inaccurate use of concepts can lead to intellectual miscommunication. Also, concepts have their general civilizational context; that is, they reflect the prevalent understanding of the human being and their role in the universe, the acknowledged ways of knowledge acquisition, and the sources of this knowledge, be they reality or divine revelation.[19]

Here, I will focus on important conclusions drawn by Abul-Fadl, Elmessiri, and Davutoğlu.

According to Abul-Fadl, the oscillating culture type associates concepts of matter and cause with tangible scientific experiences, excluding metaphysics and celebrating reason. Ethical knowledge, if not reachable as "scientific knowledge," is simply discarded as passionate dogma of no significant scientific value. Consequently, social sciences concluded that conflict is the principal driving mechanism of social order (psychologically, economically, and politically).[20]

According to the oscillating culture type, the concept of conflict is based on hegemony, dominance, and submission. This type regards power as a core value and a life goal, and conflict as driven by either material interests or utilitarian idealism. However, conflicts are not terminated once these interests are achieved, because conflict is a permanent state and a basic feature of natural and social orders.

In the median culture type, the concept of conflict is differently constructed. That type, however, does not express an idealistic view on eternal universal harmony. Rather, it admits that *tadāfuʿ* (repellence) and positive deterrence correct the imbalances in social order and drive it back towards equilibrium. Deterrence is the value, and *tadāfuʿ* is a temporary situation; a means and not an end. *Tadāfuʿ* is a Qur'anic term that refers to all kinds of opposite social interactions that lead to mobility; to adjustments or changes in positions. *Tadāfuʿ* serves the function of bringing social systems back to just equilibrium and, hence, guarantees the continuation of life on earth.

Based on this, the concept of tolerance also has contrasting connotations in the two cultural types. In the oscillating culture, human differences stimulate conflicts and necessarily lead to confrontation and disputes, thus belittling universal ideals of diversity, pluralism, and interdependence. Conflict outweighs other core societal values such as liberty, individualism, and tolerance. By contrast, the median culture recognizes human differences, diversity, and interdependence as legitimate and essential. It advocates diversity in accordance with *tawḥīd* as a comprehensive view of human being, universe, life, as well as the origin of cognitive, belief, and value systems (dominated by the values of *tawḥīd*), *ʿumrān* (promoting growth and prosperity on earth),[21] and *tazkiyyah* (self-righteousness).[22] The *tawḥīdī* philosophical anthropology stems from diversity and difference within the framework of unity and interconnectedness.

As for Elmessiri, the concept of "progress" is a very important product of the Western episteme. It is the main pillar of the modern materialist (Western) episteme and is considered by the modern Western civilization as the final end and referral point. The defining feature of the concept of progress, as produced by the Western episteme, is that it refers to a linear, one-way, universal process that is inevitable and unstoppable, presuming the prevalence of a single human history (rather than a shared humanity among different civilizations and diverse histories). Therefore, what fits a certain civilizational or historical formation is necessarily suitable for all other formations. Western societies are the culmination of this universal process of progress, where human knowledge grows and accumulates to increase human control of the surrounding environment.[23]

Elmessiri criticizes this conception as it lacks any profound reference to teleology; lacks any reflection on the purpose of progress or lacks any ethical content. By being self-referential, progress sets itself as its own reference, means, and end. Augmenting utility and maximizing pleasure are the only criteria of progress, taking no account of ethical and religious particularities. According to Elmessiri, this conception sets progress as a natural global law and the West as the most advanced civilization in the world. But the most serious consequences of accepting this conception are the recognition of Western superiority, universality, and morality as a fact, and the endorsement of the Western episteme and civilizational experience as the ideal model. This recognition and endorsement lead to the generalization of theories and concepts in various sciences, especially social sciences, without consideration of cultural particularities, thus excluding the non-Western Other from any scientific or historical records.

As for Ahmet Davutoğlu, he asserts that secularism has a long history in Western civilization, yet it has been subject to reformulations over centuries. The epistemological and axiological nexus between Western civilization and secularism has influenced the evolution of ideas, theories, and political institutions. It has had its ramifications on Western political science, particularly what concerns the justification for the existence and purpose of political regimes (also international relations). It also affected the evolution of Western views, especially the view of the state as a divine institution, and the adherence to secularism in defense of the state's autonomy against the Church, leading eventually to the emergence of the concept of "nation-state"; a concept that stands in stark contrast to the idea of the Islamic state.

Davutoğlu argues that the state of nature was used to justify the existence of the state and other political and social orders. He perceives this justification as the outcome of the centrality of nature to empirical knowledge, and the dominance of the humanistic and secular tendency in dealing with knowledge and the essence of science and existence. Davutoğlu believes that Islamic axiological normativism is central to Islamic political theorizing and a reflection of the *tawḥīdī* episteme, thus playing a significant role in the justification for the existence and purpose of the state. He regards this comparison between the two epistemes as representing politically significant theoretical and cultural endeavors. The Western challenge to the Islamic civilization is not a matter of alternative entities and institutions being created or a certain historical formation being challenged, but a challenge to a comprehensive world view that is capable of generating an alternative political culture so long as the epistemological, ontological, and political aspects remain interconnected in culture, as well as in social and political conceptions.

This previous analysis provides tools to critically analyze many dichotomies that emerged as an outcome of the dominance of a single episteme: reason/revelation, matter/value, science/religion, constant/variable, part/whole, relative/absolute, man/nature, man/God, objectivity/bias, and universality/particularity. These epistemological dichotomies have their ontological and methodological implications on theorizing and science. In fact, putting these dichotomies under scrutiny, by attempting to develop them into integrated systems, defies the accounts of the uniqueness and universality of this positivist methodology, and falsifies the claims labeling it as scientific, objective, and unbiased.

But if multiple epistemes exist, epistemological biases must arise. Bias is inevitable and does not contradict the "scientific" nature of social sciences and humanities. Therefore, not only can we criticize the dominant positivist episteme's claims to universality, hegemony, and sole validity, but we can also introduce a comparative, or alternative, theoretical contribution in social sciences that originates from an episteme that is critical and opposite of positivism. This happened already during the epistemological revision experienced by the discipline in the late 1980s. Still, how does an Islamic critique of positivism differ from a normative, yet secular, critique of positivism? An answer will be delivered in Part III of this study. Here, I will sum up the conclusions of my methodological introduction:

- Theorizing can be hierarchically ranked from top to bottom as follows: episteme (pre-method), paradigm (guiding model), theory, and research method.
- The (systemic) relationship between the epistemological, ontological, and methodological aspects differs from one paradigm to the other. For instance, different definitions of power and its essence influence the patterns of power distribution and how power relations are managed and for what purpose.
- The existence of multiple and diverse civilizational paradigms is traceable to the existence of multiple epistemes.

- The multiplicity of paradigms explains the existence of different theories on the same topic, be they theories from within the same episteme or from different comparative, contrasting, and competitive epistemes.
- Any paradigm can study whatever phenomena by resorting to systematic scientific methods or tools, because being "scientific" is not a monopoly of behavioralism and positivism. Paradigms offer different explanations of results, but also different understandings of "science" depending on their epistemological differences. Therefore, social sciences do not produce "facts," science is a process laden with implicit and explicit biases, and comparison and cumulative criticism are the bases of every new trend in science. Hence, scientific methods are expected to minimize, but not to eliminate, the effects of bias.

It follows that this study is principally concerned with finding answers to some main questions: How should we teach and conduct research to address novelty in the discipline and in reality? This concern is shared by many scholars and has been repeatedly expressed via various approaches in all the subfields of political science. Theorizing is basically a Western effort that is undergoing a phase of transformation and crisis. How should we comprehend that? And how is an Egyptian school of political science expected to take part in this transformation? Why isn't there an Arab discipline of political science? And what about an Islamic civilizational paradigm?

For clarification, I refer to two different perspectives that can be found in one of the publications of the Department of Political Science at Cairo University.[24] Chapters of this published book were written in the aftermath of the American aggression on Afghanistan and Iraq that has had vast repercussions on the world order and on our Arab region. Here again, I assert the connection between theory and reality.

On the one hand, Mostafa Elwi analyzed the crisis of theorizing in IR, and he affirmed that the discipline was basically Western, and that theorizing was only a tool for understanding ongoing events but did not precede action in any way. Elwi denied the existence of non-Western theories of IR and argued that other non-Western cultural paradigms had not crystallized yet. He also stated that IR Theory was mainly an achievement of the Western mind and admitted that although diversity and multiplicity had been characteristic of our world, this diversity was not reflected in theorizing as should had been.[25]

On the other hand, Heba Raouf emphasized that new trends in social theory, along with transformations in the types of phenomena studied by political scientists, required a paradigm shift in order to reassess the boundaries, scope, and content of political science.[26] Yet, this shift had to be needs-based, because developing a national academic theoretical framework that criticized the dominant international (Western-centric) production was not an end per se, but a means for change. Raouf argued that it was the real context, rather than pure theoretical research, that stimulated the need for conceptual change for concepts to be able to serve as an effective means to change. She raised several questions: How could theory change reality into a more just and free world? How could we develop our own perspective and introduce it globally as our own contribution to political theory? How could we manage to develop a critical perspective that redefined "*the* political" and opened up a space for research projects, methods, and issues that could benefit our Ummah and assist it in overcoming its crises? Raouf raised many questions and called for an answer from a national school concerned with the development of pedagogy and scholarship in political science. Raouf put it this way: "This demonstrates how important it is to have multiple and novel perspectives and schools, [...] so that the content of what they (the students) study becomes expressive of the new world they live in [...] and for us to be proactive and not just to wait for some post-modern schools here or there to instruct us on how to tailor theoretical studies to fit them for our own societies."[27]

NOTES

1. See for example: Elmessiri, "Fiqh al-Taḥayuz" [Fiqh of Bias]; Hamid Abd al-Majid, *Al-Waẓīfah al-ʿAqīdiyyah li al-Dawlah al-Islāmiyyah* [The Religious Function of Islamic State] (Cairo: Dār Al-Tawzīʿ Al-

Islāmiyyah, 1993), pp. 23-48; Saif AbdelFattah, "Binā' ʿIlm Siyāsah Islāmī" [Constructing an Islamic Political Science], in *Silsilat Buḥūth Siyāsiyyah* [Political Research Series] (Cairo University: Centre for Political Research and Studies, 1988); Nasr Arif, "Muqadimah" [Introduction], in *Qaḍāyā al-Manhājiyyah fī al-ʿUlūm al-Islāmiyyah wa al-Ijtimāʿiyyah* [Issues of Methodology in Islamic and Social Sciences], ed. Nasr Arif (Cairo: International Institute of Islamic Thought, 1996), pp. 7-15; Mona Abul-Fadl, "Islamization as a Force of Global Cultural Renewal: Relevance of *Tawḥīdī* Episteme to Modernity," *The American Journal of Islamic Social Sciences* 5, no. 2 (December 1988): p. 163; Mona Abul-Fadl, "Paradigms in Political Science Revisited," pp. 1-15; Mona Abul-Fadl, "Contemporary Social Theory: Towards Tawḥīdī Projections in the Principles of Theorization and the Need for an Alternative," *Islamiyyat Al-Maʿrifah* 2, no. 6 (September 1996): pp. 69-109; Ahmet Davutoğlu, "Al-Falsafah al-Siyāsiyyah" [Political Philosophy], in *Hadhā Huwa al-Islām* [This is Islam], trans. Ibrahim al-Bayoumi Ghanem (Cairo: Maktabat al-Shurūq al-Dawliyyah, 2006).

2. See for example: Milja Kurki and Colin Wight, "International Relations and Social Sciences," in Tim Dunne, Milja Kurki, and Steve Smith, eds., *International Relations Theories: Discipline and Diversity*, 3rd ed. (Oxford: Oxford University Press, 2013), pp.14-35.
3. Abul-Fadl, "Paradigms in Political Science Revisited," pp. 1-15.
4. Elmessiri, "Fiqh al-Taḥayuz," pp. 61-77.
5. Ibid, pp. 24-55.
6. Ibid, pp. 56-60.
7. The second part of this paper addresses the epistemological aspects of the Western critical approaches that criticized the positivist episteme.
8. One of the foundations of the "IR in Islam" project in the late 1980s was recalling of values and norms, and the search for non-Western paradigms in the discipline. This was manifested in one of the constitutive studies of the project.
9. Elmessiri, "Al-Namādhaj al-Maʿrifiyyah al-Idrākiyyah wa al-Taḥlīliyyah" [Cognitive and Analytical Paradigms], in *Al-Manhājiyyah al-Islāmiyyah* [Islamic Methodology], Ahmad-Fouad Basha et al., eds., vol. 2 (Cairo: Markaz al-Dirāsāt al-Maʿrifiyyah wa Dār al-Islām, 2010), pp. 795-816.

10. The term *tawḥīd* (here in the adjectival form, *tawḥīdī*) refers to the Islamic monotheistic concept meaning "the indivisible oneness of God."
11. Abul-Fadl, "Contemporary Social Theory," pp. 69-109.
12. See: Davutoğlu, "Al-Falsafah al-Siyāsiyyah"; Davutoğlu, "Al-Namādhaj al-Maʿrifiyyah al-Islāmiyyah wa al-Gharbiyyah: Taḥlīl Muqāran" [Islamic and Western Paradigms: A Comparative Analysis], *Islamiyyat al-Maʿrifah* 6, no. 22 (October 2000): pp. 11-34. The two sources are translated to Arabic from the English publication of his work *Alternative Paradigms: The Impact of Islamic and Western Weltanschauungs on Political Theory* (Lanham, MD: University Press of America, 1994), which is based on his PhD dissertation (in German).
13. See for example: Ralph Pettman, *Reason, Culture, Religion: The Metaphysics of World Politics* (New York: Palgrave MacMillan, 2004).
14. See for example: Fathi Malkawi, ed., *Naḥū Niẓām Maʿrifī Islāmī* [Towards and Islamic Episteme] (Amman: International Institute of Islamic Thought, 2000); Mohammed Amezian, *Al-Manhaj al-Ijtimāʿī: Bayn al-Waḍʿiyyah wa al-Miʿyāriyyah* [Social Methods: Between Positivism and Normativism] (Herndon, VA: International Institute of Islamic Thought, 1981); Louay Safi, *The Foundation of Knowledge: A Comparative Study in Islamic and Western Methods of Inquiry* (Malaysia: International Islamic University and International Institute of Islamic Thought, 1996); Nasr Arif, "Taqdīm" [Introduction], in *Qaḍāyā al-Manhājiyyah* [Issues of Methodology], ed. Nasr Arif, pp. 7-15; Elmessiri, "Al-Namādhaj al-Maʿrifiyyah al-Idrākiyyah wa al-Taḥlīliyyah," 2:795-816.
15. See preamble of Nadia M. Mostafa et al., *Fī Tajdīd al-ʿUlūm al-Ijtimāʿiyyah: Binā' Manẓūr Maʿrifī Ḥaḍārī (Al-Khibrah wa al-Fikrah)* [On Renewing the Social Sciences: Constructing a Civilizational Epistemological Paradigm (Idea and Experience)] (Cairo: Civilization Center for Political Studies, 2016). See also Nadia Mostafa, "Binā' al-Manẓūr al-Ḥaḍārī fī al-ʿUlūm al-Ijtimāʿiyyah wa al-Insāniyyah" [Constructing a Civilizational Paradigm in the Social Sciences and Humanities], in *Al-Taḥawwūl al-Maʿrifī wa al-Taghiyīr al-Ḥaḍārī: Qirā'ah fī Manẓūmat Fikr Munā Abū al-Faḍl* [Epistemological Transformation and Civilizational Change: A Perusal of Mona Abul-Fadl's Thought], ed. Nadia Mostafa et al. (Cairo: Civilization Center for Political Studies, 2011), pp. 21-77.

16. See for example: Dunne, Kurki, and Smith, eds., *International Relations Theory: Discipline and Diversity*; Elmessiri, "Al-Namādhaj al-Maʿrifiyyah al-Idrākiyyah wa al-Taḥlīliyyah," 2:795-816.
17. Elmessiri, "Al-Namādhaj al-Maʿrifiyyah al-Idrākiyyah wa al-Taḥlīliyyah," 2:795-816.
18. See: Dunne et al., *International Relations Theory: Discipline and Diversity*; Viotti and Kauppi, *International Relations Theory: Realism, Pluralism, Globalism and Beyond*, p. 2.
19. Ibrahim al-Bayoumi Ghanem et al., *Binā' al-Mafāhīm: Dirāsah Maʿrifiyyah wa Namādhij Taṭbīqiyyah* [*Construction of Concepts: An Epistemological Study and Applied Examples*] (Cairo: International Institute of Islamic Thought, 1998).
20. Abul-Fadl, "Contemporary Social Theory"; see also a thorough analysis in Mona Abul-Fadl, "Naḥū Manhājiyyah li al-Taʿāmul maʿ Maṣādir al-Tanẓīr al-Islāmī: Bayn al-Muqadimāt wa al-Muqawanāt" [Towards an Islamic Methodology of Dealing with Sources of Islamic Theorizing: Between Introductions and Capabilities], in *Al-Manhājiyyah al-Islāmiyyah*, no. 13 (Cairo: International Institute of Islamic Thought, 1996).
21. Social and economic development.
22. Purification of the self.
23. Elmessiri, "Fiqh al-Taḥayuz" [The Fiqh of Bias], pp. 74-77.
24. See Nadia Mostafa, ed., *ʿIlm al-Siyāsah: Murājaʿāt Naẓriyyah wa Manhājiyyah* [Political Science: Theoretical and Methodological Revisions] (Cairo University: Department of Political Science, 2004).
25. Mostafa Elwi, "Al-Ḥarb ʿalā al-ʿIrāq wa Azmat al-Tanẓīr fī al-ʿAlaqāt al-Dawliyyah" [The War on Iraq and the Crisis of Theorizing in International Relations], in *ʿIlm al-Siyāsah: Murājaʿāt Naẓriyyah wa Manhājiyyah* [Political Science: Theoretical and Methodological Revisions], ed., Nadia Mostafa (Cairo University: Department of Political Science, 2004), p. 324.
26. Heba Raouf Ezzat, "Iʿādat Taʿrīf al-Siyāsī" [Redefining the Political], in *ʿIlm al-Siyāsah: Murājaʿāt Naẓriyyah wa Manhājiyyah* [Political Science: Theoretical and Methodological Revisions], ed., Nadia Mostafa (Cairo University: Department of Political Science, 2004), pp. 413-422.
27. Ibid., pp. 421-422.

PART II

THE PARADIGM DEBATES: FROM DOMINANT PARADIGMS TO THE CRISIS OF THE DISCIPLINE

INTRODUCTION

THE CONCEPT OF CHANGE, WHAT CONSTITUTES IT, WHAT IS ITS NATURE, HAS BEEN A KEY ASPECT OF IR DEBATE. The end of the twentieth century witnessed IR Theory literature capturing much more significant analysis of change than it had done during the early decades of the century. Specifically, the paradigm debates approach demonstrated that IR as a discipline was both dynamic and responsive to international changes and global transformations. During its early days and subsequent evolution IR remained strongly concerned with issues of war/conflict and peace in connection to the great powers, and preoccupied with addressing two specific questions: How to define international relations? And how to study them?

Theoretical literature, including that of the founding Western schools, attests to the fact that continuous change is the only invariable aspect of international relations and of IR theories. In other words, IR history is marked by scholarly disputes across various successive paradigms, with debates developed in parallel with and in response to various dimensions of global change. This connection further demonstrates the significance of the paradigm debates approach. The competing nature of the paradigms, with one or other dominating, and/or the emergence of new paradigms, are all indicators of IR responding to either a state of stability or a state of change and transformation in international and global affairs.

This study does not intend to delve deeply into the details of paradigm debates in terms of either content (agents, actors, processes, issues, and the relationship between internal and external aspects) or methods of research. The aim here is to map major paradigms; to trace the phases and essence of the evolution of the debates between them; and to describe the state of the debates since the end of the Cold War till the current phase of theorizing (also sometimes referred to as the crisis of the discipline). In other words, this part of the study focuses on the problem of monopoly versus diversity, and the position of the epistemological and geographical non-Western Other in the theorizing process, thus questioning the validity of claims advocating the universality of IR Theory.

The major phases of the evolution of Western theorizing can be summed up as follows:

- The dominant Western positivist realist paradigm as a starting point of an epistemological essence.
- A growing rivalry between the realist paradigm and other positivist paradigms.
- Ontological, theoretical, and methodological revisions emerging from within Western academic centers. These revisions reached their peak after the end of the Cold War, leading IR to be designated as a discipline in crisis.
- The rise of Western and non-Western critical revisions in the first two decades of the twenty-first century.

Here, I put my methodological introduction to the test and I examine whether the discipline of IR has witnessed a division, a crisis, or rather diversity. These three terms are not synonymous, and each one of them carries specific implications for the essence, origins, and role of science. My analysis in the following part will tackle three issues: the three great debates; the repercussions of the end of the Cold War on theorizing in IR; and the characteristics of the great debates and their significance to the state of IR.

3
THE THREE GREAT DEBATES: FROM DOMINANT PARADIGMS TO COMPETING PARADIGMS

A close examination of the history of the discipline reveals that Western theorizing in IR has evolved from the initial phase characterized by the existence of dominant paradigms, throughout the three great debates, to the phase of competing paradigms (the inter-paradigm debate), characterized by the absence of a dominant paradigm.[1] The rise of major paradigms in IR has eventually coincided with transformations in the world order, including the interwar period, post-WWII times, and post-Cold War era. The Western perspectives on international relations since the beginning of the twentieth century until the end of the Cold War have developed throughout different phases: diplomatic history; political idealism during the interwar period; realism in the post-WWII period; behavioralism in the 1960s; and post-behavioralism in the 1970s and 1980s.

Alongside the three major paradigms (realism, liberalism, and behavioralism), Marxism is considered a fourth major paradigm. Great debates took place between consecutive dominant perspectives of IR during the transitional periods from one phase to another. The three great debates are: (a) Idealism versus traditional realism in the late 1930s and early 1940s, (b) Realism versus liberalism in the 1970s, then realism versus Marxism in the 1980s, and (c) Traditionalism versus behavioralism (1960s and 1970s). While the first two debates focused on the content of major assumptions and hypotheses of each paradigm (What?) (such thematic and ontological aspects as the drivers of international relations, actors, issues and processes, and the relationship between internal and external aspects), the third debate focused on methods (How?).

Theoretical literature used different vocabulary to map these debates: paradigm, image, and perspective.[2] More importantly, the impact of global changes on the different perspectives remained identifiable in the conclusions or introductions of academic research papers and the impact of viewing complex and sophisticated international and global phenomena from multiple perspectives remained noticeable as well.

A dominant paradigm in a specific period reflects the nature and features of international relations during this period; hence, a new paradigm arises as a reaction to critiques directed at the precedent dominant paradigm that prevailed during a different international context. Dominant paradigms are usually criticized for their failure to offer valid descriptions of and concrete explanations for new international phenomena.

Three major events marked great-power interactions in the twentieth century: WWI, WWII, and the end of bipolarity without an armed fight. Three major questions were often raised in this context: Is it a new era? What is its impact on theory? Did theory in any way affect, or at least predict, the big event? In fact, answers to these questions always revolved around great power politics, namely relations between the rival Western centers of power. During the early phases of this discussion, other non-Western actors (the South, the Third World) were neither mentioned in this discussion nor invited to it, despite claims of universality of the discipline. Afterwards, however, a gradual change has taken place both from within and without the Western academic circles (as will be shown later when discussing the crisis of the discipline).[3]

3.1 THE FIRST DEBATE: IDEALISM VERSUS TRADITIONAL REALISM

This debate occurred during the early days of the discipline after WWI. The momentum of the debate was during the interwar period (when idealism was the dominant paradigm), and it lasted till after the end of WWII (when the realist school prevailed). Without going deep into the details of this debate,[4] I will highlight some points:

- The first debate had initiated from within the "traditional school," before the behavioral revolution erupted. The focus of the debate was on the characteristics of the international order and ways of achieving peace and preventing war. Questioned was the validity of the idealist view that world peace could not be fragmented and, hence, that wars could be totally prevented through the elimination of their causes and the imposition of collective security. Questioned was also the counterargument claiming that peace could prevail only partially, and that world peace was unattainable because conflict over power and interests among states had been the eternal historical law. It was said that wars, therefore, could not be prevented completely, yet they could be avoided through the balance of power mechanisms and the protection of both national security and interests.

- Although traditional idealism emerged in response to the challenges caused by WWI, reformist idealist initiatives proved inadequate and failed to survive the international changes of the time. After the world economic crisis, expansionist policies by Germany, Italy, and Japan demonstrated the failure of the collective security system. Moreover, these policies paved the way for realist trends to rise after WWII, when international law, values, and arms control proved incapable of preventing the war. Therefore, the dominant view on the nature of international politics and on managing it adequately changed due to international transformations. The newly dominant view was obviously serving the interests of victorious powers. The intensity of the Cold War, the rigid bipolarity, and the ideological conflict from the 1950s till the 1970s consolidated the emergence of the realist paradigm as the then dominant paradigm.
- The debate between realism and idealism brought the issue of war and conflict versus peace and cooperation to the fore of IR. Theorizing efforts were pendulum-wise oscillating between these two sets of issues, though within different international contexts, as was later on the case during the third great debate between realism and liberalism (in the post-behavioralist period). It is also important to note that the second great debate shed light on the multiple facets of the dialectic relationship between values/ethics and realism.

3.2 THE SECOND DEBATE: TRADITIONALISM VERSUS BEHAVIORALISM[5]

"Scientific" behavioralism dominated IR in the 1960s as a response to the scientific movement in the social sciences, which sought to apply the tools and methods of the natural sciences to research and analysis. IR followed suit in pursuit of transforming international studies into organized scientific research. In doing so it tried to benefit from the behavioralist revolution in the social sciences to challenge traditional methods of studying IR and to call for a general theory.

Traditional research methods originate theorizing and hypothesis from philosophy, history and law. Here the dominant research method is deductive, depending on perception and intuition to reach general assumptions, rather than on verification and proof. In contrasting, behavioralism pursues a stronger and more accurate mode of analysis to replace subjective perception, intuitive reflection, and personal experience with verified and empirically-tested knowledge.

Behavioralists utilise an inductive approach to research based on an accumulation of knowledge and data through observation and other systematic practices. From data they move onto theory aiming to construct a general theory explaining the facts of international relations and predicting its development. This can be achieved by applying empirical tools of data collection and analysis, and using quantitative and comparative methods to test hypotheses on the correlation between variables. The end result should be generalized explanations of frequent patterns of behavior over time and place that avoid becoming involved in redundant narrative details, supposedly leading, thereby, to the construction of a general theory of IR.

Behavioralists have critiqued traditionalism generally for:

- Using primitive methods, based on unclear hypotheses, which eventually result in inaccurate descriptions.
- Using insufficient comparisons which lead to the inability to analyze, explain, and predict.
- Using details-oriented approach, specifically on the micro level.
- Overemphasizing the significance of values that cannot be empirically studied.
- Being over-dependent on intuition and deduction.

By contrast, traditionalists have criticized behavioralists for:

- Overrating the importance of quantitative methods without regard to the immeasurable, yet important, qualitative differences among phenomena.
- Turning data collection methods into an end in itself.
- Exaggerating theoretical ambitions and overestimating the ability to make generalizations and predictions to reach a general theory that reduces social phenomena to causal relations.
- Excluding values and all immeasurable variables from analysis.
- Using insufficient or superficial accounts of history (treating history as separate episodes, paying no attention to the philosophy of history and its interconnected nature).

The dominance of behavioralism declined during ensuing periods of the evolution of theorizing. In fact, the second great debate gave rise to subsequent methodological and epistemological debates among rival paradigms. In the post-behavioralist period, some "reconciliatory perspectives" worked on bridging the gap between traditional and behavioralist schools. These perspectives attempted to benefit from behavioralist – albeit limited – achievements and to include values into analysis at the same time. These reconciliatory perspectives took variant and new shapes during the revision of the state of the art in the aftermath of the end of the Cold War (a renewed interest in values and a growing criticism of behavioralism).

The beginning of the new century saw these reconciliatory perspectives develop into critical approaches that directed criticism to the epistemological and – not only – the methodological aspects of positivism. A rising and diminishing interest in methodological and epistemological aspects remained identifiable throughout the course of the evolution of theorizing, reflecting, thereby, the oscillating nature characteristic of "Western" theorizing. Meanwhile, this methodological debate, where the epistemological aspects are not absent, offered a solid ground for comparisons between Western paradigms and other civilizational paradigms, especially the Islamic paradigm, as will be further elaborated on.

3.3 THE THIRD DEBATE: REALISM VERSUS LIBERALISM[6]

The early beginnings of the third debate are usually associated with the post-behavioralist stage of Western theorizing. Post behavioralism emerged as a reaction to critiques levelled at behavioralism. As mentioned earlier, behavioralism was critiqued for its emphasis on research methods, especially the quantitative methods at the expense of the changing dynamics of international relations. Two main developments occurred during this phase:

- A call for abandoning the narrow definition of what is "scientific" and reconciliating different research tools and methods (which would eventually lead to the rise of other methods and tools) set in. The third debate in the post-behavioralist phase was not confined to the ontological aspects of IR. It was extended, though mildly, to include methodological aspects, especially as voices critical of excessive positivism and behavioralism were getting louder. Calls for renewed interest in values and criticisms of positivism grew in the 1980s and crystallized during the post-Cold War years. Nevertheless, "content" remained the core concern of the third debate.
- Renewed interest in the substance or content of IR, with special emphasis on new issues and problems, specifically economic issues. New different hypotheses on IR surfaced in response to critiques posed to the hypotheses of the hitherto dominant realist paradigm. These hypotheses addressed the entire structure of IR (units, scope, themes, and processes). When this heated debate started in the 1980s, the pivotal questions were: To what extent does the current international order reflect elements of continuity or change when compared to the World order that has prevailed since the Second World War? Isn't there a need for an alternative paradigm to the paradigm of the politics of nation-states, which revolves around conflict over power in pursuit of national interests and military national security? At that time, transformations in international politics redirected attention from power politics, superpower conflicts, and the traditional definition of security, which placed the

state as the only referent object, to actors and processes of a new era of international interdependence, emphasizing, thereby, an interest in promoting international peace and security.

The third debate revolved thus around four major issues: (a) patterns of power distribution among states and other actors; (b) change in the essence of power with increasing significance of economic aspects; (c) the process of power management (interdependence or conflict and anarchy); and (d) the state of the international order (peace or conflict).

In the early post-behavioral phase, realism was not challenged by a single opposing paradigm, but by alternative rival perspectives that challenged all together the assumptions of the realist paradigm. These emerging rival perspectives, though all post-behavioralist, were given different labels, depending on the criteria of classification emphasized:

- Interactions: Transnationalism, interdependence, global integration.
- Power distribution among states and other actors: state-centric, multi-centric, or global-centric.
- Paradigm's philosophical bases or origins (hence, emerged the labels "liberalism" and "neo-idealism" to clearly differentiate them from traditional idealism).

When the third debate started in the early 1980s, multiple terms designated multiple schools that were all calling for a new paradigm to challenge realism. Unlike the first and second debates, the third was not a debate between two rival paradigms. Rather, it was a debate between a dominant perspective and a bundle of complementary schools, initially enjoying relatively little consensus when compared to the consensus that the realist paradigm had enjoyed. It is important to note that different labels emphasize different aspects of the paradigm. So "realism" emphasizes the centrality of the nation-state as an actor; "the paradigm of power politics" emphasizes the processes of IR; "the paradigm of international conflict" emphasizes the state of IR; and "the paradigm of international security" emphasizes the issues of concern. Moreover, the term "realism" has an epistemological foundation that affects all the other – interrelated – dimensions, which are reflected upon by the paradigm (i.e., actors, drivers, issues, and processes).

The common denominator among the multiple non-realist schools is that they introduce new assumptions of IR as far as actors, issues, and processes are concerned, as will be elaborated on in the following:

a) *Non-state actors*

They play a significant role in changing the structure and content of international politics, raising new issues, and bringing to the fore the so-called "nation-state crisis."[7] This gave rise to new expressions, such as "global or international politics," that highlight the overlap between domestic and international politics and the vulnerability of states to external influence. Thus, the meaning of sovereignty changed due to the change in the essence of power and its patterns of diffusion and distribution.[8]

b) *Scope and priority of issues (substance and conception of power)*

Issues of military security are top priority for realists who assume that they are also given top priority at the governmental and international levels. Military power is considered to be the principal tool for defending the state's sovereignty, interests, and territories, as only military security protects the survival of the state and the stability of the international order through balance of power.

In other words, there is a systemic relationship between the realist assumptions on the concept of power, actors, international processes (conflict), and security. This, in effect, explains priority being given by realists to political (strategic) security issues, regarded as high politics, and, hence, more influential when compared with economic issues that are regarded as low politics. Therefore, realism does not provide a reliable framework for understanding issues like international trade, economic development, protection of human rights, and environmental issues; although realists do not deny the importance of these issues and their effect on world peace and stability.

At that time, emerging new approaches advocated that there existed no clear hierarchy of issues. These approaches recorded the alterations in the – relative and absolute – significance of military power and the growing importance of economic and transnational issues; the latter had been gradually exercising a stronger impact on transformations in world politics with gradual recognition of influence on high politics. Consequently, these new approaches emphasized the necessity of studying the economic foundations of international relations (both conflictual and cooperative). Governments became more concerned with new issues (trade preferences, blocs, oil, aids, technology, currency exchange rates, and the problems of global monetary policies). This shift in governmental policy orientations is attributed to the growing cross-border effects of these issues. In addition, employment, education, and development were issues society and the general populace were increasingly demanding be addressed. It is important to note that these issues were also international in scope with governments having increasingly to commit themselves to binding international frameworks to ensure provision of basic resources and improvement of peoples' living conditions.

Therefore, the economic, as well as political, and military dimensions became equally important for developed and developing states such that consequently in pursuit of economic development, they were forced to engage with other non-state actors by way of negotiation and cooperation, rather than use of military power. What had become apparent was that economic considerations were now governing relations of partnership or hostility as opposed to military-political ones alone. Furthermore, the nature of new and emerging issues also had an impact. The new issues of concern centered on overpopulation, food crisis, non-renewable resources, pollution, exploitation of seas, oceans and outer space, organized crime, and cross-continental diseases; in other words issues which were gaining further importance because they were seen to be increasingly threatening not only individual states, but the entire international community. Broadening the scope of foreign policy agendas, these issues made international interactions more complex. Power and influence were being redefined in a world where the use of military power (specifically among great powers) had declined because of its high cost. Economic considerations became a source of bargaining power in negotiations related to conflicts over new security interests. The values of peace, economic welfare, and social justice were gaining growing attention alongside values of military security. In these transformations, the discrepancies of power and capabilities between small and big powers were becoming more obvious.

c) *International interdependence*[9]

This emerged as a new pattern of international processes that, in turn, reflected new types of actors and issues. It was a manifestation of the increasing interconnectedness between individuals, communities, and governments across different states. It reflected a substantial feature of contemporary international politics; that being the overlap between economic and political dimensions, and the interconnection between internal and external aspects. This unprecedented interconnectedness was a result of tremendous progress made in modern transportation, communication and technological development.

The notion of international interdependence indicated the cross-border effects of economic and political processes in an interconnected system. It was multidimensional as it took place on regional, continental, and global levels. It was also cross-cutting as it covered the political, economic, military sectors and others simultaneously. Thus, it became necessary to explore innovative ways of thinking and new concepts to analyze these multidimensional, multilevel interactions. This may justify the special emphasis that was given to international interdependence, as a phenomenon and as a concept, in the analyses of the different perspectives of the pluralist paradigm. International independence was mainly concerned with two themes: the crisis of the nation-state, and the ways of managing global economic problems (more cooperation or more conflict?).

Besides, the international order had been significantly changing since the 1970s. These changes led to the dissolution of rigid bipolarity and the mitigation of Cold War conflicts. A new era of flexible bipolarity, détente, and cooperation ranked economic issues and thereto related changes in actors, power, and processes as high politics. International political economy was given advanced priority on research agendas.[10] These changes became a core interest of many non-realist schools, such as the liberal pluralist school.

Finally, in the 1980s, in the context of global economic changes and intensified peaceful and cooperative interactions among great powers, a third debate crystallized under the title of the debate between realism and liberalism and became the theme of a wide range of literature.[11] By that time, critical approaches to realism had found a common ground; they could now situate themselves under the broad umbrella of the liberal paradigm.

To sum up, the 1980s onwards has witnessed the map of IR paradigms changing. Since the three consecutive great debates, IR Theory has neither witnessed the dominance of a single paradigm, nor ongoing debates between two rival paradigms. In effect, following the three successive great debates, inter-paradigm debates have become the essential feature of IR Theory. It is noteworthy that, during that period, many publications in IR Theory introduced paradigms and paradigm debates by referring to realism, behavioralism, liberalism, and Marxism (or radicalism/globalism) altogether.[12] A substantial development of the post-behavioral phase was the acknowledgement that IR was no longer dominated by a major paradigm, be it behavioralism, traditionalism, realism, or idealism. Although, during the early foundation years of IR, realism had held a monopoly – along with idealism – over the discipline, theoretical transformations in response to environmental development and other factors had reduced realism's dominance. Neither realism nor its key themes of preventing war and managing military power dominated the IR research agenda anymore.

Meanwhile, theorizing in IR began to demonstrate a growing comparative interest in Marxist theory and thought. This for example manifested itself in works produced in Western literature on themes such as the world order and international political economy. One of the most important developments in this regard was the emergence in mid-1970s Latin America of the Dependency school, considered the first attempt to break the hold of a hitherto Western Anglo-Saxon monopoly over international theorizing. Although ideologically different to Western capitalist theorizing in IR, the school was guided by the same positivist modernist episteme. In relation to that monopoly for instance Hedley Bull, a pioneer of the English School, had criticized the existence of a Western-centric bias in IR Theory impeding the fulfillment of "the universality of the discipline." According to Bull, Marxist theorizing in IR made its way to IR Theory only after years of obviation and skepticism.[13] Martin Wight, also an English School theorist, inaugurated the theoretical tradition of the comparative study of IR Theory. This tradition, known as "3Rs," for rationalism, revolutionism, and realism, indicated the intellectual roots of the three respective schools of liberalism, Marxism, and realism.[14]

Over the ensuing two decades, critiques of Western (especially American) centrism gradually gained greater ground reaching a climax with the end of the Cold War, and especially the arrival of the new millennium, during which time Marxist-oriented critical approaches began to emerge. These same criticisms were accompanied by a call for civilizational non-Western theorizing, from the East or South. In the meantime, a body of literature in IR Theory conducted horizontal comparisons between the substance and content of the three major paradigms: realism, liberalism, and Marxism.[15]

NOTES

1. For details on the pros and cons of this historic order, see: Steve Smith, "Ten Self-Images of a Discipline," pp. 16-71; Nadia Mostafa, "Naẓriyyat al-ʿAlāqāt al-Dawliyyah" [International Relations Theory], pp. 54-82; Ole Wæver, "The Rise and Fall of Inter-Paradigm Debate," in *International Theory: Positivism and Beyond*, eds. Steve Smith, Ken Booth and Marsia Zalewski (Cambridge: Cambridge University Press, 1996), pp. 149-185.
2. See for example: M. Smith et al., eds., *Perspectives on World Politics* (London: Croom Helm, 1981); Robert O. Keohan and Joseph S. Nye, *Power and Interdependence: World Politics in Transition* (Boston: Little Brown Co, 1977); Charles W. Kegley Jr., ed., *Controversies in International Relations Theory: Realism and the Neoliberal Challenge* (New York: Palgrave Macmillan, 1995); Barry B. Hughes, *Continuity and Change in World Politics: The Clash of Perspectives* (Englewood Cliffs, NJ: Prentice Hall, 1991); Greg Fry and Jacinta O'Hagan, eds., *Contending Images of World Politics* (London: Macmillan International, 2000).
3. In the following parts, I will keep focusing on the position towards the

non-Western "Other" in theorizing, whether as an actor or as a subject of study.

4. For details, see for example: Charles W. Kegley and Eugene Wittkopf, *World Politics: Trend and Transformations* (New York: St. Martin's Press, 1983), pp. 5-13; Ray Maghroori, "Major Debates in International Relations," in *Globalism Versus Realism: International Third Debate*, eds., Ray Maghroori and Bennett Ramberg (Boulder: Westview Press, 1982), pp. 9-22.
5. For details on the second debate at that time and more recently, see for example: Hedley Bull, "Traditionalism Versus Behavioralism," in *Contending Approaches of International Relations*, eds., Klauss Knorr and James Rosenau (Princeton: Princeton University Press, 1969); J. Dougherty and R. Pfaltzgraff, *Contending Theories of International Relations* (New York: Longman, 1997); Ismail S. Maqlad, "Naẓriyāt al-Siyāsah al-Dawliyyah" [Theories of International Politics].
6. Nadia M. Mostafa, "*Naẓariyat al-ʿAlāqāt al-Dawliyyah: Bayn al-Manẓūr al-Wāqiʿī wa al-Daʿwah ilā Manẓūr Jadīd*" [International Relations Theory: Between the Realist Paradigm and the Call for a New One], pp. 54-82. See also: R. Keohan and S. Nye, *Power and Interdependence* (Boston: Little Brown and Co, 1977); James Rosenau, "Order and Disorder in the Study of World Politics: Ten Essays in Search of Perspective," in *Globalism Versus Realism*, eds. R. Maghroori and B. Ramurg (Boulder, CO: Westview Press, 1982), pp. 9-22; Jeffrey Harrod, "Transitional Power," *Yearbook of World Affairs* (1976): pp. 102-105.
7. Discussions of this crisis go back to the early 1970s, and they intensified afterwards in the context of globalization, as we shall see later. For examples of early insights on the future of the nation-state (corner stone of realist thought), see: R. H. Wagner, "Dissolving the State: Three Recent Perspectives on International Relations," *International Organization* 28, no. 3 (July 1974): pp. 435-466; Stanley Hoffmann, "Obstinate or Obsolete? The Fate of the Nation-State and the Case of Western Europe," *Tradition and Change* 95, no. 3 (Summer 1966), pp. 862-915.
8. Similarly, the first wave of discussions on the change in the notion of power began. See for example: Seymon Brown, "The Changing Essence of Power," *Foreign Affairs* 51, no. 2 (January 1973): p. 286.
9. For more details on international interdependence, see: James O'Leary,

"Envisioning Interdependence: Perspectives on Future World Orders," *Orbis* 22 (October 1978): pp. 503-537; Keohane and Nye, *Power and Interdependence*; Stanley J. Michalak, "Theoretical Perspectives for Understanding International Interdependence," *World Politics* 32, no. 1 (October 1979): pp. 136-150; Fatema Abou-Zeid, "Al-ʿAmaliyāt al-Dawliyyah min Manẓūrāt Muqāranah" [International Processes in Comparative Paradigms] in *Al-ʿAlāqāt al-Dawliyyah fī ʿĀlim Mutaghayyir: Manẓūrāt wa Madākhil Muqāranah* [International Relations in a Changing World: Comparative Paradigms and Approaches], ed. Nadia Mostafa (Cairo: Hadara Center for Political Studies, 2016), pp. 1104-1202.

10. For more details on these changes and the renewed interest in international political economy during that era, see: Nadia M. Mostafa, "*Naẓariyat al-ʿAlāqāt al-Dawliyyah: Bayn al-Manẓūr al-Wāqiʿī wa al-Daʿwah ilā Manẓūr Jadīd*" [International Relations Theory: Between the Realist Paradigm and the Call for a New One], pp. 65-66; Ahmed Shawky, "Al-Iqtiṣād al-Siyāsī al-Dawlī: Bayn al-Iqtirāb al-Naẓmī wa al-Siyāsah al-Khārijiyyah wa al-Taghayyir al-ʿĀlamī" [International Political Economy: Systems Approach, Foreign Policy and Global Change], in *Al-ʿAlāqāt al-Dawliyyah fī ʿĀlim Mutaghayyir: Manẓūrāt wa Madākhil Muqāranah* [International Relations in a Changing World: Comparative Paradigms and Approaches], ed. Nadia Mostafa (Cairo: Hadara Center for Political Studies, 2016), pp. 1204-1283.
11. See for example: eds. Viotti and Kauppi, *International Relations Theory*, pp. 1-14; ed. Kegley Jr., *Controversies in International Relations Theory*.
12. See for example: Viotti and Kauppi, eds., *International Relations Theory*; Steve Smith and Ken Booth, eds., *Globalization and World Politics* (Oxford: Oxford University Press, 1997).
13. Hedley Bull, "New Directions in the Theory of International Relations," *International Studies* 14, no. 2 (1975): pp. 286-287.
14. See this tradition among ten approaches to the study of IR Theory in: Steve Smith, "Ten Self-Images of a Discipline," pp. 16-71.
15. See for example tripartite brief comparisons in three tables in: Viotti and Kauppi, eds., *International Relations Theory*; Jack Snyder, "One World, Rival Theories."

4
THE END OF THE COLD WAR: TOWARDS A CRISIS IN THE DISCIPLINE OF IR

The Cold War period had impacted International Relations strongly following the Second World War, and so when it suddenly ended in the early 90s, this in turn was to have major implications for the discipline of IR:

a) A dominant paradigm was non-existent in prevailing literature on the state of the art and the characteristics of Post-Cold War international relations, , while the divisions between rival and competing paradigms were remarkably deepening. This transformation was also quite noticeable in the literature describing the state of globalization. That was a theoretical phase sometimes referred to as "post-internationalism."
b) Growing criticism of behavioralism and positivism reflected methodological and epistemological oscillation, which is quite characteristic of "Western" theorizing. So, the prefix "post" was widely used in the 1990s to label the multiple emerging schools of rival paradigms that prevailed in the post-Cold War IR. This, in turn, resulted in ontological and epistemological fluidity and fluctuation that hindered the formulation of a general theory of IR. In the beginnings of the 21st century, these developments were quite alarming: Does this signify the failure of a positivist "IR science"? In response, positivists and realists launched into a debate on the crisis of the discipline or the divided discipline. While such developments were conceived by positivists and realists as signs of crisis, other theoretical approaches perceived them as a move towards an epistemological paradigm shift that should influence the ontological dimension of the discipline.

In this section of the study, I trace the impact the end of the Cold War had on IR Theory during the "fluidity phase," with particular emphasis on the characteristics of international relations, on the one hand, and globalization on the other, both of which have been quite interrelated.

During the early 1990s, IR theorists were specifically interested in the characteristics of international relations. Literature of the time focused on depicting and exploring the "reality of international relations" in a manner that was strongly related to theorizing globalization. The main question raised in this transitional period – though also asked during previous transitional periods – was: Is the world witnessing a new era?

The dialectic relationship between internal and external factors was a core concern of earlier international theorizing. James Rosenau's "Linkage Politics" was a pioneer attempt to address the topic in the early 1970s.[1] In the late 1970s, Wolfram Hanrieder spoke of signs of transformation in the nation-state considering external influences.[2] The third debate between realist and non-realist approaches, which were advocating a new paradigm in the post-behavioralist era in the 1980s, was also partly an outcome of this theoretical concern with the external-internal relationship.

By the end of the Cold War, and in the aftermath of the 9/11 attacks, the reciprocated influence between internal and external factors was constantly increasing in an unprecedented way. The complex impact of this reciprocal relationship on the world order, global change, and international theorizing took multiple forms and extended to various fields. The prevalence of the term "globalization" by the end of the Cold War reflected a recognition of this erosion of strict borders between internal and external affairs; a fact obvious in the post-Cold War era.

Therefore, the in-depth study of the characteristics of the post-Cold War world order and the late twentieth century global transformations, on the one hand, and the in-depth study of globalization on the other hand, were two flipsides of the same coin, both reflecting a growing interest in "a new world order"[3] and a need for new perspectives to analyze and explain IR. Post-Cold War international theorizing (during the fluidity phase) paid attention to these two sides of the coin in an effort to explain the end of the Cold War and to examine its consequences.[4]

Two questions were raised in this regard: Does the end of the Cold War mark the beginning of a new era, or has the end of the Cold War just revealed changes that had already been taking place over the course of two decades preceding that end? Did globalization stimulate the end of the Cold War, or was globalization an outcome of the latter?

Theoretical answers to these questions only attested to the extent to which the discipline had become divided between different competing rival paradigms and their schools. These answers were but old wine in multiple new bottles, adding only additional theoretical complexity to the state of fluidity that had already been characterizing the discipline.

4.1 THE CHARACTERISTICS OF POST-COLD WAR INTERNATIONAL RELATIONS

Do we live in a new world with completely different challenges? IR scholars approached this question from multiple perspectives in search of answers to the essence of global change.[5] For the purpose of depicting the state of theory at that period, I select a sample of different theoretical writings[6] from the 1990s:[7]

Robert Adams: The end of the Cold War is a turning point indeed, yet conflictual features of IR will persist:

- The great-power relations are moving away from armed conflict to new forms of hegemony based on blocs and regional balances.
- The world map is changing because of integration as well as fragmentation.
- The end of communism as a political force in Europe.
- The spread of democracy and the challenges facing that alternative, and the relationship between the spread of democracy and world peace.
- The non-credibility of the relationship between the existence of homogenous values – shared by a global community – and the achievement of global stability.
- The survival of the state, despite the impact of economic and cultural globalization.

- Increasing tensions in the South with no signs of great power willingness to resolve them. Meanwhile, international instability is stimulated by North-South unsettled tensions.

James Rosenau: The Post-Cold War world is in disorder; it is a world of "post-internationalism." International chaos is fed by the same factors that ended the Cold War. The multiple sources of international disorder created a blurry image of this new era: increasing rivalry between non-state actors and the sovereign state; globalization of national economies; the impact of modern technology; the growing urgency of interdependence issues; the waning of the nation-state; Third World problems; the widening gap between North and South; divisions between countries of the South; and South-to-North flows.

Fred Halliday: The rules of the game have changed and the end of the Cold War was the culmination of transformations that had been growing since the 1970s. These transformations carry aspects of homogeneity and heterogeneity at the same time. Aspects of homogeneity include: ideological homogeneity after the fall of communism; economic homogeneity driven by globalization; socio-political homogeneity promoted by democratization and modernization; and diminished inclination to resort to war and violence in developed societies (which are considered the center of the world order) under the influence of growing interdependence. Heterogeneity materializes in: the global crisis of authority; the end of bipolarity; the rising role of new actors; and the de-Westernization of the world. The Third World witnesses factors of both homogeneity as well as heterogeneity and disaggregation.

Pierre Grosser: Neither the nature of, nor the patterns of conducting international relations have changed. It is only the case that the circumstances surrounding international relations since the end of the Cold War have changed, but in fact no substantial change has occurred to international relations itself. International interdependence is neither recent, nor does it replace conflicts or negate potentials of war. In addition, the non-violent change in Eastern Europe does not necessarily imply that violence in international relations has become obsolete. It simply implies that the specific circumstances in Eastern Europe and the Soviet Union at that time were catalysts for that particular pattern of change. In fact, duality and contradictions still dominate international relations: with a newly shaped world seeking unity and ideological, economic, and political homogeneity, and another world characterized by disaggregation, either because of the nature of authority and the diffusion of power, or because of the dissolving bipolar structure, or the emergence of new actors. So, the homogeneity characterizing the center of the world and the new world order is contradicted by the heterogeneity and fragmentation seen at the opposite side, where the Third World and the countries of the South are located.

Mohammed Selim: Global changes have different direct impacts on the Muslim world. Multi-level challenges (resulting from Western policies) generate various challenges that the Muslim world is required to face. There have been many transformations that have radically changed the basic foundations of the world order and resulted in the emergence of a new hierarchy of power in international relations: the third industrial revolution and the technological development in communication and information; transformations in international subsystems (e.g., the demise of the European bloc, Western Europe's orientation towards political unity, the East-Asian rise); and transformations in the global economy towards capitalist globalism. These phenomena should open opportunities for Muslim countries to benefit from Asian experiences of development and to provide alternatives, albeit limited, to Western hegemony. However, transformations in the global economic order lead to greater marginalization of the South and speed up the subordination of its economies to the capitalist industrial world.

A close examination of these writings[8] and others[9] help us to highlight the following observations:

- The emergence of optimistic views on cooperation alongside pessimistic views on conflict to theoretically foresee the future did not negate the rigorousness and complexity of real-world challenges.
- The difficulties faced by great powers that affected their ability to perform as effective global authority, at a time of growing Third World problems, were considered to augment the probabilities of global disorder.

- Theorizing about reality was confined to the framework of Western capitalist values and interests. Although multiple schools tackled democratization, capitalism, and cultural values, they still expressed a unilateral Western perspective. To them, the non-democratic underdeveloped Third World, or South, jeopardized international peace and security once it failed to embrace democracy or achieve development (i.e., it had become the source of global chaos and disorder). This was a wild repetition of the traditional image of realist conflictual international politics.

  Here it is worth recalling that this trend of theorizing was not totally new. In the mid-1970s, the literature on international interdependence argued that international relations was becoming more cooperative, yet competitive, and less conflictual than it had been after the Second World War. In contrast, other trends argued that interdependence is not applicable to North-South relations.[10] A similar former scenario, that dated back to the post-World War I era, however, maintained that the rights to self-determination and collective security within the framework of the League of Nations were not applicable to the case of the "South" or the colonized states.

  Also, following the second Gulf crisis, when a multitude of theoretical writings redirected attention to the New World Order, some perspectives kept warning that the ongoing problems and conflicts in the Third World – of which the Gulf crisis was just an example – would still threaten world stability and that the end of ideological conflict and bipolarity would not reflect itself positively on the conditions of the Third World.[11]

  Differently stated, these examples of major trends of theorizing about the New World Order were preoccupied with accommodating and protecting the interests of great powers, rather than being concerned with "global change" as such.
- As previously shown, Third World /South/underdeveloped countries (depending on the criteria of classification) were not adequately represented during earlier phases of IR theorizing. These countries were just remotely observed by post-Cold War Western analyses of the New World Order and globalization, which were

largely interested in depicting and explaining great power politics in the new world. Meanwhile, some timid critiques of IR Western-centrism began to look for non-Western perspectives (as will be detailed later).

- Sophistication, complexity, and the growing interconnection between internal and external affairs could be attributed to many factors: the importance of global civil society, the privatization of international relations, increased global interconnectedness, intensified interactions among individuals, states, and peoples, and the mushrooming of transnational and subnational loyalties.

  The interaction between internal and external dynamics or external penetration of national borders went beyond the economic and political issues and remarkably extended to cultural and social aspects. Not only did this interaction affect the political elites, it also manipulated the cognitive orientations of peoples. Peoples' recognition of Western superiority was deepened; reinforcing the conviction that the West was destined to victory and, hence, should be imitated by non-Westerners. Therefore, major paradigms became more attentive to religious and cultural origins of globalization. This theoretical shift was associated with reflections on the impact of globalization on the emergence of new approaches to IR.

4.2 GLOBALIZATION: THE CONCEPT AND ITS IMPACTS FROM THE PERSPECTIVE OF COMPETING PARADIGMS

Globalization is a buzzy term that strikingly prevailed in a wide range of international studies in the 1990s. Reflecting on the characteristics of international relations, hitherto, revolved around addressing the question: Do we live in a new era? However, my own analysis of globalization – at that time – revolved around answering the questions: How different is this era? What are the magnitude and implications of this difference? My approach to globalization[12] was that of a researcher seeking to diagnose the then prevalent state of research by constructing the concept of globalization, and mapping the aspects, levels, and problematics of its study. Two main motivations were driving this approach.

The first motivation was the prevalence of the concern with globalization in almost all disciplines of political science, social sciences, and humanities, and the spread of the concept, coupled with other important concepts such as the globalization of: capitalism, human rights, business, trade, investment, culture, identity, values, etc. However, despite these abundant and diverse perspectives on globalization, no definition of globalization was agreed upon; and neither a description of globalization, nor of its potential impact on IR was endorsed. The only consensus available was that on the ambiguity of the concept and its confusion with overlapping concepts.

The second motivation was related to the reception of the term in the Arab world. After the term had been coined and circulated in Western academia, responses in Arab and Muslim circles varied between a spectrum of rejection and harsh criticism, on the one hand, and justification and acceptance, on the other; which in fact closely mirrored the early 90s responses to the terms "New World Order" and "international legitimacy." Driven by curiosity to explore the underlying reasons for this duality of positions, I used the competing-paradigms approach to investigate the influence of paradigm differences on the approach to globalization in IR. Indeed, IR scholarship on globalization was a highly significant indicator of the degree of division and plurality that was characterizing the paradigmatic state of IR at that stage. Earlier scholarship on the characteristics of post-Cold War international relations was an indicator of the degree of division and plurality then prevalent in the discipline. Debates were no longer confined to those between two dominant paradigms. Globalization was not a new paradigm, but a concept that needed initial construction. A comparative selective review of the immense literature on globalization published through the 1990s[13] featured two sets of problematics; those related to the definition (identification and explanation) and those related to assessing the impacts of globalization.

Is globalization a process, a condition, or a final desired status? Is it a mere intellectual phenomenon or does it also have material expressions and manifestations? Does it originate from a main single source or from various overlapping sources? Is it driven by economics, technological innovations, global environmental crises, or by all of these and other factors? Does globalization entail a deeper homogeneity or just a broader familiarity with diversity? Does it represent a unified world or separate systems connected by material or symbolic ties? Is it characterized by distinct cultural practices or is it just an aggregation of local cultures? What are its possible implications on the dialectic relationship between internal and external factors, between neighboring and distant international actors, and between us and them? Is it a one-way or a multi-directional process? What are the prospects of the nation-state? Does the survival of the nation-state reinforce globalization or challenge its dynamics? Does regionalism obstruct globalization? Is the gap between the wealthy and the deprived an outcome of globalization? Finally, should we welcome or reject globalization? Will it improve people's lives or should they resist it?

A) Problematics of Definition: Identification and Explanation

Based on a comparative literature review,[14] I can draw here some important conclusions. Globalization was defined in comparison to or in association with other terms that denoted global processes at that time, such as interdependence, transnationalism, liberalization, internationalization, universalism, and global society. These terms differed according to the different priority they gave to economic aspects relative to other aspects like communication technology. Hence, various disciplines, such as political economy, political sociology, IR, and political systems, offered distinct definitions and descriptions of globalization in a manner that triggered several questions: Which of these aspects are the causes and which are the outcomes? Which of these aspects are manifestations and which are explanatory forces? Which discipline is most capable of introducing an inclusive understanding and diagnosis of globalization?

Comparative analysis of the assumptions of realism, neo-liberalism, and international interdependence on globalization revealed the emergence of novel assumptions that challenged the traditional conception of the levels of analysis in IR and political science. While assumptions about the traditional levels of analysis often distinguished between internal and external factors and clearly differentiated between the chaotic nature of international relations and the organized authoritative hierarchical nature of internal structures, globalization embodied the overlap between internal and external affairs and the intersection between economic, social, and political processes. Moreover, as the state was considered to be a historical social entity, whose role was determined by the historical era to which it belonged, the role and functions of the state were expected to change in the globalization era.

Jan Aart Scholte argued that the issue of "borders" was central to the debates on globalization, along with other associated issues like governments, economies, identity, and community. He articulated an operational definition of globalization based on the distinction between three border-related indicators: cross-border relations, open-border relations, and trans-border relations. While the first two indicators were respectively connected to the concepts of interdependence and liberalization, Aart Scholte believed that trans-border relations were the most meaningful indicator of globalization as they reflected a real demographic transformation driven by radical changes in communication and information technology during the last decades of the twentieth century.

As for the explanatory factors behind globalization, some definitions of globalization emphasized the international political economy approach, while others applied more comprehensive and generic approaches that added non-economic factors to analysis (i.e., factors other than the globalization of capitalism or the global economy). Comprehensive definitions still considered economics as an essential driving force, yet insufficient to single-handedly provide a thorough analysis of globalization as a phenomenon, a process, or a state. These comprehensive approaches were keen to emphasize the sociocultural aspects, while analyzing international relations, alongside the traditional political and security aspects that dominated the scene during the peak of the Cold War and political economic aspects that had become a field of interest since the early 1970s. Thus, the globalization of culture and societies was no longer separable from political and economic globalization. This conception, however, assumed that globalization was not a recent product of the end of the Cold War, but an old phenomenon traceable to the beginnings of capitalism and, hence, dating back to centuries ago.

It is important to note that such comprehensive definitions of globalization were mainly delivered by IR theorists. The discipline was, hence, expected to offer a comprehensive view on the systemic relationship between the various aspects of globalization (its manifestations, processes, and driving forces) which were addressed separately by other disciplines. It can, therefore, be argued that the growing attention to social, cultural, and religious aspects in international studies was a real value-added contribution of the studies of global change by the end of the 20th century. This raises a question: Can the study of global change become an autonomous field of study to which different disciplines contribute? One very significant indicator of the growing attention paid to the social, cultural, and religious aspects in academic political studies was the emergence of the clash of civilizations thesis and the ensuing debate which carried blatant cultural and civilizational aspects.[15]

B) The Repercussions of Globalization

This topic is often tackled in literature addressing the crisis of the nation-state and the state of the world order.

The State of the World Order

Is the world heading towards convergence and homogeneity or towards chaos, multiplicity, divergence, and heterogeneity? Are there some forces that push towards a mixture of convergence and divergence? Discussions and answers to these questions were integral to studies on global distribution of wealth and welfare, the founding values of political regimes (especially democracy), and cultural identity and ethical normative aspects. The term "borderless world" was celebrated by numerous studies due to the neoliberal assumptions about the necessity and inevitability of transformations towards a single-market global economy, with increasing direct investments, where everyone would be enjoying the positive impact of trade liberalization. By contrast, there were other studies that put under scrutiny these assumptions and questioned the validity of both what concerned the global economy and what concerned the local social and political consequences of globalization.

Meanwhile, other studies underlined emerging dichotomies: localization/globalization, homogeneity/hegemony, and convergence/divergence. In all of these dichotomies, the dilemma of the self/the other or us/them was present across different civilizational contexts and with reference to diverse value systems. Social and cultural aspects were central to these dichotomies, and some related studies were keen to prove the expansion of the divisive effects of economic globalization that were created by economic disparities between the North and the South. In addition, some studies highlighted that structural reform policies had domestic social consequences that widened the socio- economic gaps inside the same country. These studies also illustrated that internal divisions led to a growing inclination towards the strengthening of local identities, and that globalization fed differences and divergence, while giving lip service to eliminating borders of time and space and calling upon homogeneity and equity.

The Crisis of the Nation-state

This discussion is not entirely new, and globalization theorists were not pioneers in bringing this crisis to debating platforms. Structural integrationists, trans-nationalists, global idealists, and even Marxists, all had had their earlier contributions to the discussion on the crisis of the nation-state, though in different contexts and with different details. Globalization theorists did not provide a unified discourse on the crisis of the nation-state. The neoliberal arguments on the demise of the nation-state were countered by the arguments of other schools adopting a different perspective (e.g., mercantilists advocated the strengthening, rather than the weakening, of the nation-state). Some sociologists rejected the assumption that the very existence of the state, as well as its role, had been the products of history, which happened to be changing in the globalization era; while others admitted that the state power and authority were undergoing deep transformations that had an impact on the former's nature and degree. Other sociologists argued that the competitive state had replaced the welfare state. In the meantime, some criticized the lack of democratic surveillance over the institutions of government, while others believed that the state still existed, yet in a different manner; having lost some aspects of its traditional territorial sovereignty. According to these theorists, the state was still supposed to remain the main agent in service of globalization, and the new state had to be prepared to play a multi-level competitive role (i.e., competition with other states, competition with multinational companies, and even regulating competition between companies themselves).

The influence of "global capitalism" or the globalization of capitalism on the role of the state was detectable in many areas. According to Jan Aart Scholte, this influence appeared in some shared rules by which all types of states abided, regardless of the degree of influence or the kind of response to this influence that they adopted. These rules included: the survival and non-withering of states; the end of the traditional notion of state sovereignty; the crystallization of externally-provoked internal conflicts; and the increase in multilateral interactions.

IR paradigms introduced diverse assessment of the impact of globalization on the nation-state.[16] The debate on the effects of globalization on international relations could be stratified into at least two main strands (as illustrated in one of the comprehensive studies on globalization and international politics).[17] One strand advocated a process of standardization: one world, global economy, universal culture, etc. The statements upheld by this strand can be summarized as follows:

- Vast and rapid economic transformation created new global policies.
- States are neither closed entities, nor are they in full control of their economies anymore.
- Interdependence in the global economy is growing due to flourishing international trade and capital mobility.
- The worldwide communication revolution affected people's awareness of the self and the other, thus creating a "cosmopolitan culture," shared specifically by urban populations.
- The world becomes more homogeneous as differences between people diminish. Time is no longer a barrier and massive transnational and global interactions are taking place among various national actors and global networks in various fields.

These views were advocated by neoliberals and had their impact on the discourse of the leaders of major global financial institutions such as the International Monetary Fund as well as the discourse of American economic and financial officials.

Views adopted by the second strand, contrastingly, revolved around rejecting Western hegemony over global processes. These views can be summarized as follows:

- Globalization is a catchy word describing eventually the final stage of capitalism. There is no single cosmopolitan economy. Non-state actors are but tools used by governments to implement the policies of the latter. Global trade and investment remain concentrated in the hands of the three great economic powers: Europe, North America, and Japan.
- Globalization has an uneven impact on humanity. It is beneficial only to the advanced world, and it reflects Western values and economic views without any consideration for the values and interests of non-Western societies. The content of globalization discourse reflects the Western worldview to the detriment of other cultures and civilizations.
- Some people will not share in the benefits of globalization, yet they will be expected to stand its harmful effects. That is why globalization is seen as not only imperialist, but also exploitative.
- A universal Western culture is non-existent so far, and human rights, women's rights, and religion remain to be areas of intercultural contestation.

These views have been common among realists, nationalists, and structuralists, and they are also shared by contemporary strands of Islamic thought, with a special focus on the systemic relationship between the civilizational and cultural aspects.[18]

In conclusion, in light of this overview of the different strands examining the manifestations and impact of globalization, the following observations on the new aspects of the state of international relations in an age of globalization can be recorded.

1. IR Theory literature portrays globalization as a multifaceted

phenomenon: capitalist-economic, democratic-political, and normative-cultural. It is also portrayed as a sustained and ongoing historical process that has been stimulated by many driving forces, but that has been particularly intensified and deepened since the 1990s due to two main factors:

- An enormous technological revolution that achieved a breakthrough in communication and information technology which, in turn, has had a substantial influence on the essence of power. The power of knowledge, innovation, and information have become equally crucial as military and economic power.[19]
- The end of the Cold War and the subsequent termination of bipolarity and ideological animosity, which have led to the emergence of the Western capitalist civilizational model as the unchallenged victorious model.

Taking these factors into consideration, it can be argued that the West has deliberately transformed globalization since the end of the Cold War into an institutionalized and legalized system for the purpose of monopolizing new elements of global power. This is quite evident from the official statements of leaders of Western industrial countries, assessing globalization quite positively.[20] While other discourses of semi-globalist Western circles have tended to criticize globalization (such as the European Union's official statements), they have still perceived it as convenient for new regional blocs.[21] Moreover, the discourse of hegemony has been inherent in the theoretical literature, whether explicitly or implicitly. That discourse has addressed the various aspects of the hegemony of the Western model; economic, political, and cultural hegemony.

A discussion of the manifestations and impact of globalization is inseparable from an answer to the following questions: What is being globalized? By whom? And for whose interest? It is true that most Western IR scholars – while reflecting on the characteristics of IR since the end of the Cold War or on globalization – have not seemed fascinated by the potential positive effects of globalization; those promised by neoliberals or by the advocates of the "end of history" thesis. However, their reflections and critiques remained mostly confined to the Western model, especially what concerns the universality of democracy and market economy, and their credibility as prerequisites for international peace and security.

In short, the ongoing worldwide interactions and mutual influences – taking place within the context of globalization – are not merely an outcome of structural factors. They are run by the rules of a single civilizational model, controlled by one leading power: the USA (at least before discussions on the decline of the American power set about). So, it is vital to distinguish between globalization as a process, globalization as an ideology, and globalization as policies, especially since the end of the Cold War. In this sense, globalization is different from "complex international interdependence" that was considered as the core of international processes by the "pluralists" (as mentioned earlier) and acquired increasing attention in the 1970s and 1980s, though in a different international context.

In fact, the growing interest in globalization did not forge new questions and answers. The real novelty was a deeper change in the relationship between internal and external factors. Globalization carried along such great changes in terms of magnitude and scope that the cultural became now included in "the political." This means that, unlike complex international interdependence, globalization can only be studied at a systemic macro level.

2. The rise of sociocultural analyses of globalization, alongside political and economic analyses, enriched the literature of global change, going gradually beyond the debate on the manifestations of globalization to embrace a debate on the normative aspects of these manifestations and their consequences. This conferred on the theoretical and intellectual debates (among the strands of neorealism or neoliberalism for example) clear normative aspects.

The contemporary globalization era is, thus, marked by the revival of values and normative aspects in international studies (a fact that opens a space for an Islamic theoretical perspective with a special interest in normative aspects). By no means should this imply that the importance of civilizational and cultural aspects grew separate from a concern for the political and economic aspects in studies of global change. On the contrary, these aspects are weaved together in recent international analyses. Culture and civilization are present in discussions about democratization, human rights, market economy, and structural adjustment. With reference to the previous analysis of the characteristics of contemporary international relations (in terms of actors, issues, tools, levels of analysis, patterns of interaction, forces, and factors), the rising interest in sociocultural aspects, in interaction with political and economic aspects, is strongly justified.

Nevertheless, amidst these three inseparable aspects – cultural, political, and economic – culture is considered particularly useful to the analysis of contemporary international relations in the South, at the heart of which lies the Muslim world. After Western political, military, and economic hegemony has been accomplished, only cultural hegemony is still missing. Structures of the South that did not resist economic dependence but remained resilient to a Westernized democratization, are fighting a harsh battle against cultural hegemony, they are not only defending their back lines, but they are in fact striving not to retreat completely.

3. The South appears in the general analyses of globalization and amid discussions about the impact of globalization on the world order. The South is usually called upon in literature dealing with the impact of global economic developments on the North-South gap, the potentials, and pros and cons of democratization, or the impact of globalization on the state in the North as compared to its impact on the state in the South. However, these discussions usually revolve around the ways of safeguarding the North against threats from the South. None of the above-mentioned analyses is concerned with how to protect the South from the negative effects of globalization!

To conclude the previous two-step analysis, analysis of the literature on the characteristics of the post-Cold War international relations and the literature on globalization reveals that the relationship between internal and external factors is becoming increasingly complex due to the increasing vulnerability of the internal to the impact of the external in a manner that impedes the fair distribution of the benefits and advantages of globalization to everyone.

In other words, analysis throughout this part has revealed that the impact of globalization and the resulting external challenges that were prevalent by the end of the 20th century are the same external challenges that face the Muslim world in the globalization era, with wide and deep external penetration affecting the internal. This proves the urgency of discussing the potentiality of an Islamic paradigm of IR in general, and of studying the consequences of globalization on the Muslim world in particular.

NOTES

1. James S. Rosenau, *Linkage Politics: Essays on the Convergence of National and International System* (New York: Free Press, 1969).
2. Wolfram F. Hanrieder, "Dissolving International Politics: Reflections on the Nation State," *American Political Science Review*, no. 4 (1978).
3. Studies on the new international order had noticeably risen in the 1990s in Arab and foreign academic circles. For comparative analysis of some of these studies, see: Wadoudah Badran, "Al-Ruʿā al-Mukhtalifah li al-Niẓām al-ʿĀlimī al-Jadīd" [Different Perspectives on the World Order], in *Al-Niẓām al-Dawlī al-Jadīd* [The New International Order], ed., Mohammed Elsayed Selim (Cairo: Cairo University Center for Political Research and Studies, 1994); Nadia M. Mostafa, "Al-Manṭiqah al-ʿArabiyyah wa al-Niẓām al-Dawlī al-Jadīd" [The Arab Region and the New International Order], in *Taqrīr al-Ummah fī ʿĀm* [The Ummah Over a Year] (Cairo: Center for Civilizational Studies, 1993); Nadia M. Mostafa, "Azmat al-Khalīj al-Thāniyyah wa al-Niẓam al-Dawlī al-Jadīd" [The Second Gulf Crisis and the New International Order], in *Azmat al-Khalīj wa al-Abʿād al-Dawliyyah wa al-Iqlimiyyah* [The Gulf Crisis and the International and Regional Aspects], ed., Ahmad Rashidy (Cairo: Cairo University Center for Political Research and Studies, 1991); Hassanein Tawfik, *Al-Niẓām al-Dawlī al-Jadīd* [The New International Order] (Cairo: Egyptian General Book Authority, 1992); Ahmad Youssef Ahmad, ed., *Al-Waṭan al-ʿArabī wa al-Taghayyirāt al-ʿĀlamiyyah* [The Arab World and Global Changes] (Cairo: Institute of Arab Research and Studies, 1991).

4. See details in: Nadia M. Mostafa, "Al-Taḥaddiyāt al-Siyāsiyyah al-Khārijiyyah li al-ʿĀlim al-Islāmī" [External Political Challenges to the Muslim World], in *Aʿmāl Mashrūʿ al-Taḥaddiyāt al-Lati Tuwājih al-ʿĀlam al-Islāmī* [Proceedings of the Project on Challenges that Face the Muslim World] (Cairo: League of Islamic Universities, 1999), pp. 27-77.
5. Ken Dark, "Defending Global Change," in *The Ethical Dimensions of Global Change*, ed., Barry Holden (UK: Palgrave Macmillan, 1996), pp. 7-17.
6. For detailed analysis, see: Nadia M. Mostafa, "Al-Taḥaddiyāt al-Siyāsiyyah al-Khārijiyyah li al-ʿĀlim al-Islāmī" [External Political Challenges to the Muslim World], pp. 32-49.
7. The respective examples are: Robert Adams, "A New Age in International Relations," *International Relations* 67, no. 3, (July 1991); James Rosenau and Mary Durfee, *Thinking Theory Thoroughly*, pp. 31-69; Fred Halliday, "The End of the Cold War and International Relations," in *International Relations Theory Today*, eds., Ken Booth and Steve Smith, pp. 39-61; Pierre Grosser, *Les Temps de la Guerre froide:* Réflexions *Sur l'histoire de la Guerre Froide et Sur les Causes de Sa Fin* (Bruxelles: Editions Comlexe, 1995), pp. 193-263; Mohammed Selim, "Al-Taḥawalāt al-ʿĀlamiyyah wa Athāruhā ʿalā al-ʿĀlim al-Islāmī" [Global Transformations and their Impacts on the Muslim World] in *Qaḍāyā Islāmiyyah Muʿāṣirah* [Contemporary Islamic Issues], ed., Hassan El-Alkeem (Cairo: Cairo University Center for Asian Studies, 1997).
8. Ibid., pp. 46-49.
9. See also: Bahgat Korany, *Al-ʿAlāqāt al-Dawliyyah ʿalā Mushārif al-Qarn al-Ḥādī wa al-ʿIshrīn* [International Relations at the Threshold of the Twenty-First Century] (Cairo: Cairo University Center for Political Research and Studies, 1996); Zbigniew Brzezi ski, *Out of Control: Global Turmoil on the Eve of the 21st Century*, Trans. Malek Fadel (Beirut: Lebanese Company for Print and Publication, 1998).
10. For more details on this scenario, see: Nadia M. Mostafa "Naẓariyat al-ʿAlāqāt al-Dawliyyah: Bayn al-Manẓūr al-Wāqiʿī wa al-Daʿwah ilā Manẓūr Jadīd" [International Relations Theory: Between the Realist Paradigm and the Call for a New One].
11. For detailed discussions of these perspectives, see: Wadoudah Badran, "Al-Ruʿā al-Mukhtalifah li al-Niẓām al-ʿĀlimī al-Jadīd" [Different

Perspectives on the World Order]; Nadia M. Mostafa, "Al-Taḥaddiyāt al-Siyāsiyyah al-Khārijiyyah li al-ʿĀlim al-Islāmī" [External Political Challenges to the Muslim World]; and Nadia M. Mostafa, "Azmat al-Khalīj al-Thāniyyah wa al-Niẓam al-Dawlī al-Jadīd" [The Second Gulf Crisis and the New International Order].

12. Nadia M. Mostafa, "Al-Taḥaddiyāt al-Siyāsiyyah al-Khārijiyyah li al-ʿĀlim al-Islāmī" [External Political Challenges to the Muslim World], pp. 50-72.

13. Nadia M. Mostafa, "Al-ʿAwlamah wa Ḥaql al-ʿAlāqāt" [Globalization and the Discipline of International Relations], in *Al-ʿAwlamah wa al-ʿUlūm al-Siyāsiyyah* [Globalization and Political Science], eds., Saif Abdel-Fattah and Hassan Nafaa (Cairo: Cairo University Faculty of Economics and Political Science, 2000); James Rosenau, "The Dynamics of Globalization: Toward an Operational Formulation," *Security Dialogue* 26, no. 3 (1996): pp. 247-262; Philip Cerny, "Globalization and Other Stories: The Search for a New Paradigm for International Relations," *International Journal* 51, no. 4 (December 1996): pp. 616-637; Claire Turenne Sjolander, "The Rhetoric of Globalization: What's in a World?," *International Journal* 51, no. 4 (December 1996): pp. 603-615; Jan Aart Scholte, "Global Capitalism and the State," *International Affairs* 73, no. 3 (1997): pp. 427-440; Paul Hirst, "Global Economy: Myths and Realities," *International Affairs* 73, no. 3 (1997): pp. 409-425; Philip Cerny, "Globalization and the Changing Logic of Collective Action," *International Organization* 49, no. 4 (Autumn 1995): pp. 595-900. Besides the former six basic references, which will be comparatively reviewed, another group of literature can be cited here: S. Smith, P. Owens and J. Baylis, *The Globalization of World Politics: An Introduction to International Relations* (Oxford: Oxford University Press, 1997); Ali Mazrui et al., "Globalization," *Special Issue of the American Journal of Islamic Social Sciences* 15, no. 3 (1998); Hans-Peter Martin and Harald Schumann, *The Global Trap: Globalization and the Assault on Prosperity and Democracy*, Trans. Adnan Abbas Ali (Kuwait: ʿĀlam al-Maʿrifa, 1998); United Nations Program, "Al-ʿAwlamah: Umum Faqīrah wa Qawm Fuqarā'" [Globalization: Poor Nations and Poor People], *Al-ijtihād* 38 (Winter 1998), pp. 65-100.

14. See details in Nadia M. Mostafa, "Al-Taḥaddiyāt al-Siyāsiyyah al-

Khārijiyyah li al-ʿĀlim al-Islāmī" [External Political Challenges to the Muslim World], pp. 55-60.

15. See: Amany Ghanem, "Al-Abʿād al-Thaqāfiyyah wa al-ʿAlāqāt al-Dawliyyah: Dirāsah fī Khaṭāb Ṣadām al-Ḥaḍārāt" [Cultural Aspects in International Relations: A Study of the Clash of Civilizations Discourse], in *Al-ʿAlāqāt al-Dawliyyah fī ʿĀlim Mutaghayyir: Manẓūrāt wa Madākhil Muqāranah* [International Relations in a Changing World: Comparative Paradigms and Approaches], ed. Nadia Mostafa (Cairo: Hadara Center for Political Studies, 2016), pp. 1509-1627.
16. See: Marwa Fikry, "Global Transformations and the Nation-State: A Theoretical Study," in *Al-ʿAlāqāt al-Dawliyyah fī ʿĀlim Mutaghayyir: Manẓūrāt wa Madākhil Muqāranah* [International Relations in a Changing World: Comparative Paradigms and Approaches], ed. Nadia Mostafa (Cairo: Hadara Center for Political Studies, 2016), pp. 460-545.
17. "Introduction," in *The Globalization of World Politics*, eds. J. Baylis, P. Owens and S. Smith.
18. See for example: Nadia M. Mostafa, "Taḥaddiyāt al-ʿAwlamah wa al-Abʿād al-Thaqāfiyyah al-Ḥaḍāriyyah wa al-Qiyamiyyah: Ru'yah Islāmiyyah" [Challenges of Globalization and the Cultural and Civilizational Alternative Aspects: An Islamic Perspective], in *Mustaqbal al-Islām* [The Future of Islam] (Damascus: Dar al-Fikr al-Arabī, 2004).
19. Alvin Toffler, *Transformation of Authority Between Violence, Wealth and Knowledge* (Benghazi: Al-Dār al-Jumāʿīriyyah, 1992); Samah Abdel-Sabour, "Smart Power in Foreign Policy: Theory and Practice," in *Al-ʿAlāqāt al-Dawliyyah fī ʿĀlim Mutaghayyir: Manẓūrāt wa Madākhil Muqāranah* [International Relations in a Changing World: Comparative Paradigms and Approaches], ed. Nadia Mostafa (Cairo: Hadara Center for Political Studies, 2016), pp. 264-331.
20. See for example: United Nations, "G-7 Summit Economic Communique," *Presidents and Prime Ministers* 5, no. 4 (1996): p. 12.
21. John Pinder, "Globalisation vs. Sovereignty? The European Response: The 1997 Rede Lecture and Related Speeches, by Sir Leon Brittan QC." European Foreign Affairs Review 6, no. 1 (2001): pp. 143-44.

5
DEBATES BETWEEN COMPETING PARADIGMS: A DIVIDED DISCIPLINE

Did the world change after the end of the Cold War? The previous two chapters have demonstrated that theorizing in IR has undergone radical changes and has experienced a state of fluidity that has been especially reflected in a state of "post-isms"; fluidity at both levels of content or substance, and research methods. The debates between competing IR paradigms can be summarized as follows.[1]

5.1 THE CHAOTIC DESIGNATION OF PARADIGMS

In IR the same paradigm often appears under a spectrum of different designations signalling a chaotic approach to the body of thought. For instance, Realism, one of the dominant schools of thought in international relations theory, is also termed as international chaos, state-centrism, power struggles, and power politics, all different names given to the same realist paradigm. Similarly, liberalism, international community, international interdependence, and multilateralism are various designations of the liberal paradigm. The same applies to Marxism, sometimes called global structuralism, class conflict or world-system. In fact, these are not synonyms, but chaotic designations. Identifying the main assumptions and hypotheses of a paradigm is dependent on answers to primary questions about actors, themes, processes, outcomes, and philosophical or intellectual roots of the paradigm. Thus, each of the above-mentioned designations focuses in fact on one of these questions. The same applies to the designation of methodologies and methods such as behavioralism, positivism, empiricism, materialism/traditionalism, subjectivism, intuitionism, and normativism, which are all names addressing different aspects of the methodological process, including the epistemological and philosophical foundations, information and data collection, hypotheses formulation, etc.

5.2 THE MULTIPLICITY OF SCHOOLS AND STRANDS

Paradigms are neither static, nor inadaptable wholes, yet, each paradigm preserves a hard core that makes the paradigm clearly distinguishable from other paradigms. Traditional idealism included multiple schools and strands, and so did neo-idealism (in the post-behavioralist phase), which was considered to be an extension of idealism but with special attention given to economic aspects. In the same manner, globalization, as perceived by the liberal paradigm, is a multidimensional version of idealism with a focus on cultural aspects. Similarly, neo-realism differs from traditional realism in terms of the source and scope of international chaos. Pessimist interdependence is a realist school concerned with the conflict-stimulating effects of the dominance of economic aspects. The clash of civilizations is another realist school that analyzes the impact of cultural and religious aspects on inter-state conflicts. Hence, a boost in IR theoretical literature did not entail academic richness as much as it signified a crisis and failure to formulate a general theory. This is attributable to a narrow-sighted theoretical oscillation between the different aspects of the phenomena.

5.3 THE EROSION OF BOUNDARIES BETWEEN PARADIGMS

The absence of a dominant paradigm in IR and the existence of a multiplicity of schools and strands within each paradigm, meant that in a complex and rapidly changing international context, swift and flexible divisions occurred. This not only revealed the ability of paradigms to adapt to new contexts, on the one hand, but was evidence of areas of intersection between the different paradigms, on the other, falsifying, thereby, the claim that each paradigm held a monopoly with reference to concern over a specific aspect of the international phenomena that no other paradigm shared.

For example, state, power, and even conflict are addressed by all paradigms. The real question is: How do theories differ from one another and why? (What is the difference between nation-state, welfare state, prosperity state, competition state, class-state? What is the difference between hard power, soft power, smart power? What is the difference between the conflict of powers, conflict of rivals, and class conflict?)

Also, the crisis of the nation-state, for example, is no longer an exclusively non-realist business. It was even addressed in the 1970s, and therefore, cannot be regarded as a recent outcome of the globalization age. Similarly, the interest in economic, cultural, and normative aspects is not confined to non-realist schools. As for behavioralists and realists, they neither have a monopoly over the study of the behavior of international units, nor the study of reality. In other words, the rigid separation between paradigms has become critically questionable, and each paradigm contains a considerable degree of internal diversity and variety that is not necessarily reflected by the labels given to it.

5.4 CAN PARADIGM DEBATES BE SETTLED?

Can paradigm debates be settled? Can one paradigm be judged as absolutely more valid or correct than other paradigms? In regard to these two questions, there prevails a consensus on some points:

- Paradigms are not assessed according to independent or external criteria. Each paradigm or school has its own criteria of assessment that is framed from within the paradigm. In the absence of an external criteria of assessment, assessment remains contingent on the researcher's own values and beliefs. Researchers make judgements according to their own epistemological formation and experiences, not only according to available information or with reference to givens of reality or the paradigm's own explanatory capabilities.
- It would be unrealistic to envision one single paradigm as capable of treating all international incidents efficiently, or to claim that a specific incident should be addressed by one paradigm only. Yet, despite the fact that the mere existence of paradigm debates suggests that paradigms offer competing explanations of international

relations, followers of each paradigm tend to focus on the paradigms' significant issues, while ignoring other paradigms, even seeking to marginalize them, especially those belonging to a different episteme.

- As Rosenau affirmed in 1981, paradigms are different perspectives on realities of international relations. The supremacy of one perspective over others at a point in time is basically attributable to changes in realities, which drive research on the nature and depth of these changes. In other words, paradigms are not various perspectives of different worlds. Rather, they are different perspectives of the same world. Hence, each of these perspectives is valid in reference to that specific aspect of the world that it deals with (and most importantly, in reference to its own particular episteme).

5.5 THE APPROACH OF SUCCESSIVE COMPETING PARADIGMS AND THE PERPETUAL MOVEMENT OF SCIENCE

This approach generates the false impression that theory is constantly changing; and that theorists are constantly realizing their mistaken assumptions and simply shifting to adopt a new perspective. It is a completely erroneous impression because the great debates among consecutive paradigms do not entail the replacement of one dominant paradigm by another rising competitive paradigm. Paradigms do not fade away. They continue to exist and sometimes develop their own new strands and schools, such as neo-realism, neoliberalism, and neo-Marxism.

Therefore, paradigm debates contradict Thomas Kuhn's theory on scientific revolutions. Kuhn's findings seem valid in the natural sciences, rather than the social sciences. In natural sciences, when qualitative shifts or scientific revolutions take place, they mark the termination of a phase and the beginning of a new one, representing, thereby, a linear forward-moving progress. However, in IR Theory, and despite the rise of realism, followed by the rise of liberalism, etc., competing paradigms continue to exist, or rather to coexist. In IR, there is no such thing as a progress that leads to the formulation of a general theory in one phase that is succeeded by another theory in a following phase, and so on. Rather, endless debates are run among concurrent paradigms and schools without necessarily resulting in a win-lose situation. While some consider this to be a normal reflection of the complex and changing nature of the international phenomena, others describe it as the crisis of Western (positivist behavioralist) theorizing that has often claimed the ability to introduce a single general theory of IR capable of bypassing the particularities of different states, nations, and peoples.

Thus, it seems there will never be an answer to the question: When will the qualitative revolution erupt, which can end divisions in IR? The question itself turns out to be inaccurate. It would be more accurate to ask: How can diversity and plurality become welcome in IR? Can non-Western paradigms ever be recognized as competitive rivals to Western paradigms?

Once diversity becomes an acknowledged reality of the discipline, it will lead to a different understanding of international reality. Diversity and plurality can guide towards the desired global change, and towards a more democratic and just world. The origins of the discipline, as a Western social science, reflected the realities of the victorious powers in the two world wars. These powers ruled the world with their theories, but their world failed to be democratic, just, or humane, and ended up in a desperate need of a paradigm shift to achieve global change, or vice versa (taking into consideration the reciprocal relationship between theory and reality).

5.6 THE GENERAL PATTERN OF THE EVOLUTION OF PARADIGM DEBATES

I describe this pattern as a permanent pendulum-wise oscillation, entailing a continuous redefinition of *the* political (i.e., a redefinition of the discipline's boundaries, scope, and substance), taking place at the ontological as well as methodological levels, thus reflecting the reciprocated relationship between content and methodology.[2]

The military aspects of security issues were given priority under the hegemony of the realist paradigm. Later on, issues of international political economy (international interdependence and dependency) came to the fore, and the religious and cultural aspects of IR have gained special attention during the globalization era.[3] Different IR paradigms adopted different positions on the importance of religious and cultural aspects, in comparison to the traditional military or economic aspects, as well as different positions on the impact of these aspects on the study of theory and reality.

The normative, cultural, civilizational, and religious approaches to IR managed to include new levels of analysis alongside the traditional levels of the state and international system. They also contributed to the widening of the scope of the discipline to include new issues. Just as the rivalry between realism and pluralism in the post-behavioral phase had marked the beginning of a redefinition of "the political," in the sense of redirecting attention to non-state actors and to new economic issues, theorizing in the globalization phase managed to consider the deserted religious and cultural variables in an attempt to override the excessive secular and materialistic orientation of the discipline. During this phase, the state-centric levels of analysis were challenged by more inclusive levels like those of the world community or the global civil society.

Moreover, the ontological oscillation (related to the content and substance of IR), though remaining within the confines of the positivist episteme, was gradually and cumulatively coupled with a methodological oscillation; from the great debate between behavioralism and traditionalism, to post-behavioralism and the call for a renewed interest in values in the 1980s,[4] to post-positivism that has been reflecting on the chances of an epistemological shift in IR since its emergence.

Hence, the quest for IR Theory attests to its oscillating nature that is actually the result of the oscillating nature of the dominant materialist positivist episteme, from which dominant IR Theory departs and which is characterized by conflicting dichotomies (as has already been highlighted in the introduction of this study). These dichotomies become particularly visible once the common denominators of the different paradigms are reflected upon: actors (state and non-state actors); power (military, economic, cognitive); international processes (conflict, dependence, globalization); the relationship between internal and external factors; state (stability and change); and issues (traditional and new). Different theorizing on each of these denominators contributed to "redefining *the* political," which was not a newly emerging trend but a recurring trend throughout the course of the evolution of the discipline. This continuous redefinition of "*the* political" entailed constant change in the credibility of the state borders, authority, role, and functions as the sole domain of "*the* political." This, in turn, justified not only the emergence of new actors, but also of new processes that transcended the traditional notion of sovereignty.

However, after the end of the Cold War, the extent to which "*the* political" was being redefined inspired the following questions: Is the discipline experiencing a crisis of disintegration?[5] Is there still an "IR Theory"?[6] Has an epistemological paradigm shift become a necessity to accommodate new post-positivist critical approaches emerging from within Western academic circles and emerging theoretical contributions from non-Western civilizational circles (an Islamic civilizational paradigm for instance)? These questions have accompanied the evolution of the discipline, from the narrow definitions of politics, political phenomena, and stability, and the narrow definitions of "science," to the wider and more generic perspective on international relations, dictated by cosmopolitan realities (where a segregation between the aspects of the international phenomenon, and a separation between reality and values are not possible).

5.7 THE IMPACT OF WESTERN-CENTRISM ON THE DISCIPLINE OF IR: CLAIMS OF UNIVERSALITY IN QUESTION

The successive paradigms of IR were initially all Western, associated – as suggested by some – with the origin of IR as "the discipline of victorious powers in the two world wars."[7] This fact became a source of growing criticism. In the mid-1970s, Hedley Bull, one of the founders of the English School, criticized the American-centric international relations theory, and referred to the emerging Scandinavian-based School of Peace Research.[8] In the early 1980s, Wittkopf and Kegley reminded their readers of the Western frame of reference of IR paradigms.[9] In the mid-1980s, Holsti asserted that international theorizing was mainly the outcome of Anglo-American efforts that reflected a Western-centric historical experience and that the presence of some theorizing, either from the Third World (dependency) or the Soviet Union (Marxism), could not be considered as an interactive and reciprocal process of theorizing.[10] Besides, Stanley Hoffman quite early on asserted that a universal IR Theory cannot be exclusively Western.[11]

This trend grew even further following the end of the Cold War, with the rising prominence of post-positivist and post-modernist revisions of IR. For example, Steve Smith regarded paradigm debates as a narrow, Western, and racist understanding of theorizing in IR that totally neglected the concerns of developing countries.[12] Ole Wæver criticized the dominance of Anglo-Saxon studies and the sense of superiority that dominated Western academia, and hence rejected the claims of the universality of IR.[13] These growing criticisms of Western centrism drove some renowned scholars to wonder whether IR was still an American social science.[14]

These scattered, albeit cumulative, observations and early alarms were implicitly included in early revisions of IR Theory. Yet, in a later phase, revisionist efforts, driven by various motivations, advocated the importance of paradigmatic plurality and asserted the need for comparative civilizational paradigms (as further elaborated in the fourth part of this study). Meanwhile, scholars from other civilizational circles (especially those advocating an Islamic civilizational paradigm), driven by their own motivations, goals, and self-perceptions that were quite different from those of the competing Western paradigms, were also asserting the need for comparative civilizational paradigms.

The preceding seven characteristics defined an academic context that justified and even urged for an Islamic civilizational theoretical contribution to IR. Then, revisionist post-positivist and post-modernist schools provided further justifications and motivations for such a contribution, in addition to those stemming from the Islamic system's epistemological, theoretical, and methodological particularity, and those stemming from its need to address the reality and interests of the Ummah (the community of Muslims tied together by the bonds of Islam) and the world. However, attempts to construct this corresponding comparative civilizational theoretical contribution had already begun in the mid-1980s at Cairo University. At that time it was a fledgling endeavor with the methodological and epistemological revisions of IR not yet powerfully self-revealing (as will be demonstrated in the fourth part of this study).

NOTES

1. See: S. Smith, "Introduction, Diversity and Disciplinarity," pp. 1-12; S. Smith, "Ten Self-Images of a Discipline," pp. 16-71; Rosenau and Durfee, eds., *Thinking Theory Thoroughly*, p. 81; Viotti and Kauppi, *International Relations Theory*, pp. 1-14; Ole Wæver, "The Rise and Fall of the Inter-paradigm Debate," pp. 149-185; M. Elwi, "Al-Ḥarb ʿalā al-ʿIrāq wa Azmat al-Tanẓīr fī al-ʿAlaqāt al-Dawliyyah" [The War on Iraq and the Crisis of Theorizing in International Relations], pp. 316-329; Nadia M. Mostafa, "Iʿādat Taʿrīf al-Siyāsī: Ru'yah min Dākhil Ḥaql al-ʿAlāqāt al-Dawliyyah" [Redefining the Political in IR: A Vision from within the Discipline], in *ʿIlm al-Siyāsah: Murājaʿāt Naẓriyyah wa Manhājiyyah* [Political Science: Theoretical and Methodological Revisions], ed., Nadia M. Mostafa, pp. 423-434; Heba R. Ezzat, "Iʿādat Taʿrīf al-Siyāsī" [Redefining the Political], pp. 413-422.
2. Nadia M. Mostafa, "Iʿādat Taʿrīf al-Siyāsī: Ru'yah min Dākhil Ḥaql al-ʿAlāqāt al-Dawliyyah" [Redefining the Political in IR: A Vision from within the Discipline], pp. 423-434.
3. See for example: Fred Halliday, "Culture and International Relations: A New Reductionism?," in *Confronting the Political in International Relations*, eds., M. Ebata and B. Neufeld (UK: Basingstoke, Macmillan, 2000), pp. 47 -71.
4. See for example: Charles R. Beitz, "Recent International Thought," *International Journal* 43, No. 2, *Ethics in World Politics* (Spring 1988): pp. 183-204; Ken Booth, "Security in Anarchy: Utopian Realism in Theory and Practice," *International Affairs* 67, no.3 (July 1991): pp. 527-545.
5. Burchill and Linklater, "Introduction," in *Theories of International Relations*, trans. Mohammed Soffar, pp. 7-50.
6. Ole Wæver, "Still a Discipline after All These Debates?," in

International Relations Theories, eds., Dunne, Kurk and Smith, pp. 288-308.

7. Burchill and Linklater, "Introduction," in *Theories of International Relations*, trans. Mohammed Soffar, pp. 7-50; Steve Smith, "The Discipline of International Relations: Still an American Social Science?," *British Journal of Politics and International Relations* 2, no. 3 (2000): pp. 374-402; Robert M.A. Crawford and Darryl Jarvis, *International Relations- Still an American Social Science?: Toward Diversity in International Thought* (Albany: State University of New York Press, 2001), pp. 1-26, 369-380; Knud Eric Jørgensen, "Towards a Six-Continents Social Science: International Relations," in *Journal of International Relations and Development* 6, no. 4 (December 2003), pp. 330-343.
8. Hedley Bull, "New Directions in the Theory of International Relations," pp. 282-283.
9. See the introduction in Charles W. Kegley and Eugene Wittkopf, *World Politics: Trend and Transformations* (New York: St. Martin's Press, 1983).
10. K. J. Holsti, "A Long Road to International Theory," *International Journal* 39, no. 2 (1984): pp. 337-365.
11. Stanley Hoffmann, ed., *Contemporary Theory in International Relations*.
12. S. Smith, "Ten Self-Images of a Discipline," pp. 17-37.
13. Ole Wæver, "The Sociology of Not So International Discipline: American and European Developments in International Relations," *International Organization* 52, no. 4 (1998): pp. 687-727.
14. Steve Smith, "The Discipline of International Relations," pp. 374-402.

PART III

THE CRISIS OF THE DISCIPLINE AND THE RISE OF CRITICAL APPROACHES: AN EPISTEMOLOGICAL TURN IN WESTERN THEORIZING

INTRODUCTION

PREVIOUS CHAPTERS OF THIS BOOK have in part tracked the temporal development of IR: traditionalism, behavioralism, post-behavioralism, and the post-Cold War era. Also outlined has been the paradigmatic development of IR: from the stage of dominant paradigms and the three great paradigm debates (the debate between realism and idealism, followed by the debate between traditionalism and behavioralism, and then by the debate between realism and liberalism/pluralism, on the one hand, and radicalism/Marxism, on the other) to the stage of competing paradigms. Chapters also explored the development of international relations, since its inception as an independent discipline in the early twentieth century, until it entered a stage of crisis and fluidity by the end of the twentieth century. This development mainly relates to the ontological, theoretical, and methodological aspects of the study of IR, rather than to its philosophical or epistemological foundations.

It is true that the early manifestations of concern with the epistemological aspects could be identified in the immediate post- Cold War period, as several references were made to post-positivism or to the debate between positivism and post-positivism (associated with the renewed interest in values or critiques addressed to behavioralism and empiricism, etc.). However, the features of a fourth great debate did not begin to crystallize and cumulate except throughout the 1990s. It was since the first decade of the third millennium, that many researchers began to characterise the debate that was going on as "the fourth debate" in IR.

This "Fourth Great Debate" was a debate between advocates of the competitive dominant paradigms (i.e., mainly neo-realism and neo-liberalism) and post-positivist theories of international relations (e.g., post-structuralism, constructivism, feminism, and post-colonialism). The debate does not revolve around ontological dimensions such as main actors, processes, issues, or concepts, but rather the epistemological dimensions of understanding and theorizing; as post-positivists suggest alternative ways to understanding reality, aside from positivism, and direct criticism to the international reality itself. This development has highlighted the impact of epistemological differences on theorizing in a clearer and more direct way than used to be the case during the second great debate between behavioralism and traditionalism, which was concerned with the methodological aspects of the study of IR. As mentioned in Part II of this book, the second great debate focused on methods and approaches rather than epistemological dimensions and their implications; the debate remained captive to "positivism" (i.e., oscillating between two different approaches to research methods that disagree on tools, rather than on the philosophy of science and knowledge). That second debate took place during the "behavioralist revolution," which was characterized by the dominance of a reductionist fragmentary view and a belief in materialist determinism, and sought to imitate natural sciences according to Newtonian laws. As for the fourth great debate, it has been taking place within the context of the "revolution against positivism," which is characterized by a paradigm shift in natural sciences towards "holism," the unity of sciences, relativism, and indeterminism. Thanks to recent advances in "hard" sciences, it becomes scientifically plausible to deny the ability to reach absolute and governing scientific laws in social sciences. This shift in natural sciences has had its impact on theorizing in social sciences and humanities, giving rise to a growing critique of the centrality of positivism in the epistemology and philosophy of science. In fact, philosophical and epistemological debates and disagreements had always existed in Western thought and philosophy, before they began having an impact on the paradigms of social sciences – the dominant as well as the newly emerging critical ones.[1]

All debates of social sciences are neither conclusive, nor mutually exclusive (as has already been explained). In its attempt to describe the state of the IR discipline since the end of the twentieth century, IR literature developed three distinct positions: (1) treating these debates as myths created by international relations scholars; (2) abandoning the quest for greater theories in favor of moderate theories that can confront contemporary world problems directly and effectively; and

(3) portraying theoretical diversity as a healthy phenomenon and calling for the enrichment of theoretical and epistemological diversity in the discipline. However, all three positions agree that the IR discipline experiences a crisis reflected in a number of failures: the failure of behavioralism to develop a general comprehensive theory in IR; the failure of realism to maintain its monopoly over the description and explanation of the reality of international relations; and the failure of the positivist epistemology to maintain the monopoly over the definition of "science."

There is a general consensus that the IR discipline is experiencing a crisis as evidenced in the current fragmentation of the discipline, the state of its paradigms, and the logic governing its debates and their various aspects (ontological, methodological, and epistemological). The aspects of this crisis can be delineated as follows:[2]

- Paradigms are always in flux, responding to an ever changing and complex international reality. This situation led to the chaos of competitive and contrasting paradigms and to urgent questions about the consequences of this permanent state of flux: Do these paradigms represent perspectives on different aspects of the same world or on different worlds? Does this shift serve the practical goals of politically, intellectually, and theoretically dominant powers? What are the reasons behind this shift from priority being given to the political-military aspects, then to the economic, and then to the cultural and civilizational?
- There is a methodological polarization between the advocates of empiricism and behavioralism, on the one hand, and the advocates of normativism, on the other. A compromise or synthesis is urgently required in order not to exclude values, culture (subjectivity in general), and hence emerges the possibility of "normative realism," "realistic normativism," and "realistic idealism."
- When approaching complex international phenomenon, the IR discipline is dominated by reductionist and oscillating understandings. This state prevents a deep and precise understanding of current and future transformations, since it omits some aspects while highlighting others, be they military, economic, cultural, material, external,

or internal. These analytical shortcomings could be remedied by the adoption of a holistic view that shows sensibility to the fluidity of the borders between the internal and the external, or the borders between the discipline of international relations and other disciplines of social sciences and humanities. A remedy of these analytical shortcomings also necessitates interdisciplinary cooperation between the IR discipline and other fields of knowledge.

- IR is dominated by the oscillation between the priority of conflict between powers and interests, or wars, on the one hand, and the priority of interdependence, cooperation, and the homogeneity of interests, on the other hand, barely giving any attention to the systemic relationship between these two processes.

In short, the current crisis raises the following questions: How can a holistic view – that combines the material and the non-material, the internal and the external, the rational and the normative aspects – be reached (i.e., how can a holistic view of content and methodology be achieved?)? What is the role that non-Western civilizational paradigms (including the Islamic paradigm) play in this revision process? What are the implications of this crisis and its impact on the state of the discipline and the desirable future of the world?

Considering the ongoing review of the discipline, especially since the end of the Cold War, the current stage witnesses the rise of new approaches to the study of IR Theory.[3] The current stage in the discipline raises several questions: What is new about these approaches ontologically, epistemologically, and methodologically in comparison to the traditional/mainstream competitive paradigms in IR? What is the contribution that they make to lead the discipline out of its crisis? How does a map of these approaches look like? What are their common characteristics? What is their impact on the discipline and international reality? What are the criticisms addressed to them? Does the IR discipline witness a real transformation due to these new approaches, or is it still captivated by its Western positivist, secular epistemological model? Where can we place an Islamic Civilizational Paradigm among these approaches, especially in comparison to the dominant/mainstream paradigms?

The post-positivist approaches have made a different contribution to the discipline of IR because they incorporate values, history, and thought. They are also open to other sciences and fields of knowledge, and even to non-Western cultures and civilizations, thus transcending the logic of opposite dichotomies that has for long governed the contribution of dominant paradigms in IR Theory: the internal/the external, the normative/the realist, the material/the non-material, the individual/the group/the state, etc.

The Egyptian School of IR, especially the IR academic community at the Faculty of Economics and Political Science at Cairo University, aims at bridging the gap between the study of theory and that of international affairs. It aims at de-alienating students from theory, changing their perceptions of its difficulty and correcting their misconceptions of the possibility of studying IR issues without a need for theory, thereby, aiming at making it easy for students to move back and forth between theory and reality (i.e., to grasp the essence of the reciprocal relationship between theory and reality). Three other objectives are also relevant:

1. Pursuing what is new in the IR discipline; since students should not only consume old views under the pretext of them being the mainstream. Students should be able to examine these views critically.
2. Enabling students to recognize that the IR discipline is not the monopoly of the positivist realist paradigm and its schools. The other schools that compete with it are not located on the margins of the discipline; they raise important questions about the credibility of the positivist realist school and its suitability for understanding international relations, especially in our contemporary world.
3. De-alienating the emerging critical approaches from the discipline itself, refuting, therewith, the claim that these approaches cannot provide solutions to world problems. This opens the door for students to explore the contributions of diverse cultural entities around the world, especially of their own Islamic and Arab civilization, in order to find innovative solutions to world problems.

The present study attempts to bridge a serious gap, whether in the process of teaching or in the supervision and writing of theses and dissertations.[4] This gap results from what Muhammad al-Sayyid Selim described as the dominance of "the international anarchy paradigm" over other paradigms in the IR discipline at the Faculty of Economics and Political Science at Cairo University, thus leading to the relative failure in keeping pace with developments in the Western discipline, not to mention the poor attention paid to theoretical aspects and to the introduction of a grand non-Western intellectual perspective to IR.[5]

The study at hand has also other concerns and interests and, hence, raises the following questions: Where is the Arab school of political science?[6] Where is political science from an Arab or Islamic perspective?[7]

NOTES

1. See for example: Yomna T. El-Kholy, *Falsafat al-ʿIlm fī al-Qarn al-ʿIshrīn: al-Uṣūl, al-Ḥaṣād, al-Afāq* [Philosophy of Science in the Twentieth Century: Origins, Harvest, and Future Horizons] (Kuwait: ʿĀlam al-Maʿrifah, 2000).
2. See: Nadia M. Mostafa, "Ishkāliyyāt al-Baḥth wa al-Tadrīs fī ʿIlm al-ʿAlaqāt al-Dawliyyah min Manẓūr Ḥaḍārī Muqāran" [Problematics of Research and Teaching International Relations from a Comparative Civilizational Paradigm], pp. 862-863; The editorial introduction in *ʿIlm al-Siyāsah Murājaʿāt* [Political Science Reviews], pp. 9-18.
3. While teaching the obligatory course in IR Theory at the pre-doctorate level, Dr. Amira Abou Samra and I began to tackle this stage in the spring semester of the academic year 2015-2016.
4. Most theses and dissertations in masters and doctorate programs, upon which this study depends, have contributed to the comparisons among the three great paradigms, and between these paradigms and new theoretical approaches. Some of them have made contributions to a third additional comparison with an Islamic civilizational perspective.
5. Muhammad al-Sayyid Salim, "Ishāmāt Kuliyyat al-Iqtiṣād wa al-ʿUlūm al-Siyāsiyyah fī Ta'ṣīl ʿIlm al-ʿAlāqāt al-Dawliyyah" [Contributions of the Faculty of Economics and Political Science to Rooting the Discipline

of International Relations], *Majalat al-Siyāsah al-Dawliyyah* [Journal of International Politics], .

6. Muhammad Si Basheer, "Naḥū Inshā' Madrasah ʿArabiyyah fī al-ʿUlūm al-Siyāsiyyah" [Towards the Foundation of an Arabic School of Political Science], *Majalat al-Dīmuqrāṭīyah* [Journal of Democracy], no. 51 (July 2013).
7. Muhammad al-Taweel, "ʿIlm Siyāsiyyah min Wajhat Naẓr ʿArabiyyah/Islāmiyyah: Fī al-Hājah ilā Ta'sīs Maʿrifī Mutaḥayuz" [Political Science from an Arabic/Islamic Perspective: On the Need for a Biased Epistemological Foundation] (May 2014), http://massaealjiha.com/index.php/plus/opinion/104744-56-08-08-05-2014.

6
THE GROUNDS FOR THE CRITICISM OF POSITIVISM AND WESTERN-CENTRISM AND THE MAP OF CRITICAL THEORETICAL APPROACHES

6.1 THE GROUNDS FOR THE CRITICISM OF POSITIVISM AND WESTERN-CENTRISM

Growing critical theoretical approaches in IR criticizing positivism and Western-centrism have an underlying basis in factors some of which are related to the establishment of IR as a discipline after WWI and its historical and complex development in the era of globalization.[1] The establishment of the IR discipline at the hands of the victorious in WWI was not separate from the remarkable reactions against the horrors of this war. This historical fact imprisoned and confined the discipline since its inception to the issue of war and peace, reducing the major concern of IR to one question: How can we prevent the outbreak of war and achieve peace?

Thus, the idealists and traditional realists monopolized the establishment of this discipline, even though they were using two contrasting approaches. From the idealist perspective, the international conflicting order could be turned into a more peaceful and just world order, through such effective means as democracy and collective security. In other words, the idealists believed that changing the world order was possible and achievable. As for the realists, they believed that the conflicting nature of world order could not be changed. However, the outbreak of war could be avoided through managing power balances and conflict of interests. Realists relied on the view that the world, in its actual state, differed from what it should be, and that theory had to help researchers as well as politicians identify the peace-threatening obstacles that needed to be overcome. Obstacles themselves, however, could not be prevented or eliminated. Thus, a revision of the origin of the IR discipline took the form of a criticism of its reduction to the issue of the struggle for power, crises, and wars. In other words, criticism was directed at the kind of image upon which this discipline was established and which made it captive to this conflicting dichotomy and other dichotomies as well. This criticism was initiated by Martin Wight, the founder of the English School, who rejected the conceptions of both realists and idealists.[2]

In as far as epistemology is concerned, however, the most important point is that this criticism emerged out of the view that this dichotomy of war and peace did not dominate theorization because it was a true reflection of "the reality of international relations"; rather, the dichotomy prevailed because it was a mere reflection of the view of the world and the perceptions adopted by the dominant powers. It could have been possible to pay attention to other explanations of the outbreak of WWI, if it were not for the dominance of realist conflict-based explanations. In fact, there existed other explanations and answers, but they did not receive due attention due to the politicized nature of this discipline since its inception (i.e., its monopolization by the victorious powers in two world wars).

Other grounds for criticizing positivism and rationalism were related to the differentiation between explanatory theory (rationalism) and constitutive or critical theory (reflectivism or interpretivism). A dissatisfaction with the significance of the debate between the dominant paradigms has given rise to the great fourth debate between rationalist positivist theories and critical theories. The differentiation between these two sets of theories is based on several assumptions. Among these is that what is present out there is not a given and does not exist as such, independently from the perspective adopted for perceiving it; also, the assumption that theory does not exist in a vacuum or is created *ex nihilo*. More importantly, each theoretical perspective that claims to be scientific and universal has political interests behind it. Hence, the strong ties between power, knowledge, and the Western (American) centrism of the discipline are meant to preserve the status quo and serve the interests of those in power positions.

Steve Smith[3] argues that thinking about IR Theory by magnifying the importance of the debate between paradigms is wrong. Defining international relations as the study of war, associated with the dominance of realism, reflects implicit assumptions and preconceived views about what deserves explanation in international relations. Theorizing eventually reflects a "political act" because the theory, which is deemed more suitable, depends on what the IR theorist wants to interpret. This, in turn, depends on the theorist's values and beliefs concerning the essence of international relations.

Therefore, a distinction is made between the foundational epistemological grounds of explanatory theories and those of constitutive theories, or between rationalist theories (neorealism and neoliberalism), on the one hand, and reflectivist theories on the other. Rationalism is the essence of positivism, and reflectivism is against positivism. The debate between them is essentially epistemological and methodological, not ontological, because the debate revolves around how we can know what we claim to know. Hence, the demarcating lines between theories since the mid-1980s have been drawn from the attitudes towards the positivist assumptions about knowledge.

Since the emergence of the inter-paradigm debate in the 1980s, there has mushroomed a proliferation of theories, most of which have opposed the dominance of rationalist approaches, especially on epistemological grounds.[4] Rationalist positivism sees the world as separate from the theories that try to explain it. The empirical scientific approaches, grounded on positivism, are seen as more capable of understanding the essence of the world as it is.[5] As for reflectivism, it assumes that every observation of international relations is done according to a perspective or theory, whether intentionally or unintentionally; and therefore, what are considered to be facts from a positivist perspective are no more than a product of implicit powerful assumptions about the world. Also, theories are derived from different intellectual traditions with historical extensions into philosophy and political theory.[6] Finally, theories serve different functions. Rationalist positivist theories suggest concepts and frameworks that can be applied to the world to better understand it. By contrast, there are theories that criticize the current dominant positivist order and open different horizons for emancipating individuals from the injustices done to them by that order: green theory, Marxism, Critical Theory, and postcolonialism. As for feminism, poststructuralism, international political theory, the English School, and constructivism, they seek to redefine the essential issues of the discipline and the ways in which they are related to the question of identity.[7]

The function of theory, according to the most powerful assumptions of positivism, is to explain the world that is completely separate from theory, hence, theory is just a means to describe the world out there and to find solutions to its problems. In return, there are constitutive theories that constitute the world, which they seek to explain. This means that theories are not separate from the world; they are an integral part of it. Theories cannot be neutral because every theory is based on assumptions about the essence of the world, whether ontological (what needs to be explained?) or epistemological (what is the explanation and how is it attained?). Every theory has a temporal, spatial, cultural, and historical context. Whereas positivists believe that non-positivism is illegitimate because it is not neutral, they fail to recognize that they commit exactly the same "mistake," which is being unneutral, when they maintain that a separation is possible between theory and the world (i.e., between the observer and the observed).[8]

The differentiation between these two conceptions of theory was introduced in a pioneering study by Steve Smith in the mid-1990s, in which he criticized the debate of paradigms as an approach to the study of international theory, and identified ten other images of "explanatory theories" versus "constitutive theories."[9] This differentiation is shared by Smith and other scholars,[10] who argue that explanatory theories are those that are involved in testing hypotheses, in proposing causal explanations, and in identifying main trends and patterns in international relations. They also show that the roots of the differentiation between these theories and constitutive theories date back to previous decades.[11]

So far, my analysis has implicitly referred to the link between positivism, realism, and the American hegemony over the discipline and the centrality of the American global role. This relationship has given additional support to scattered theoretical efforts that have warned against the implications of Western centrism for the universality of IR Theory since the mid-1970s. That is the case, because critical approaches have focused over the last two decades on the consequences of American centrism at both the epistemological and practical levels. Their criticism of positivism was, therefore, accompanied by an interest in integrating non-Western civilizational paradigms into IR Theory.

6.2 THE MAP OF CRITICAL THEORETICAL APPROACHES: ASSUMPTIONS AND HYPOTHESES, AND THE RATIONALIST POSITIVIST COUNTER-CRITICISM

A) Why is There a Need for the Map?

The general foundational grounds discussed above are common among many approaches or theories that fall under the broad umbrella of the criticism of positivism. However, each of these theories or approaches has its own hypotheses and assumptions that make it distinct from the others. Also, some of them still have some intersections with positivism. That is why it is important to start with outlining the map in order to avoid generalizations which undermine the credibility of some theoretical studies that address these theories or approaches, especially in light of a proliferating interest in them. In fact, this state of chaotic interest in these approaches stimulates critical reflection on the part of scholars who observe it from outside the Western circle of academic production.

Since the end of the 1980s, Steve Smith distinguished between neorealism and neoliberalism as explanatory positivist theories, on the one hand, and constitutive theories, on the other. Marxism, postcolonialism, and green theory were also distinguished and classified as explanatory theories that seek change; while feminism, poststructuralism, constructivism, the English School, and globalization were differentiated and regarded as theories that pay attention to identity. Moreover, Smith placed feminism and poststructuralism under reflectivism, and constructivism and the English School under positivist rationalism.[12]

In addition to realism, liberalism, and Marxism, some scholars combine, in one and the same reference,[13] the English School, historical sociology, critical theory, poststructuralism, constructivism, feminism, green theory, and international political theory. Viotti distinguishes between the three competitive major paradigms, to which he adds the English School and what he calls "interpretive understandings," as opposed to explanatory and constructivist understandings. According to this typology, interpretive understandings include critical theory, social constructivism, and postmodernism.

Muhammad al-Sayyid Selim classifies postmodernism or post-international relations as the third perspective which competes with the perspectives of both international anarchy and international society. He does not classify specific theories or trends under that category, but he formulates a general set of defining features:[14] First, this perspective accepts the differences between human units as essentially important. It also focuses on details that the discipline ignores because of being preoccupied with the search for a general theory or general laws in IR. In addition, this perspective underlines the role of logical assessment and intuition in understanding social phenomena, a role we have lost due to the dominance of the concept of rationalism. It also asserts that any discipline is not superior to other disciplines because there are no standards of differentiation between fields of knowledge or cultures. This perspective dispenses with standards and highlights diversity and differences.

The postmodernist perspective, according to Selim, emphasizes, then, that there are no fixed laws, patterns, or generalizations. Social reality is highly ambivalent. The rule in social life is arbitrariness, spontaneity, and relativity. Social life is full of details that cannot be grasped by any single theory. The positivist scientific methodology is only one methodology among many others, and it is not necessarily the single correct methodology. It is important to focus on the human dimension of social phenomena, since the rationalist and positivist scientific method can lead to results that harm human beings, as clearly seen in environmental degradation and the production of weapons of mass destruction.

Contrary to old typologies, Selim maintains that among the most important expressions of this perspective are the studies of Lewis Gaddis after the end of the Cold War, Rosenau's writings on governance without government in a turbulent world (1992), along with the emergence of reflexive rationalism. According to Selim, this latter paradigm converges with postmodernism in renouncing the belief in the validity of scientific knowledge and its generalizability, in admitting that the modern mind can produce knowledge that harms human beings, and in their readiness to accept and coexist with alternative philosophies of science. However, reflexive rationalism diverges from postmodernism in asserting that rationalism is still the basis for the philosophy of science and that it is possible to reform the negative consequences that may result from rationalism by "rationalizing rationalism." In the meantime, postmodernism has renounced rationalism and searched for a new and alternative deconstructive philosophy. Here, Selim refers to Alker's study "The Humanistic Moment in International Studies," where Alker defends a new paradigm of the discipline called civic humanism. This new philosophy approaches social problems from a humanistic perspective, that is, from a non-racist perspective that explores human problems while sticking to the scientific method. The humanization of the discipline, according to Alker, does not mean renouncing the scientific method.

Muhammad al-Sayyid Selim's reading of "the postmodernist paradigm" highlights samples of the rising critical approaches, especially those that aim to refine positivist rationalism through an engagement with the human and normative aspects. His reading reflects an interest in a synthesizing view that differs from previously mentioned classifications and identifications, from within Western academic circles, of these emerging "critical" approaches.

Reflecting on the state of the art, this author (Nadia Mostafa) – throughout two decades since the end of the Cold War – simply recognized the existence of critical and constructivist trends without paying much attention to differences between them. Hence, it is important to admit that the general state of the discipline is characterized by the rise of post-positivist critical approaches. However, it is also of academic importance to distinguish between the different strands and schools associated with these approaches.[15] In the meantime, the following question still holds: What about a contribution to the criticism of positivism and realism from non-Western civilizational traditions?

B) Main Assumptions of Three Interpretive Approaches

Viotti focused only on three strands of interpretive understandings: social constructivism, Critical Theory, and postmodernism.[16] After the end of the Cold War, two questions came to the fore with the emergence of social constructivism: Why did one of the two poles collapse without a war? What will the future power relations between the major powers look like?

The constructivist criticism of realism and liberalism began in the early 1980s, asserting that knowledge is influenced by subjectivity, and that reality is not out there; hence, it showed interest in values, rules, identities, and their impact on our perception of ourselves and on the ways in which we relate to the world. Social constructivism serves, therefore, as a link between positivism, as reflected in the materialist concerns of realist and liberal theories, on the one hand, and post-positivism, radical postmodernism, or poststructuralism, which maintain that "only ideas matter," and that "science is merely power disguised as knowledge" (the power of ideas, understanding, and interpretation).

In contrast to neorealists and neoliberals who assume that identities and interests are givens, constructivists argue that the identities and interests of states do cause problems in the international arena. Hence, constructivists tend to emphasize the significance of subjectivity and intersubjective exchanges and actions of "individuals" as "agents" of state and non-state actors.

The international structure is not a given; rather, it is a social structure influenced by many factors such as science, norms, and law. This structure can influence the identities and interests of agents, as well as international outcomes in various fields such as humanitarian intervention and weapons of mass destruction.

In contrast to the materialist approach (the neorealist and neoliberal search for structures), constructivism emphasizes the social dimension of structures.

The world is regarded as a permanently incomplete project, always becoming, rather than being, as opposed to the much narrower realist view of change. Constructivists rethink ontological and epistemological issues. They call for a reconsideration of the positivist causal theorizing in order to create space for a way of thinking that enables subjectivity to play its role in the process of understanding. Given the subjectivity of human beings, constructivists tend to underline the impossibility of pure objectivity. This does not mean that they totally reject the possibilities of scientific research; rather, they look for normative-rationalist models to explain behavior, with particular emphasis on the researchers' ontological and epistemological preferences as well as the actors' and agents' normative priorities and beliefs.

As for Critical Theory,[17] it underlines "emancipatory politics," that is, social and political transformation through an exploration of the relationship between power and freedom. To achieve this transformation, it is essential to scrutinize the current understanding of international politics, of existing realities of IR and their development over time. To avoid pure idealism (i.e., a sole occupation with "what ought to be"), IR scholars are expected to explain and criticize the political order based on the principles vested in political institutions and cultural practices. More importantly, they are expected to do so with the assistance of the comparative historical sociology of states, an approach that strongly supports these assumptions.

The theme of ""emancipation" is a common concern of the Frankfurt School, which used a Marxist critique of political economy and turned it into a critique of ideology. Critical Theory maintains that the relations of power and freedom should become the center of theoretical attention. In this respect, Critical Theorists are influenced by Karl Marx, especially his analysis of human inequality and his normative aspiration to eliminate exploitation. Critical Theory has been affected by various other philosophical influences, such as the revolutionary spirit advocating the escape from ideological constraints (Rousseau); the search for universal moral principles (Kant); the denouncing of the oppression of classes or other socioeconomic structures (Marx); understanding the role of human psychology in relations of dominance (Freud); and rejecting economic determinism and accepting the Gramscian/Marxist course that adopts a normative approach to criticizing, challenging, and overthrowing existing structures of domination.

It is important to criticize the status quo, but what is more important is to explore the possible ways for changing it. Indeed, normative and ethical considerations should not be discarded in our theories of international relations; they should be recognized as being part and parcel of these theories. Instead of dedicating our mind to reflecting on technical and instrumental means to maintain the stability of society, we have to seriously address the following important question: What is the good and just society which should transcend and expand beyond the state to the global space if we wish to create a universal/cosmopolitan society? Linklater argues that a three-dimensional transformation (sovereignty, territory, and national conceptions of citizenship) requires the universalization of certain moral, political, and legal principles, the reduction of material inequality, and the respect for ethnic, cultural, and gender differences.

The relationship between knowledge and interest is another important research area in international critical studies. Critical Theory maintains that knowledge seeking is inherently political, since theorizing "without a purpose" is an impossibility, even a shame. Theory, as Robert Cox succinctly stated, is always for someone and for some purpose.

Therefore, Critical Theorists are interested in the purposes served by different theories, arguing that beliefs held by positivists necessarily reflect themselves in biased claims about "truth" and are in fact part of grand global ideological schemes that seek to legitimate particular world orders. One of the tasks of Critical Theorists is to unmask such biases and expose the class or elite whose interests these theories, or more accurately these ideologies, are designed to serve. In other words, Critical Theorists put their cards on the table while being self-reflective.

Critical Theory attempts to refute the work of realists and liberals, including the assumptions of the latter about the influence of external events and uncontrollable factors on the behavior of individuals, such as anarchy, distribution of capabilities, and balance of power, arguing instead that individuals are the conscious initiators of these events. On the other hand, Critical Theorists argue that both realism and liberalism are problem-solving approaches. They are biased toward stability and maintaining the status quo of international politics (How to manage international relations? How to keep the international system within stable bounds to avoid its disintegration?). The goals of realists or liberals do not include transforming international relations in a way that serves the interests of the majority of humankind. Hence, the goal of Critical Theorists is to uncover underlying purposes and other motives of realist and liberal theories which confer legitimacy on states and power relations among them.

From the point of view of some Critical Theorists, these are not really theories, but ideologies that serve state, class, or elite interests. For example, in his criticism of neoliberal institutionalism, a theory which aims at maintaining international stability, Robert Cox argues that neoliberalism serves as a mediator between the state and the capitalist world economy as it provides insights on the ways for maintaining their mutual coexistence and the ways for resolving crises between them. In addition, Richard Ashley criticized Kenneth Waltz's systemic explanation of the behaviors and relations of states.[18]

As for postmodernism, its advocates argue that what we see, what we choose to see or measure, and the mechanisms or methods we employ, are all of human construction, as they essentially rely on perceptions and cognitive processes influenced by prior understandings and meanings.[19] Moreover, "the language we use necessarily reflects a set of implicit values that are an integral part of any culture, found in the narratives or stories people commonly employ to depict understandings of their observations and experiences in the world around them."[20] Therefore, postmodernists typically linguistically deconstruct what is said and written as a way to understand international relations.

Like Critical Theorists and feminists, postmodernists assume a strong "connection between power and knowledge" in the analysis of international relations. According to Foucault, "the production of knowledge is a political process that has a mutually supportive relation to power."[21] This does not mean an "emphasis on the material basis of power," as realists do, but it means a focus on how actors and commentators "impose authoritative interpretations on events."[22] For example, central to much postmodernist work in IR is the development of the concept of sovereignty and the associated terms and assumptions on the state, anarchy, borders, and security.[23]

At the level of methodology, some postmodernists trace the significance of power-knowledge relations over time (genealogy) and unveil false discourses in the study of international relations. For example, they reconsider the discourse of sovereignty and anarchy. According to postmodernists, knowledge is always conditioned by a particular time and place.[24] Therefore, understanding how particular historical interpretations continue to influence and guide current thinking and behavior requires searching for historical explanations. Hence, history does not merely serve the purpose of building a dynamic image of the past and uncovering unknown facts, but rather serves the purpose of exposing an endless repetitive game of domination."[25] Therefore, postmodernist study of discourses and texts reflects a need for understanding the world as a whole and adopts an ontological position advocating that different interpretations do not represent but constitute the world. Postmodernists call attention to competing historical perspectives, stressing that there is no single historical reality, as there is no objective standard for truth.

This epistemological position differs from that of Thomas Kuhn who presented the concept of paradigm as a lens that influences scientific work. Kuhn assumed the existence of a discoverable objective reality out there, while different lenses are used to test and interpret facts in different ways. By contrast, postmodernists argue that these lenses represent the "real world," simply because postmodernists reject the idea that there is a single truth awaiting to be discovered. Again, a state of anomie is at work, and it is therefore important to differentiate postmodern ideas from an Islamic Paradigm that can also be considered as "critical."

Postmodernists "reject the idea that the only way to gain knowledge is through a positivist methodology,"[26] the methodology used by traditional approaches in IR, including realists and liberals. That is why they seek also to interpret art, literature, and theater. Many postmodernists express a normative commitment to the idea that the sovereign state is not "the only means to organize political and social life."[27] They "take issue with the ontological perspective of realists and liberals that privileges the state as the unit of analysis";[28] they simply do not consider the state to be a given for theorizing in international relations.

It can be argued that postmodernists dive beneath the surface. They deconstruct words, phrases, statements, and texts, in search for underlying and implicit meanings in communications and discourses as a means for understanding. They regard us as subjective creatures; we human beings are the source of knowledge about the world around us. Here again, this assumption can be subjected to scrutiny by an Islamic, civilizational critical paradigm, which questions the claim that the sources of knowledge are limited to human beings only.

Steve Smith argues that rationalist positivists (neorealists and neoliberals) regard critical theoretical approaches as illegitimate social science. According to Robert Keohane, in his position as the president of the International Studies Association, the problem with reflectivist approaches is that they focus on criticizing dominant paradigms, without providing positive alternatives. Therefore, they remain minor, dissident, and self-centered approaches in the field. Steve Smith, on his part, argues that reflectivism lacks a research agenda, whereas Stephen Walt, the realist, considers neo-constructivism to be one of the main alternatives to realism and liberalism. However, neo-constructivism, according to him, is not one of the reflectivist approaches, because it owns a great deal of rationalism. In the meantime, through its focus on individuals, ideas, and discourses, constructivism can complement the paradigms that focus on power and internal powers as having a vision for change. Here, Smith argues that the insidious problem lies in the fact that mainstream theorists deny the legitimacy of alternative theories to positivism, not that they reject their ontological premises reflected in the kind of international issues they focus on (such as poverty, gender, race, international law, and environment), which give no priority to traditional issues such as inter-state wars.

One of the icons of realism and the established scholars in the discipline, Kal Holsti (2002), argues that the increasing plurality and proliferation of theories is not a positive matter, because it causes the field to lose its defining hard core. On the other hand, Steve Smith argues that the plurality of theories is a healthy phenomenon that has many epistemological and ontological benefits. This proliferation allows for thinking about and researching more aspects of international relations, and it allows for the diversity of the methods of thinking about the world, away from the monopoly of positivism and realism, and in a way that allows for a deep engagement with other social and human sciences.[29]

Whereas the realists and positivists hold critical approaches as partly responsible for the crisis of the international relations discipline, a crisis manifest particularly in the absence of a dominant paradigm and fierce theoretical competition, the advocates of these critical approaches regard them as a means for treating "the crisis of the discipline" and its main symptoms:[30] reductionism, decontextualization, and the epistemological, ontological, and methodological oscillation which characterized the course of the development of international relations theory over decades, and marked the crisis of the discipline at the beginning of the third millennium. Just as there were reconciliatory views, at the ontological as well as methodological levels, during the heyday of the traditionalist-realist debate and the realist-pluralist debate, reconciliatory views are present during this fourth debate as well. For example, Smith argues that if realism and liberalism are necessary for explaining international relations, they alone are not sufficient for a full understanding.

Fred Halliday presents a view that reconciles the requirements of explanatory and constitutive theories as follows:[31]

> First, there needs to be some preconception of which facts are significant and which are not. The facts are myriad and do not speak for themselves. For anyone, academic or not, there needs to be a criterion for determining what is significant. Secondly, any one set of facts, even if accepted as true and as significant, can yield different interpretations: the debate on the "lessons of the 1930s" is not about what happened in the 1930s, but about how these events have been interpreted. The same applies to the end of the Cold War in the 1980s. Thirdly, no human agent, again whether academic or not, can rest content with facts alone: all social activity involves moral questions, of right and wrong, and these can, by definition, not be answered by facts. In the international domain, such ethical issues are pervasive: the question of legitimacy and loyalty (should one obey the nation, a broader community, even the world, the Cosmo polis, or some smaller sub-national group); the issues of intervention (whether sovereignty is a supreme value or whether states or other agents can intervene in the internal affairs of states); the question of human rights and their definition and universality, etc.[32]

These reconciliatory visions remind of two issues that were addressed during the construction process of an Islamic Civilizational Paradigm. First, the conclusion that Mona Abul-Fadl drew from her analysis of the sources of Islamic theorizing, in which she described an Islamic Civilizational Paradigm as "realist idealism" or "realist normativism."[33] Realist normativism is a natural outcome of the features of the Islamic episteme (vertical-monotheistic), which transcends conflicting dichotomies. That stands in stark contrast to the positivist episteme (oscillating, secular) which values these dichotomies, especially dichotomies that are epistemologically positivist.

Second, there are two key epistemological questions that the Islamic epistemological system reveals about the construction of an Islamic, civilizational paradigm in general, and in international relations in particular: the relationship between the constant (foundations) and the variable (human interpretation), and the relationship between values and reality. These two questions derive from the nature of the sources of an Islamic Civilizational Paradigm in comparison with corresponding Western secular paradigms, whether positivist or critical. The Islamic Civilizational Paradigm recognizes a "constant" or a hard core derived from divine transcendental sources; putting the Islamic Civilizational Paradigm in clear opposition to the Western civilizational paradigm. This "constant," in its relationship with the variable, has its impact on the nature of values and the relationship between values and reality, in a way that produces harmony and equilibrium between the binaries: values/reality, material/immaterial, and other binaries (as has been previously illustrated in the methodological introduction of this study, and as will be discussed in detail in the fourth part of this book).

In conclusion, this brief introduction to rising theoretical approaches in the field has revealed the following:[34] all of them are of a normative nature, and they are open to other social sciences as well as humanities. They criticize reality, not only dominant theories, in an attempt to change reality by changing the tools available for looking at it. They search for non-Western critical theoretical contributions, departing from different civilizational and religious frames of reference. The latter can, in turn, supply their own epistemological, ontological, and methodological revisions of the Western -positivist or reflectivist- discipline of IR.

NOTES

1. See: Scott Burchill and Andrew Linklater, "Introduction," in *Theories of International Relations*, pp. 15-19; Steve Smith, "Introduction: Diversity and Disciplinarity," pp. 1-12; Steve Smith, "The Discipline of International Relations: Still an American Social Science?," pp. 374-395.
2. See: Scott Burchill and Andrew Linklater, "Introduction," in *Theories of International Relations*, pp. 15-19; Steve Smith, "Introduction: Diversity and Disciplinarity," pp. 1-12; Steve Smith, "The Discipline of International Relations: Still an American Social Science?," pp. 374-382.
3. Steve Smith, "Introduction: Diversity and Disciplinarity," pp. 4-6.
4. One of the most important channels of their publication is the *European Journal of International Relations*.
5. Steve Smith, "Introduction: Diversity and Disciplinarity," p. 5.
6. Ibid., pp. 9-11.
7. Ibid., p. 10.
8. Ibid., pp. 10-11.
9. Steve Smith, "Ten Self-Images of a Discipline," pp. 1-37.
10. Scott Burchill and Andrew Linklater, "Introduction," pp. 29-33.
11. It is even related to the roots of the epistemological, philosophical, and historical debate between empiricism and utopianism and the development of this debate over decades. In this context, see for example: Yomna T. El-Kholy, *Falsafat al-ʿIlm fī al-Qarn al-ʿIshrīn: al-Uṣūl, al-Ḥaṣād, al-Afāq* [Philosophy of Science in the Twentieth Century: Origins, Harvest, and Future Horizons]. See also, Scott Burchill and Andrew Linklater, "Introduction," pp. 31-33; and Scott Burchill et al., *Theories of International Relations*, 3rd ed. (Hampshire: Palgrave MacMillan, 2005). pp. 17-18.
12. Steve Smith, "Introduction: Diversity and Disciplinarity," p. 5.
13. Scott Burchill et al., *Theories of International Relations*.
14. Muhammad al-Sayyid Salim, "Taṭawur al-Iṭār al-Naẓrī li ʿIlm al-Siyāsah

al-Dawliyyah" [The Development of the Theoretical Framework of the Discipline of International Politics], *Majalat al-Siyāsah al-Dawliyyah* [Journal of International Politics], no. 161 (July 2006): pp. 46-51.

15. The proliferation of new media publications and of the numerous labels of theoretical trends makes following them, from outside Western circles, a challenging methodological issue given the difficulty involved in keeping pace with all that is produced and published in numerous circles. On the other hand, Western academic circles can follow one another naturally and cumulatively, because the traditions of scientific circles and epistemological dialogues are an essential component of the constitution of these groups. As a result, they produce forms of science that present "old wine in new bottles." See a detailed map of the critical trends in the discipline of international relations in an unprecedented manner in Arabic, in: Amira Abou Samra, *Mafhūm al-ʿĀlamiyyah fī al-ʿAlaqāt al-Dawliyyah: Dirāsah Muqāranah Ishāmāt Naẓriyyah* [The Concept of Universality in International Relations: A Comparative Study of the Contributions of a Critical Theory] (PhD diss., Cairo University, 2014).
16. Paul R. Viotti and Mark V. Kauppi, *International Relations Theory*, pp. 276-278.
17. Ibid., pp. 331-333.
18. Ibid., p. 333.
19. Ibid.
20. Ibid., pp. 333-334.
21. Ibid., p. 334.
22. Ibid.
23. Ibid.
24. Ibid.
25. Ibid.
26. Ibid., p. 335.
27. Ibid.
28. Ibid.
29. Steve Smith, "Introduction: Diversity and Disciplinarity in International Relations Theories," pp. 7-11. For mutual criticisms, see Paul A. Viotti and Mark V. Kauppi, *International Relations Theory*, pp. 335-337.
30. See Nadia M. Mostafa, "Ishkāliyyāt al-Baḥth wa al-Tadrīs" [The Problematics of Research and Teaching], pp. 862-863; Heba Raouf Ezzat, "Iʿādat Taʿrīf al-Siyāsī fī al-ʿAlāqāt al-Dawliyyah: Ru'yah min

Dākhil Ḥaql al-ʿAlāqāt al-Dawliyyah" [Redefining the Political in International Relations: A View from within the Field of International Relations], in *ʿIlm al-Siyāsah: Murājaʿāt Naẓriyyah wa Manhājiyyah* [Political Science: Theoretical and Methodological Revisions], edited by Nadia Mostafa (Cairo University: Department of Political Science, 2004), pp. 423-433.

31. Cited in Scott Burchill and Andrew Linklater, p. 30.
32. Scott Burchill et al., *Theories of International Relations*, 3rd ed. (Hampshire: Palgrave MacMillan, 2005), p. 16.
33. See: Mona Abul-Fadl, "Naḥū Manhājiyyah li al-Taʿāmul maʿ Maṣādir al-Tanẓīr al-Islāmī: Bayn al-Muqadimāt wa al-Muqawanāt" [Towards an Islamic Methodology of Dealing with Sources of Islamic Theorizing: Between Introductions and Capabilities], in *Al-Manhājiyyah al-Islāmiyyah*, no. 13 (Cairo: International Institute of Islamic Thought, 1996); "Introduction," in *Fī Maṣādir Dirāsat al-Turāth al-Siyāsī al-Islāmī* [On the Sources of Studying Islamic Political Heritage], Nasr Arif (Herndon, VA: International Institute of Islamic Thought, 1993).
34. The studies in this book as a whole provide details about these approaches, whether with reference to their origins, especially the master thesis and doctoral dissertation of Amira Abou Samra, or to their applications in the study of other topics related to power, the state, non-state actors, war, alliances, international political economy, levels of analysis, etc.

7
THE DEFINING FEATURES OF CRITICAL THEORETICAL APPROACHES

Critical theoretical approaches in IR are growing in number and embody a wide range of interests. These include rising interest in values and their relationship to reality; an increasing interest in civilizational, cultural, and religious dimensions, as well as the essence of the relationship between these and between real politics, on the one hand, and theoretical levels of analysis, on the other (especially as new levels of analysis that transcend the nation-state and world order emerge); a serious interest in interdisciplinary approaches and interdisciplinary connections with other social sciences and humanities; a keen interest in non-Western civilizational paradigms and their contribution to IR Theory; and finally, a growing interest in, and call for, world change emerging as a result of the previous four fields of interest. These fields of theoretical interest are systemic in nature because they intersect, converge, and have accumulating essences and effects.

Identifying this system of fields of interest has been the product of cumulative research efforts in the review of the state of the discipline, whether at the level of postgraduate teaching and academic publishing[1] or at the level of academic seminars held by the Department of Political Science, whose proceedings were issued in publications that underline these features or some of them.[2] With regard to the state of the discipline, the editorial introduction to one of the proceedings of the academic seminar of the Department of Political Science highlights two major aspects.

On the one hand, a renewed interest in values in the political study is gaining grounds. In the context of successive societal and global developments, political sciences and social sciences in general face methodological and theoretical challenges that necessitate significant revisits of the state of the discipline in all fields. Hence, the different paradigms of political science face theoretical, methodological, philosophical, and ontological revisions. The area of values is one of the most important areas where these multiple revisions intersect, resulting in serious developments in the methodologies of political study.

On the other hand, politics is redefined. The essence, the framework and circles of political phenomenon – as a social/human phenomenon – experience radical transformations in their philosophy, forms, and levels. These transformations redefine "the political" and consequently the scope and boundary of political science. They also incorporate political science into the larger framework of social theory: the relations, nature, and tools of power, political actors, their internal and external influence and their interrelationship; the new tools in the era of technology, info-media, and their impacts, structures, and transformations; the emergence of new forms of networks, alliances, and interactions, particularly the transformation in the nature and philosophy of the state as a major cornerstone in the field of political science, and the reconsideration of its circles of action, its powers, and political administration systems; and last but not least, the nature and systems of democracy in a changing world.

The material components of the concept have changed, or their meanings are being reconceived and re-conceptualized. As for the symbolic and relational components, they witness semantic transformation. The very concept of politics, upon which the discipline, its subfields, approaches, and methods are based, has witnessed serious broadening and qualitative transformations that oblige scholars and researchers to reflect on them, reconsider their views, and perhaps reclassify the traditional fields of political science.

Here, I will explore the findings of the proceedings of the academic seminar of the Department of Political Science at Cairo University over the course of two consecutive years:[3]

- All the major fields of political science witness a revision of the scope and boundaries of the discipline and its methodology. This state is characterized by a critique of behavioralism accompanied by a renewed interest in values, and an engagement with cultural dimensions along with the traditional political, economic, and military ones. This is done with the assistance of various approaches or levels of analysis, be they related to the individual or the group, or to the national or international level.

- The relationship between political science, social sciences, and humanities has been reinforced, and obtained multiple significance, in terms of research issues, actors, and processes at the level of domestic as well as international systems. This transformation entails the need for a redefinition of the units and levels of analysis as well as the concepts of power and politics themselves.
- The plurality of competitive paradigms in each field and the absence of a dominant paradigm represent the most important manifestations of the crisis experienced by political science and social theory. At the same time, the ramification, complexity, and diversity of theorization do not necessarily mean that there is something new in terms of topics and methodologies. Most sessions and discussions of the seminar raised the question of novelty, and answers mostly agreed that new theoretical and research trends are largely no more than a reproduction of what already exists, or revisions – imposed by international and domestic changes – taking place within the confines of the existing paradigms.
- The theoretical frameworks for studying applied topics are not ready-made. Their preparation requires comparative readings of the theories related to the topic of research and its different aspects so that the researcher can determine the theoretical framework that best suits his research topic and problem, on the one hand, and that helps achieve scientific accumulation in terms of comparison and generalizations, on the other. The theoretical framework can also highlight the creativity of the researcher, not only when designing the theoretical framework in the first place but also when applying and employing it in the study in a way that achieves scientific accumulation at the levels of theory and application. This theorctical and methodological matter is pivotal to the development of scientific research and the application of its outcomes, whether theoretical or otherwise. Attention given to this matter is the principal criterion for assessing the "scientific" quality of political studies, and whether they are an art or a science. In addition, the issue of the

relationship between political thought and political action was quite often discussed, and two questions were raised: To what extent does thought translate the problems of reality? To what extent does it provide alternatives serving the purpose of change?

- The importance of theoretical frameworks becomes clearer considering another question: To what extent do decision-making and policymaking centers benefit from the results of theoretical and scientific research? Why is there no link between thought and theorization, on the one hand, and action, on the other, in the South like that in the North? Does this relate to the inability of political thought and theory to provide visions and alternatives for change, or are the centers of decision-making and policymaking isolated from the centers of thought and research in the South?
- The issue of particularity and universality was manifest in a wide range of forms and levels, raising a number of questions: First, what is the relationship between the center of global power and dominant/mainstream paradigms and schools that claim universality? Second, how relevant are Western paradigms and theories for studying the conditions of the South? Third, what are the reasons behind the ineffective contribution of the South to the development of paradigms and theories that reflect cultural particularity, on the one hand, and the particularity of real problems, on the other? Finally, if there is a crisis of theorization, does this crisis reflect the crisis of the West and, consequently, the non-universality of its theories and paradigms, as well as the need for new epistemological, theoretical, and methodological alternatives that respond to the requirements of the highly complex reality?
- Discussions revealed the diversity of the intellectual backgrounds of the faculty members who presented lectures during the seminar sessions, as well as the diversity of the intellectual backgrounds of those who contributed to discussions and commented on the lectures. While this attests to epistemological, theoretical, methodological, and intellectual diversity, it also raises an important question about the education that graduate students and new generations of postgraduate students and young staff members receive: Do they experience this diversity, revealed in the seminars, during

their years of study and research? That is because acquaintance with diversity and plurality is one of the first pre-requisites for the high-level scientific preparation of young researchers and young staff members.

To conclude, the general trends of discussions held over two successive years in the academic seminars revolved around sets of binaries: the intersection between fields/the boundaries of the field, thought/action, crisis/revision and renewal, science/values, particularity/universality, and the plurality of paradigms/the dominance of a paradigm. All these dichotomous binaries lie at the heart of the great fourth debate in the age of post-dominant paradigms and the rise of critical theoretical approaches that have not yet achieved a paradigmatic shift.[4] In this context, four observations concerning the scope of the interests of the fourth debate are worth noting.

First, a horizontal review of the state of the discipline over more than two decades has revealed these accumulating features of the fourth great debate. A vertical review has revealed that these rising critical theoretical approaches still have not achieved a sufficient epistemological breakthrough in the discipline that justifies describing their impact on the discipline as a paradigm shift.

Second, these interests, characteristic of the fourth great debate, have not grown suddenly, and have not become dominant interests in the field yet. However, the fourth debate has indeed become more elaborate since the first decade of the third millennium. In fact, the early manifestations of the fourth debate, though traceable to the late 1980s, have been growing steadily since the end of the Cold War. These critical theoretical approaches have relied on a wide range of publications, scientific journals, scientific associations, and academic departments to disseminate their production in international theorization, seeking, thereby, to assert their own legitimacy and to crystallize their own research agendas.

Third, these five different fields of interest that have drawn the attention of the rising critical theoretical trends have also attracted the attention of the competing dominant paradigms in one way or another, who showed interest in them, yet, without giving up on their own basic epistemological and ontological hypotheses and assumptions. Critical theoretical approaches address these fields of interest by raising philosophical and epistemological concerns, and, hence, ontological, theoretical, and methodological concerns in a way that seeks to break the taboos, myths, and images into which these great paradigms have shaped the discipline, including, to mention but a few, war and peace, Western centrism of interests, balance, stability, maintenance of the status quo, the state, the international system, and materialist positivism. The rising post-positivist critical approaches seek to call upon "values" to effect global change for the sake of human liberation and emancipation, while taking into consideration particularities within "universality." Moreover, the dominant paradigms have addressed these five fields of interest from the perspective of adjustment, rather than that of transformation, while resorting to the same assumptions of realism and liberalism they have always upheld.

Fourth, these five fields of interest represent/form a system, because they overlap, intersect, and cumulate at the levels of essence and impact. The present study does not claim to be dealing with the debate revolving around these fields of interests between the mainstream/dominant paradigms and the critical theoretical approaches in detail. Rather, the study limits itself to reflecting on the most relevant problematics raised in the course of the debate and reasons behind the growing interest in these fields.[5] Taking into consideration the systemic relationship between these fields of interest, the study raises the following question: When does a paradigm shift in the study of international relations take place? The question on the possibility of an upcoming paradigm shift had not been raised for two, even almost three decades in a way comparable to that experienced since the end of the Cold War; although, the 1980s saw the beginnings of the methodological revision (criticism of excessive behavioralism) and witnessed the beginnings of the ontological revision (with the rise of pluralism, liberalism, and interdependence). However, an epistemological revision, posing a challenge to the field, was not visible until the end of the Cold War.

7.1 RENEWED AND RISING INTEREST IN VALUES

The current interest in values, their position in the epistemological debate, and their relationship to action, did not emerge suddenly.[6] Though explicitly absent, that interest was implicitly present in the 1980s, in discussions reflecting on the causes of the failure of IR theories to develop the promised "general" theories, and reflecting on possible alternatives such as a diversity of minor and intermediate theories.[7]

Wadoudah Badran quite early called attention to the fact that the most important characteristic of post-behaviorialist studies of international relations in the 1980s was their acceptance of possible plurality of theoretical approaches to the study of international relations, and their interest in values in addition to behavior in a way that entailed a call for restructuring the discipline. The debate about positivist empiricism (the possibilities of a value-free science) in IR joined, thereby, revisions that were taking place in all social sciences.[8]

The late 1980s and the early 1990s saw many calls, driven by various reasons, for paying attention to values and normative dimensions.[9] Whereas some analyses pointed out that one of the most important causes behind the failure of IR in reaching a general theory and the absence of a dominant paradigm in the field was the neglect of values, history, and philosophy by behavioralism as well as post-behavioralism, other analyses assumed that the end of the Cold War initiated a growing interest in reviewing positivism in general, and advancing post-positivism in particular.[10]

John Gaddis's study[11] on the impact of the end of the Cold War on international relations theory marked the beginning of a stage of methodological and epistemological revisions. The main contention in his study is that the different behavioralist, structuralist, and evolutionary approaches/paradigms failed to forecast the end of the Cold War or the transformation of world order at a time dominated by the strict "scientific" methodology and the neglection of theorizing derived from history, values, and philosophy. Gaddis harshly criticized behavioralism and his critique was far harsher than that of traditionalists during the second great debate because his critique accompanied the crisis that the discipline was experiencing after more than half a century of behavioralist revolution in IR Theory.

Gaddis severely criticized a concept of "science" that copied the methods of the natural and physical sciences. He also criticized the structuralist and evolutionary approaches concluding in his twofold argument: failure to predict the end of the Cold War is explicable either by the inability of theories to make universal statements or by the invalidity of such universal statements.

He also highlighted that at the time when social sciences were claiming objectivity, legitimacy, and predictability, because of adopting the traditional methods of physical and natural sciences (determinism and causality), interest of physicists, biologists, and mathematicians were turning to relativism, indeterminacy, disparities between theories, irregularity, and unpredictability. Gaddis argued that soft sciences were becoming harder just as hard sciences were becoming softer.[12] Moreover, the complexity of phenomena, their ties to human reality, and the necessity of taking time and place into consideration are all factors that impose themselves on the analysis of human and social phenomena, because human beings are not mere gases or solid matter that can be subjected to scientific analysis. Gaddis' argument called for the necessity of values in politics, of making use of history, philosophy, and sociology, modelling of human action, and of integrating "the general and the specific, the regular and the irregular, the predictable and the unpredictable."[13]

Since the end of the Cold War, the rise of interest in ethics and values has been accompanied not only by a debate on appropriate research methods (similar to the one that took place between behavioralism and traditionalism) within the same positivist episteme, as was the case during the second great debate, but also with epistemological revision questioning the more general view of the world; a revision strongly influenced by the warless end of the Cold War, and the failure of all behavioralist predictions in this regard. For example,[14] it is argued that if theory is a cognitive, epistemological translation of our understanding of reality and a guide for action toward dealing with it, then the end of the Cold War has affected both theory and reality in a way that has revealed the insufficiency of positivist realism alone for explaining this reality. This has led to a reconsideration of the basics of thinking about international relations so that it does not reflect the concept of orthodox Western victory or derive from the philosophical foundations of Western modernity, but from a broader view of the world and of possible ways for understanding it, and from the need for a new approach to theoretical as well as practical study.

Though all departing from a criticism of positivism, the degrees and approaches of the growing interest in values have varied since the beginning of the third millennium. The two following approaches are but examples. First, values, ethics, ideas, and beliefs are seen as different approaches of a new epistemological outlook that should reflect the methodology for studying international relations and the content of this study, especially that the relationship between IR Theory and ethics has come to the fore after September 11.[15] This approach is founded on a belief in the necessity for reinstating values and identity for the purpose of establishing a universal IR Theory. The main argument of this approach is that a non-normative social science cannot be established because there are no absolute truths in international relations. We are part of these truths, and our perceptions create the social world. This refutes the myth of neutrality; paradigms and theories of the discipline are biased towards some values and interpretative models. This mitigates the monopoly over universality and reality claimed by positivist rationalism, which is actually in service of Western and American practices, value system, and interests.

The discussions and debates about the causes, motives, and consequences of September 11 have revealed the drawbacks of the Western model in the field of international relations. This necessarily produced a call for a plurality that does not eliminate existing paradigms but recognizes the diverse means of understanding social reality and the legitimate engagement with values and ethics. The drawbacks of theorization are summarized in a set of binary oppositions: focusing on the role of the state, as opposed to that of the individual or of humanity; separating the state's interior from its exterior; separating the political from the economic; mis-assuming that humanity is driven by the forces of liberal democracy and the market; ignoring the issues of gender and ethnicity; giving priority to the military and security agenda; focusing on wars as the major manifestation of violence and neglecting other forms such as structural violence; giving primacy to the stability of the structure of the international order, not to change; marginalizing the question of identity; developing theories assuming the homogeneity of identities irrespective of cognitive biases; and showing interest in explaining the world, rather than understanding non-Westerners' worldviews and cognitive structures. Obviously, renewed interest in values is strongly linked to the other four fields of interest characteristic of the rising critical theoretical approaches in the field.

Second, Christian Reus-Smit and Duncan Snidal called for reuniting values and social sciences as a way to serve action and to assist the mission of science in guiding change.[16] The major argument upheld by their call assumes that if the discipline of international relations wants to remain of any worth, it should deal with the most persisting problems in international politics at the levels of both reality and theory. For IR to have a truly scientific content, it must turn into what is more than an explanatory project. It should deal with the murky space between empirical research and normative research, expressing not only what is, but also what ought to be.

This call persistently reminds us of the reasons behind the dominance of the explanatory theories that displaced organized and conscious normative thinking away from the scope of the IR discipline and expressed their bias for a value-free science. This call also uncovers the opposite biases of the theoretical efforts which gave primacy to normative considerations and neglected realistic ones in IR. Therefore, if normative theory is to provide scientific contribution that transcends abstract idealisms, it should take the reality-related concerns into its consideration.

Christian Reus-Smit and Duncan Snidal declared their structural and rational biases. However, they refused to confine themselves to any particular classification, and they searched for a common ground that united them despite their differences. Moreover, both authors sought to help the field rediscover its identity by asserting that a separation between normative considerations and empirical research, or vice versa, only impedes the ability of the discipline to deal with pressing problems in international politics. To them, the widespread division between normative theories and empirical theories is rejected. In fact, this division contradicts reality because, regardless of whichever theory we are talking about, theories are never devoid of normative considerations, whether explicit or implicit.

The two scholars argued that current international changes had made the contemporary moment suitable for reuniting the scientific and normative. These changes were challenging the focus given to the state as the main international actor, the dominance of the security dilemma, and the dominance of positivism. The two scholars argued that the traditional security dilemma left the stage for new security problems such as ethnic conflict, terrorism, international political economy issues, human rights, and climate change. All these issues raise questions regarding values, justice, and freedom, and they challenge the traditional logic of thinking about international relations.

In brief, the major assumption of this argument is that if the IR discipline has been always accused of its limited effect on public politics, this is not due to its focus on theory, though this is the favorite justification adopted by many scholars, but because it lost its identity as a practice-oriented discipline that brings together values and social science. There is a need for reclaiming this identity of the field; an identity that seeks global change for the sake of humanity, rather than adjustments to maintain the balances and interests prevalent in the status quo.

7.2 THE RISE OF INTEREST IN RELIGIOUS, CULTURAL, AND CIVILIZATIONAL DIMENSIONS

The rise of the role of religion, culture, and civilization in the study of IR Theory[17] represents one of the most important fields of interest of post-Cold-War and post-positivist revisions. It is closely related to values and lies at the heart of redefining the political. This interest is not confined to the critical, theoretical approaches; it is also shared by dominant paradigms, though from a totally different perspective. A good example can be found in the wave of debates about the relationship between civilizations, a relationship of clash or dialogue, and the impact these debates have on the study of international relations.[18]

The rise of interest in these dimensions, which engage with human beings and values in different historical and geographical contexts, is not only a product of post-positivist epistemological revisions, but also of global changes since the end of the Cold War and in the context of globalization (as has already been discussed). Although an interest in these dimensions was never really absent, these changes have pushed that interest to the top of the list of theoretical and practical priorities and debates.

While reviewing the literature that tackles this religious, cultural, and civilizational dimension in IR Theory, from different schools and approaches and under the title of "redefining the political,"[19] I find myself experiencing the same methodological state that I had experienced when I was reviewing the literature of the 1970s and 1980s on the then growing interest in international political economy (i.e., at the time of the rise of interest in economic dimensions (low politics) in international relations).

Two observations need to be made here. First, referring to religion, culture, and civilization combined certainly does not mean that they are synonymous, but the relationship between these three concepts is debated among theories in the field of culture and civilization.[20] Scholars with civilizational perspectives have paid attention to these debates.[21] The second, is the multiplicity of the levels of the influence that these dimensions exert on the study of international relations. Moreover, the rise of interest in these dimensions was the result of six developments, which, in turn, resulted in several epistemological, methodological, and theoretical problematics.

First, interest in these dimensions was fueled by the powers of globalization and the powers of divisions, conflicts, and the religious, ethnic, and national bloody wars that broke out throughout the world after the end of the Cold War. That interest became also evident in literature explaining the end of the Cold War. That literature was not confined to military and economic dimensions, but extended to embrace cultural explanations. The renewed interest in these dimensions was also present in literature that reflected on the state of the international system, which appeared as if it was dominated by a civilizational model without any clear and decisive alternative (i.e., the model of Western dominance under the leadership of the United States of America). Finally, interest in the normative dimension, which is related to the cultural dimension, was renewed in the literature that sought to explain the behavioralist and empiricist failures of the IR Theory to forecast the end of the Cold War.

Second, the main paradigms adopted different perspectives on the relationship between the cultural dimension and other dimensions (i.e., whether they considered the cultural dimension to be an independent or a dependent variable in international relations and the kind of influence it had on international relations: leading to conflict or cooperation). This debate revolved around whether the cultural factor had an independent explanatory ability or not.

Hence, the following question arises: Which is the dependent variable and which is the independent one? Culture or politics? Some schools and theoretical approaches, such as mercantilism, Marxism, and liberalism, raised earlier similar questions and tried to give answers to it: Which comes first; economy or politics? Now, we find ourselves confronted with schools in IR that lead research into the meaning of and reasons for the rise of cultural and civilizational dimensions in the field of international relations theory.

Equivalent to the debate on values, here too a debate arose, reflecting on the following questions: Is a paradigm shift taking place in the study of international relations as a consequence of the rising role of religion and culture at the level of theory and practice? Are cultural and religious variables independent or dependent variables? Do differences between cultures and religions necessarily lead to conflicts? What are their impacts on the stability, security, and peace of the world? What are the different types of relations between religions and cultures on the one hand, and interests and power balances on the other?[22]

Third, since the theory of culture has not provided simple and easy answers regarding the essence of culture and its relationship to religion and civilization, and since the maps of cultural analysis are complex and complicated, the interest in the cultural dimension in political science is reflected in the form of a diversity of schools and approaches. Political theory and its revisions contribute a great deal to this issue of the relationship between the cultural and political, a relationship also reflected upon and debated by international relations and comparative systems throughout the history of the development of these fields.[23] This shows that the renewed interest in culture has epistemological as well as practical reasons.

Fourth, renewed interest in the cultural dimensions led to a growing interest in the study of methodological problematics. How can we study it in a methodologically scientific way despite its normative character? The introduction of this dimension into the study of international relations is deeply related to the redefinition of "the political": at the levels of the concept of power, actors, and issues. Opening up to the cultural dimension necessarily entails rethinking international politics at the levels of the individual and society, that is, going beyond the levels of states or international system (making reference to new actors below or above the level of the nation-state). It also entails reflecting on the relationship between the self and the other and considering new sources of threat, which are quite different from the traditional geo-strategic sets of threats. These new sources are related to the view of the world and the religious and cultural basics of its division. Opening to the cultural dimension also entails paying attention to a new agenda of priorities such as the dialogue of religions, cultural and educational policies as tools for foreign policy; fundamentalisms and their impact on global peace, religion and international relations; the normative justifications for using military power in international interventions; and the renewal of religious discourses. These concepts, actors, issues, and processes attest to the interconnectedness between national and foreign interactions in global affairs. This, in turn, broadens the scope of the political in international relations, making it no longer confined to the traditional topics of state power only. Meanwhile, traditional approaches and methods seem no longer able to explain many phenomena or understand the state of the world.

Fifth, one of the most important areas for studying the impact of the rise of cultural dimensions is the one related to peoples, nations, groups, and individuals. It is an area in which power and authority are practiced across borders, spaces, processes, and nontraditional interactions at the global level, in which dialogue and cooperation are pursued for the sake of a new world order. Literature, departing from new concepts of power, authority, actors, and processes, has been growing.

This literature is thus setting the foundations for a view of the discipline and its management, one that appeals to negotiatory, dialogic, and cooperative processes in order to deal with "a world in crisis." This literature explains the relevance of these processes by the effects of globalization on time and place. It questions the boundaries of the traditional nation-state and widens the scope of interaction between peoples and nations in a way that leads us to new levels of analysis and to new processes of world change. Here, I will explore two examples of this literature.

Harold Saunders[24] presents a concept of "politics" as relations, whose study requires a paradigm based on a multilevel process of continuous interaction, that is a "relational paradigm" that has "relationship" at its core. The concept of relationship does not focus on the components of the relationship (the actors); rather, it focuses on the multilevel process of continuous interaction in political, social, and economic life. The concept carries an analytical and operational framework which reflects a new paradigm of thinking; a paradigm that can be applied in practice for the purpose of solving world crises, especially the crises of a violent, conflictual nature. Therefore, the concept of "relationship" embodies an accumulative experience of an interaction that has a special nature and value. It is a different way of approaching human relations, and it calls upon non-traditional tools that lead to what Saunders terms "the citizens' century."

As for Petito and Michalis,[25] they present a view that is more holistic and systemic, and more critical of the theoretical Western centrism (realist positivism), which lacks interest in the issues, problems, and challenges that the concept of civilizational dialogue imposes on the future of the world and international relations. Dialogical initiatives have become a sort of a global social movement that reflects human diversity and seeks human solidarity, not uniformity or global hegemony. They are the peaceful tool of managing the future of multicultural and globalized global society. In the meantime, unification powers and division powers continue to compete for the post-cold-war and post-September-11 world. In this competition, the power of ideas plays a principal role, and dialogue becomes a means of criticizing the dominant, Western, normative system and looking for a new and shared normative structure of the global society.

Sixth, some debates about the weight of religion, culture, and civilization, and hence of ideas, values, and history in the study of international relations reveal how theories differ in their answers to these questions, inter alia, because they differ in how they address changes in reality.[26] Moreover, some of these debates direct their attention to the theoretical challenge that religion poses to IR Theory and constitute, thereby, an epistemological attack on the excessive materialism and secularism of the discipline.[27] Calls for recognizing the theoretical challenge that religion poses to IR Theory eventually go beyond the traditional (or renewed) interest in the effect of religion on the issues of international relations or the corresponding processes, be they conflictual or cooperative.

What is special about this pattern of renewed interest in religion in international relations is its harsh criticism of the traditional realist model's exiling of religion and approach to addressing a renewed interest in religion since the emergence of the "clash of civilizations" thesis and other similar theses, that all too often associate the resurgence of religion with new Cold War mindsets, the danger of fundamentalist politics, even the threat of global terrorism; or more generally with a novel anarchy witnessed by the world.[28] By contrast, this pattern of renewed interest in religion shows "how an engagement with worldwide religious traditions might lead to creative theoretical and political accomplishments," about which "IR Theory has oddly remained silent."[29] It is not enough to make "minor adjustments to the prevalent theoretical frameworks available to deal with the role of ideas, culture, and identity;" what is required is "the elaboration of new theoretical and analytical approaches"[30] that can explore and explain the relationship between religion and politics. In this context, "the return of religion from the (Westphalian) exile brings with it the promise to emancipate IR from its own theoretical captivities."[31] Transcending the debates about culture and multiculturalism in contemporary religious thinking is required; we should explore how "contemporary religious thought provides new ways of thinking"[32] which go beyond the Westphalian stage and the studying of international relations from a secular perspective.

The manifest, growing interest in the religious, cultural, and civilizational dimensions, as drivers or subjects of study or processes in international relations, must raise the question about the contribution to this debate from a comparative, Islamic, civilizational paradigm. In this paradigm, Islam lies at the heart of the cultural and civilizational configuration. Moreover, this growing interest must raise the question about the practical goals of such political theorization in comparison with its counterparts in the realist and positivist political theorization. Here, I will introduce the argument of Alsayed Abd al-Muttalib Ghanim.[33]

Ghanim wonders about the purpose of the diverse and sophisticated political theorizing, which is preoccupied with the relationship between the cultural and political through different stages. He also shows interest in the relationship between the dominant political theorizing under the umbrella of realism and rationalism and the goals of the political action of great powers. Warning against falling into the trap of reaction to the renewed interest in the cultural and normative dimensions, Ghanim draws attention to the existence of an alternative argument that expresses a civilizational view that is different from that of the modernist and postmodernist liberal thesis. He stresses the importance of what our heritage has to say about the relationship between the normative and the political. His discussion answers two important questions: What should we read? And where do we start from? He reminds us of the interconnectedness of the normative, the religious, the civilizational, and the cultural. Ghanim raises another important question: When will it be time to move on from the stage of thinking about the need for revising the discipline to the stage of making real contributions to the discipline; ones that reflect our needs and priorities?

Ghanim's thought-stimulating questions led his audience to reflect on another crucial question: Does the current engagement with the cultural dimension in international relations serve the interests of great powers in the international system only, or is it one of the resistance mechanisms embedded in the structure of world order and its levels as well? In other words, can an engagement with culture in IR serve the interests of the materially weak in the system?[34]

Hence, it is necessary, while reflecting on the consequences of the crisis of the discipline, to raise the following questions: Are we, in the discipline of political science in general and the discipline of international relations in particular, in an "artificial" state of crisis; one that results from the "luxury" of theoretical debating afforded by the revisionary trends in the field, or that is maybe driven by hidden goals pursued by the great powers, from whose territories these revisions have emerged; goals including the maintenance of internal stability and external hegemony? Or, are we, instead, in a "real" state of crisis, resulting from political science undergoing a process of "correction," not only of "adjustment"; a process taking the discipline back to its natural track, from which the study of political science has long deviated, a process that – if persistent and successful – might guide political science to become more credible and more capable of performing its main tasks of studying the political phenomenon and looking for solutions to world problems?

These complex questions call for investigation into the three remaining fields of interest of the fourth great debate. These are: the interest in the contribution of non-Western civilizational paradigms to IR Theory in resistance to the Western centrism of the IR discipline, interdisciplinarity and global change. These latter three have been inseparable from an increasing interest in the civilizational, cultural, and religious dimension paving the way for a non-Western contribution to the field.

Non-Western contributions to the field of IR departed from early criticisms (during the 1980s and early 1990s) of dominant paradigms' claims of the universality of their assumptions and theories. With the start of the new millennium, critical revisions unveiled American dominance over the world, on the one hand, and Western dominance over the main assumptions and agenda of IR in addition to a bias for a positivist and secular episteme, on the other.[35] In what follows, I explore the third field of interest of the great fourth debate.

7.3 THE WESTERN-CENTRISM OF THE INTERNATIONAL RELATIONS DISCIPLINE: THE CRITICISM OF CLAIMS OF UNIVERSALITY

Critique of the claims to universality in IR Theory has its own epistemological and ontological foundations. Some scholars have even considered international relations to be the relevant field for civilizational studies,[36] which explore comparative perspectives (Western, Islamic, etc.) on the different dimensions of the study of political and social phenomena at domestic and international levels.[37] The interest in civilizational analysis directs IR discipline towards adopting a transcendent interdisciplinary perspective, encouraging it to pay attention not only to non-Western contributions, but also to levels of analysis and agendas of issues that engage with history and anthropology, thus confronting IR Theory or "the Global Theory of IR" with new challenges. This point, however, requires a special investigation that goes beyond the scope of this study.[38]

Questions have been raised concerning the ability of non-Western contributions to fill a gap in IR Theory, a gap partly revealed by academic discourse on "the crisis of the discipline." The Project of International Relations in Islam (1986-1996) pioneered reflection on the purpose and need for such a contribution and in engaging critically with Western theories and approaches at various levels, while attempting to establish the foundations for a comparative Islamic civilizational paradigm in the discipline. A later stage of the development of the paradigm (1996-2016) was accompanied by the crystallization of some Western critical interest in studying comparative non-Western contributions to IR, including an Islamic contribution.[39]

Many aspects of divergence between these "Western" critical attempts and the attempt of the Egyptian school of political science at constructing an Islamic Civilizational Paradigm of International Relations are identifiable and will be highlighted in some detail in the fourth part of this study. It suffices here to refer to the features of one of the most popular and holistic among these critical attempts. This comes in the form of an edited book,[40] whose introduction[41] establishes the foundation of the need for non-Western contributions in IR upon a set of epistemological motives and justifications, which lie at the heart of the "critical perspective." The book contends that IR theorizing is related to power and hegemony, as reflected in the claims to universality adopted by its main schools, and that theoretical perspectives cannot be separated from the context of time and space. Therefore, it is necessary to distinguish between explanatory and constitutive theories. There are no universal theories, because of the cultural differences and political interests underlying theoretical concepts. Moreover, one of the most important indicators of Western hegemony is that all dominant theories have Western philosophical and historical roots and reflect the Western-centric view of world history.

The introduction to the edited book attributes the dominance of Western theories to a set of causes that also explain the reasons for the absence of non-Western contributions. The great powers, which emerged victorious following the two world wars, claimed to have discovered the right way to understand the reality of international relations. The West possessed the tools of hegemony, in the Gramscian sense. These are Western imperialism's tools of intellectual influence, that have been utilized during the years of imperialist expansion, or colonialism and its aftermath. Non-Western theorization exists, but it is unknown to Western academic circles due to the many linguistic, cultural, and political barriers that prevent it from becoming part of Western academic debates. Moreover, there are local cultural, political, and institutional conditions that work against the production of a non-Western theory in international relations.

The theoretical framework suggested by the book for studying theoretical contributions from Asian civilizational circles, consists of four elements: (1) traditions of political thought and the political thought of the military, political, and religious classical figures or symbols; (2) the intellectual approaches of contemporary Asian leaders and their foreign policy to the organization of the international order; (3) the application of some Western theories to local contexts and dilemmas to assess the former's relevance; and (4) the study of particular events and experiences and the development of concepts that can be used as tools of analysis of international relations, in a way that allows for locating Asia within the world order and comparing it with other parts of the world.

The selection of Asia in particular, from among the different "civilizational circles" or strategic regions, is worth reflecting on. As the book's introduction shows, this selection is related to the new international power balance manifest in the rise of Asia, the discourse on "Asian Values," and the labelling of the 21st century as "the Century of China." Ironically, choosing Asia (China, Japan, India, Indonesia, Korea, etc.) in effect reflects the same traditional geographical materialist logic related to power balances, influence, and nation-states, rather than any particular interest in normative aspects that are related to people's lives. That choice reflects the same logic of power balances and the adjustment, rather than the transformation, of the existing international system to accommodate new powers, which happen to have a different non-Western civilizational background. This argument re-advocates what realists are advocating and what critical theorists claim to be criticizing. In other words, here too, power balances have their impact on IR Theory, and this raises the following questions: What kind of world change do critical theorists ask for? Is it a change towards accommodating and locating non-Western powers within the existing world order, just reflecting a new dichotomy of power balances (Western/non-Western, namely Asian)? Or does the change that critical theorists request involve a pursuit of global values and interactions that transcend dichotomies?

What is the human common (and constant) ground towards which global change must be directed, so that it transcends national boundaries and closed civilizational entities and, thus, paves the way for a universal pluralist dialogue that helps solve the problems of the world and humanity as a whole, neither the Western world, nor the non-Western world alone? Does the "Islamic Civilizational Paradigm" have a contribution to make in this regard? Is an Islamic Civilizational Paradigm just creating a new dichotomous depiction of reality? It is remarkable that the edited book does not refer to Islam as one of its case studies. However, the book does not ignore Islam completely, referencing Islam in a chapter titled "International Relations Theory and the Islamic Worldview."[42]

7.4 INTERDISCIPLINARITY: THE ENGAGEMENT WITH THOUGHT AND HISTORY IN INTERNATIONAL THEORIZING AS AN EXAMPLE

Among the titles that have been dominating the scene of IR publications in Western circles are: theory of international politics, historical sociology, international relations philosophy, the political thought of international relations, the social theory of international relations, and international political economy.[43] Some of these titles appeared in the 1990s in the course of revisions that took place in the field in the aftermath of the end of the Cold War; that was the stage of revision sometimes labelled as "post-positivism."[44]

These interdisciplinary studies became one of the most important outcomes of the great fourth debate between critical theoretical approaches and dominant paradigms.

The establishment of international relations as an independent discipline after WWI was concomitant with its separation from other fields that were closely related to it, especially law, history, and philosophy. The scientific development of the discipline in the behavioralist stage and during the heyday of positivism was the reason behind its separation from these fields and their methods. However, as a consequence of the crisis of the discipline and the critiques of dominant paradigms, the ties of international relations to these and other fields of study have been renewed, but with new methodological approaches and new research objectives beyond traditionalism. One of the most important features of the crisis of the discipline, according to behavioralists and positivists, is the fluctuation of the demarcating boundaries between the discipline of international relations and other social sciences in general, thus threatening the essence of this "independent" discipline, its scope, boundaries, and methodology.

The epistemological, ontological, and methodological revisions (the criticism of positivism, the criticism of the assumptions of realism and liberalism, and the renewed interest in values and the civilizational, cultural, and religious dimensions) necessitated a broadening of the scope of the discipline and a reconsideration of the concept of the political. The return of the ties between the IR discipline and other social sciences is referred to with various terminologies, which are quite often used interchangeably without distinction: transdisciplinarity, cross-disciplinarity, interdisciplinarity, and multidisciplinarity. Omaima Abboud[45] argues that these terms fall within the scope of "the inter-disciplinary perspective" and the concept of "interdisciplinarity" in general. To what extent can interdisciplinarity create a new epistemology that can affect some social change and produce knowledge that transcends the limits of a single field? The great renewed interest in the concept of interdisciplinarity in the last two decades in the social sciences highlights the call for new approaches to the issues of social reality, which academic traditions with their limited and sometimes limiting standards failed to accommodate, especially in the context of the post-Cold War period and globalization.

These interdisciplinary relations between the disciplines, according to Omaima Abboud, take many names. Sometimes they are described as the inter-fertilization and interaction of disciplines in favor of a new category which can be called meta-discipline. They are also referred to as the convergence of disciplines, intermediate space, or hybrid space. These relations are also sometimes portrayed as a blurring of the boundaries of disciplines or a penetration of disciplines away from the traditional division of labor and in favor of the integration of knowledge and action.[46]

One important study[47] identifies four types of interdisciplinary studies. First, informed disciplinarity that is concerned with knowing and reading about another field of knowledge. Second, synthetic interdisciplinarity that focuses on the research problems and concerns that are common among different fields of knowledge. Third, transdisciplinarity that underlines the interconnection, unity, clarity, and consistency across different fields of knowledge for the purpose of solving the problems common among science, technology, and society. Fourth, conceptual interdisciplinarity that explores new intellectual fields and spaces without methodological or academic restrictions.

Omaima Abboud argues that multiple theoretical challenges are posed by the renewed interest in the interdisciplinary perspective. One of the most important challenges is the paradox between the acknowledgement of most Western literature that the boundaries of any discipline are unstable, non-closed, and non-independent, on the one hand, and the widespread existence of institutional, academic, scientific, and interdisciplinary structures that seek to maintain the independence of sciences and epistemological systems, on the other hand.

Besides, the gradual transition, from traditional interdisciplinary study and research that adopt a problem-solving perspective to research and study, has revealed many theoretical and methodological problematics related to the interdisciplinary approach, its nature, goals, and outcomes.[48] These problematics are also manifest now at the level of IR Theory, where a field of international interdisciplinary studies is widely growing. The interdisciplinarity in the field is no longer confined to the relationship between IR Theory and other branches of political science (the first wave of interdisciplinarity that took place in the 1960s and 1970s), which revolved around the connection between the internal and the external or the differences and similarities between internal interdisciplinarity and political international interdisciplinarity, but the interdisciplinarity in the field now also extends to the connection between IR theory and other social sciences, at the top of which are history and economics.

These interdisciplinary studies raise a problem of classification: Are they explanatory, constitutive, normative, or empirical approaches? Some of the most important interdisciplinary fields are international political theory and historical sociology. Burchill and Linklater define them as follows:[49]

> international political theory covers a range of ethical, philosophical and historical questions that used to be raised in domestic settings, rather than in the domain of international politics. Though not necessarily prescriptive, international political theory seeks to understand the grounds on which a range of ethical choices and normative preferences in international politics are made. Issues such as just-war theory, global justice, and humanitarian intervention now occupy a central place in the theory of international relations. When is it legitimate to use force? What is the basis of a good international society? Are there any human rights that should be central to any decent international order? Do affluent peoples have an obligation to

> assist the victims of famine and poverty in other societies? When do our obligations to people in other political communities – and to humanity generally – supersede our duties to fellow nationals? International political theory analyses the arguments that are advanced in attempt to answer such questions and reflects on the presuppositions and politics which reside in the foundations of these discussions.[50]
> International political theory acts as reminder of the existence of a precious history of international thought and the need for a serious consideration of its inceptions and formulations. In this context, historical sociology is expected to identify and understand long-term patterns and processes of change in international relations.... Like international political theory, historical sociology has many different strands and traditions. Some embrace grand historical narratives with an eye to uncovering distinctive patterns and themes, while others can be considered an antidote to "presentism" – providing historical context to ensure that the analysis of supposedly unique contemporary events takes account of their relationship with processes that might stretch back for decades or centuries, and in some cases for millennia.[51]

In the field of thought and history, international interdisciplinary studies are an epistemological and ontological necessity for non-Western efforts and contributions to international theorizing. As previously shown, this is because Western theorizing depends on Western philosophical roots and Western historical practices. Moreover, some of the scholars interested in interdisciplinary studies admit that their studies are confined to Western thought in its different ages and do not extend to cover the thought of other civilizations.[52]

It is remarkable that the Project of International Relations in Islam already as early as the mid-1980s[53] proved that Western international theorizing ignored the Islamic experience at the levels of thought and history. This conclusion motivated an engagement with these two fields in the foundational works of this project (1986-1996)[54] and then again during the ensuing process of implementing and constructing a comparative Islamic Civilizational Paradigm.[55] The paradigm's engagement with thought and history reflects its peculiar nature and characteristics, because the motives, goals, objectives, and even methodological tools of a comparative approach to these two fields (thought and history) vary from one paradigm to the other, be they realist, liberal, Marxist, modernist positivist, or non-positivist Islamic.[56]

7.5 GLOBAL CHANGE: THE RELATIONSHIP BETWEEN POWER AND KNOWLEDGE AND THE GROWING SIGNIFICANCE OF NORMATIVE DIMENSIONS

The precepts and characteristics of the critical theoretical approaches as well as their four previously discussed fields of interest collectively reveal the importance of a fifth field of interest, the field of global change. However, the way in which these approaches deal with global change differs tremendously from the way in which the dominant paradigms of IR deal with it. That is because the new critical theoretical trends pay attention to the significance of normative dimensions, or because they associate change with transformation, rather than mere adjustment. Thus, an interest in "global change" is not totally new.

What is new in the world? Who is responsible for it? Who is affected by its positive or negative consequences (as being new does not necessarily mean being better)? Most importantly, what are its causes? How does it happen? These questions of what, why, when, how, and where have been recurrent throughout history. Philosophers, thinkers, and politicians always raise these questions and argue about them, whether by resort to thought, theorization, diplomacy, weapons, or money.

Temporal and spatial contexts differ, so do events and facts, so do details, processes, and tools. However, there are major temporal and thematic benchmarks that indicate successive changes and transformations, because of which the "global system" moves from one stage to the other. In our Islamic Arab civilizational space, we are located at the heart of these transformations, with their ups and downs, as subjects as well as objects.

Moreover, a set of conceptual dichotomies frame the processes of change, whether in their cooperative or conflictual forms, across the world, between the powerful and the weak, the rich and the poor, the young and the old, peoples and governments, etc. At the top of the list of opposite dichotomies which underlie methodological, theoretical, and epistemological debates about the "reality of the world we live in" are the following sets: reality/thought, action/theory, inside/outside, structures/institutions, power/knowledge, science/values, reason/revelation, individual/society, state/society, the homeland/the nation, religion/politics, economy/politics, national security / human security, major peace / minor peace, world order/world community, global order/global group, universality/particularity, freedom/justice, independence/dependence, conflict/cooperation.

Some intellectual approaches and political movements seek to maintain structures, institutions, and dominant normative systems, arguing that the dominant is indeed the global, because it is the better. By contrast, other approaches and movements seek change, even transformation, in world order, because the prevalent or dominant is not necessarily the better or the global. Instead, it is the product of Western civilizational centrism that claims universality in the name of modernity and secularism. By the same token, the conceptual systems derived from this Western centrism, at the top of which are the nation-state, sovereignty, democracy, and human rights, are not universal concepts, and have all been exposed to criticism. The development of the intellectual, theoretical, and epistemological debate about each of these dichotomies and their multiple interrelations is related to developments in the reality of international relations and the state and characteristics of world order. This fact is quite manifest in the content and issues addressed by the paradigm debates.

For example, since the end of the Cold War and the fall of bipolarity, the paradigm debate has experienced three waves that have been correlated with main international benchmarks. The first wave lasted from the end of the Cold War until September 11, 2001. The second wave lasted until the outbreak of the Arab Spring uprisings, late 2010. We are still experiencing the third wave. While the first wave witnessed democracy and human rights being tested in the Americas, Eastern Europe, the Balkans, and the republics of the former Soviet Union, the second wave witnessed the rise of violations of democracy and human rights in the Islamic world in the name of the American or global War on Terror. The third wave is still putting to the test the dichotomies of democracy/interests, values/interests, and revolution/terrorism.

Thus, while the last three decades have witnessed theoretical anticipations for the future of the international system in terms of structure, the nature of power, and power balances and processes, our Islamic Arab civilizational circle has not been absent from these predictions. Among these theoretical predictions, two main opposing trends can be identified: a conservative trend that seeks to maintain the status quo, and another radical trend that seeks change in the form of deep transformation. Whereas, the first wave witnessed the call for the multiplicity or plurality of civilizational paradigms as a means of achieving true universality in the IR discipline, the second wave witnessed the maturation of change seeking critical theories. These advocated global change at the levels of international issues, frameworks, structures, and institutions, as well as theoretical change to better deal with reality and explore its explicit and implicit biases. Thus, throughout the second wave, debates about "global change" have crystalized at these levels. It is important to note that critical theoretical endeavors link reality and theory. They believe that global change becomes possible once we change our perspective on reality and once we unveil implicitly embedded biases in social sciences; biases that reflect the relationship between authority, power, and knowledge. Western civilizational paradigms claim universality and exercise monopoly over the "scientific" definition of concepts.

In other words, Western critical theoretical efforts serve the purpose of guiding and changing, not merely of observing and explaining, because change – according to them – is affected not only through the reformation of international system's institutions, but also through treating the root causes of problems, rather than their manifestations or symptoms. And among the most important problems is the malfunctioning of the value system of the international system. In fact, the discourse on global change is a two-sided coin. The first side addresses the state of world order crises from the perspective of comparative paradigms in IR, while focusing on the critical ones that seek international/global change. As for the second face, it raises comparative arguments about democracy and global justice.

The 2008 crisis of the global capitalist system unleashed events and ideas about "global change." These represented political, economic, and even cultural contexts for the debates on democracy and global justice, between Western paradigms and a change seeking Islamic Civilizational Paradigm, though still under construction. Moreover, Arab Spring revolutions and uprisings have provided a vibrant field for testing the concepts and practices of global democracy. They have allowed for reflections on the significance of the historical experiences of revolutions in the Arab and Muslim world and the patterns of foreign interventions in these revolutions. They have also allowed for reflections on the significance of the theoretical literature of the two decades preceding the revolutions, in which the concepts of revolutions were missing for the sake of the concepts of democratic transition, gradual reform, non-violence, peace, and dialogue. And they have allowed for reflections on the position of revolutions in international relations theory.[57] If these revolutions had succeeded, they would have set the beginning for global change towards a more democratic, just, and humane world. Moreover, the counterrevolutions and coups that faced these revolutions constitute a live test for the credibility of comparative democratic concepts and the extent to which foreign interventions affect domestic experiences of change towards freedom and justice.

So, what is new about the crises of world order at the beginning of the 21st century? What is new about change? The last quarter of the 20th century had witnessed the accumulation of indicators of change in the international system, leading later on to the end of the Cold War and the end of the structure of bipolarity, interpreted at that time as a victory without war and declaration of the hegemony of the Western civilizational model under American leadership. Although the end of the Cold War had produced serious reflections about the future of American hegemony in light of globalization, the third millennium carried along the greatest challenge to this hypothetical hegemony, that was the attacks of September 11, 2001. The United States exploited this event to reinforce the hegemony of the American empire in the world: the centrality of American military power, the control of global economy, and the dissemination of Western values (political, economic, and cultural).[58]

Thus, a series of regional wars during the first decade of the 21st

century in Afghanistan and Iraq, under the pretext of the war on terror, came as an activation of the American strategy of the 21st century. These wars exhausted the global American power, politically, economically, and militarily. Besides, the American administration's value system, marketed under the title of the "Greater Middle East Project," came under deep internal as well as external scrutiny. The project claimed to protect and spread the system of American values throughout the world as a means for achieving security, stability, and prosperity.[59]

With the global financial and economic crisis of 2008, the question was asked anew, though in another form: Will the global capitalist system witness a transformation, because this crisis and its consequences are unprecedentedly serious? Or is this crisis merely another crisis of the many recurring crises of the global capitalist system throughout the century, one whose consequences the capitalist system will succeed in managing and containing?

The debate on the indicators of the US leadership of the world after the end of the Cold War and the movement of the international system towards unilateralism was replaced by the end of the first decade of the third millennium by a debate on the chances that a continued American leadership had and the obstacles that it faced due to its domestic and foreign crises. Thus, with the end of the first decade of the third millennium, the increasing difficulties facing the American and global economy, and the frequent political and military crises at the global level, the following two questions seemed strongly correlated: Will the world order experience a structural transformation leading the United States to lose its position as the unilateral leader of the world? Will the global capitalist system, in turn, experience a radical transformation?

In other words, the questions throughout the main stages of transition of the 20th century basically revolved around the position of the leading power of the international system, be it European, American, or Asian (Japanese or Chinese); an international system characterized by a global capitalist order that adjusted itself to its frequent crises and came out victorious each time. These questions often asked about the causes that led to the regression of Europe and then the disintegration of the Soviet Union. Now, questions underline two interconnected issues simultaneously: the state of the American world leadership and the orientation of the American global role, on the one hand, and the consequences of the global capitalist order and the state of world order, in terms of its stability and security, on the other hand.

With the end of the first decade of the third millennium, it became clear that the world was undergoing a double crisis: the crisis of global capitalism and liberalism and that of world leadership. There was also a third crisis, the crisis of the system of values in the world. The latter manifested itself in the debates about the type of relations between religions, cultures, and civilizations, whether they take the form of conflict or cooperation. These debates emerged in the 1990s and have come to the fore since the events of September 11, 2001, whether in academic or political circles. They accompanied the then aggravating internal and regional conflicts that had obvious religious, ethnic, and national dimensions, thus reflecting the rising weight of cultural and normative dimensions in international relations. These dimensions have jumped to the fore of the new policies of global powers since 2001. For although these global policies seemed to be basically run by Western diplomatic and military power, albeit under American leadership, they were strongly interwoven with cultural dimensions, needed to justify and implement the strategy of the war on terror. This strategy targeted people too, not only regions and governments. Therefore, the goals and objectives of this strategy required new tools and methods that dealt with the issues of culture and identity as an integral part of the issues of global policies. This paved the way for unprecedented debate, in terms of degree and frequency, about the systems of contrasting (conflicting or competing) civilizational values.[60]

Calls for the "multiplicity of civilizational paradigms" emerged as a means to solve the crisis of the current global civilization and to achieve a more secure and just world.[61] The debate about the future of global change in political and academic circles has revolved around three synchronous crises since 2008, even more since 2011. First, there is the crisis of world leadership associated with the decline in American power and the rise of other power centers. Second, there is the structural crisis of the global capitalist order. And finally, there is the crisis of the ruling system of values: representative liberal democracy vs. social justice, and the centrism of Western civilization vs. the multiplicity of civilizational paradigms as sources for prospective change and transformation in world order. That is because the international (or global) system is not merely a structure of political power (distribution of global power); it involves also social and economic structures and value systems. There are also the environmental factors that represent inputs for this order, whether they are national, regional, or systemic factors. Perhaps the most important of these factors are the successive industrial, technological, and post-industrial revolutions, the information and communication revolution, as well as globalization and its processes. These factors, inter alia, have always had systemic impacts upon international relations (e.g., the impact of atomic weapons on the international system, and the impact of the information and communication revolution on global economy and nation-states). The neglect of these factors, and the change they go through, causes some researchers to miss the distinction between indicators of systemic change or transformation, its causes, and its outcomes.[62]

The above mentioned three crises indicate the degree of complexity which the study of change/transformation in international system has reached, in contrast with three decades ago when Ole Holsti, along with others, made a qualitative breakthrough in the field of systemic studies.[63] However, it was a breakthrough under the hegemony of the realist paradigm over the study of international relations and the early beginnings of the third great debate between the realist paradigm and what was then called post-behavioralism or pluralism. The critical perspectives have been contributing to the current debate for more than two decades. Hence comes the significance of recalling the international system's value system as a third dimension in addition to the other two dimensions upon which realism focused (i.e., the structure of military and political power and that of economic power).

The debate has thus turned to the "transformation" of world order, not merely the "change" of some of its components. The debate highlights the indicators, causes, and outcomes of transformation at the level of the leadership of the system, the structure of the global capitalist system, or the prevalent system of values and norms. Academic debate during the first decade of the 21st century, especially on the part of the Critical School and the Social Constructivist School, revolved around the following topics: the global systemic crisis, crisis and transformation, globalization and global crisis, and the growing interest in the South.

The previous round of debates before the outbreak of the global financial crisis of 2008, which took place within/under global change studies,[64] revolved around global governance, global democracy, and global citizenship. These debates were frequently associated with the rising paradigm of globalism, a paradigm that leaped forward to challenge the realist paradigm. Despite its obviously different ontological and methodological assumptions, some scholars considered this paradigm only as a new means for the current world order to adjust with its frequent crises, first internally and then externally, in an attempt to overcome the two crises of democracy and citizenship in the West by giving them new global dimensions. In the West, this call for globality is still governed by the same philosophical assumptions about democracy adopted by the liberal capitalist paradigm.

The difference between the two rounds of debates, the one that has been taking place since 2008 and the one that took place after the end of the Cold War, clearly reveals the difference between the discourse of change and the discourse of transformation.[65] In other words, whereas the literature in the late 1980s and early 1990s had disagreed on whether the United States would become the sole leader of the global order, and whether the post-Cold War world would be unilateral or multi-polar, literature during the first decade of the 21st century was quite different. At that time, the global political arena was dominated by two approaches. The first approach explained the global American strategy (under the neo-conservatists) as an expression of the imperialist stage of the development of American politics. The second approach warned against the political, economic, and even ethical implications of the huge American military involvement abroad because, rather than signaling the imperialist behavior of the U.S., it could serve as a cause for the decline and the fading of the American global power.

It is, however, almost agreed upon (since 2008), especially in the literature of the critical schools of IR, that we do not focus on the causes of the rise or fall of great empires throughout history in order to give advice to the United States or teach it a lesson, as Paul Kennedy[66] did, though at a time when the United States was at the apex of its victory over the Soviet Union. Instead, we argue that the United States has indeed entered a stage of crisis and that its global power has already started retreating. Moreover, we argue that the United States has been exerting every possible effort to halt this deterioration. However, in the meantime, both the global capitalist system and the dominant system of values have also entered the stage of an unprecedented structural crisis.

The crisis of globalization represents the overall framework from which these crises have emerged. In terms of its diagnosis and the evaluation of its impact, globalization was an important site for debate between the three competing dominant paradigms (realism, liberalism, and structuralism),[67] especially after the end of the Cold War. Growing criticism has revealed the negative impact of globalization as a process, an ideology, or a set of policies.

The critical constructivist school exposes these three interrelated crises. In addition to the material and structural factors, the school recalls the role of ideas, values, beliefs, and identity, and their effect on understanding current global transformation and the future of Western centrism in world order in the face of rising cultures and civilizations that challenge this centrism. These developments have given rise to a third generation of literature on the study of the historical development of international systems. The first generation is known as the static holistic school, while the second generation is known as the dynamic school in the study of global transformations.[68]

These interrelated crises, around which the third generation of the literature on the development of international systems and global transformation revolves, have produced a two-fold argument. First, the current crisis of the world order is also a normative crisis, not merely a crisis of material power. Throughout the first decade of the (unilateral) American hegemony, which coincided with the first decade of the third millennium, there was growing evidence of the retreating effectiveness of material power. Moreover, after the conflict between the two Western models – the liberal capitalist model and the authoritarian communist model – it has become evident that the model of "the triumphant without war" has not been accepted as the universal model and that it has tried to assert its hegemony by force, through military power and structural violence.[69] However, the indicators of the decline and deterioration of this model have followed through in a way contending this time the following question: when and how will transformation take place?

The question now is about "transformation," rather than change. Here, normative dimensions play a significant role. These dimensions have been increasingly called upon throughout the last three decades, in which revisions of IR Theory have been taking place. Values, ideas, beliefs, and identity, not to mention culture and religion have become a common denominator in the titles of publications on international relations. An engagement with values and ethics has become a necessity for guiding action, resulting in, inter alia, the call for the multiplicity of civilizational paradigms vis-a-vis Western civilizational centrism, as previously discussed.

Finally, what is that additional input into the global change debate that a comparative Islamic Civilizational Paradigm can have? How is the paradigm, compared to critical approaches, to be applied to the study of issues of global change such as global democracy and global justice? These questions, along with those that we have raised so far in this study, lead us to the fourth and final part of this study, reflecting on the grounds, characteristics, and assumptions of a comparative Islamic Civilizational Paradigm.

To conclude, the interest of the critical theoretical approaches in these five different fields discussed throughout the previous sections reflects mainly their postmodern and secular nature. Hence, the Islamic Civilizational Paradigm can still provide a critical contribution of a different nature, as a paradigm with Islamic foundations and intellectual and historical roots relevant to the experience of the Muslim Ummah. As a non-secular and non-Western paradigm, it raises many questions about values from an Islamic perspective, about religion, cultural and civilizational dimensions, and about the levels of analysis and the engagement with history and thought when studying international relations. Finally, it also raises many questions regarding the issue of global change from an Islamic perspective in comparison with the dominant paradigms in the discipline and with the critical theoretical approaches

Is the world experiencing a shift towards a real transformation, or is it just experiencing a new crisis in the relationship between power and knowledge resulting from shifts in the authority and power centers in the world and their oscillation between states, on the one hand, and peoples, nations, groups, and individuals, on the other? Is it, rather, a crisis in the relationship between power and knowledge, resulting from attempts by existing hegemonic centers to restore their full hegemony through the exploitation of all tools and approaches, especially the non-traditional ones that were not given much attention by realism and positivism?[70] Whatever the answers to these questions, we can conclude here by saying that a growing interest in civilizational, religious, and cultural approaches to the study of international relations has been strongly tied to the renewed interest in values and norms and has paved the way for non-Western, civilizational, theoretical contributions to the discipline of international relations.

NOTES

1. See: Nadia M. Mostafa, "ʿAmaliyat Bināʾ Manẓūr Islāmī li Dirāsat al-ʿAlaqāt al-Dawliyyah: Ishkāliyyāt Khibrat al-Baḥth wa al-Tadrīs" [The Process of Building an Islamic Paradigm for the Study of International Relations: Problems of Research and Teaching Experience]; "Ishkāliyyāt al-Baḥth wa al-Tadrīs fī ʿIlm al-ʿAlaqāt al-Dawliyyah min Manẓūr Ḥaḍārī Muqāran" [Problematics of Research and Teaching International Relations from a Comparative Civilizational Paradigm],], in *Fiqh al-Taḥayuz: Ru'yah Maʿrifiyyah wa Daʿwah li al-Ijtihād* [Fiqh of Bias: An Epistemological Perspective and a Call for Ijtihād] (Cairo: International Institute of Islamic Thought and Dar Al-Salam, 2016), pp. 319-393; "Ishkāliyyāt al-Baḥth wa al-Tadrīs fī ʿIlm al-ʿAlaqāt al-Dawliyyah min Manẓūr Ḥaḍārī Muqāran" [Problematics of Research and Teaching International Relations from a Comparative Civilizational Paradigm], in *Al-Manhajiyyah al-Islāmiyyah* [Islamic Methodology], ed. Ahmad-Fouad Basha et al. (Cairo: Markaz al-Dirāsāt al-Maʿrifiyyah wa Dār al-Islām, 2010), pp. 817-914; "Al-ʿAlāqāt al-Dawliyyah fī al-Fikr al-Siyāsī al-Islāmī: al-Ishkāliyyāt al-Manhājiyyah wa Kharīṭah wa al-Namādhij al-Fikriyyah wa Manẓūmat al-Mafāhīm" [International

Relations in Islamic Political Thought: Methodological Problematics, Intellectual Models Map, and Conceptual System]; *Al-Dīmuqrāṭīyah al-ʿĀlamiyyah min Manẓūrāt Gharbiyyah wa Naḥū Manẓūr Islāmi fī ʿIlm al-ʿAlāqāt al-Dawliyyah* [World Democracy from Western Perspectives and Towards an Islamic Perspective in the Discipline of International Relations], Silsilah al-Waʿī al-Ḥaḍārī [Civilizational Awareness Series] (Cairo: Civilization Center for Political Studies, 2011); *Al-ʿAlāqāt al-Dawliyyah fī Tarīkh al-Islāmī Manẓūr Ḥaḍārī Muqāran* [International Relations in Islamic History: A Comparative Civilizational Perspective] (Cairo: Civilization Center for Political Studies and Dār al-Bashīr for Culture and Sciences, 2015); Nadia M. Mostafa, "Arabic Islamic Debates on Dialogue and Conflict between Cultures," in *Human Values and Global Governance: Studies in Development, Security and Culture*, ed. Bjorn Hettne, vol. 2 (New York: Palgrave MacMillan, 2008), pp. 96-191.

2. See Nadia M. Mostafa, ed., *ʿIlm al-Siyāsah: Murājaʿāt Naẓriyyah wa Manhājiyyah* [Political Science: Theoretical and Methodological Revisions]; Omaima Abboud ed., *Al-Manẓūr al-Baynī wa al-ʿAlāqāt al-Bayniyyah fi al-ʿUlūm al-Siyāsiyyah: Iʿādat Naẓr wa Qirā'ah Jadīdah* [Interdisciplinary Perspective and Interdisciplinary Relationships in Political Science: Re-View and a New Reading] (Cairo: Cairo University Faculty of Economics and Political Science, 2012); Amira Abou Samra ed., *Madākhil al-Taḥlīl al-Thaqāfī lī Dirāsat al- awāhir al-Siyāsiyyah wa al-Ijtimāʿiyyah: al-Munṭaliqāt wa al-Mafāhīm fī al-ʿUlūm al-Ijtimāʿiyyah wa al-Siyāsiyyah* [The Cultural Analysis Approach to the Study of Political and Social Phenomena: Origins, Fields, and Concepts in Social and Political Sciences] (Cairo: Cairo University Faculty of Economics and Political Science, 2011).

3. Amira Abou Samra ed., *Madākhil al-Taḥlīl al-Thaqāfī lī Dirāsat al-Ẓawāhir al-Siyāsiyyah wa al-Ijtimāʿiyyah: al-Munṭaliqāt wa al-Mafāhīm fī al-ʿUlūm al-Ijtimāʿiyyah wa al-Siyāsiyyah* [The Cultural Analysis Approach to the Study of Political and Social Phenomena: Origins, Fields, and Concepts in Social and Political Sciences], pp. 15-17.

4. The proceedings of the first scientific conference of the assistant teaching staff at the Department of Political Science, Cairo University, entitled *Al-Thawrah wa al-ʿUlūm al-Siyāsiyyah* [Revolution and Political Science], were an opportunity to test the new theoretical approaches in political science. See: Ikram Badr-Eddin, Nadia M. Mostafa and Amal Hamada,

eds., *Al-Thawrah al-Miṣriyyah wa Dirāsat al-ʿUlūm al-Siyāsiyyah* [Egyptian Revolution and the Study of Political Science] (Cairo: Cairo University Faculty of Economics and Political Science and the Arab Center for Political Research and Policy Study, 2011).

5. Most studies in this book tackle epistemological, theoretical, and methodological details because their topics lie in this scope, as previously shown in the general introduction to the book, and in a way that is basically based on comparison as a method in these studies.

6. See the study of Amira Abou Samra, *Al-Buʿd al-Miʿyārī li Istikhdām al-Quwah al-ʿAskariyyah: Dirāsah Muqāranah fī Ishāmāt Naẓriyyah Naqdiyyah* [The Standard Dimension of the Use of Military Force: A Comparative Study of the Contributions of a Critical Theory], in *Al-ʿAlāqāt al-Dawliyyah fī ʿĀlim Mutaghayyir: Manẓūrāt wa Madākhil Muqāranah* [International Relations in a Changing World: Comparative Paradigms and Approaches], ed. Nadia Mostafa (Cairo: Hadara Center for Political Studies, 2016), pp. 1628-1734.

7. Ismail S. Maqlad, "Naẓriyāt al-Siyāsah al-Dawliyyah" [Theories of International Politics], pp. 27-55. On contested areas of theorization and the causes of theoretical explosion, see Scott Burchill and Andrew Linklater, "Introduction," in *Theories of International Relations.*

8. Wadoudah Badran, "Dirāsat al-ʿAlāqāt al-Dawliyyah fī al-Adabiyyāt al-Gharbiyyah wa Baḥth al-ʿAlāqāt al-Dawliyyah fī al-Islām" [Study of International Relations in Western Literature and the Project of International Relations in Islam], in Nadia M. Mostafa, *Al-Muqadimmah al-ʿĀmah li Mashrūʿ al-ʿAlāqāt al-Dawliyyah fī al-Islām* [General Introduction to the Project of International Relations in Islam], vol. 1, pp. 79-131.

9. For instance, see: Charles R. Beitz, "Recent International Thought," *International Journal* (Spring 1988); Ken Booth, "Security in Anarchy," pp. 527-545; P. Viotti and M. V. Kauppi, *International Relations Theory*, pp. 533-545; Martha Finnemore, "Norms, Culture and World Politics: Insights from Sociology's Institutionalism," *International Organization* 50, no. 2, (Spring 1996): pp. 325-345; Robert Jackson, "Is There a Classical International Theory," in *International Relations Theory Today*, eds., Ken Booth and Steve Smith; Miles Kahler, "Rationality in International Relations," *International Organizations* 52, no. 4, (Autumn 1998); Seymon Brown, *International Relations in a*

Changing Global System: Toward a Theory of the World Polity (Boulder, CO: Westview Press, 1992); Saif AbdelFattah, *Madkhal al-Qiyam: Iṭār Marjaʿī li Dirāsat al-ʿAlāqāt al-Dawliyyah fī al-Islām* [Introduction to Values: A Referential Framework for the Study of International Relations in Islam], vol. 2 (Cairo: International Institute of Islamic Thought, 1996).

10. For instance, see: Steve Smith, Ken Booth, Marysia Zalewski, eds., *International Theory: Positivism and Beyond*, (New York: Cambridge University Press, 1996).
11. John Lewis Gaddis, "International Relations Theory and the End of the Cold War," *International Security* 17, no. 3, (Winter 1992): pp. 29-53.
12. Ibid., p. 54.
13. Ibid., p. 56.
14. Jim George, *Discourses of Global Politics: A Critical (Re) Introduction to International Relations* (Boulder, CO: Lynne Rienner Publishers, 1994), pp. 1-20.
15. Steve Smith, "Singing Our World into Existence: International Relations Theory and September 11," *International Studies Quarterly* 48, no. 3 (September 2004): pp. 499-515.
16. Christian Reus-Smit and Duncan Snidal, "Reuniting Ethics and Social Sciences," *The Oxford Handbook of International Relations* 22, no. 3 (Fall 2008).
17. On the role of culture, see: Ali Mazrui, *Culture Forces in World Politics* (London: James Currey; Portsmouth, NH and Nairobi: Heinemann, 1999); Youssef Lapid ed., *The Return of Culture and Identity in International Relations Theory* (London: Lynne Rienner Publishers, 1996); Fred Halliday, "Culture and International Relations: A New Reductionism?"; Marysia Zalewski and Cynthia Enloe, "Questions about Identity on International Relations," in *International Relations Theory Today*, K. Booth and S. Smith, eds., pp. 279-305; Simon Murden, "Culture and World Politics, in *Globalization and World Politics*, eds., S. Smith and K. Booth; Valerie M. Hudson ed., *Culture and Foreign Policy* (London: Lynne Rienner Publishers, 1997); Martin W. Sampson, "Culture Influences on Foreign Policy," in *New Directions in the Study of Foreign Policy*, eds., Charles F. Hermann, Charles W. Kegley, James N. Roseneau (London: HarperCollins, 1987); Naeem Inayatullah and David L. Blaney, *International Relations and the*

Problem of Difference (New York: Routledge, 2004); R. James Ferguson, "The Contested Role of Culture in International Relations." On the role of religion, see: Barry Rubin, "Religion and International Affairs," *The Washington Quarterly* (Spring 1990); Jeff Haynes, *Religion in the Third World Politics* (Boulder, CO: Lynne Rienner Publishers, 1994), pp. 122- 145 [Ch. 5, Links Between Religion and Foreign Policy in the third world]; Georges Weigel, "Religion and Peace: An Argument Complexified," in *Order and Disorder after the Cold War*, ed., Brad Roberts (Cambridge: MIT Press, 1996); Jeff Haynes, "Religion," in *Issues in World Politics*, eds., Brian White, Richard Little, Michael Smith, 2nd ed. (London: Palgrave, 2001), pp. 153-170; Paylos Hatzopoulos and Fabio Petito, eds., *Religion in International Relations: The Return from Exile* (London: Palgrave Macmillan, 2003); Peter L. Berger, ed., *The Desecularization of the World: Resurgent Religion and World Politics* (Washington D.C.: W.B. Eerdmans, 1999); John D. Carlson and Erik C. Owen, *The Sacred and the Sovereign: Religion and International Politics* (Washington D.C.: Georgetown University Press, 2003); Jonathan Fox and Shmuel Sandler, *Bringing Religion into International Relations* (New York: Palgrave Macmillan, 2004).

18. See: The study of Amany Ghanem, "Al-Abᶜād al-Thaqāfiyyah wa al-ᶜAlāqāt al-Dawliyyah: Dirāsah fī Khiṭāb Ṣidām al-Ḥaḍārāt" [Cultural Aspects in International Relations: A Study of the Clash of Civilizations Discourse]; Essam Abdelshafi, *Al-Siyāsah al-Amrīkiyyah Tujāha al-Mamlakah al-ᶜArabiyyah al-Saᶜūdiyyah: Dirāsah fī Ta'thīr al-Buᶜd al-Dīnī* [American Politics Toward the Kingdom of Saudi Arabia: A Study of the Effect of the Religious Dimension 2000-2005] (PhD diss., Cairo University, 2009); the second chapter entitled "Al-Fikr al-Istirātījī al-Gharbī" [Western Strategic Thought], in *Al-Taḥaddiyāt al-Siyāsiyyah al-Khārijiyyah li al-ᶜĀlim al-Islāmī* [External Political Challenges to the Muslim World], Nadia M. Mostafa (Cairo: League of Islamic Universities, 1999).
19. Nadia M. Mostafa, ed., "Iᶜādat Taᶜrīf al-Siyāsī fī al-ᶜAlāqāt al-Dawliyyah: Ru'yah min Dākhil Ḥaql al-ᶜAlāqāt al-Dawliyyah" [Redefining the Political in International Relations: A View from within the Field of International Relations], pp. 427-430.
20. See: Nadia M. Mostafa and Amira Abou Samra, *Madākhil al-Taḥlīl al-Thaqāfī lī Dirāsat al-Ẓawāhir al-Siyāsiyyah wa al-Ijtimāᶜiyyah:*

al-Munṭaliqāt wa al-Mafāhīm fī al-ʿUlūm al-Ijtimāʿiyyah wa al-Siyāsiyyah [The Cultural Analysis Approach to the Study of Political and Social Phenomena: Origins, Fields, and Concepts in Social and Political Sciences] (Cairo: Cairo University Faculty of Economics and Political Science, 2011).

21. See two studies on this relationship in one of the parts of the project of rooting civilizational studies: Fawzi Khalil and Fouad Alsaid, "Al-Thaqāfah wa al-Ḥaḍārah: Maqārabah bayn al-Fikrayn al-Gharbī wal al-Islām" [Culture and Civilization: A Comparison of Western and Islamic Modes of Thought], in *Al-Ta'ṣīl al-Naẓrī li al-Dirāsāt al-Ḥaḍāriyyah: al-ʿAlāqāt bayn al-Ḥaḍārah wa al-Thaqāfah wa al-Dīn* [Theoretical Rooting of Civilizational Studies: Relationships among Civilization, Culture, and Religion], Mona Abul-Fadl and Nadia M. Mostafa, eds., vol. 4 (Cairo: Cairo University Program of Civilizational Studies and the Dialogue of Cultures; Damascus: Dār al-Fikr, 2008).

22. Nadia M. Mostafa, "Arabic Islamic Debates on Dialogue and Conflict between Cultures," in *Human Values and Global Governance: Studies in Development, Security and Culture*, ed. Bjorn Hettne, vol. 2, pp. 97-121.

23. See: Nadia M. Mostafa and Amira Abou Samra, *Madākhil al-Taḥlīl al-Thaqāfī lī Dirāsat al-Ẓawāhir al-Siyāsiyyah wa al-Ijtimāʿiyyah* [The Cultural Analysis Approach to the Study of Political and Social Phenomena], especially the first chapter entitled "Al-Jadīd fī Naẓriyat al-Thaqāfah" [The New in the Theory of Culture] and the second chapter entitle "Al-Dhākirah wa Ṣaʿūd al-Ihtimām bi al-Buʿd al-Thaqāfī fī al-ʿUlūm al-Siyāsah" [Memory and the Rise of Interest in the Cultural Dimension in Political Science]. There are contributions by: Ahmad Zayed, "Al-Jadīd fī Naẓriyat al-Thaqāfah: al-Mafhūm wa al-Itijāhāt wa al-Manāhij" [The New in the Theory of Culture: the Concept, Approaches, and Methods], pp. 33-47; Kamal Almonoufi, "Taʿqīb ʿalā Aḥmad Zayid" [Comment on Ahmad Zayed], pp. 48-67; Heba Raouf, "Bayn al-Ḥadāthah wa mā baʿd al-Ḥadāthah: Ṣaʿūd al-Ihtimām bi al-Buʿd al-Thaqāfī" [Between Modernism and Postmodernism: the Rise of Interest in the Cultural Dimension], pp. 71-110; Omaima Abboud, "Masīrat al-Thaqāfī wa al-Siyāsī fī al-Naẓriyyah al-Siyāsiyyah al-Lībirāliyyah" [The Progress of the Cultural and Political in the Liberal Political Theory], pp. 73-94; Sayed Ghanim, "Taʿqīb ʿalā Hibah Ra'ūf

wa Umaymah ʿAbūd" [Comment on Heba Raouf and Omaima Abboud], pp. 101-103.

24. Harold H. Saunders, *Politics is about Relationship: A Blueprint for the Citizens' Century* (New York: Palgrave MacMillan, 2005).
25. Michael Michális and Fabio Petito, eds., *Civilizational Dialogue and World Order: The Other Politics of Cultures, Religion and Civilizations in International Relations* (New York: Palgrave Macmillan, 2009), pp. 3-29.
26. Fred Halliday, "Culture and International Relations: A New Reductionism?," pp. 47-71.
27. Paylos Hatzopoulos and Fabio Petito, eds., *Religion in International Relations: The Return from Exile.*
28. Ibid., pp. 2-3.
29. Ibid., p. 3.
30. Ibid., p. 3.
31. Ibid., p. 3.
32. Ibid., p. 5.
33. Cited in the editorial introduction in Nadia M. Mostafa and Amira Abou Samra, *Madākhil al-Taḥlīl al-Thaqāfī lī Dirāsat al-Ẓawāhir al-Siyāsiyyah wa al-Ijtimāʿiyyah* [The Cultural Analysis Approach to the Study of Political and Social Phenomena], pp. 16-17.
34. Nadia M. Mostafa, "Daʿwah li al-Tafkīr al-ʿIlmī: al-Gharb wa al-ʿĀlim wa al-ʿAlāqah bayn al-Sulṭah wa al-Maʿrifah" [A Call for Scientific Thinking: The West and the World and the Relationship between Power and Knowledge], in *Ḥalaqāt Tajadud al-Ihtimām bi al-Qiyam wa al-Abʿād al-Ḥaḍāriyyah fī al-Dirāsāt al-Siyāsiyyah al-Dawliyyah: Kayf? wa li-Mādhā?* [Series of the Renewal of Interest in Norms and Civilizational Dimension in International Political Studies: How? Why?], Hadara Center for Political Studies], .
35. See: Steve Smith, "The Discipline of International Relations: Still an American Social Science?," pp. 374-402.
36. For instance, see: Giorgio Shani, "Provincializing Critical Theory: Islam, Sikhism and International Relations Theory," *Cambridge Review of International Affairs* 20, no. 3 (September 2007); Navnita Chadha Behera, "Re-imagining International Relations in India," in *Non-Western International Relations Theory: Perspectives On and Beyond Asia*, eds. Barry Buzan and Amitav Acharya (New York: Routledge,

2010), pp. 92-116; Amira Abou Samra, *Mafhūm al-ʿĀlamiyyah fī al-ʿAlaqāt al-Dawliyyah: Dirāsah Muqāranah Ishāmāt Naẓriyyah* [The Concept of Universality in International Relations: A Comparative Study of the Contributions of a Critical Theory] (PhD diss., Cairo University, 2014), pp. 231-290; Elizabeth Shakman Hurd, "The Political Authority of Secularism in International Relations," *European Journal of International Relations* 10, no. 2, (June 2004): pp. 235-262; Candice Moore, "Multiple Perspectives on Hierarchy," *International Studies Association Convention* (San Francisco, 2008).

37. In this respect, see: Mona Abul-Fadl and Nadia Mahmoud Mostafa, eds., *Al-Ta'ṣīl al-Naẓrī li al-Dirāsāt al-Ḥaḍāriyyah: al-ʿAlāqāt bayn al-Ḥaḍārah wa al-Thaqāfah wa al-Dīn* [Theoretical Rooting of Civilizational Studies: Relationships among Civilization, Culture, and Religion], vol. 4 (Cairo: Cairo University Program of Civilizational Studies and the Dialogue of Cultures; Damascus: Dār al-Fikr, 2008). It includes the following seven parts: Mona Abul-Fadl, Omaima Abboud and Sulaiman Alkhateeb, "Al-Ḥiwār maʿ al-Gharb: Ālīyātuh, Ihdāfuh, Dawāfiʿuh," [Dialogue with the West: Its Mechanisms, Goals, and Motives]; Ruqayyah al-Alwani, Father Christian van Neseen and Sameer Marcus, "Mafhūm al-Ākhar fi al-Yahūdiyyah wa al-Masīḥiyyah" [Concept of the Other in Judaism and Christianity]; Alsayed Omar, "Al-Anā wa al-Ākhar min Manẓūr Qur'ānī" [The Self and the Other from a Qur'anic Perspective]; Fouad Said and Fawzi Khalil, "Al-Thaqāfah wa al-Ḥaḍārah: Muqārabah bayn al-Fikrayn al-Gharbī" [Culture and Civilization: An Approach between Western and Islamic Modes of Thought]; Abdel Khabeer Ata Mahrous and Amani Saleh, "Al-ʿAlāqāt al-Dawliyyah: al-Buʿd al-Dīnī wa al-Ḥaḍārī" [International Relations: The Religious and Civilizational Dimension]; Hassan Wajih, "Ḥiwār al-Thaqāfāt: Idārat al-Ajindāt wa al-Sīnārīyūhāt" [Dialogue of Cultures: Management of Agendas and Contested Scenarios]; Saif AbdelFattah, "Al-ʿAwlamah wa al-Islām: Ru'yatān li al-ʿĀlam" [Globalization and Islam: Two Worldviews].

38. Cultural analysis in international relations is a new growing field of study that reflects a high degree of interdisciplinarity in studying contemporary international relations, depending on historical, religious, and cultural roots. There is a growing number of publications in scientific journals and proceedings of conferences during the last decade. See

for example: Riham Bahi, "Al-Ḥaḍārāt fī al-Siyāsah al-Dawliyyah: Manẓūr Taḥt al-Ta'sīs" [Civilizations in International Politics: An In-Progress Perspective], in Nadia M. Mostafa and Amira Abou Samra, *Madākhil al-Taḥlīl al-Thaqāfī lī Dirāsat al-Ẓawāhir al-Siyāsiyyah wa al-Ijtimāʿiyyah* [The Cultural Analysis Approach to the Study of Political and Social Phenomena], pp. 535-554; Brett Bowden, "Politics in a World of Civilizations: Long-term Perspectives on Relations between Peoples," *Human Figurations: Long-term Perspectives on the Human Condition* 1, no. 2 (July 2012), ; Peter J. Katzenstein, ed., *Civilizations in World Politics: Plural and Pluralistic Perspectives*, trans. Fadel Jaktar (Kuwait: National Council for Culture, Arts and Letters, 2012), pp. 7-72, 281-317.

39. See for example: Giorgio Shani, "Provincializing Critical Theory: Islam, Sikhism and International Relations Theory"; Ralph Pettman, Reason, *Reason, Culture, Religion*, pp. 103-104; Richard Falk, "False Universalism and the Geopolitics of Exclusion: The Case of Islam," *Third World Quarterly* 18, no. 1 (March 1997); Amitav Acharya and Barry Buzan, *Non-Western International Relations Theory: Perspectives on and beyond Asia*. London; New York: Routledge, 2010.
40. Ibid.
41. Amitav Acharya and Barry Buzan, *Non-Western International Relations Theory*, pp. 1-25.
42. Shahbranou Tadjbakhsh, "International Relations Theory and the Islamic World View," in *Non-Western International Relations Theory*, eds. Amitav Acharya and Barry Buzan, pp. 174-196.
43. For instance, see: Dunne, Kurk and Smith, eds., *International Relations Theories*.
44. For instance, see: Robert Jackson, "Is There a Classical International Relations Theory," in *International Theory: Positivism and Beyond*, eds. S. Smith, K. Booth, M. Zalewski, pp. 203-221; Jean Bethke Elshtain, "International Politics and Political Theory," in, *International Relation Theory Today*, eds. S. Smith and K. Booth, pp. 263-279.
45. Omaima Abboud, "Muqadimah Taḥrīriyyah" [Editorial Introduction], in *Al-Manẓūr al-Baynī wa al-ʿAlāqāt al-Bayniyyah fi al-ʿUlūm al-Siyāsiyyah: Iʿādat Naẓr wa Qirā'ah Jadīdah* [Interdisciplinary Perspective and Interdisciplinary Relationships in Political Science: Re-View and a New Reading], eds. Nadia M. Mostafa and Omaima Aboud, pp. 11-13.

46. Ibid., p. 13.
47. Ibid. For more information, see: Warleigh-Lack, Alex, and Cini Michelle, "Interdisciplinarity and the Study of Politics," *European Political Science* 8, no. 1 (March 2009), pp. 4-15.
48. Omaima Abboud, "Muqadimah Taḥrīriyyah" [Editorial Introduction], pp. 14-18.
49. Scott Burchill and Andrew Linklater, eds., *Theories of International Relations*, pp. 33-35.
50. Scott Burchill and Andrew Linklater, eds., *Theories of International Relations*, 5th ed. (New York: Palgrave MacMillan, 2013), p. 19.
51. Ibid., p. 20.
52. Chris Brown, Terry Nardin, and Nicholas Rengger, *International Relations in Political Thought* (Cambridge: Cambridge University Press, 2002).
53. Nadia M. Mostafa, *Al-Muqadimmah al-ʿĀmah li Mashrūʿ al-ʿAlāqāt al-Dawliyyah fī al-Islām* [General Introduction to the Project of International Relations in Islam].
54. Nadia M. Mostafa, *Madkhal Minhājī li Dirāsat Taṭawur Waḍʿ wa Dawr al-ʿĀlim al-Islāmī fī al-Niẓām al-Dawlī* [Methodological Introduction for the Study of the Position and Role of the Islamic World in the World Order].
55. See: Nadia M. Mostafa, "Al-ʿAlāqāt al-Dawliyyah fī al-Fikr al-Siyāsī al-Islāmī: al-Ishkāliyyāt al-Manhājiyyah wa Kharīṭah wa al-Namādhij al-Fikriyyah wa Manẓūmat al-Mafāhīm" [International Relations in Islamic Political Thought: Methodological Problematics, Intellectual Models Map, and Conceptual System]; *Al-ʿAlāqāt al-Dawliyyah fī Tarīkh al-Islāmī Manẓūr Ḥaḍārī Muqāran* [International Relations in Islamic History: A Comparative Civilizational Perspective], pp. 37-112.
56. On these comparative frameworks and their position in comparative international theorization, see the third part of the present study. On historical and intellectual examples from an Islamic, civilizational perspective compared with Western examples, see Nadia M. Mostafa: "Al-ʿAlāqāt al-Dawliyyah fī al-Fikr al-Siyāsī al-Islāmī: al-Ishkāliyyāt al-Manhājiyyah wa Kharīṭah wa al-Namādhij al-Fikriyyah wa Manẓūmat al-Mafāhīm" [International Relations in Islamic Political Thought: Methodological Problematics, Intellectual Models Map, and Conceptual System]; *Al-ʿAlāqāt al-Dawliyyah fī Tarīkh al-Islāmī*

Manẓūr Ḥaḍārī Muqāran [International Relations in Islamic History: A Comparative Civilizational Perspective].

57. In the studies of this book, see: Amani Ghanim and Amira Abou Samra, "Al-Thawrah wa Naẓariyyat al-ʿAlāqāt al-Dawliyyah" [The Revolution and International Relations Theory] in *Al-ʿAlāqāt al-Dawliyyah fī ʿĀlim Mutaghayyir: Manẓūrāt wa Madākhil Muqāranah* [International Relations in a Changing World: Comparative Paradigms and Approaches], ed. Nadia Mostafa (Cairo: Hadara Center for Political Studies, 2016), pp. 1891-1944. It was previously published as Amany Ghanm and Amira Abou Samra, "Al-Thawrah wa Naẓariyyat al-ʿAlāqāt al-Dawliyyah" [The Revolution and International Relations Theory], in *Al-Thawrah al-Miṣriyyah wa Dirāsat al-ʿUlūm al-Siyāsiyyah*, eds. Nadia M. Mostafa and Amira Abou Samra (Cairo: Cairo University, 2011), pp. 459-519.

58. For critiques and reviews of the literature of IR discipline on great powers strategies and on change in the structural of international order (change or continuity?) since the end of 1980s, at the end of the Cold War and bipolarity, in light of globalization, and since September 11, 2001, see: Nadia M. Mostafa, "Al-Quwatān al-Aʿẓam wa al-ʿĀlam al-Thālith min al-Ḥarb al-Bāridah ilā al-Ḥarb al-Bāridah al-Jadīdah," [The Two Greatest Powers and the Third World: From the Cold War to the New Cold War], *Majalat al-Fikr al-Istirātījī al-ʿArabī* [Journal of Strategic Arab Thought] (October 1986); "Al-Manṭiqah al-ʿArabiyyah wa al-Niẓām al-Dawlī al-Jadīd" [The Arab Region and the New World Order] (Cairo: Center for Civilizational Studies, 1993); "Azmat al-Khalīj al-Thāniyyah wa al-Niẓam al-Dawlī al-Jadīd" [The Second Gulf Crisis and the New International Order] (Cairo: Center for Civilizational Studies, 1993); "Al-Quwā al-Thānawiyyah wa al-Niẓām al-Dawlī" [Secondary Powers and World Order] (Cairo: Center for Civilizational Studies, 1993); "Āsiyā al-Wusṭā wa al-Qawqāz bayn al-Quwā al-Islāmiyyah al-Kubrā wa al-Rūsiyā: Anmāṭ wa Muḥadadāt al-Taṭawur al-Tārīkhī li al-Tafāʿalāt al-Dawliyyah: Iṭār Muqtaraḥ li al-Taḥlīl al-Siyāsī li al-Tārīkh al-Islāmī" [Central Asia and Caucasia between Great Islamic Powers and Russia: Types and Determinants of the Historical Developments of International Interactions: A Proposed Framework of the Political Analysis of Islamic History], in *Al-Waṭan al-ʿArabī wa Kūmanwalth al-Duwal al-Mustaqillah* [The Arab World and

the Commonwealth of Independent States], ed. Mostafa Elwi (Cairo: Institute of Arab Research and Studies, 1994); "Al-Taḥaddiyāt al-Siyāsiyyah al-Khārijiyyah li al-ʿĀlam al-Islāmī" [Foreign Political Challenges of the Islamic World] (see especially the first and second chapters); "Al-Taḥaddiyāt al-Siyāsiyyah al-Khārijiyyah li al-ʿĀlam al-Islāmī" [Foreign Political Challenges of the Islamic World], in *Al-Ummah fī Qarn* [The Nation in a Century], eds. Nadia M. Mostafa and Saif AbdelFattah (Cairo: Hadara Center for Political Studies and International Shorouq Publishing House, 2002); "The First War in the 21st Century: A Preliminary View," *Journal of International Politics*, 2003.

59. On these wars and their regional and global consequences, see: Nadia M. Mostafa and Saif AbdelFattah, eds., "Tadāʿiyāt al-Ḥādī ʿAshar min Sibtambir ʿalā Ummat al-Islām" [The Consequences of September 11 on the Nation of Islam], *Ḥawlīyat Ummatī fī al-ʿĀlam* [Journal of My Nation in the World], no. 5 (2004); Nadia M. Mostafa and Hassan Nafaa, eds., *Kharīṭat Azmah wa Mustaqbal Ummah* [Transgression on Iraq: A Map of Crisis and the Future of a Nation] (Cairo: Center for Research and Political Studies & Department of Political Science at the Faculty of Economics and Political Science, 2003); Nadia M. Mostafa and Saif AbdelFattah, "Al-ʿUdwān ʿalā al-ʿIrāq" [Transgression on Iraq], *Ḥawlīyat Ummatī fī al-ʿĀlam* [Journal of My Nation in the World], no. 6 (2005); Nadia M. Mostafa and Saif AbdelFattah, eds., Ghazzah bayn al-Ḥiṣār wa al-ʿUdwān" [Gaza between Besiege and Transgression], *Ḥawlīyat Ummatī fī al-ʿĀlam* [Journal of My Nation in the World] (2010); Nadia M. Mostafa, Saif AbdelFattah, Amani Ghanim and Medhat Maher, *Al-ʿUdwān wa al-Muqāwamah al-Ḥaḍāriah fī Ḥarb Lubnān: al-Dalālāt wa al-Mālāt* [Transgression and the Civilizational Resistance in the Lebanese War: Implications and Consequences], (Cairo: Cairo University Program of Civilizational Studies and Dialogue of Cultures at the Faculty of Economics and Political Science, 2007); Nadia M. Mostafa and Saif AbdelFattah, eds., *Al-ʿUmmah wa Mashrūʿ al-Nuhūḍ al-Ḥaḍārī: Ḥāl al-Ummah* [The Nation and the Project of Civilizational Renaissance: The State of the Nation], *Ḥawlīyat Ummatī fī al-ʿĀlam* [Journal of My Nation in the World], no. 8 (2009).

60. On the dimensions of these theoretical and applied debates, see: Nadia M. Mostafa, "Jadālāt Ḥiwār/Ṣirāʿ al-Ḥaḍārāt: Ishkāliyyat al-ʿAlāqah bayn al-Siyāsī—al-Thaqāfī fī Khiṭābāt ʿArabiyyah wa Islāmiyyah" [Debates of the Dialogue/ Clash of Civilizations: The Problematics of the Cultural-Political Relationship in Arab and Islamic Discourses], *Majalat al-Siyāsah al-Dawliyyah* [Journal of International Politics], no. 168 (April 2007).
61. See for example: Fabio Petito, "Dialogue of Civilizations as an Alternative Model for World Order," in *Civilizational Dialogue and World Order: The Other Politics of Cultures, Religion and Civilizations in International Relations*, eds. Michael Michális and Fabio Petito (New York: Palgrave Macmillan, 2009), pp. 47-67; "Dialogue of Civilization as an Alternative Model for World Order," http://www.e-ir.info.
62. On the distinction between the causes and outcomes of global systemic change or transformation after the end of the Cold War in the literature of IR Theory, see Chapter One in Marwa Fikry, *Athīr al-Taghayyurāt al-ʿĀlamiyyah ʿalā al-Dawlah al-Qawmiyyah Khilāl al-Tisʿīnīyāt: Dirāsah Naẓariyyah* [The Impact of Global Changes upon the National State in the 1990s: A Theoretical Study] (master's thesis, Cairo University, 2006).
63. Ole R. Holsti, Randolph M. Siverson, and Alexander L. George, eds., *Change in International System* (Boulder, CO: Westview Press, 1980).
64. On this concept, its dimensions and applied domains as a sub-discipline of IR, like the sub-disciplines of security studies and studies of political economy, see: Ken Dark, "Defining Global Change," in *The Ethical Dimensions of Global Change*, ed. Barry Holden (London: Palgrave Macmillan, 1996), pp. 8-19.
65. On the difference between the two concepts, see: Marwa Fikri, *Athīr al-Taghayyurāt al-ʿĀlamiyyah ʿalā al-Dawlah al-Qawmiyyah Khilāl al-Tisʿīnīyāt: Dirāsah Naẓariyyah* [The Impact of Global Changes upon the National State in the 1990s: A Theoretical Study] (master's thesis, Cairo University, 2006); Shareef Abdulrahman, *Naẓariyat al-Niẓām wa Dirāsat al-Taghiyīr al-Dawlī* [Systems Theory and the Study of International Change] (master's thesis, Cairo University, 2003).
66. Paul Kennedy, *The Rise and Fall of the Great Powers* (New York: Vintage Books, 1987).

67. On the dimensions of this debate, see the "Introduction" in S. Smith and K. Booth, eds., *Globalization and World Politics*. On the dimensions of the Islamic civilizational perspective on globalization, see: Nadia M. Mostafa, "Taḥaddiyāt al-ʿAwlamah wa al-Abʿād al-Thaqāfiyyah al-Ḥaḍāriyyah wa al-Qiyamiyyah: Ru'yah Islāmiyyah" [The Challenges of Globalization and Cultural, Civilizational, and Normal Dimensions: An Islamic View]. On the comparison of this view with other perspectives on international relations discipline, especially in terms of the interrelationships between cultural and political factors, see: Nadia M. Mostafa and Saif AbdelFattah, "Muqadimah" [Introduction], *Ḥawlīyat Ummatī fī al-ʿĀlam* [Journal of My Nation in the World], no 1 (1999); Nadia Mostafa, "Arabic Islamic Debates on Dialogue and Conflict between Cultures."
68. For more detail, see: Nadia M. Mostafa, "Madkhal Manhājī li Dirāsat Taṭawur Waḍʿ wa Dawr al-ʿĀlam al-Islāmī fī al-Niẓām al-Dawlī" [A Methodological Approach to the Development of the Position and Role of the Islamic World in the International System] (Cairo: Al-Maʿhad al-ʿĀlamī li al-Fikr al-Islāmī, 1996); "Al-Tārīkh wa al-Dirāsat al-Niẓām al-Dawlī: Ru'yah Naẓariyyah wa Manhājiyyah Muqāranah" [History and the Study of International System: Comparative Theoretical and Methodological Perspectives], in *Al-ʿAlāqāt al-Dawliyyah fī Tarīkh al-Islāmī: Manẓūr Ḥaḍārī Muqāran* [International Relations in Islamic History: A Comparative Civilizational Perspective], pp. 37-112.
69. This does not prevent some scholars from maintaining the triumph of realism. See for example: Malik Awni, "Intiṣār al-Wāqiʿiyyah: Asāṭīr al-Taʿāwun al-Dawlī fī Idārat al-Taghiyīr al-ʿĀlamī" [The Triumph of Realism: Myths of International Cooperation in Managing Global Change], Majalat al-Siyāsah al-Dawliyyah (June 2015).
70. Nadia M. Mostafa, "Daʿwah li al-Tafkīr al-ʿIlmī: al-Gharb wa al-ʿĀlim wa al-ʿAlāqah bayn al-Sulṭah wa al-Maʿrifah" [A Call for Scientific Thinking: The West and the World and the Relationship between Power and Knowledge].

PART IV

A COMPARATIVE ISLAMIC CIVILIZATIONAL PARADIGM OF INTERNATIONAL RELATIONS: THE MAP OF PROBLEMATICS AND CHARACTERISTICS

INTRODUCTION

MY EXPLORATION OF AN Islamic Civilizational Paradigm in a separate part of this study implies that it is neither separate from, nor subsequent to, all the previous developments in the discipline of international relations. Rather, my exploration has now reached the end of the cumulative thread that is woven throughout the parts of this study, that is, the critical vivid interaction with Western dominant paradigms, and the assiduous attempt to contribute something "new" from an Islamic civilizational perspective.

A comparison between "the Western," on the one hand, and "the Islamic" and the "non-Western," on the other, has been present in my exploration from the very beginning, from the methodological introduction of this study. That comparison appeared in the conclusion of the second part of the study, and its preliminary features were elucidated in the third part. Here, in the fourth and concluding part of my study, I will elaborate on some aspects of an Islamic Paradigm in order to answer two basic questions: First, taking into consideration the impact of epistemological differences on comparative paradigms and on the dimensions of the debate raised between them (actors, processes, issues, etc.), what is the novel contribution that an Islamic Paradigm can make, when compared to dominant paradigms in the discipline? Second, what are the similarities and differences between this Islamic paradigm and Western critical approaches?

Western critical approaches' invitation to non-Western paradigms to contribute to theorization in IR implicitly acknowledges the existence of differences between Western and non-Western paradigms. These differences might be identifiable once we explore the characteristics of these paradigms that go beyond their mere agreement upon criticizing Western secular positivism and upon interest in values and civilizational, religious and cultural dimensions or their openness to social sciences and humanities. In other words, once we explore the nature, sources and consequences of this criticism itself. Such an exploration is expected to raise two major questions: Does an Islamic

Paradigm – as a new critical paradigm that differs, though, from Western critical approaches – represent a quest for "a real universality" that acknowledges epistemological and theoretical plurality and diversity, or rather a quest for a new world and a different reality? What are the characteristics of this paradigm in comparison with Western paradigms, be they positivist or critical? Before answering these questions, a few foundational observations need to be introduced.

First, the assiduous attempt to construct an Islamic Paradigm of International Relations is part of the response of the Egyptian and Arab political science community to the problematic of particularity vs. universality in political science in general. As discussed earlier, many questions have been raised about the possibility of the existence of an "Arab political science," the crisis of political science from an Arab perspective, and the state of the study of international relations in the Arab world. All of which have recognized, in one way or another, that we are just consumers of a Western scientific product. However, these questions have largely remained captive to "realist positivism," in clear opposition to the attempts at constructing an Islamic Civilizational Paradigm. The "Islamic frame of reference," from which this paradigm departs, affects the relationship between the contributors to the paradigm and the receivers of its assumptions in the field of social sciences in general and political science and international relations in particular, as will become manifest from the criticisms directed at the paradigm that will be explored in following sections.

Second, the attempt at constructing an Islamic Paradigm of IR is not a reaction to the critical wave that has been rising since the end of the Cold War. Rather, it is a constructive response rooted in a civilizational experience, having both epistemological and practical motives and objectives. The attempt started about half a century ago and has so far developed within the Egyptian community of political science.[1]

Third, this growing and developing attempt has not been separate or isolated from both the dominant and critical "Western" approaches in the field of international relations. Rather, it has always sought to engage with them: reflectively, critically as well as comparatively; and therefore, deeply understanding the criticism of critical approaches to the Western IR is as significant to the Islamic Paradigm as its own criticism to the Western IR. In other words, engagement with criticisms to Western theorizing – regardless of their origin – has been one central approach relevant to the construction of a comparative Islamic Civilizational Paradigm in the discipline of international relations. Other approaches adopted in the construction of the paradigm have been critical as well, such as the approach calling upon the historical Islamic experience (thought and practice), or the approach calling upon Islamic jurisprudence.

As Mona Abul-Fadl argues in a pioneering study,[2] we do not defend or popularize Islam; rather we criticize Western paradigms to break the taboos associated with the claims of universality and monopoly on science upheld by some Western schools. That is why it did not come as a surprise that some smart graduate students came to raise the following questions: Why don't we begin our study of IR Theory with the Islamic Paradigm directly? Why do we deal with it after dealing with the development of Western paradigms, and in comparison with them? The answer is that an ultimate goal of the construction of an Islamic paradigm is for it to be a comparative paradigm within the field of IR, not merely another area of Islamic Studies.

Fourth, the school of the Islamic Civilizational Paradigm believes in the importance of subjective theoretical and epistemological dimensions in the production of useful science and that useful science must reflect ontological and epistemological subjectivity and serve the goal of guiding action towards desired change. Therefore, the efforts of constructing this paradigm have not been separate from the existing reality of the Ummah and the world. Thus, "the state of the Ummah and its position in the global system" have given rise to an interest in constructing a comparative Islamic Civilizational Paradigm of international relations. Moreover, the efforts of constructing this paradigm have recognized the necessity of epistemological plurality and epistemological dialogue.

Fifth, decades have passed since the inception of the Project of International Relations in Islam in 1986 from the premises of the Department of Political Science at the Faculty of Economics and Political Science at Cairo University. The project departed from explicit epistemological biases that undermine the claims of objectivity and universal scientific neutrality of dominant IR theories.[3] Writing now from within the Islamic Civilizational Paradigm is indeed totally different from writing "about" it in 1996, when the Project's publications first appeared. Writing at the current stage is indeed also different from writing about the paradigm throughout the previous stages of its development.[4] Moreover, there are numerous means for activating and applying the Islamic Paradigm of International Relations, and they are not confined to academic publications.[5]

The following is worth highlighting: The criticism of the state of the discipline and the process of comparative theorizing from an Islamic perspective was started by the Egyptian School of an Islamic Paradigm much earlier than the current wave of Western critical theorizing under the fourth great debate. It developed from a call for a comparative Islamic paradigm (not an Islamic IR Theory), to a call for a comparative civilizational paradigm, and finally to a call for a critical Islamic civilizational paradigm.

This whole process of academic production by the Egyptian School has not received a wide degree of visibility within Western and international academic circles equivalent to that received by corresponding critical schools. That is partly due to the fact that the School basically addressed Arab and Egyptian academics, and it called for criticizing the dominant Western paradigms in the discipline, which were also subjected to deep revisions and criticism from within their own Western circles. Critical revisions are supposed to provide the necessary grounds for constructing a new paradigm, whether departing from an Islamic frame of reference or any other alternative to it.

The same reasons that some Western critical theorists have depicted as being behind the limited presence of non-Western theorizing in IR[6] are the same reasons behind the obstacles that have been faced by the Egyptian School in its strive for visibility, circulation, and engagement with other schools. There are also other reasons related to the Egyptian and Western academic contexts in general and the impact of these contexts on the patterns of interaction with an "Islamic" paradigm in IR.[7]

A process of criticism, which explores the Western theoretical product and maps its trajectory, has interacted with an authentic building process through three consecutive stages over three decades, during which the efforts of foundation, construction, activation, and application have cumulated.

The first stage was marked by the search for the bases of legitimacy for the proposed paradigm within the discipline, seeking to legitimate it as a paradigm of social sciences, rather than a field of Islamic Studies or a mere source among different sources for Islamic political theorizing. In fact, the set of motives behind and justifications for the project at the time of its inception in 1986 expanded and developed throughout the second stage of its construction that lasted from the mid-90s till the beginnings of the third millennium, especially after the events of September 11, 2001. The project proved its legitimacy and took the lead in calling for plurality and the overcoming of unilateral definitions of science. The credibility of the project was further asserted during a third stage (during the two first decades of the third millennium) when emerging Western critical approaches began also to increasingly call for emancipation from the crisis-ridden impact of the hegemony of positivism over the discipline.

The current stage of the crisis of the divided discipline, whose ontological and methodological dimensions are in permanent oscillation, proves the credibility of the non-positivist Islamic normative paradigm. At the time of its inception, this paradigm was not in need of justifications for its legitimacy as a comparative paradigm in the discipline, as much as for an academic context that accepts epistemological plurality and conducts a real epistemological dialogue. However, a rising interest in the normative and religious dimensions in Western international theorizing poses still a new challenge for the Islamic Paradigm, and an additional motive for highlighting the uniqueness of its sources, methodology, content, and objectives.

Whereas different features of "international relations in Islam" had attracted the attention of Western theoretical literature before the end of the second millennium,[8] the last two decades have witnessed the onset of a new stage of interest in an Islamic paradigm,[9] both in terms of theory and practice. Although this interest in a comparative Islamic perspective has become an accepted norm within Western academic circles, some Egyptian and Arab academic circles still question the "scientific" credibility of an "Islamic" paradigm. However, differences need comprehensive comparative studies,[10] as those conducted, for instance, on the comparison between orientalist literature and the Islamic perspective on the relationship between war and peace in Islam[11] or the relations among religions, cultures, and civilizations.[12]

Therefore, the answer to the questions raised above lies in tackling the following issues: the nature of the paradigm, its epistemological characteristics and sources (how?); the relationship between the constant and the variable, or between values and reality; and the map of the different aspects of comparison with Western paradigms (what?); the motives for building the paradigm and its objectives (why?); the relationship between theory and reality, between power and knowledge; and finally, the position of the paradigm in the discipline (potentials and criticisms). However, I do not claim that my conception of the Islamic civilizational paradigm is the only one available, nor the most original one. Rather, this conception only reflects my personal experience with the construction of an Islamic paradigm in IR. The proposed paradigm represents an open and interactive system, whose supporters neither consider it to be perfect, nor absolute. They only claim that it should always stay guided by its religious frame of reference, which is a fixed and constant frame of reference, whose interpretations may vary in an innovative way to reflect on the relationship between the revealed text and reality; between the normative and the material; and between what ought to be, what really exists, and what can be. Mona Abul-Fadl describes this paradigm as a "normative-realistic" paradigm, whose characteristics reflect the characteristics of the median, Islamic, epistemological pattern. Moreover, it is described as an Islamic Civilizational Paradigm, not merely as an Islamic Paradigm, a label that deliberately seeks to avoid confusing it with a jurisprudential Islamic paradigm. In short, the following methodological introduction to an Islamic Civilizational Paradigm aims at explaining the steps, stages, and outcomes involved in the construction of this paradigm, in a way that makes a critical engagement with and an evaluation of this process possible, allowing the paradigm to move on to upcoming stages of its development and growth.

NOTES

1. In this regard, see: Nadia M. Mostafa, ed., *Fī Tajdīd al-ʿUlūm al-Ijtimāʿiyyah: Binā' Manẓūr Maʿrifī Ḥaḍārī* [On the Renewal of Social Sciences: Building an Epistemological and Civilizational Paradigm] (Cairo: Dār al-Bashīr li al-Thaqāfah wa al-ʿUlūm, 2016).
2. Mona Abul-Fadl, *Where East Meets West: The West on the Agenda of the Islamic Revival* (Herndon, VA: International Institute of Islamic Thought, 1992). See a distinguished reading of this pioneering work in Muhammad Basheer Soffar, "Al-Sharq fī Qalb al-Gharb: al-Badīl al-Thālith" [The East at the Heart of the West: The Third Alternative], in *Al-Taḥawwūl al-Maʿrifī wa al-Taghiyīr al-Ḥaḍārī: Qirā'ah fī Manẓūmat Fikr Munā Abū al-Faḍl* [Epistemological Transformation and Civilizational Change: A Perusal of Mona Abul-Fadl's Thought], ed. Nadia Mostafa et al. (Cairo: Civilization Center for Political Studies, 2011), pp. 361-395.
3. Nadia M. Mostafa, "Al-Dawāfiʿ, al-Ahdāf, al-Munṭaliqāt" [Motives, Goals, and Precepts], in *Al-Muqadimmah al-ʿĀmah li Mashrūʿ al-ʿAlāqāt al-Dawliyyah fī al-Islām* [The General Introduction to the Project of International Relations in Islam], ed. Nadia M. Mostafa (Cairo: International Institute of Islamic Thought, 1996).
4. See: Saif AbdelFattah, *Dawrat al-Manhājiyyah al-Islāmiyyah fī al-ʿUlūm al-Ijtimāʿiyyah: Ḥaql al-ʿUlūm al-Siyāsiyyah Namūdhajan* [The Role of Islamic Methodology in Social Sciences: The Case of Political Science] (Cairo: Hadara Center for Political Studies and International Institute of Islamic Thought, 2002); Nadia M. Mostafa, "ʿAmaliyat Binā' Manẓūr Islāmī li Dirāsat al-ʿAlaqāt al-Dawliyyah: Ishkāliyyāt Khibrat al-Baḥth wa al-Tadrīs" [The Process of Building an Islamic Paradigm for the Study of International Relations: Problems of Research and Teaching Experience]; Nadia M. Mostafa, "Ishkāliyyāt al-Baḥth wa al-Tadrīs" [The Problematics of Research and Teaching], pp. 319-394; Ahmad-Fouad Basha et al. ed., *Al-Manhājiyyah al-Islāmiyyah* [The Islamic Methodology] (Cairo: Markaz al-Dirāsāt al-Maʿrifiyyah wa Dār al-Islām, 2010), pp. 817-914. In this context, also see the proceedings of the scientific seminars of the Department of Political Science (2002-2014).

5. See: Nadia M. Mostafa, "Al-ʿAlāqāt al-Dawliyyah fī al-Islām: Min Khibrah Jamāʿah ʿIlmiyyah ilā Maʿālim Manẓūr" [International Relations in Islam: From the Experience of a Scientific Group to the Aspects of a New Civilizational Paradigm], *Majalat al-Muslim al-Muʿāṣir* [Journal of the Contemporary Muslim], no 133/134 (2009), pp. 5-56; Nadia M. Mostafa, ed., *Fī Tajdīd al-ʿUlūm al-Ijtimāʿiyyah: Bināʾ Manẓūr Maʿrifī Ḥaḍārī* [On the Renewal of Social Sciences: Building an Epistemological and Civilizational Paradigm] (see in particular the second part "Bināʾ Jamāʿah ʿIlmiyyah fī al-ʿUlūm al-Siyāsiyyah min Manẓūr Ḥaḍārī" [Building a Scientific Group in Political Science from a Civilizational Perspective]).
6. Amitav Acharya and Barry Buzan, eds., *Non-Western International Relations Theory*, pp. 1-25.
7. See: Nadia M. Mostafa, "Ishkāliyyāt al-Baḥth wa al-Tadrīs fī ʿIlm al-ʿAlaqāt al-Dawliyyah min Manẓūr Ḥaḍārī Muqāran" [Problematics of Research and Teaching International Relations from a Comparative Civilizational Paradigm] (especially the second part: "Al-Abʿād al-Manhājiyyah li Dirāsat Ahdāf Manẓūr Islāmī..." [Methodological Dimensions of the Study of the Goals of an Islamic Paradigm...], pp. 862-912.
8. For instance, see: James Piscatori, *Islam in a World of Nation-States* (New York: Cambridge University Press, 1991); Harris Proctor, ed., *Islam and International Relations* (London: Pall Mall Press, 1963); Muḥammad Ibn Al-Ḥasan Shaybānī and Majid Khadduri, *The Islamic Law of Nations: Shaybānī's Siyar* (Beirut: Al-Dār al-Mutaḥidah li al-Nashr, 1975); Bernard Lewis, "Politics and War in Islam," in *Heritage of Islam*, eds. Joseph Schacht and Clifford Bosworth (Kuwait: National Council for Culture, Arts and Letters, 1998); Thomas Arnold, *The Preaching of Islam: A History of the Propagation of the Muslim Faith* (Cairo: Maktabat al-Nahḍah al-Miṣriyyah, 1970).
9. See for example: Richard Falk, "False Universalism and the Geopolitics of Exclusion: The Case of Islam"; Ralph Pettman, *Reason, Culture, Religion: The Metaphysics of World Politics*; Jonathon W. Moses, "The Umma of Democracy," *Security Dialogue* 37, no. 4 (2006); Giorgio Shani, "Provincializing Critical Theory: Islam, Sikhism and International Relations Theory."

10. Some of the studies of this book present their contributions in this respect, whether they relate to universalism, level of analysis, concepts, or issues. Moreover, graduate students at the master and doctorate levels are assigned the task of what is new in the literature in this field and present it critically and comparatively.
11. See the comparative criticism of the views of Thomas Arnold, Bernard Lewis, Majid Khadduri, and Marcel Boisard, in Nadia M. Mostafa, "Al-ʿAlāqāt al-Dawliyyah fī al-Fikr al-Siyāsī al-Islāmī: al-Ishkāliyyāt al-Manhājiyyah wa Kharīṭah wa al-Namādhij al-Fikriyyah wa Manẓūmat al-Mafāhīm" [International Relations in Islamic Political Thought: Methodological Problematics, Intellectual Models Map, and Conceptual System], pp. 179-191.
12. Nadia M. Mostafa, "Arabic Islamic Debates on Dialogue and Conflict between Cultures," pp. 96-121.

8

THE CHARACTERISTICS AND SOURCES OF AN ISLAMIC CIVILIZATIONAL PARADIGM[1]

The previous chapters have highlighted the significance and functions of "paradigms" and "episteme," the various methodological and ontological aspects of the study of a paradigm, as well as the particularity of the Islamic episteme when compared with the Western episteme. They have also highlighted the criticisms addressed to the Western episteme from within and without its own academic circles, and the different epistemological and ontological assumptions associated with these criticisms. This is how I have argued for the possibility of constructing comparative paradigms in IR that depart from different epistemological grounds than those of positivism (even of post-positivism). The nature and characteristics of an Islamic Paradigm can be summed up in the following complex statement: an Islamic Civilizational Paradigm of IR is a normative paradigm, however of a special nature. It stands in clear opposition to the materialist, utilitarian, and positivist nature of Western dominant paradigms. The particularity of this paradigm is traceable to the uniqueness of its sources and origins compared to those of Western paradigms. It is also attributable to the differences between epistemes. The special normative nature of the paradigm is highly reflected in the methodology and tools of the paradigm as well as its assumptions about the basic dimensions of the study of international relations: the origin and drivers of relations, actors and units and levels of analysis, types of interactions and issues of concern to the study of international relations, the relationship between the external and the internal, and the relationship between the material and the non-material.

This is basically what differentiates an Islamic Civilizational Paradigm from the Western secular paradigms, whether they are materialist or normative and critical. These differences raise the following complex questions: How can a holistic view of the international phenomena be attained, one that encompasses the different binaries, the material and the non-material, the internal and the external, rationalism and normativism, etc.? In other words, how can a holistic view of both content and methodology be attained? What does the Islamic Civilizational Paradigm contribute to criticism of IR Theory? What are the comparative characteristics of the Islamic Paradigm? How do they reflect the particular character of the paradigm's sources and nature? What is the cumulative product of the paradigm? These questions highlight two sets of methodological problematics: (1) the relationship between the constant and the variable sources of the Islamic Civilizational Paradigm; and (2) the relationship between values and reality from an Islamic perspective.

8.1 THE RELATIONSHIP BETWEEN THE CONSTANT AND THE VARIABLE SOURCES OF THE PARADIGM

This problematic relates to the relationship between the different sources of the paradigm, whether they take the form of constant foundational sources (Qur'an and Sunnah) or *ijtihād* (variable independent reasoning). Involved here is also the problematic relationship between revelation and reason in light of the givens of reality and its constantly changing requirements.[2] The foundational sources, namely the Qur'an and Sunnah, are the two revealed sources and the only constant sources of Islamic Shariʿah. Throughout centuries of *ijtihād*, Muslim scholars and jurists have developed several methods and approaches for dealing with these two foundational sources such as *ijmāʿ* (consensus), *istiḥsān* (juristic discretion towards that which is deemed to be good), and *qiyās* (analogical reasoning).

The sources of the Islamic Paradigm fall into three categories. The first category includes sources dealing directly with the foundational sources. Here, the different jurisprudential standings on the origin of the relationship between Muslims and non-Muslims as well as the relationship among Muslims themselves are addressed, the differences between jurisprudential schools and their underlying causes are explained, and the different characteristics of these schools, which some Orientalist studies identify as the "traditional theory of international relations in Islam," are depicted. Addressed here also are the main issues and questions relevant to the study of the Islamic perspective of international relations across time and space, including the unity of the Muslim Ummah, jihad, and the relations with non-Muslims. Attention is also paid to the study of the general principles, fundamentals, and rules that define the normative dimensions of the Islamic Paradigm. Hence, this category of the paradigm's sources – dealing directly with the foundational sources – includes the general, non-changing, and governing rules and principles of Shariʿah; time-and-place-conditioned jurisprudential rulings; and the primary and secondary systems of values related to international relations.

The second category of sources deals with history and underlines real experiences throughout successive Islamic ages. It aims to understand how these experiences and the position of Muslims in the world have developed from the stage of conquests, unity, and civilizational building, to that of regression and defense, and then to that of civilizational backwardness and colonization. Here, some methodological problematics require special attention. First, how can we explain the deviation between the teachings embodied in foundational sources and some Muslim practices? Second, how can we understand the general trajectory from rise to fall? Third, how can we explain the differences between the schools of the Islamic interpretation of history and other schools interpreting history (e.g., nationalism, leftism, liberalism, etc.)? Finally, how can we employ "the historical experience" to better understand reality and to identify possible routes for change and reformation? It is important to note that the historical experience of the Prophet's leadership in Madinah and the leadership of the guided caliphs are regarded as ideal models to be referred to for a better understanding of the practice and application of the Shariʿah and the principles, rules, and fundamentals embodied therein.

As for the third category of sources, it relates to Islamic thought, and it raises the methodological problematic of the relationship between the Islamic thought's three central issue areas: unity, independence, and reform as tackled by the iconic figures and eminent thinkers of the Muslim Ummah throughout successive Islamic ages. Here, the relationship between the thought of key Muslim thinkers and the temporal and spatial context is investigated, in a way that addresses the problematic of the constant and the variable in Islamic thought regarding foreign relations. Another important problematic is also addressed, which involves the relationship between the external and the internal levels in intellectual and original works of Islamic thought, as values guiding internal relations had always been extended to external relations as well and had been considered of universal worth and validity. While an Islamic traditional jurisprudential and intellectual perspective of international relations remained captive to a division of the globe into two or three abodes, it remained guided by the system of values associated with this division: *daʿwah* (or the notion of enlightenment about Islam and Islamic values through various noncoercive, tactful, and polite means, such as through education and/or exemplification of Islamic teachings and values), jihad (striving – whether morally, spiritually, or physically – toward that which is good or of benefit and with the aim of earning the pleasure of God), and *nuṣrah* (giving support). It is important to note that the notion of "abodes" (or "houses" or "divisions") in premodern Islam (i.e., the notion of *Dār al-Ḥarb/Dār al-Islām*) are not constructs explicitly found in the Qur'an and Hadith/Sunnah. Rather, they are a human product that flourished in the early centuries of the encounter between Muslims and non-Muslims and, hence, were a product of a specific historical context. With the beginning of direct contact with the West, there emerged a need for the differentiation between the internal and the external levels as a response to external aggression and occupation. Important here is that the Islamic view of the universe and the world guided the different reflections on the two previous problematics.

In fact, we cannot separate the foundational sources (the sources of the worldview and episteme, i.e., the Quran and Sunnah) from history (practical experience), and thought (systems of values, priorities of interest, and responses to international changes). However, the distinction between the three categories, as sources for founding and constructing a contemporary Islamic perspective on international relations, is a methodological necessity to facilitate analysis. The exploration of the sources of a "contemporary" Islamic perspective on international relations is a multilevel construction process that requires necessary methodological tools. Dealing with these sources should not involve direct literal citation, but rather contemplation, understanding, comparison, and critical reading. This is in order to come up with innovative interpretations of contemporary applicability that are not only based on jurisprudential rulings, but also on the deep understanding of political thought, history, as well as the rapidly changing contemporary reality. Dealing with the foundational sources of this Islamic perspective requires non-specialists in religious studies or in political science to acquire the methodological skills needed for dealing with the sources of exegesis, hadith, jurisprudence, history, and thought so that they can explore "international relations" in this vast and extended collection of sources of thought and practice.

In order to address these different sets of sources of an Islamic paradigm of international relations, the Project of International Relations in Islam followed three methodological tracks. The first track acknowledged that the construction of an Islamic Paradigm of International Relations must begin from the foundational sources of Shariʿah, which supply both definitive rulings (not open to different interpretations) and systems of general rules, principles, and fundamentals guiding the relations between Muslims and non-Muslims, as well as relations among Muslims themselves. Therefore, one main study of the Project of International Relations in Islam explores the "religious foundations and the principles governing external relations in Islam."[3] The study concludes that Muslims, irrespective of the form of political organization they are subjected to (be it an Ummah within a single state, many nation-states, a community etc.), are all commanded by the inclusive and general provisions of Shariʿah to communicate with others in order to convey the *daʿwah*. By discussing the three major jurisprudential standings on the driver of relations among Muslims and non-Muslims, the study reaches the innovative conclusion that the driver is not conflict nor *merely* peace for peace's sake, but *daʿwah* in the sense of enlightenment about Islam and Islamic values through various noncoercive, tactful, and polite means, such as through education and/or exemplification of Islamic teachings and values. To put it differently, *daʿwah* is more of a caring and compassionate driver to IR relations between Muslims and non-Muslims than merely peace for peace's sake and of course conflict; but where *da*ʿ*wah* is not successful, peace is still an objective. The unity of humankind is the foundational principle that governs these relations, and there are many principles that derive from this unity, such as equality, justice, keeping promises and commitments, supporting other Muslims, non-reciprocal treatment in cases of violations of promises and commitments, and finally the principles of *walā'* (allegiance) and *barā'* (dissociation).

A second methodological track involved exploring the normative foundations of the paradigm. Therefore, a second main study of the project is preoccupied with the introduction of values as a frame of reference for studying international relations in Islam.[4] The study sets some key foundations of an Islamic Paradigm by criticizing the concept of values in Western as well as Islamic theoretical studies, highlighting the importance of reinstating values in the face of rationalism and claims of scientific objectivity in social sciences, as well as the need for reflecting on the foundations of the concept and the theoretical potentials of the system of Islamic values.

First, values are the soul of the epistemological structure of any Islamic perspective. Therefore, values serve different functions as: a civilizational concept, a methodological approach, a frame of reference, a standard of perfection, the foundation for a worldview, and a normative and guiding model. Hence, values are considered to be an umbrella term that is inclusive, connective, and comprehensive. They are not mere theoretical ideals or abstracts, but they guide processes of foundation, mobilization, activation, and application. According to this perspective, there is a close relationship between values and practice, theory and action, and deeds and science.

Second, the paradigm rests on a value system consisting of seven elements: an elevating faith; a motivating Shariʿah; governing values, intermediate values, derived values; an inclusive Ummah; a witnessing and active civilization; conditional *sunan* (eternal laws); and safeguarding *maqāṣid* (the higher objectives of Shariʿah). This particular view of values corresponds to the distinction well known to contemporary international theoretical studies between the elements of the worldview, the driving forces of IR and relevant issue areas, and the units and levels of analysis.

Third, relying on this seven element value system, different models can be introduced; models that measure reality against the foundational perspective (activation) and models that move from the foundational perspective to reality (application) to address various areas of research: *daʿwah* as the driver of relations between Muslims and non-Muslims, and the reconstruction of the concept of power, the concept of war, and the standards for classifying abodes, processes, and actors.

Aside from the methodological dimensions related to the foundational sources and the methodological dimensions related to the civilizational normative foundation of an Islamic Paradigm, a third methodological track, addressed by the Project of International Relations in Islam, involved reflecting on the methodological experience of dealing with the foundational sources as well as different sources from Islamic heritage. Therefore, the Project of International Relations in Islam includes two other methodological studies; the third part[5] and seventh part[6] of the Project. The third part offers a precise recording of the real experience of the research team with dealing with the books of jurisprudence, the life of Prophet Muhammad, and exegesis; an experience driven by the general purpose of studying international relations in Islamic foundational sources and exploring the major jurisprudential standings on specific issues and topics such as war, peace, and the state. The importance of this methodological part derives from the fact that it represents the experience of those specialized in the different subfields of political science (international law, theory and thought, and political systems) when dealing with these sources; an experience serving the goal of bridging the gap between the study of social sciences and that of religious and Islamic disciplines. As for the seventh part, it records the methodological experience of dealing with the sources of Islamic history that are necessary for following on the development of the position of the Ummah within the international system, in comparison with the methodological experience of (Western) international systemic studies that have focused on Western histories. In order to complete the project, an additional part was published a few years later. This part also records the methodological experience related to dealing with the sources of Islamic thought, which make it possible to follow the development of international Islamic thought and to reflect on its possible contribution to international theorizing in comparison with Western experiences in this field (international thought and international political theory).[7]

While taking into consideration the above explained categorization of the sources of the paradigm and the resulting methodological tracks, addressing the problematics of the relationship between the constant and the variable necessitates a differentiation between the foundational sources, the constructional sources, and the assisting sources for the construction of the paradigm. Each set of these sources raises its own problematics in terms of the relationship between the constant and the variable.

Foundational Sources and the Problematic of the Constant and the Variable

Of prime importance here is the identification of the relationship between the different strands of jurisprudential schools on war and peace and the general principles and bases guiding the relations between Muslims and other nations.[8] In addition to the importance of recognizing the multiplicity of schools, intellectual standings, and the jurisprudential differences among them, one must realize the justifications for this multiplicity, as well as its underlying causes. An explanation of this multiplicity is a matter of foundational, epistemological, and methodological importance. It became subject to debates between Islamic perspectives and Orientalist ones. Orientalist studies treat this matter of multiplicity as an expression of the relationship between the "traditional theory of international relations in Islam" (theory of war) and the corresponding modern theory (theory of peace), or as an expression of "the gap between theory and practice." International relations in Islam, from the view of these Orientalists and those who agree with them, are basically and merely confined to questions of war and peace.

However, Orientalist readings of this gap (i.e., of this change in the jurisprudential theorizing about war and peace) deserve some critical reconsideration, with particular reference to four main scholars: Bernard Lewis, Majid Khadduri, Thomas Arnold, and Marcel

Boisard.[9] Generally speaking, their Orientalist contribution can be described as, to borrow Saif AbdelFattah's words, the "trap of objectivity," "the fairness of objectivity," or "fair objectivity." This conclusion is arrived at based on a comparative reading of these four sources[10] and it revolves around three pivots: First, foreign relations are an extension of domestic affairs. Second, it is necessary to show that jurisprudence is not the whole of thought, and thought does not consist only of jurisprudence. In fact, jurisprudence or jurisprudential theorizing itself has its elements of thought that cannot be ignored when explaining the development of this theorizing. Finally, explaining the development of jurisprudential theorizing and the development of thought cannot dispense with articulations of the development of historical events.

These four scholars relate the development of political jurisprudence on political power (caliphate, imamate, sultanate, and emirate) to the development of political jurisprudence on war and peace, jihad, or *daʿwah*. Finally, the developments of the balance of power between Muslims and the world, whether rise or fall, are present in the background or constitution of these theses, in a way that sheds light on their view of the elements of thought included in these jurisprudential developments. However, the four studies remain unequal in terms of their "degree of objectivity." Whereas Majid Khadduri and Bernard Lewis departed in their analysis from the approach of war, peace, and jihad, Thomas Arnold departed from the approach of *daʿwah*, and Marcel Boisard from the approach of "humanity." These approaches differ in methodology, goals, and perspective, and so do the contents and outcomes of these studies. While the first study can be classified under the label of "the trap of objectivity," the third and fourth studies can be classified under the label of "fair objectivity," and the second in an intermediate position between the two.

Thus, a map of Islamic jurisprudential schools on the foundation of international relations in Islam clearly reveals multiplicity and disagreements. As shown, a modern Orientalist approach to explaining this multiplicity could be subjected to criticism. An attempt at identifying the foundations of the relationship between Muslims and non-Muslims leads us to the more constant aspects of this relationship, to the principles and bases governing the relationship with the other, and to the Islamic system of values. In fact, most political science researchers who have shown interest in this matter, like Ahmad Abdelwanees, Ibrahim al-Bayoumi Ghanem, AbdulHamid AbuSulayman, and Saif AbdelFattah,[11] distinguish between these variable jurisprudential schools and the constant Qur'anic principles, foundations, and values, in addition to the Qur'anic provisions and divine eternal laws.[12]

Finally, the problematic of the constant and the variable in the foundational sources of the paradigm has important methodological implications for the study of international relations from an Islamic perspective, as well as important implications for the paradigm itself. That is because the study of the religious framework requires special methodological tools, including the consulting of commentaries on hadiths and Qur'anic exegesis. It also requires a subsequent and crucial step, that is, introducing a contemporary *ijtihād* (innovative interpretation), based on the available jurisprudential heritage, on the main issue upon which the paradigm revolves (i.e., the issue of the origin of relations or the main driver of relations, and the rules, principles, and fundamentals that govern them).

By contrast, the sources of Western dominant paradigms, be they realist or pluralist or structuralist, as well as their intellectual and philosophical roots, are variable human sources derived from the experiences of Western political thought. It is noteworthy that there is a tendency to attribute the different strands and variations of these paradigms to three major philosophical and intellectual schools. Major characteristics between different sets of school have a basic common denominator embodied in the assumptions of the paradigm, to which they belong; assumptions that have been elaborated throughout the history of this paradigm. This leads us to compare the Western and the Islamic historical and intellectual sources of international theorizing.

Constructional Sources of Theorizing: Islamic Thought as a Source of Intellectual and Philosophical Foundations

Islamic thought represents the source of the philosophical and intellectual – alongside the jurisprudential – foundations of the Islamic

Civilizational Paradigm. Moreover, the inherited and modern models of political thought, alongside their associated systems of concepts, reflect the changes experienced by the Ummah in its international relations, and its position in the world from an Islamic perspective that is comparable against an original ideal view of the Ummah. Islamic thought of international relations serves as a source of theorizing as it helps researchers discover more about the international dimension of Islamic projects of renaissance and grasp the essence of concepts such as *jihad*, the Ummah, state, war, peace, etc., as understood over centuries by Muslim thinkers.

All these aspects raise two main problematics that fall within the circle of our interest. We deal with thought as a complementary, constructional source in the process of founding and theorizing an Islamic view of international relations. First, how can we explain the causes of Muslims' strength or weakness; those of the rise and fall of the Islamic state, or nations and peoples in general? This problematic requires addressing the way in which the international dimension emerged in Islamic thought, and how this dimension is recognized and treated. It is a holistic and systemic problematic that relates to the development of the international system as a whole.

The second problematic relates to the system of relations between three major issue areas of the paradigm: the internal model, relations among Muslims, and relations with non-Muslims. Have studies of Islamic thought revealed standings on the relationship between these three areas? This three-dimensional relationship should be of interest because it enables us to move from the traditional narrow field of Islamic political thought (focusing on the internal system of authority and the relationship between the ruler and the ruled) to the broader field of Islamic political thought that involves reflections on the international dimension, whether as an extension of the internal or in interaction with it. This broader field also involves reflections on relations among "Islamic entities or states," which used to be addressed as a part of the internal or domestic relations at the time of the caliphate.

When comparing Islamic political thought as a source of international theorizing to Western political thought as a source of international theorizing (as in the domain of international political theory or elsewhere), two facts are worth noting. First, the interest in Islamic political thought performs two functions in the process of international theorizing that are not performed by Western political thought. The first function is to remedy Western paradigms' neglect of Islamic thought, and the second function is to contribute to the construction of an Islamic Civilizational Paradigm of International Relations that transcends traditional Islamic studies about "international relations in Islam." Second, approaching Islamic political thought involves a two-fold process: approaching thought as a source of theorizing, and approaching thought as a reflection of the development of the state of the Ummah.

By drawing upon Islamic philosophical and intellectual roots of political theorizing in comparison with the Western roots, the founding scholars of the Egyptian School of the Islamic Civilizational Paradigm have made pioneering contributions.[13] Here, it is relevant to consider the differences between the objectives of engagement with Western thought as opposed to those of engagement with Islamic thought as a source for international theorizing. These differences are partly attributable to differences in the epistemes, the goals of theorizing, and even the nature of thought as a source for theorizing. The motives and goals of engagement with Western thought in the process of theorizing are so numerous that we can differentiate between many theoretical strands in this field, ranging from strands seeking to validate their assumptions to those seeking to discover maps of political thought.[14] As for Islamic thought, which serves as one of the sources for constructing the Islamic Civilizational Paradigm, it reflects the history of the enforcement of Shariʿah, the history of its interaction with the reality of Muslims, and the way they have perceived and applied it, whether they have been close to or distant from the "original ideal." Thus, this field reflects the manner of the interaction between the constant and variable, and between the material and the normative. It is the existence of "the constant" in the Islamic episteme that guides the different motives and aims of engagement with Islamic thought in contrast to those of engagement with Western thought.[15]

Approaching Islamic political thought remains a necessity for complementing the "civilizational" dimensions of the Islamic Paradigm. The development of thought is a mirror of the development of the state of the Ummah, and therefore, the Islamic Paradigm relies on thought as a constructional tool of the paradigm. The Islamic Paradigm's claims of civilizational particularity stand in obvious contrast to claims of universality and monopoly on scientific production raised by Western paradigms. This Civilizational Paradigm responds to the criticisms uncovered by the critical revisions of the state of the discipline by calling upon the multileveled Islamic civilizational experience (jurisprudential, intellectual, and historical).

As such, international Islamic thought aims to achieve a set of key goals: to provide an understanding of the general frames that surrounded the production of Islamic jurisprudence, and, hence, to contribute to making sense of the development of jurisprudence as a product of the interaction between the original text and reality.[16] Both religious jurisprudence and practice have developed within external and internal political, social, and economic contexts. Although neither jurisprudence nor practice fall directly under the category of Islamic thought, both depart in fact, even if implicitly, from some kind of Islamic thought. Writings that explicitly fall under the category of thought are ones that address the existing reality, from the thinkers' perceptions and frames of reference.

Despite their different approaches, Muslim thinkers present the results of their testing of the values and rulings of Islam in real life. Therefore, the study of Islamic thought, its development, and diverse models, provides the "civilizational thought" that helps us explore, beyond legal jurisprudence, the relations between Muslims and the world, the relations among Muslims themselves, and the Muslim ways of life.

Hence, studying Islamic thought from a civilizational perspective helps us understand the junctures in the history of the Ummah, whether identifiable in its interactions with other nations, in interactions between its different component parts, or in its internal conditions. Studying Islamic thought helps us also expose the falseness of some Orientalist assumptions which view the Islamic perspective of international relations as a conflictual perspective, based on violence, war, and rejection of the other. When we compare these intellectual historical junctures with their counterparts at the level of practice in Islamic history, we find that they provide us with a map of the shifts and the ups and downs of Muslim thought, as will be further explained later.

Finally, reading Islamic political thought as a constructional source for the Islamic Civilizational Paradigm has its methods and tools that raise important considerations and necessitate the drawing of temporal, spatial, and thematic maps of international Islamic political thought.[17] Moreover, there are various approaches to contemporary and traditional Islamic political thought as a source for theorizing and theoretical perspective.[18] Because of its development, which serves as a reflection of the state of the Ummah, Islamic thought has been particularly significant for understanding the problematics of the current conditions of the Ummah and the world.

Supporting Sources: History as an Intermediate Link between Jurisprudence (the Foundational) and Thought (the Constructional)

The experience of Islamic historical trajectory, when compared with the Western one, presents an additional source that is necessary for constructing a comparative Islamic Civilizational Paradigm. Most importantly, employing history in constructing this Islamic Civilizational Paradigm fulfills many goals and objectives, especially when compared with the employment of history by Western theoretical paradigms. In light of the relationship between history and modern social sciences in general, the relationship between history and international relations in particular, and the role of history in the study of the development of the international systems by Western paradigms,[19] we can draw four basic conclusions.[20] First, Western paradigms confine themselves to the experience and history of the European system, especially since Westphalia. They deal – partially or wholly – with the position of the Ottoman Empire in the international system, especially during the last three centuries of its existence, which happened to be concurrent with the modern European colonial expansion and its development since the Renaissance. However, the Ottoman Empire is dealt with, not as an Islamic caliphate that has distinctive motives and goals, but as one of the numerous powers that were parties to the traditional system of multipolarity that had prevailed until the Second World War.

In contrast, Western historians interested in the international dimension of Islamic history before and after Westphalia, and early Muslim historians and contemporary researchers of the different ages of Islamic history, have dealt with aspects of Muslim history. However, they have not dealt with the development of the position of the Islamic state within the structure of the international system, or in comparison with other non-Muslim powers. Therefore political science researchers from an Islamic perspective need to direct their attention to the neglected international Islamic political history. Instead of studying the diplomatic history, they need to approach history with the tools of systemic analysis, calling upon the theoretical dimensions of studying international systems.

Second, Western historical models have provided us with various circular and, increasing as well as decreasing, linear evolutionary models of history that are derived from Western civilizational perspectives on the essence, nature, and interpretation of history.[21] Hence, what different understandings of the nature of history, the direction of its development, and the explanation of its evolution does an Islamic perspective hold?

Third, the employment of Western historical experience in the discipline of international relations serves the objectives of political action in the present and the future. That is why calling upon historical experience has usually emphasized incidents related to war and peace, changes in the global balances of power, and the position of leading Western powers, especially the outbreak of war has attracted great attention. Hence, the purpose behind calling upon history has been to explore the conditions that would maintain the continuity of Western hegemony and the dominance of global American values. As most historical studies in IR are basically an Anglo-Saxon product, the South in general has been marginalized in these studies that have focused on the leading powers in the system.

Fourth, when addressing the Western historical experience, special emphasis is given to a set of structural and material variables, these include political, military, economic, and social variables. Different variables are given different priority by different paradigms, frames of reference, or intellectual schools (realist, liberal, Marxist, etc.). While some scholars have focused on the variables of stability and instability, others have paid attention to the variables of economic and military power (how they impact the rise and fall of great powers within the system) or to the variables of economic development and regression and their impact on the succession of the cycles of dominance.

By contrast, non-material, basically normative, variables have not been given attention by the static holistic models or the evolutionary holistic models which employ history in the study of the development of the international system. These variables, however, have been given remarkable attention by the International Society School, among whose pioneers are the English scholars Martin Wight and Hedley Bull. The school contributed to the rising interest in normative dimensions in theoretical international studies that focus on the contemporary international system, rather than its historical development.

International society theorists are, therefore, normatively oriented and, hence, differ from the positivist theorists of the international system, because the former explore ethical and legal dimensions and norms, and regard international society as an empirical reality, rather than an abstract concept (like the system). The studies of "global community," "global society," and "cosmopolitan society" contribute to this normative trend, which transcends behavioralist and positivist structuralism. Since the 1990s, a growing number of studies has focused on the normative dimensions of studying change in the contemporary global system and has sought to develop a normatively oriented theory to understand this system. Critical Western approaches that have paid attention to historical sociology have come close to this orientation.

Then, how can we employ history in a way that challenges this Western European centrism and contributes to the construction of a comparative Islamic Civilizational Paradigm that calls on history out of different objectives?[22] The Islamic Civilizational Paradigm's employment of history has a basic central objective, entailing several complementary objectives that can be achieved indirectly. The central objective is to determine the position of the Islamic state within the structure of the distribution of world powers throughout the successive historical stages of the development of the international system. This is done in a way that explains the rise and fall of the successive Islamic caliphates, the rules that govern this process and the different factors behind it, and the different kinds of relations with non-Muslim powers. A complementary and derived objective is to explore and determine behavioral types related to three main areas: interactions between central Islamic actors and other non-Muslim actor units, interactions among different Islamic actors, and the factors behind the rise, the fall, or the demise of great Islamic states. These areas lie at the heart of relevant issues to the study of current Islamic international relations, including: the development of relations between Muslims and non-Muslims, the rules governing the conflictual/cooperative relations in light of the concept of jihad, the spread of the nation-state model accompanied by the fragmentation of the Ummah because of international political pressures, and the declining commitment to Islamic legal rules and principles.

These objectives, therefore, evoke the need for adopting a systemic approach to history, as a part of the systemic studies of international relations. This, in turn, means that when we read and analyze Islamic history in its international dimension, we focus on generalities rather than particularities, on historical patterns, rather than individual incidents, and on major shifts, rather than specific occurrences. However, at the same time, we should focus on specific issues and topics that have important implications for the Islamic state as they relate to the political and social factors that gave rise to successive external challenges to the Islamic state throughout its history and, hence, influenced the path and development of the Islamic international system and the world system as a whole.

This central objective fills an important gap in Western literature on the historical development of international systems, which has omitted the international experience and practice of Islamic history. It also contributes to fill another gap in the literature of international relations, that pays attention to other levels aside from the international system, or in the literature occupied with relationship between history and politics in general. This kind of literature employed Islamic history for different research purposes. It does not address the temporal development of diplomatic history as such, but combines historical narration and theoretical frameworks in order to study change in foreign policies and in the international system.

To this kind of literature belong studies that seek to derive general conclusions on holistic issues, such as the relationship between the "Islamic theory" and international Islamic practices, especially in relation to two main issues: the development towards international Islamic political plurality, and the development towards peaceful relations between Muslims and non-Muslims. Although these studies are quite diverse, they usually highlight the disparity between what they term "Islamic idealism," "Islamic traditional perspective," or "the classical theory of international relations in Islam," on the one hand, and the practices of Muslims throughout history, on the other. The justifications that these studies present for this disparity and its implications vary.[23]

The selection of this central objective responds to the objectives and methodology of political analysis, where history is dealt with as a means, rather than an end in itself. At the same time, this central objective responds to the calls of some Arab historians for historical studies to adopt a new methodology. This new methodology should focus, as Emad Eddin Khalil argues, on generalities and conjunctures and should transcend the details and particularities. Although details are quite abundant in old historical sources, especially details related to the political and military aspects of our history, what remains needed is an analytical study of the trajectory of Islamic history throughout its long course.

Answering back these calls might achieve real progress in the field of historical research, and international political analysis from the international systems approach can indeed add to an understanding of the general features and significance of the development of international Islamic political history (among Muslim actors, and between Muslim and non-Muslim actors). By combining historical events and the assumptions and generalizations about the process of change in the international system, an international systems approach to history analyzes patterns rather than individual events or specific occurrences, thus highlighting the different factors that influenced the position of the Islamic state (or states) within the structure of the distribution of world powers.

As revealed by the above discussion, and while taking into consideration the philosophy and rules governing the study of history and its interpretation, the employment of Islamic history in international relations studies from an Islamic Civilizational Paradigm can be of a value added, especially in light of the normative nature/character of this Paradigm. The employment of history by the Islamic Civilizational Paradigm is based on the foundations of the Islamic interpretation of history. The foundations, standards, and rules of the Islamic interpretation of history differ from their counterparts in other interpretations (idealist or materialist), which represent the Marxist and liberal traditions of Western civilization, both of which have different subsidiaries and schools. The mere comparative study of these interpretations of history and the detailed study of the Islamic interpretation of history constitute a fertile, deep, and complex field. Many studies have contributed to this field of comparison, dealt with it from different approaches, and tackled it from integrated angles.

Elsewhere, I have provided the details of this comparison, as well as the dimensions and strands of the Islamic interpretation.[24] Here, we can say that the study of the developments of each system of international interactions, or of the transformation or shift from one system to another, should be guided by the following three questions: What is the role of Islamic beliefs and rules? What is the impact of political, economic, and other conditions? What is the impact of non-Muslim cultural considerations or non-Muslim material factors? The answers to these questions help us explain the major shifts in Islamic history away from the Islamic original ideal; a problematic quite often referred to as the relationship between theory and practice in Islam or as the difficult equation, especially with right and faith on the one side and power and politics on the other side of the equation.

The West sees a difference between theory and practice in Islam, especially when reflecting on Islamic interrelations (within the Muslim Ummah) and between Muslims and non-Muslims. It refers to these interrelations to equate Islam with Muslims, and to represent Islam as equivalent to the thought and practices of Muslims. This disparity between theory and practice, once understood in light of the Islamic interpretation of history, especially in light of the divine eternal laws (*sunan*), seems quite compatible with the Muslim perspective. What Muslim practices have reached after long periods of accumulations attests to the validity of the eternal laws as an integral part of the Islamic interpretation of social interactions. The worlds, which materialists have perceived from a one-dimensional perspective, follow in fact the eternal laws of Allah, those embedded in the universe, life, and people. Evolutionists and empiricists did not create these laws; rather they only discovered some of them, and they largely misunderstood and misinterpreted many of them. The Islamic interpretation of history, guided by an understanding of these eternal laws, verifies the correctness of the understanding of the different political, economic, and social factors. In other words, Western studies claim that historical experience has changed the essence of Islam and that the teachings of Islam were only applied for forty years. When responding to this reasoning, we should know that the requirements of practical necessity and the pressures of actual reality do not annul the foundations of Islam or the great goals it sets for Muslims. Though Muslim practices have not reached this goal (e.g., Islamic unity under the umbrella of the Ummah), this distraction away from the original ideal does not prove the failure of that ideal or the incorrectness of its goals, allowing for the loss of credibility in Islam as a way of life, applicable across time and space. Rather, it proves that when Muslims do not follow the teachings of Islam, this is reflected on their own practices, and the eternal laws of God – including the laws guiding the fall or weakness of nations and civilizations – become applicable to them, regardless of time or space.

In other words, our understanding of the criteria and rules governing Islamic interpretation of history render the grounds of our judgement of the difference between theory and practice in Islam (between idealism and the reality of practice, between traditional jurisprudence and contemporary reality, etc., whatever the names might be) different from the grounds used by research approaches in the West. The Islamic "idealism" they conceive is not the one meant by Islam.

The right starting point for applying some of the tools and frames of analysis of modern social sciences (here the international systems analysis), without falling into the same pitfalls that those who have previously employed these tools and frames in the study of Islamic history have fallen into, is to understand the criteria and rules that govern these tools and frames. Developments in the approaches to the study of history within Western scientific circles have emphasized the particularity, plurality, Islamic fragmentation, conflict, and dissatisfaction. These developments have also shed light on the importance of transition from the traditional orientalist methods of historical study, based on narration and verification, to analytical methods that might help explain the gap between theory and practice in Islam. The criteria and governing rules of Islamic interpretation should guide a correction process, where the goal of reading history should not be confined to the search for generalized patterns. In order for the process of categorization, generalization, and interpretation not to fall into the trap of disregarding the particular Islamic content, the exploration of different patterns and the derivation of general conclusions from specific incidents should not proceed in isolation from temporal and spatial contexts.

In short, the comparison between the Islamic Civilizational Paradigm's approach to the study of history and that of other paradigms reveals two major observations.[25] First, they differ because of their different frames of reference, their different standards against which the historical experience is evaluated, and the different manners in which the nature of the frame of reference and the sources of the paradigm are reflected on the understanding of the factors driving towards transformation, and the weight assigned to the material and immaterial variables influencing this transformation. Crucial in this context is to distinguish between three cases: (1) a case in which conflict over power and national interest is the driving force (whether military or economic power and whether conflict is managed by war or economic tools); (2) a case in which class struggle is the driving force; and (3) a third case in which *daʿwah* (i.e., enlightenment about Islam and Islamic values through various noncoercive, tactful, and polite means), which is managed by the tools of war or peace, is the driving force, serving the goal of civilizational *tadafuʿ* (opposite forces checking one another in a way that sustains life on earth). Thus, the identification of the factors of strength and weakness, or rise and fall, in the first two cases remain captive of material variables or the factors of material power in principle, while the weight given to immaterial factors, alongside the material ones, increases tremendously in the third case.

Second, the different frames of reference and sources of the paradigms are reflected on their views of the direction of historical development. The Marxist school presents a model of linear historical development and determinism, while realism and Mercantilism present circular models and historical structuralism. Some scholars, especially from outside the Islamic circle, argue that the Islamic perspective advocates a model of history based on improvement;[26] based on the conviction that when a greater number of individuals and peoples submit to the will of Allah, their lives improve, especially that many Muslims trust their model and believe that Islam is destined to win. However, other interpretations of the movement of history from within Islamic circles present two opposite arguments.[27] On the one hand, Ashʿarites argue that each moment of history is worse than the moments preceding it, because it lies farther away from the moment of grace, that is, the times of the Prophet and the guided caliphates. This understanding corresponds to the decreasing linear perception of history. Ashʿarites build their understanding on a set of hadiths such as the one which says, "The best people are those of my generation, and then those who will come after them (the next generation), and then those who will come after them (i.e., the next generation), and then after them. There will come people whose witness will precede their oaths, and whose oaths will precede their witness."[28]

Muʿtazilites, on the other hand, elaborated on the concept of "preference" and introduced instead the concept of "equilibrant force." If a moment being better than another is determined, according to the Ashʿarites, by its closeness to, or distance from, the ideal moment, then the concept of "equilibrant force" is based on the fact that the movement of history shows that we can conceive moments "close to" the moment of grace that can stop the movement of deterioration to some extent. Therefore, Saif AbdelFattah speaks of the conditional development of history according to divine eternal laws revealed in the original sources, the Qur'an and Sunnah, which help us describe, analyze, interpret, and evaluate the causes of nations' civilizational fluctuations between the states of glory and empowerment and those of weakness and deterioration. Thus, divine eternal laws lie at the heart of the Islamic civilizational perspective, as they provide a foundational methodological approach to reflect on the civilizational course and its development.[29]

To sum up on the problematics of the relationship between the constant and the variable and its impact on the system of interrelated historical, intellectual, jurisprudential, and epistemological sources of the Islamic Civilizational Paradigm (in comparison with their Western counterparts), it is noteworthy that because of the difference between the Western positivist episteme and the Islamic episteme, the sources of knowledge of the Islamic Paradigm differ from those of its Western counterparts (both positivist and critical) in two respects. The first relates to the existence of the constant or the origin that does not have an equivalent in Western experience. The second relates to the nature of the engagement with both thought and history. Both are called upon, not as fields of social sciences to which the study of international relations opens up (as in critical approaches), but as fundamental constructional sources that complement the foundational sources (derived from the constant original sources, the Qur'an and Sunnah), upon which the Islamic paradigm is founded.

In light of the nature of the paradigm itself, these sources (thought and history) have functions and roles that exceed their role as mere sources for theorizing. They also constitute more than a fundamental part of the infrastructure of the Project of International Relations in Islam, since its launch in 1986, which preceded calls for international political theory or international political systemic history within the Western circles of the discipline.

8.2 THE PROBLEMATICS OF THE RELATIONSHIP BETWEEN VALUES AND REALITY FROM AN ISLAMIC PERSPECTIVE

The Islamic Civilizational Paradigm, albeit normative because of its sources and nature, provides a perspective on the surrounding world based on the paradigm's legal foundation, system of values, and its set of guiding principles. However, this perspective is not confined to reflecting on what ought to be; rather, it is also closely related to reality and engages with it. Values play a role, and serve a function in the Islamic perspective, because they are a frame of reference, a methodological approach, and an ideal against which reality is measured when explained, evaluated or changed. Moreover, these values differ from their Western counterparts. Here, two questions come to the fore: How do values from the perspective of an Islamic Paradigm of International Relations differ from values from the perspective of Western paradigms interested in values? How do these differences get reflected in the paradigm's attitude towards reality?

As for the first question, Wadoudah Badran has pinpointed, since the launching of the Project of International Relations in Islam, the different aspects of this difference regarding the source, level, and scope of values, the extent to which they are obligatory, and their relationships. She argues that due to theoretical differences between "Western" researchers who advocate the importance of the role of values in international relations, no agreement on a common definition of ethical guidelines for international behavior could be identified. By contrast, the Project of International Relations in Islam could identify at least a minimum degree of agreement on the essence of values among different Muslim researchers, since the values that can govern international relations are determined by the Qur'an and Sunnah. Moreover, ethics in Islam are strongly informed by the notions of *sunan* (divine eternal laws) and *maṣlaḥah* (public interest or what is of benefit to people while in accordance with the *maqāṣid* (higher objectives) of Shariʿah).[30]

Western scholars interested in values raise the question of the relationship between individual ethics and international collective ethics. Whereas some scholars identify a possibility for analogy between the two types of ethics, others believe they are not analogous. Here, we can observe that the question of whether the ethics at the collective level are analogous to those at the individual level is a product of the absence of general principles that guide the collective action in Christian culture. As for Islam, it provides separate guidelines for each of these levels. Indeed, the study of international relations in Islam reveals that there is no need for analogy, because each of the two levels has its own organizing rules and guiding principles.[31]

Although some Western scholars recognize the importance of values in foreign policy, they assert that there are no abstract and universal principles that govern them, except in some exceptional cases. Research into international relations in Islam reveals a very different conclusion. Islam looks at universality in a way that runs counter to that of the West. The religiously forbidden (*ḥarām*) transcends time and place and derives its boundaries and limits from heavenly revelation, while taking permanently changing conditions into consideration. In other words, the Project of International Relations in Islam can show that the abidance by Islamic ethics in international action was the norm, and their violation was the exception.[32]

Some scholars interested in the normative dimension of international relations argue that methodological transition must be from what already exists to what should be, not vice versa. In this context, some Western studies claim that ethics of the decision maker are ethics of responsibility, rather than belief. What the politician believes in must undergo a cost-benefit analysis, because what is good in political calculations is a derivative of what is possible. The study of international relations in Islam adopts a different logic about the relationship between ethics and reality, because the starting point is the Islamic teachings against which we can judge reality.[33]

As for the second question, and as has been previously demonstrated by reference to Saif AbdelFattah's argument about the civilizational normative framework of the Project of International Relations in Islam, the system of values from an Islamic Paradigm, compared to its Western counterpart, is a frame of reference, a methodological approach, and the ideal against which reality is measured when explained, evaluated, or changed. It is an integrated and interwoven seven element system that includes – among other elements – values, *sunan* (divine eternal laws), *maqāṣid* (the higher objectives of Shariʿah), the Ummah, and civilization. It is, therefore, argued that the goals of theorizing from the perspective of the Islamic Civilizational Paradigm are not separable from a deep understanding of reality because the latter is a basic ground for the paradigm.[34] However, we must not separate an understanding of reality from an understanding of the jurisprudential rulings. In other words, the Islamic Civilizational

Paradigm does not separate the changing practice from the constant system of values which it calls upon when interpreting, evaluating, contemplating, or guiding change in reality. If the deep understanding of jurisprudential rulings and the system of values, rules, and principles are the measure, reality is the measured object around which experimentation, interpretive innovation, and renewal revolve. In contrast, Western paradigms do not have this normative measure. Therefore, the Islamic Paradigm occupies an intermediate position, on a continuum, between the extreme of the normative idealism that presents ideas and values for their own sake, and the extreme of the historical materialism that is committed to experimentation and aspires to maintain the equilibrium of the status quo.

Therefore, we cannot say that the Islamic Civilizational Paradigm of International Relations is a mere idealistic or utopian paradigm, because it is occupied with how these relations should be, while this "utopian idealism" was not applied, as some claim, except in the first forty years of the age of the caliphate. In fact, the Islamic Paradigm determines the goals as much as it determines the rules and conditions governing action—in turn, the outcomes. In other words, it is not ethical idealism in the narrow sense of the term, but it has its implications for behavior and for the doctrine of *istikhlāf* (vicegerency). Thus, the deep understanding of reality is not less important than the deep understanding of the Islamic legal foundations and the normative civilizational foundations. Instead of having reality as the only guiding principle, the system of Islamic values, while serving as a methodological approach and a frame of reference, provides a holistic inclusive frame of analysis to assess and guide thought and action, thus curbing extreme materialism, rigid rationalism, and empiricism that deprive analyses of any non-materialist logic or objective. From the standpoint of the Islamic system of values, human rights, for instance, become a necessity, not just a cause. And jihad (as understood in its comprehensive meaning of striving or struggling toward moral or spiritual refinement, or a physical struggle in defense against aggression, oppression, persecution—otherwise, striving against what is referred to in the Arabic as *fitnah*), for example, becomes a value, not a mere tool or a means.[35]

Some scholars seek to explain the foundations of the position of "reality" in Islamic political heritage and its different approaches, be they jurisprudence (al-Mawardī and al-Juwaynī), philosophy (al-Farābī), or historical sociology (Ibn Khaldūn). According to Heba Raouf, "it is important to understand the origins of the conceptions of Islamic jurists, philosophers, and historians of the essence of politics and the methodology required for studying the political field and its relationship with other fields of life. In this respect, they were aware of the jurisdiction of the religious frame of reference over reality, and of the ability of reality to raise new questions that necessitate *ijtihād* and call upon different tools for addressing them."[36]

What is relevant about the study of the political field from an Islamic perspective is not the understanding of the "changing reality," as Medhat Maher argues, but the methodology of studying this reality, its transformation or repetition, and its complexity.[37] Islamic political heritage does not provide theories or ways to organize thinking about political reality. Whereas the divine revelation is an epistemological source to be grasped by means of the revealed text, reality is a source for another kind of knowledge to be grasped by means of the senses, observation, and hearing. In other words, the study of the political field from an Islamic perspective distinguishes between the method of perceiving reality and that of representing and conceptualizing it. These are known as perception and treatment. Perception refers to receiving and comprehending reality so as to create a mental image of it. Many factors affect this act of perception, the most important of which are the cultural background and life experiences of the jurist who approaches the political field. As for treatment and representation, they refer to the recording of this perception and to its fashioning into specific molds. The "research approach" controls this process, be it a jurisprudential, philosophical, or historical approach.

This depiction of the Islamic Paradigm as a "normative paradigm of a special nature" (i.e., neither oblivious to reality, nor to the material world), this depiction of the relationship between reality and values, along with this depiction of the system of Islamic values, together represent a rebuttal to some of the aspects of criticism and rejection that the Islamic Paradigm has been exposed to. Such criticism and rejection derive from a perspective that confines religion to places of worship and refuses to recognise any relationship between reason and revelation. It is, thus, a perspective based on a narrow understanding of reason and religion and is strongly influenced by the Christian European historical experience. This perspective fails to grasp the essence of Islam as a belief, religion, way of life, and system of values, eternal laws, and rulings. In fact, this perspective remains confined to a narrow meaning of empirical methodology, which corresponds to a narrow definition of what is scientific and does not open up to the current revision of the definition of science already identifiable within Western academic circles themselves. These revisions, from within Western academic circles, have often questioned the separation between the scientific methodology and values in a way that has renewed the prospects of the Western normative theory. This theory, however, does not dismiss a contradiction between divine revelation, on the one hand, and reason and science, on the other, although it adopts the assumption that knowing about empirical reality is not confined to material or physical tools of knowledge. As a matter of fact, it does not assume that reality and facts are out there to be studied, and stresses that realities and facts are not the truth itself. This is comparable to an Islamic perspective, which departs from the assumption that revelation in the Qur'anic discourse does not only relate to *al-ghayb* (the absent, invisible, and unknowable/the unseen), but also to the witnessed and experienced reality.[38]

As we have seen in the third part of this book, some critical approaches to IR have tended to criticize excessive realism and excessive idealism and to cast doubts about their credibility as well as the kind of relationship they advocate between values and standards, on the one hand, and reality, on the other. No wonder some describe this orientation as idealist-realist.[39] In other words, these critical approaches have tended to revisit the dominant methodological traditions in IR by focusing on the problematics of the relationship between "the ideal and the real" and also between "the ideal and the material." As we have also seen in the third part of this book, some critical approaches have tended to criticize the methodological traditions in IR in light of the problematics of the relationship between "the empirical and the normative." There are approaches that criticize extreme empiricism and emphasize the impossibility of separating the scientific and the normative.[40] Some scholars have even regarded the normative and the realist dimensions as integrated.[41]

Despite the existence of an intermediate zone of intersection between these Western critical theoretical approaches and the assumptions upheld by an Islamic Civilizational Paradigm on the inseparability of values and reality, religion remains, from the perspective of these critical approaches, a marginal source of the system of values that is the focus of their interest. Moreover, these approaches have a narrow view of values and equate them with ethics, thus regarding values as a variable or a mere research approach, rather than as a frame of reference, or a standard that has obliging power because of its source; a view that stands in obvious contrast to that of the Islamic Civilizational Paradigm of the definition and function of the system of values.[42]

In brief, the special realist-normative nature of the Islamic Civilizational Paradigm must leave an impact on the different levels of analysis, whether they are holistic and systemic, or particular and related to certain concepts, distinct events, or perspectives on specific incidents. For example, a diagnosis and explanation of the reality of the Muslim Ummah in the international system is measured against the Islamic Civilizational Paradigm's seven element comprehensive approach to values. This reality may be close to, or distant from, the different values that should govern the relations between Muslims and non-Muslims, the relations among Muslims, or the politics of an individual state within the Ummah.

This special normative nature of the Islamic Paradigm is reflected on its basic concepts, on the one hand, and on the comparative concepts with Western paradigms. Whereas the concepts of *tawḥīd*, *daʿwah*, jihad, *ʿumrān*, and *istikhlāf* are special fundamental Islamic concepts, the concepts of interest, power, and conflict, for example, are among the comparative concepts. The meanings and implications of these concepts differ widely from theirs in the Western perspective, whether the latter is realist or Marxist, for instance. The external functions of the Islamic state, the interests of the Ummah or Muslim states, the tools serving and protecting these interests, and the factors of strength and weakness, all have, according to the Islamic Civilizational Paradigm, non-material (normative) dimensions in addition to their traditional material dimensions in which Western paradigms are principally interested.

It should be clear by now that the preceding discussion is not concerned with the study of values from an Islamic Civilizational Paradigm, rather it is concerned with the nature of the Islamic Paradigm, as a normative paradigm based on religious foundations and its peculiar normative approach in which values serve as a frame of reference and as a methodological approach. It is, therefore, that the relationship between values and reality distinguishes the paradigm from other paradigms. The Islamic Civilizational Paradigm does not only refer to Islam (the faith and the civilization) as a source of values and ethics for the international system in which Muslims live with the rest of the world. Rather, the Islamic Civilizational Paradigm addresses another level by providing an outlook of the world, its problems, interactions, and variables impacting its formation, departing, therein, from an Islamic normative-legal frame of reference that governs, explains, and evaluates the reality, and even specifies the necessary conditions for its change. This frame of reference is not optional, but obligatory, dictated by the nature of its constant original sources, from which different legal reasonings have sprung over time and place.

To sum up, the preceding account has sought to clarify, in light of the nature and characteristics of an Islamic Civilizational Paradigm, the aspects of divergence between values as perceived by an Islamic Civilizational Paradigm, on the one hand, and values as perceived by positivist paradigms and critical approaches, on the other hand. The preceding account has also tried to underline the aspects of divergence between critical theorists' openness to social sciences and humanities and the Islamic perception of thought and history as fundamental and complementary constructional sources. An attempt has also been made at explaining the reasons for calling this paradigm "the Islamic Civilizational Paradigm."[43]

The term "civilizational"[44] implies a holistic approach to political, economic, and other dimensions; a comprehensive perspective encompassing the past, present, and future and the multiplicity of levels of the universal and particular; integration, rather than opposition, between the binaries (including divine revelation and reason, values and reality, the constant and the variable); and the integration between jurisprudential rulings and the views of the world and humankind. The Islamic Civilizational Paradigm goes beyond the jurisprudential foundation to the civilizational foundation. Most writings that tackle IR Theory in Islam approach international relations in Islam only from the perspective of jurisprudential rulings, or the Islamic principles guiding international relations. However, Islamic Shariʿah is much broader than these two domains. In addition to the original sources embodied in the Qur'an and Sunnah, it also includes values and divine eternal laws. In other words, combining foundational, constructional, and experimental sources produces an approach that is much broader than the traditional approaches that fundamentally rely on a single source, such as jurisprudence or history, in their provision of an Islamic perspective on international relations. Moreover, the contemporary inclusive *ijtihād* provided by the paradigm, which suggests *daʿwah* as the driver of relations between Muslims and the world, is in fact a holistic civilizational kind of *ijtihād* which reflects on the functions of the state, the international position of the Ummah, war and peace as tools of international relations, etc.

The Qur'anic perspective of international relations is not to be found in the Qur'anic verses that serve as sources for Islamic legal rulings only, but also in the verses providing the holistic Islamic perspective on the human being, the universe, life, and time. This Qur'anic perspective allows for a new *ijtihād* from a comprehensive civilizational approach that moves beyond the narrow and partial jurisprudential approach, which revolves only around the issues of managing war or peace. That is because the spacious civilizational approach engages with all types of civilizational interactions including other central issues, aside from fighting, war, and peace. Thus, the Qur'anic perspective provides the foundation for the relations among nations, or so to say, a "perspective on the global system." In other words, the relationship between the jurisprudential foundation and the civilizational foundation exists because a foundational perspective on international or foreign relations between the Muslim Ummah and the world is not limited to the issues of war and peace. Rather, it includes other issues of a civilizational nature, including the overlapping and intersecting ideas of *taʿāruf*, *ʿumrān*, and *tadāfuʿ*. Likewise, approaching these civilizational issues should not be confined to jurisprudential rulings, which largely relate to specific occurrences, times, and places. Rather, they need to be addressed with the help of more holistic approaches (i.e., the *maqāṣid* (objectives) of Shariʿah, *sunan* (divine eternal laws), values, and doctrinal foundations).

Therefore, a theoretical perspective on the changing conditions of people and the way for managing these conditions requires an understanding of reality that is guided by an Islamic holistic perspective. An understanding of reality is not only needed for the purpose of guiding new jurisprudential rulings that relate to partial matters on which fatwas and rulings are needed, but also for the purpose of developing a holistic perspective of the changing conditions of people, a perspective that grasps the essence of these conditions from different angles and approaches: internal, external, and intermediate. Thus, what can be described as "the interconnected and extended trajectory of civilizational thought" is as important as the interconnected and extended trajectory of jurisprudence.

NOTES

1. Here, I draw and build on the following works: Nadia M. Mostafa, "ʿAmaliyat Binā' Manẓūr Islāmī li Dirāsat al-ʿAlaqāt al-Dawliyyah: Ishkāliyyāt Khibrat al-Baḥth wa al-Tadrīs" [The Process of Building an Islamic Paradigm for the Study of International Relations: Problems of Research and Teaching Experience]; "Ishkāliyyāt al-Baḥth wa al-Tadrīs" [The Problematics of Research and Teaching]; "Al-ʿAlāqāt al-Dawliyyah fī al-Islām: Naḥū Ta'ṣīl min Manẓūr al-Fiqh al-Ḥaḍārī" [International Relations in Islam: Towards a Rooting from the Perspective of Civilizational Jurisprudence], *Majelat al-Muslim al-Muʿāṣir* [Journal of the Contemporary Muslim], no. 133/134 (2009), pp. 121-190; "Manẓūmat al-Daʿwah, al-Quwah, al-Jihād: Min Mafāhīm al-ʿAlāqāt al-Dawliyyah fī al-Islām" [The System of *Daʿwah*, Power, and Jihad: Among the Concepts of International Relations in

Islam], *Majelat al-Muslim al-Muʿāṣir* [Journal of the Contemporary Muslim], no. 137/138 (October 2010), pp. 95-104; "Binā' al-Manẓūr al-Ḥaḍārī fī al-ʿUlūm al-Ijtimāʿiyyah wa al-Insāniyyah" [Constructing a Civilizational Paradigm in the Social Sciences and Humanities], pp. 31-77; *Al-ʿAlāqāt al-Dawliyyah fī Tarīkh al-Islāmī Manẓūr Ḥaḍārī Muqāran* [International Relations in Islamic History: A Comparative Civilizational Perspective], pp. 17-35; *Qirā'āt fī Fikr Aʿlām al-'Ummah* [Readings in the Thought of the Public Figures of the Nation] (Cairo: Hadara Center for Political Studied and Dār al-Bashīr for Culture and Sciences, 2014), pp. 13-32; Abdel Khabeer Ata, "Al-Buʿd al-Dīnī fī Dirāsat al-ʿAlāqāt al-Dawliyyah (Dirāsat fī Taṭawur al-Ḥaql): ʿAmaliyat al-Ta'ṣīl al-Ḥaḍārī li Dawr al-Buʿd al-Dīnī fī Dirāsat al-ʿAlāqāt al-Dawliyyah," [The Religious Dimension in Studying International Relations (A Study in the Development of the Field): The Process of the Civilizational Rooting of the Role of the Religious Dimension in Studying International Relations] in *Madākhil al-Taḥlīl al-Thaqāfī lī Dirāsat al-Ẓawāhir al-Siyāsiyyah wa al-Ijtimāʿiyyah: al-Munṭaliqāt wa al-Mafāhīm fī al-ʿUlūm al-Ijtimāʿiyyah wa al-Siyāsiyyah* [The Cultural Analysis Approach to the Study of Political and Social Phenomena: Origins, Fields, and Concepts in Social and Political Sciences], eds. Nadia M. Mostafa and Amira Abou Samra (Cairo: Cairo University, Faculty of Economics and Political Science, Department of Political Science, 2011), pp. 201-238; Abdel Khabeer Ata, "Tajribat al-Jāmiʿah al-Islāmiyyah fī Mālīziyā fī Tadrīs al-ʿUlūm al-Siyāsiyyah min Manẓūr al-Takāmul bayn al-Ijtimāʿiyyah wa bayn al-ʿUlūm al-Sharʿiyyah" [The Experience of the Islamic University in Malaysia in Teaching Political Science from the Perspective of the Integration between Social Sciences and Religious Studies], in *Namādhij ʿĀlamiyyah fī Tadrīs al-ʿUlūm al-Siyāsiyyah* [Global Examples in Teaching Political Science], ed. Mostafa Manjoud (Cairo: Cairo University, 2002), pp. 171-207; Abdel Khabeer Ata, "Al-Buʿd al-Dīnī fī Dirāsat al-ʿAlāqāt al-Dawliyyah (Dirāsat fī Taṭawur al-Ḥaql): ʿAmaliyat al-Ta'ṣīl al-Ḥaḍārī li Dawr al-Buʿd al-Dīnī fī Dirāsat al-ʿAlāqāt al-Dawliyyah" [The Religious Dimension in Studying International Relations (A Study in the Development of the Field): The Process of the Civilizational Rooting of the Role of the Religious Dimension in Studying International Relations], in *Madākhil al-Taḥlīl al-Thaqāfī lī Dirāsat al-Ẓawāhir al-Siyāsiyyah wa al-*

Ijtimāʿiyyah: al-Munṭaliqāt wa al-Mafāhīm fī al-ʿUlūm al-Ijtimāʿiyyah wa al-Siyāsiyyah [The Cultural Analysis Approach to the Study of Political and Social Phenomena: Origins, Fields, and Concepts in Social and Political Sciences], edited by Nadia M. Mostafa and Amira Abou Samra (Cairo: Cairo University, Faculty of Economics and Political Science, Department of Political Science, 2011), pp. 83-164; On other contributions by Muslim researchers, see for instance: Muhammad WaqieAllah, "Madākhil Dirāsat al-ʿAlāqāt al-Siyāsiyyah al-Dawliyyah" [Approaches of Studying International Political Relations], *Majalet al-Islāmiyyah al-Maʿrifah* 4, no. 14 (October 1998); Mustapha Kamal Pasha, "Islam as International Relations" (paper presented at The Annual Meeting of the International Studies Association, Montreal, Canada, 2006) ; Amr Sabet, "The Islamic Paradigm of Nations: Toward a Neo-classical Approach," *Peace and Conflict Studies* 8, no. 2 (November 2001).

2. Diverse fields of knowledge contribute to the study of this problematic which political scientists with critical visions are extremely interested in. On the relationship between reason and heavenly revelation and its position in comparative research in epistemological and Western system, as well as its implications for paradigms, see, for instance: Ahmet Davutoğlu, *Political Philosophy*; Louay Safi, *The Foundations of Knowledge* (Herndon, VA: IIIT, 1997).
3. Ahmad Abdelwanees, "Al-Asās al-Sharʿī wa al-Mabādi' al-Ḥākimah li al-ʿAlāqāt al-Khārijiyyah li al-Dawlah al-Islāmiyyah" [The Religiously Legal Foundation and the Principles Governing Foreign Relations of the Islamic State], in *Mashrūʿ al-ʿAlaqāt al-Dawliyyah fī al-Islām*, ed. Nadia M. Mostafa, 1:131-222.
4. Saif AbdelFattah, *Madkhal al-Qiyam: Iṭār Marjaʿī li Dirāsat al-ʿAlāqāt al-Dawliyyah fī al-Islām* [Introduction to Values: A Referential Framework for the Study of International Relations in Islam].
5. Ahmad Abdelwanees, Saif AbdelFattah, and Abdelaziz Saqr, *Methodological Approaches to Research in International Relations in Islam*. Op. Cit., vol. III.
6. Nadia M. Mostafa, "Madkhal Manhājī li Dirāsat Taṭawur Waḍʿ wa Dawr al-ʿĀlam al-Islāmī fī al-Niẓām al-Dawlī" [A Methodological Approach to Studying the Development of the Position and Role of the Islamic World in World Order].

7. "Al-ʿAlāqāt al-Dawliyyah fī al-Fikr al-Siyāsī al-Islāmī: al-Ishkāliyyāt al-Manhājiyyah wa Kharīṭah wa al-Namādhij al-Fikriyyah wa Manẓūmat al-Mafāhīm" [International Relations in Islamic Political Thought: Methodological Problematics, Intellectual Models Map, and Conceptual System].
8. See: Ahmad Abdelwanees, "Al-Asās al-Sharʿī wa al-Mabādi' al-Ḥākimah li al-ʿAlāqāt al-Khārijiyyah li al-Dawlah al-Islāmiyyah" [The Religiously Legal Foundation and the Principles Governing Foreign Relations of the Islamic State], pp. 131-222; Saif AbdelFattah, *Madkhal al-Qiyam: Iṭār Marjaʿī li Dirāsat al-ʿAlāqāt al-Dawliyyah fī al-Islām* [Introduction to Values: A Referential Framework for the Study of International Relations in Islam].
9. See their works: Marcel Boisard, *Humanism in Islam*, Trans. Afeef Demashqeyyah (Beirut: Dār al-Adāb, 1983); Muḥammad Ibn Al-Ḥasan Shaybānī and Majid Khadduri, *The Islamic Law of Nations: Shaybānī's Siyar*; Bernard Lewis, "Politics and War in Islam"; Thomas Arnold, *The Preaching of Islam: A History of the Propagation of the Muslim Faith.*
10. See the details of this critical analysis in Nadia M. Mostafa, "Al-ʿAlāqāt al-Dawliyyah fī al-Fikr al-Siyāsī al-Islāmī" [International Relations in Islamic Political Thought].
11. See: AbdulHamid AbuSulayman, *Towards an Islamic Theory of International Relations: New Directions for Methodology and Thought*, Translation, revision, and commentary by Nasser Albreik (Herndon, VA: International Institute of Islamic Thought, 1992); Ahmad Abdelwanees, *Al-Uṣūl al-ʿĀmah li al-ʿAlaqāt al-Dawliyyah fī al-Islām fī Waqt al-Silm* [General Foundations of International Relations in Islam in the Time of Peace]; Saif AbdelFattah, *Madkhal al-Qiyam: Iṭār Marjaʿī li Dirāsat al-ʿAlāqāt al-Dawliyyah fī al-Islām* [Introduction to Values: A Referential Framework for the Study of International Relations in Islam]; Ibrahim al-Bayoumi Ghanem, "Al-ʿĀmah li al-Naẓariyyah al-Islāmiyyah fī al-ʿAlāqāt al-Dawliyyah" [General Principles of the Islamic Theory of International Relations], *Majalet al-Muslim al-Muʿāṣir* [Journal of the Contemporary Muslim], no. 100 (July 2001).
12. On the concept of divine canons, see for instance: Muhammad Amara, "ʿIlm al-Sunan al-Ilāhiyyah ʿind al-Imām Muḥammad ʿAbduh" [The Discipline of Divine Canons According to Imam Muhammad Abduh], in *Mafhūm al-Sunan al-Rabāniyyah: Min al-Fihm ilā al-Taskhīr—Dirāsah*

fī aw` al-Qur'ān al-Karīm [The Concept of Divine Canons: From Understanding to Predestination—A Study in the Light of the Holy Quran], Ramadan Khamees Alghareeb (Cairo: Maktaba al-Shurūq al-Dawliyyah, 2006), pp. 5-19.

13. On the comparison of the approaches to a tripartite system by scholars (Hamed Rabie, Mona Abul-Fadl, and Saif AbdelFattah) for revolutionizing the study of Islamic political heritage as a source for theorization in general and in the field of international relations in particular, see: Nadia M. Mostafa, "Dirāsat al-ʿAlāqāt al-Dawliyyah fī al-Fikr al-Siyāsī al-Islāmī" [The Study of International Relations in Islamic Political Thought], in *Al-Manẓūr al-Bayanī wa al-ʿAlāqāt al-Bayaniyyah fī al-ʿUlūm al-Siyāsiyyah* [Interdisciplinary Paradigm and Interdisciplinary Relations in Political Science: Revisiting and a New Reading], ed. Omaima Abboud, pp. 86-100.
14. On the details of the comparison among these Western trends, see: Ibid., pp. 86-100.
15. Ibid., pp. 83-86.
16. Ibid., pp. 105-110.
17. In this respect, see: Ibid., pp. 110-122; Nadia M. Mostafa, *Al-ʿAlāqāt al-Dawliyyah fī al-Fikr al-Siyāsī al-Islāmī: al-Ishkāliyyāt al-Manhājiyyah wa Kharīṭah wa al-Namādhij al-Fikriyyah wa Manẓūmat al-Mafāhīm* [International Relations in Islamic Political Thought: Methodological Problematics, Intellectual Models Map, and Conceptual System] (Cairo: Hadara Center for Political Studies and Dar Al-Salam for Printing, Publication, and Distribution, 2013), pp. 243-293; *Qirā'āt fī Fikr Aʿlām al-Ummah* [Readings in the Thought of the Public Figures of the Nation], (Cairo: Hadara Center for Political Studies and Dār al-Bashīr for Culture and Sciences, 2014), pp. 13-32.
18. For instance, see: Saif AbdelFattah, "Turāth al-ʿAlāqāt al-Dawliyyah fī al-Islām" [Heritage of International Relations in Islam], in *Nadwat Turāth al-ʿArab* [Arabs' Political Heritage], ed. Faisal Alhafyan (Cairo: Institute of Arabic Manuscripts, 2002); Ahmad Nabeel Sadeq, *Ishām Ibn Khaldūn fī al-Naẓariyyah al-Dawliyyah bayn al-Fikr wa al-Ḥarakah* [Ibn Khaldūn's Contribution to International Theory between Thought and Action] (master's thesis, Cairo University, 2011); Fatma Mahmoud Ahmad Muhammad, *Anmāṭ al-ʿAmaliyāt al-Dawliyyah: al-Mandhūrāt wa al-Namādhij Dirāsah Maqārinah* [Types of International Relations:

Paradigms and Models: A Comparative Study], (PhD diss., Cairo University, 2017); On international relations in theses and dissertations, see: Horeyya Mujahed, ed., *Taḥlīl al-Abʿād al-Islāmiyyah fī al-Rasā'il al-ʿIlmiyyah* [Analysis of Islamic Dimensions in Academic Theses and Dissertations] (Cairo: Cairo University and UNESCO, 2016).

19. On the details of this system in Western theoretical efforts, see: Nadia M. Mostafa, *Al-ʿAlāqāt al-Dawliyyah fī Tarīkh al-Islāmī: Manẓūr Ḥaḍārī Muqāran* [International Relations in Islamic History: A Comparative Civilizational Perspective], pp. 37-68.
20. Ibid., pp. 68-79.
21. John Lewis Gaddis. "International Relations Theory and the End of the Cold War," *International Security* 17, no. 3, (Winter 1992): pp. 29-53.
22. Nadia M. Mostafa, *Al-ʿAlāqāt al-Dawliyyah fī Tarīkh al-Islāmī Manẓūr Ḥaḍārī Muqāran* [International Relations in Islamic History: A Comparative Civilizational Perspective], pp. 73-78; On the methodological problematics of this employment and its theoretical framework, see: Ibid., pp. 78-100; On the outputs of the systemic political analysis of Islamic history, see "Al-Taḥlīl al-Naẓmī li al-Tārīkh al-Islāmī wa Dirāsat al-ʿAlāqāt al-Dawliyyah: al-Anmāṭ al-Tārīkhiyyah wa Qawāʿid al-Tafsīr" [Systemic Analysis of Islamic History and the Study of International Relations: Historical Types and the Rules of Explanation], in *Al-Tārīkh al-Islāmī wa Binā' Manẓūr Ḥaḍārī li al-ʿAlāqāt al-Dawliyyah* [Islamic History and Building a Civilizational Paradigm of International Relations], pp. 350-420.
23. On the details of the discussion of samples of these studies, see: Nadia M. Mostafa, "Madkhal Minhājī li Dirāsat Taṭawur Waḍʿ wa Dawr al-ʿĀlam al-Islāmī fī al-Niẓām al-Dawlī" [Methodological Approach to Studying the Development, Position, and Role of the Islamic World in the International System], p. 32. These samples are: James Piscatori, *Islam in a World of Nation-States* (Cambridge, UK: Cambridge University Press, 1988); Daniel Pipes, *In the Path of God: Islam and Political Power* (New York: Basic Books, 1983); Majid Khadduri, *War and Peace in the Law of Islam*. Baltimore: Johns Hopkins Press, 1955.
24. Nadia M. Mostafa, "Madkhal Manhājī li Dirāsat Taṭawur Waḍʿ wa Dawr al-ʿĀlam al-Islāmī fī al-Niẓām al-Dawlī" [A Methodological Approach to Studying the Development of the Position and Role of the Islamic World in World Order], pp. 93-104.

25. Nadia M. Mostafa, "Ishkāliyyāt al-Baḥth wa al-Tadrīs fī ʿIlm al-ʿAlaqāt al-Dawliyyah min Manẓūr Ḥaḍārī Muqāran" [Problematics of Research and Teaching International Relations from a Comparative Civilizational Paradigm], in *Al-Manhajiyyah al-Islāmiyyah* [Islamic Methodology], pp. 909-911.
26. Alban Gregory Widgery, *Interpretations of History*, Trans. Abdelaziz Tawfiq Jaweed (Cairo: General Egyptian Book Organization, 1996), 1:163-164.
27. Abdellatif Almutadayyin, *Imārat al-Taghallub fī al-Fikr al-Siyāsī al-Islāmī* [Emirate of the Conqueror in Islamic Political Thought] (master's thesis, Cairo University, 1998), p. 84.
28. Muḥammad ibn Ismāʿīl al-Bukhārī, "Sahih Al-Bukhari - Sunnah.com - Sayings and Teachings of ...," Sunna.com, accessed June 2, 2020, https://sunnah.com/bukhari/81/18.
29. On the definition, classification, and sources of divine canons and their position in the system of the normative approach to studying international relations in Islam see: Saif AbdelFattah, *Madkhal al-Qiyam Iṭār Marjaʿī li Dirāsat al-ʿAlaqāt al-Dawliyyah fī al-Islām* [Introduction to Values: A Referential Framework for the Study of International Relations in Islam].
30. Wadoudah Badran, "Dirāsat al-ʿAlāqāt al-Dawliyyah fī al-Adabiyyāt al-Gharbiyyah wa Baḥth al-ʿAlāqāt al-Dawliyyah fī al-Islām" [Study of International Relations in Western Literature and the Project of International Relations in Islam], pp. 82-91.
31. Ibid.
32. Ibid.
33. Ibid.
34. Hamed Abd al-Majid, *Al-Waẓīfah al-ʿAqīdiyyah li al-Dawlah al-Islāmiyyah* [The Belief Function of the Islamic State] (Cairo: Dār al-Tawzīʿ wa al-Nashr al-Islāmiyyah, 1993), pp. 23-48.
35. For more on the concept of "jihad," see Mohammad Hashim Kamali, "Issues in the Understanding of Jihād and Ijtihād," *Islamic Studies* 41, no. 4 (2002): 617–34.
36. Medhat Maher, *Fiqh al-Wāqiʿ fī al-Turāth al-Siyāsī al-Islāmī: Namādhij Fiqhiyyah wa Falsafiyyah wa Ijtimāʿiyyah* [Jurisprudence of Reality in Islamic, Political Heritage: Jurisprudential, Philosophical, and Social Models] (Beirut: Arab Network for Research and Publication, 2015), pp. 11-14.

37. Ibid., pp. 19-21.
38. Louay Safi, *The Foundations of Knowledge.*
39. Ken Booth, "Security in Anarchy," pp. 527- 546.
40. For instance, see: Fred Halliday, "The Future of International Relations: Fears and Hopes," in *International Theory: Positivism and Beyond* (Cambridge, UK: Cambridge University Press, 1996), pp. 318-327.
41. Christian Reus-Smith and Duncan Snidal, "Reuniting Ethics and Social Science: The Oxford Handbook of International Relations," *Ethics & International Affairs* 22, no. 3 (2008): pp. 261-271, 239-240.
42. On this comparison, see: Saif AbdelFattah, *Madkhal al-Qiyam: Iṭār Marjaʿī li Dirāsat al-ʿAlāqāt al-Dawliyyah fī al-Islām* [Introduction to Values: A Referential Framework for the Study of International Relations in Islam]; Saif AbdelFattah, "Qiyam al-Wāqiʿ wa Wāqiʿ al-Qiyam: Mā al-Maʿnā al-ʿIlmī li al-Qiyam?" [The Norms of Reality, the Reality of Norms: What is the Scientific Meaning of Norms?], in *Al-Qiyam fī al-Ẓāhirah al-Ijtimāʿiyyah* [Norms in the Social Phenomenon], ed. Nadia Mahmoud Mostafa et al. (Cairo: Cairo University Center for Civilizational Studies and Dialogue of Cultures and Hadara Center for Political Studies, 2012), pp. 43-65; Taha Jabir al-Alwani, "Al-Qiyam bayn al-Ru'yah al-Islāmiyyah wa al-Ru'yah al-Gharbiyyah fī Manhaj al-Maʿrifī al-Qur'ānī" [Norms between the Islamic Vision and the Western Vision in the Quranic Epistemological Method], in *Al-Qiyam fī al-Ẓāhirah al-Ijtimāʿiyyah* [Norms in the Social Phenomenon], ed. Nadia Mahmoud Mostafa et al. (Cairo: Cairo University Center for Civilizational Studies and Dialogue of Cultures and Hadara Center for Political Studies, 2012), pp. 103-147.
43. Nadia M. Mostafa, "Al-ʿAlāqāt al-Dawliyyah fī al-Islām: Naḥū Ta'ṣīl min Manẓūr al-Fiqh al-Ḥaḍārī" [International Relations in Islam: Towards a Rooting from the Perspective of Civilizational Jurisprudence], pp. 127-129; "Al-ʿAlāqāt al-Dawliyyah fī al-Fikr al-Islāmī" [International Relations in Islamic Thought], in *Al-Manẓūr al-Baynī wa al-ʿAlāqāt al-Bayniyyah fi al-ʿUlūm al-Siyāsiyyah: Iʿādat Naẓr wa Qirā'ah Jadīdah* [Interdisciplinary Perspective and Interdisciplinary Relationships in Political Science: Re-View and a New Reading], Omaima Abboud ed., pp. 102-105.
44. On this concept, see: Saif AbdelFattah, "Ishkāliyyāt wa Maqārabāt fī Mafhūm al-Ḥaḍārī, al-ʿUdwān wa al-Maqāwamah al-Ḥaḍāriyyah fī

Ḥarb Lubnān: Al-Dalālāt wa al-Mālāt" [Problematics and Approaches in the Concepts of the Civilizational, Transgression, and Civilizational Resistance in the Lebanese War: Implications and Consequences], in *Al-ʿUdwān wa al-Muqāwamah al-Ḥaḍāriah fī Ḥarb Lubnān: al-Dalālāt wa al-Mālāt* [Transgression and the Civilizational Resistance in the Lebanese War: Implications and Consequences], eds. Nadia M. Mostafa, Saif AbdelFattah, Amani Ghanim and Medhat Maher (Cairo: Cairo University Program of Civilizational Studies and Dialogue of Cultures at the Faculty of Economics and Political Science, 2007), pp. 239-249.

9
THE ASSUMPTIONS OF AN ISLAMIC CIVILIZATIONAL PARADIGM: A COMPARATIVE MAP[1]

The preceding exploration of the characteristics and sources of the normative Islamic Paradigm of International Relations lay the foundation for its comparison to Western critical approaches, which are also normative and civilizational, albeit departing from a totally different frame of reference. Here, I compare the Islamic Paradigm with the three major Western paradigms of realism, pluralism, and structuralism in terms of basic substance and assumptions. These include: the origin of international relations and their driving force; actors and levels of analysis; the types of issues that should be given priority; comparative concepts; the perspective on world division and the classification of states; and the relationship between the external and the internal.

Whereas studies of international relations have tackled these aspects as part of the theoretical debates between the three dominant traditional paradigms,[2] other Arab and Western studies have tackled them as topics pertaining to Islamic Studies. The Project of International Relations in Islam has researched the religious foundations of some major topics of international relations: the state as a unit of analysis; the rules guiding international relations at times of war and those guiding it at times of peace; concepts of *daʿwah*, jihad, and power; the application of the normative approach to the study of power, the division of abodes, and war; and the problematics of employing Islamic history and thought in the study of international systems and international relations in general. The volumes of the Project of International Relations in Islam, published in 1996, provided the infrastructure for later efforts that became concerned with activating and implementing the foundational theoretical frameworks in order to contribute to the construction of the comparative Islamic Paradigm of International Relations.

Whereas the first step revolved around identifying the foundations of the paradigm (a process that involved reflecting on the origins, sources, principles, and fundamentals necessary for its construction), the next step has been to activate that foundational knowledge (i.e., to use these foundational methodological and epistemological findings in research and academic study), and the third step has been to apply the revealed or deduced approaches, rules, principles, and tools of analysis and explanation. Thus, application is the first "practical" step, to be taken by researchers and faculty staff members in their studies, publications, articles, classrooms, field research, and reports. Application follows the foundation and the activation stages. That is the stage of giving advice and conducting studies that evaluate existing reality and assess the correctness, efficiency, and effectiveness of conduct. This third stage addresses influential figures and practitioners in governments, institutions, media, education, families, individuals, and different groups of society.[3]

Significant and numerous contributions have been made towards the activation of an Islamic Civilizational Paradigm, notably through academic research and dissertations produced. A strong and essential focal point of analysis has been a comparison of the assumptions and hypotheses of the Islamic Civilizational Paradigm against those formulated by the three traditional, dominant Western paradigms as well as the multiple schools of thought underlying them. Comparison has also involved consultation of both Arab and Western literature in the field of Islamic Studies to complement and support research, where the scope of topics addressed has fallen into the purview of International Relations.[4]

Spanning over two decades the outcome of this comparative research is summarised in the following section. Key elements of analysis include: the origin and drivers of international relations and the concept of power; actors and level of analysis; international processes; and finally, the relevance of cultural issues when compared to their economic and political counterparts..[5]

9.1 MAPPING THE ASSUMPTIONS OF THE PARADIGMS: A HORIZONTAL COMPARISON

This map is confined to the major substantial and ontological assumptions of the paradigms, since methodological dimensions have been discussed earlier when addressing the normative nature of the paradigm and its sources compared to those of Western paradigms.

First, regarding the origin and drivers of international relations, a comparison between the concept of power as understood by the different paradigms reveals a relationship between the Islamic concepts of conflict, cooperation, and *daʿwah* in the following ways: a struggle for power to achieve national interest and through the mechanisms of balance of power, as in realism; a struggle for welfare, whereby welfare is considered to be the basis of power and the driver towards the homogenization of interests through increased international interdependence and a growing role for international institutions in cooperation and globalization, as in pluralism or neoliberalism; class struggle within the global capitalist system as a driver towards a final, ideal stage in which the capitalist system collapses, as in Marxist radicalism; and finally, *daʿwah* as the origin and driver of relations between Muslims and non-Muslims, reflecting the nature of Islam as being a message for the whole world.

Second, regarding international processes, types of interactions and relations, and their tools, whereas realism highlights conflictual types of processes and stresses the importance of military power and acknowledges the possibility of war, pluralism and liberalism belittle the importance of military power in conflict management and highlight the mechanisms of collective as well as multilateral peaceful international competition management. Marxism, in its turn, considers global class struggle to be the driver of international relations and a main determinant of international interactions. Marxist analysis revolves around the various mechanisms and tools for managing structural and non-structural violence.

From an Islamic perspective, a comprehensive understanding of the concept of jihad is essential for understanding the driver of international relations. Broadly speaking, jihad involves any inward or outward effort (self-exertion, struggle, or striving) toward a good or beneficial cause that is hoped to be pleasing to God. The means of jihad, therefore, may be through one's moral/spiritual capacity (e.g., the struggle for self-discipline and restraining oneself from sin, such as refraining from backbiting, slander, etc.), or intellectual capacity (e.g., resolving an issue through research), or physical capacity (e.g., developing environmentally friendly technology or fighting in self-defense) [the examples of course are numerous, and these capacities are not mutually exclusive and often coalesce]. Many scholars emphasize this broad definition of jihad. Mohammad H. Kamali, for example, clarifies that limiting the concept to its military aspects only has narrowed the original broad meaning of the concept:

> Even in Madinah the Prophet (peace be upon him) resorted to *jihād* as a defensive measure, and the theory of *jihād* as a war of offensive character was a subsequent development in the works mainly of the jurists who probably indulged in legitimising the policies of expansion of the military strategists of the powerful 'Abbāsid state. In the course of time, juristic writings on *jihād* became so pre-occupied with its military aspect that the term *jihād* was eventually restricted only to this meaning to the near-total exclusion of its wider connotations.[6]

The controversial interpretations of some Qur'anic verses about jihad (especially the verse known as the verse of the sword), have resulted in multiple answers to the question of whether – according to the Muslim perspective – war or peace are the drivers of relations between Muslims and non-Muslims. For the Islamic Civilizational Paradigm, the driver of relations between Muslims and non-Muslims is not war nor *merely* peace for peace sakes. The paradigm introduces a new *ijtihād,* according to which the driver of these relations is considered to be *da'wah* in the sense of enlightenment about Islam and Islamic values through various noncoercive, tactful, and polite means, such as through education and/or exemplification of Islamic teachings and values. As stated earlier, *da'wah* is more of a caring and compassionate driver to IR relations between Muslims and non-Muslims than merely peace for peace sakes and of course conflict; but where *daʿwah* is not successful, peace is still an objective. The paradigm stresses the importance of understanding jihad as involving conflictual (i.e., physical struggle in defense against aggression, oppression, persecution – otherwise, against *fitnah*) as well as peaceful types of interactions, both of which are applicable under certain conditions and following certain guidelines. Both war and peace are only two possible variations of the relationship between Muslims and non-Muslims that do not necessarily even mutually exclude each other.

In regard to *daʿwah* serving as a driver of relations between Muslims and non-Muslims according to the Islamic Civilizational Paradigm, it involves not only the invitation to the Muslim creed, but also the introduction of Muslim values to the world and where non-Muslim response to *daʿwah* determines the features of the relationship between Muslims and non-Muslims. Hence, the relationship between Muslims and non-Muslims does not revolve around a search for hegemony or material gains for the sake of increasing influence, rather it entails different kinds of interactions, all of which should serve the purpose of promoting *daʿwah* and introducing the Muslim value system to the world for the sake of a more just and humane world.

According to the Islamic Civilizational Paradigm, power is essential, as an absolute abandonment of force is neither desired, nor possible. However, understanding the role of power in international relations (when to use it, how and for what purpose) is inseparable from the concepts of *daʿwah* and jihad. Reflecting on the Islamic foundations of the concept of *daʿwah* leads to reflecting on the Islamic foundations of the concepts of power and jihad, in a way that highlights the realistic-normative characteristics of the Islamic Civilizational Paradigm, where Muslim practice – of *daʿwah*, jihad, and power, among other things – should be guided by the robust Islamic value system.[7] Likewise, in Western paradigms, there is a clear systemic relationship between the concepts of power and struggle and their tools. However, it is a relationship of a different nature.

Calling upon the comprehensive meaning of the concept of jihad is essential for responding to claims that the Islamic conquests resorted to violence in order to spread Islam and imposed Islam on conquered places using military force.[8] The comprehensive meaning of the concept of jihad is also essential for responding to claims that jihad is the equivalent of war and that Muslims have only been manipulating the revealed texts so as to advocate the use of military power at times of their strength and to advocate peace at times of their weakness.[9] The comprehensive meaning of jihad reveals that jihad has both its conflictual and peaceful tools and that although jihad does not dismiss war or the resort to force, whenever necessary, the Muslim foundational perspective regulates jihad, and sets its limits and guidelines.[10] This is not to mention that Muslims are requested to provide *ijtihād* that corresponds to the needs of their changing reality and protects their interests, across time and space, at times of weakness or strength.[11]

Third, in terms of the level and unit of analysis or actors: realism emphasizes the nation-state; pluralism and liberalism call for including other non-state actors into analysis; Marxism presents class as an actor; Marxist structuralists propose the level of holistic structures such as "world-system"; and neo-constructivists underline holistic levels of analysis such as "global community." The Islamic Paradigm proposes the "Muslim Ummah" as a level and unit of analysis, while recognizing its internal organizational variations, be they states or communities.

Fourth, every paradigm has its own conception of the nature and sources of power, as a result of which different priorities are assigned to different issues of international relations. Realism is mainly interested in military and security political issues; pluralism and liberalism in economic issues; and Marxism in economic variables and capabilities that act according to Marxism as the independent variable that explains international interactions in terms of materialistic determinism and historical dialectics. The Islamic Civilizational Paradigm integrates civilizational, cultural, economic, and political dimensions, and gives priority to immaterial variables, without foregoing material ones. That is a reflection of Islam's holistic, non-reductionist vision of the universe, manifest in concepts such as *daʿwah* or comprehensive power, and in the paradigm's conception of the types of interactions, for example. These concepts and conceptions, while being holistic and comprehensive in nature, challenge the logic of conflictual dichotomies and seek integration between opposites in a way that reflects the "value" of *tawḥīd,* which serves as the base of the Islamic episteme.

Finally, regarding the relationship between the internal and the external: realism underestimates the influence of the external upon the internal, while pluralism and structuralism, with their different emphases on interdependence, dependency, or globalization, highlight this influence of the external on the internal. The Islamic Civilizational Paradigm maintains a relationship of continuous mutual influence, wherein both the internal and external aspects receive equal importance, and wherein the relationship proceeds from the internal to the external.

9.2 MAPPING THE ASSUMPTIONS OF THE ISLAMIC CIVILIZATIONAL PARADIGM

Though it does not underestimate the differences between the different schools of each paradigm, the previous map remains confined to the broad differences between the assumptions and hypotheses of different paradigms.[12] The preceding horizontal comparison shows that the methodological and thematic dimensions of each paradigm constitute a system, wherein the driver of international relations directly relates to the concept of power, the relevant processes and issues, and the units and levels of analysis. The methodology of each paradigm is a reflection of its system of interrelated assumptions about IR, whereas that system reflects this methodology as well (as has been demonstrated by the discussion of the interplay between the methodology and the substance and the ontological assumptions of the Islamic Paradigm). This interrelationship between the methodology of the paradigm and the substance of its assumptions can be further highlighted by a vertical comparison between the different assumptions of the paradigms.

Whereas a detailed vertical comparison between the assumptions of the various paradigms about these four aspects remains beyond the scope of this study, it might still be of use to stop at some general characteristics of the conceptual system of *da*ʿ*wah*-jihad-power, the system of actors, including the units and levels of analysis, the system of processes, and the system of issues. A map of the assumptions of the Islamic Civilizational Paradigm goes beyond the general traditional jurisprudential foundational perspective of international relations, where international relations revolve around peace or war, to tackle broader and more spacious systems of concepts. Thus, these systems of concepts do not only highlight the different aspects of comparison between the different paradigms, but they also reveal the subjective, particular, and civilizational character of the Islamic Paradigm.

These various and diverse concepts can be divided into two groups: The first group includes foundational, key concepts common among the discipline of international relations and other disciplines from an Islamic perspective, such as *tawḥīd*, *tazkiyyah*, and *ᶜumrān*. The second group includes concepts peculiar to the discipline of international relations, including concepts that derive from the particular and unique character of Islamic origins and heritage (jihad, *daᶜwah*, *taᶜāruf*, *tadāwul*, *tadāfuᶜ*, *nuṣrah*, *ḥadarah*, Ummah, Muslim Ummah)[13] and the concepts comparable to those of other paradigms, some of which are original and key concepts in these paradigms, such as power, conflict, war, peace, and cooperation.

There is a need for identifying the systems of concepts and for drawing their maps, whether as intellectual concepts per se or as intellectual sources for constructing the theoretical frameworks for studying international relations from a comparative Islamic Civilizational Paradigm. For example, a map including the following four comparative conceptual systems can be drawn: *daᶜwah*, power, and jihad; community, the Ummah (each group for whom a messenger was sent, whether they believed or disbelieved), the Muslim Ummah (the whole community of Muslims bound together by ties of Islam), the Islamic state, and the nation-state; jihad, war, peace, cooperation, conflict, *tadāfuᶜ*, universalism, and globalization; and diversity, plurality, *taᶜāruf*, dialogue, and *tadāwul* (rotation).

The first three of these systems revolve around drivers of international relations, levels of analysis and actors, and tools and processes respectively. These are the different pivots of the modern study of international relations, to which we seek to introduce an Islamic Civilizational Paradigm. However, the Islamic Civilizational Paradigm's contribution is not confined to reflecting on the realist-normative dimensions of these three systems, taking into consideration that the three of them represent a traditional political perspective, focusing on the foreign relations of the Islamic state, which is the perspective adopted by Islamic political jurisprudence and revolving around war, peace, and the division of abodes. Although the comparison of these systems of concepts with their equivalent counterparts in Western paradigms reveals many of the particular characteristics of the Islamic Civilizational Paradigm, they are not the only conceptual systems available to highlight the civilizational and normative particularity of the Islamic Civilizational Paradigm and how distinct it is even when compared to Western normative paradigms.

A fourth system must be added to these systems; it may even become the first if we reorder them from the perspective of the Islamic Civilizational Paradigm. This fourth system is a product of the characteristics of the Islamic worldview[14] and reflects the principles, foundations, rules, and values that guide the relations between Muslims and non-Muslims and provide the necessary frame of reference and methodological approach for the study of international relations. Consequently, this Islamic Civilizational Paradigm breaks the monopoly of the traditional political jurisprudential paradigm on the study of international relations in Islam (jihad, war, and peace), without underestimating the necessity and vitality of jurisprudence for such a study, while asserting that it cannot alone provide a full picture of international relations in Islam. Therefore, extending the scope of the study of the political thought of international relations to include other sources, aside from jurisprudence, can help build this fourth system of concepts, which does not substitute other systems, but complements them. This fourth system introduces a constructional perspective that neither takes war nor peace as the base of international relations but shows when to resort to war and when to resort to peace and the rules for managing each of the two conditions, departing therein from an Islamic civilizational perspective upholding *taʿāruf* and a realist-normative Islamic Paradigm centered mainly on these four systems of concepts.

Although the study focuses here on these four systems of the Islamic Paradigm, a brief engagement with the corresponding dimensions in other Western paradigms is to ensue in order to point out what is particularly special about the normative nature of the Islamic Paradigm, guided, therein, by the nature of the Islamic episteme and belief system. The core features of the Islamic Civilizational Paradigm can be summed up as follows:

- It is neither idealist nor merely "theoretical"; it neither ignores existing reality, nor aims to consecrate it;
- It departs from an integrated epistemological system, guided by an extensive historical experience, to explain and evaluate existing reality with the goal of changing it;
- It adopts a holistic perspective that includes the material, immaterial, realist, idealist, and the internal, as well as the external political, economic, military, and cultural dimensions.

This map highlighting the products of the activation of the paradigm is to be followed by a more comprehensive and holistic map of the outcomes of the application of the paradigm when addressing the contemporary global and Islamic reality, as reflected in the efforts of the Egyptian political science community working on the construction of an Islamic Civilizational Paradigm.

9.3 DAʿWAH, POWER, AND JIHAD

Since the characteristics of each paradigm are manifest in a system of relations among its different dimensions, the concept of power or jihad in Islam cannot be understood apart from the concept of *daʿwah*, which provides, according to some Muslim scholars and political theorists and also according to the normative approach adopted by the Islamic Civilizational Paradigm, the religious foundation of international relations in Islam. The contributions of Ahmad Abdelwanees[15] and Saif AbdelFattah[16] explain in detail the religious foundations for regarding *daʿwah* as the driver of international relations, on the one hand, and the normative approach, on the other. The activation of the seven element value system approach (an elevating faith; a motivating Shariʿah; governing values, intermediate values and derived values; an inclusive Ummah; a witnessing and active civilization; conditional *sunan*; and safeguarding *maqāṣid*) has revealed the following: *daʿwah* (the invitation to or enlightenment about Islam and Islamic values through various noncoercive, tactful, and polite means, such as education and/or exemplification of Islamic teachings and values) is an ongoing process of jihad (striving – whether morally, spiritually, or physically – toward that which is good or of benefit and with the aim of pleasing God) that is related to the individual, the Ummah, external relations, internal relations, war, and peace. Taking into consideration the set of Islamic concepts such as *amānah* (responsibility/trust), *taklīf* (entrusting obligations), *ʿimāratul-arḍ* (to promote growth and prosperity on earth), and *istikhlāf* (vicegerency), which derive from a faith-based view that revolves around the value of monotheism and encompasses integrated sub-views about humankind, universe, and life, it is inconceivable that international relations finds its base in either war or peace, which are mere liminal poles on a continuum, while remaining totally oblivious to the Islamic values.

The seven element normative approach, which is the frame of reference for the Project of International Relations in Islam, maintains that peace and war alone cannot form the grounds for Muslim relations with the non-Muslim other. It goes against human nature and disposition for Muslims to be in a constant state of war and chaos, or to receive aggression and injustice passively while being expected to maintain peace. History attests to the fact that war was not the only tool of Muslim communication with the other, not even in the heyday of Muslim strength.[17] Therefore, *daʿwah* provides the grounds for Muslim/non-Muslim relationship, because the goal of this relationship is not to exclude or exterminate the other, but for "*ummat al-ijābah*" (the nation that accepted the message) to deliver the message of Islam to "*ummat al-daʿwah*" (the nation invited to the message). Consequently, a definition of jihad, equating it with a state of fighting or killing, needs to be scrutinized in a way that remedies biases implicit in discourses speaking about Islam either as a religion of peace or a religion of war. In other words, both the historical context and the state of the capabilities of power determine when does war or when does peace seem to be an effective option so that civilizational action remains committed to *daʿwah* as an invitation to or enlightenment about Islam and Islamic values through various noncoercive, tactful, and polite means and to jihad as a value and a tool at the same time. *Daʿwah* sets the guidelines for power and defines its sources, goals, and impact. How this works is to be explained in the following section.

Power, its sources, distribution structures, interaction types, and issues lie at the heart of the study of major Western paradigms and their debates. That is because power is a central concept to the discipline of international relations and Western political science in general. Although the critical processes of self-reflection taking place within these disciplines have challenged this centrality, the concept of power has remained a key concept for Western paradigms. Power lay at the heart of realism when the latter dominated the study of international relations.[18] It was also an integral part of the concern of the paradigm of pluralism, interdependence, and transnationalism and its debate with realism during the post-behavioralist stage.[19] And now it is a central part of the stage of globalization, cosmopolitanism, or the information age.[20] During these stages, priority shifted, respectively, from military power, to economic power, and then to information and informatics power. These shifts were also accompanied by shifting perspectives on the types and tools of relations and the development of international power balances among the leading powers of the contemporary international system (throughout bipolarity, its end, and post-Cold War polarity).[21]

The changing concepts of power reveal the extent of theoretical flux[22] in response to ongoing changes in international reality and – once again – the extent to which binaries related to power, including its elements and manifestations (military-economic, military-cultural, military-normative, etc.), are treated as oppositional. Finally, they reveal how the internationally dominant Western powers evoke different concepts of power to further their political, economic, and cultural forms of dominance. That is why a reconstruction of the concept of power constitutes a main field of contribution for other civilizational paradigms and serves the goals and policies of non-hegemonic powers that seek to instill guided global change.

The normative approach to the study of international relations in Islam[23] is an attempt at reconstructing the concept of power of Western intellectual traditions which, although various and experiencing processes of self-reflection to reinstate values in international relations as already explained earlier, reflect in their entirety the grand features of the dominant Western episteme (positivist-materialist). The reconstruction of the concept of power from the perspective of an Islamic Paradigm – which was striven for by Saif AbdelFattah – departed from a reassessment of the major philosophical assumptions behind Western concepts of power. These assumptions include: giving priority to the materialist dimensions of power; a Darwinian conception of evolution and development that regards the most powerful as the best; worship of power as a part of an atheist philosophy that advocates the "death of God" and separates political values from ethical ones (even the minority of strands that admit the relevance of ethics to politics, they usually constrain this relevance by considerations of national interest or ideology); power as an end in itself and a value of utmost priority; and the consolidation of the status-quo under the guise of stability, security, and peace. This confers legitimacy on the actions of the materially powerful and delegitimizes the practices of power, once called upon by the less powerful to challenge the prevalent definitions of stability, security, and peace. In other words, these philosophical assumptions imply that realism and rationalism dictate the respect for power, legitimize the persistence of relations of subordination, impose research agendas that ignore the fact that there is no universal definition of interest and that forego the essence of policies and principles such as calls for peace, coexistence, and tolerance.

By contrast, an Islamic concept of power is based on the following assumptions: the possession of power is a matter of *istikhlāf*, as human beings practice the successive authority upon earth. It furthers the purpose of *ʿumrān*, as it is the responsibility of human beings to promote growth and prosperity on earth. Hence, power should neither serve transgression, nor falter in the face of injustice. Such a conception of power even necessitates a redefinition of the concept of politics itself so that it comes to mean "to set things aright/to foster reform or betterment." Thus, this concept of power as a tool for reform and construction, and this concept of politics, as a process of reform and betterment, are quite different from their Western counterparts, which advocate balance and stability for the sake of maintaining the status-quo. The

Islamic concept of power is open to a set of many other concepts such as right and justice, and not limited to those of interest, power balances, interest balances, and conflict. In this context, power is a means to an end; it is a precondition for a duty, where duty is right and justice. Power is not the practice of coercion; it is a practice of *istikhlāf* and it is not separate from normative action or its consequences, as it combines both material and non-material elements.[24]

It is important to note that while the inner struggle toward moral and spiritual refinement and striving for the acquisition of knowledge occupies a central place with the concept of jihad (as evidenced in its Qur'anic usage, especially in the early Makkan revelations emphasizing the peaceful meaning of jihad, and as understood from several hadith),[25] and while the best form of external jihad is giving sincere advice – in a courteous manner – to rulers "so as to avert them from oppression and injustice,"[26] it does not preclude armed jihad at times of necessity. Medieval scholars of Islamic law outlined two types of armed jihad. Both types can be said to be defensive in purpose. One of them was a defensive action (i.e., against invaders, oppression, persecution – essentially fighting for social justice and against the suppression of human liberties), while the other (though defensive in purpose) was preemptive in action (i.e., military action commissioned by a political authority: after all non-violent means have been exhausted; after a fair declaration of war; wherein a credible threat exists; and never with those inclined to peace nor in violation of a peace treaty or truce). [It is worth noting here that these medieval views are informed by the pre-modern context wherein, absent of a peace treaty, war was a default. For Muslim states today, the mechanisms of, inter alia, international law would apply and inform the permissibility of preemptive action.]

Nevertheless, contrary to Western understanding of jihad as a war of aggression, and by contrasting the numerous discourses and approaches to the concept, and once the concept of jihad is placed within the system of *daʿwah*-power-jihad, it could be argued that an alternative third understanding of jihad is possible, and its assumptions can be summarized as follows:

By being a tool for spreading *daʿwah*, jihad cannot be equated with war, whether offensive or defensive. Moreover, it cannot be equated with the Western concept of the "holy war," although it does not exclude armed conflict or propose peace as a permanent option. As the different meanings of jihad are context-bound, it is vital to avoid reductionism and to consider why, when, and how the military power is used, and why, when, and how peaceful means become the option. An answer to these questions should not ignore the strict rules governing fighting in Islam and the real-world challenges that surrounded Muslims. Jihad has many forms, each having its own preconditions and justifications. Such an understanding of jihad is driven from an integrated understanding of the Qur'an's depiction of the relationship between Muslims and non-Muslims in terms of Qur'anic values, ethics, and eternal divine laws.[27] Therefore, jihad is a process that employs the tools of peace and war for the service of *daʿwah*. This concept of jihad is both realistic as well as normative, as it accommodates the various contexts and conditions of Muslims at times of strength and weakness, whereby jihad becomes an action that corrects unjust and unequal relations, militarily or peacefully.

9.4 ACTORS AND UNITS AND LEVELS OF ANALYSIS

In terms of the levels and units of analysis or main international actors, realism focuses on the nation-state, while liberalism and pluralism include non-state actors.[28] The critique of the nation-state and debates about its nature, role, and functions have dominated the post-Cold War age of globalization, calling upon debates about the concept of power and its mechanisms. As for the Islamic Civilizational Paradigm, it emphasizes the "Muslim Ummah," without dismissing the possible existence of organizational variations within the Ummah, be they states, groups, or individuals.

Scholars who approach international relations from the Islamic Civilizational Paradigm usually compare between the Islamic state, as an external or international actor, and the nation-state, in the realist sense, and how each of them emerges, its functions, and factors affecting its power, rise, and weakness.[29] The Islamic Civilizational Paradigm highlights the importance of normative dimensions, highlighting the functions of the state related to faith, jihad, and *ʿumrān* vis-a-vis the functions of the state from the perspective of Western paradigms, where the state appears as the protector of national interests, as the provider of welfare, and as a competitive state. This is not to mention the differences between the Qur'anic term "state" and that to be found in Western sources. Moreover, the definition of the "Islamic state" in contemporary international reality is beset by other problematics that propose a need for some "foundational standards against which to assess the reality,"[30] in addition to critiques of the consequences of transferring the model of the nation-state to the contemporary Muslim world.[31] More importantly, what distinguishes the Islamic Civilizational Paradigm from other paradigms is its holistic level of analysis: the Ummah as a level of analysis.

Whereas the post-behaviorialist stage set off a discussion of the crisis of the nation-state, the globalization stage incited debate on the future of the nation-state in a way that not only paid attention to non-state actors but also to levels of analysis that transcend the traditional state and international levels of analysis. This opened the opportunity for the Islamic Paradigm to make its own contribution to this debate. The interest of the various jurisprudential, epistemological, intellectual, and political approaches in the concept of the Muslim Ummah has long preceded the interest of the Islamic Civilizational Paradigm or even the Project of International Relations in Islam in it. Although many religious, social, and political studies have elaborated on the concept,[32] it was thanks to the pioneering efforts of Hamed Rabie and Mona Abul-Fadl that the concept's relevance for political science has received attention.

Hamed Rabie's studies reflect an obvious concern for the Islamic dimension, among other dimensions, of the study of international relations. That is why, during the 1970s and early 1980s, Rabie developed an agenda of the issues that he thought were relevant to the Muslim Ummah and were worth attention. Rabie also considered theorizing in international relations from Islamic sources. His agenda and methodology could therefore be placed under the title "the normative civilizational approaches to the study of the issues of the Muslim Ummah."[33]

As for Mona Abul-Fadl, she considered it a mission for the researcher to turn the Ummah from a mere subject of study into a concept, where a romanticized perception of the Ummah was replaced by voluntary conscious interactions. This voluntary and conscious conduct should be guided by the necessary normative and ethical considerations that are indispensable for any human civilizational development.[34] Mona Abul-Fadl suggested a reflection on the Ummah as a means for solving the problems of identity and belonging, and as an approach to tackling the questions of government, political systems, and Islamic international relations. She refused to treat the Ummah as a historical legacy; instead, the Ummah, according to her, had a responsibility towards humankind and a civilizational role to play. Abul-Fadl suggested the following questions must be addressed: What is the significance of the Ummah for Islam? What is the position of this collective entity in comparison to other collective entities? What are the constitutional and vital characteristics of this entity? What preserves the essence of these characteristics and ensures their sustainability?

Mona Abul-Fadl maintained that the Ummah was that distinct, fundamental collective entity, created by faith and *daʿwah*, that embodied the subjective, objective, material, and immaterial aspects of the shared and diversified existence of the Muslim community. The fate of the Ummah was, therefore, inseparable from the path of faith/*daʿwah*.

Historically, "the Abode of Islam," an integrated Islamic social and political system, formed and unified the Muslim Ummah which consisted of diverse peoples and nations under a caliphate that signified the political unity of the Ummah, and after whose demise, the Islamic community disintegrated into disparate nationalisms having only a religious tie, and it seemed that nothing remained of Islam except the belief in the one and same God. This contemporary situation raises the following questions: How relevant is the concept of Ummah to our contemporary reality? Has it become part of the collective unconscious of the Muslim peoples who are torn by political boundaries and national regimes? Has the Ummah turned into a historical phenomenon, a good memory, or an abstract and idealistic notion? Should we revive the interest in the Ummah, liberate the concept from the burdens of contemporary reality, and try to explain and justify its continued existence as a political and civilizational community despite the loss of its material and organizational foundations?

The Ummah, defined as the Muslim community, should be perceived as an origin or a foundation, as it is the repository of the Islamic message, from which the "Imam" (the head of the Muslim community) and the state are derived; and therefore, the absence of the Imam does not negate the presence of the Ummah, because it is the latter, according to the Muslim creed and law, that gives rise to regimes in Islam. Hence, Islam's teachings do not constrain the Ummah to a specific organizational structure because the Ummah is a fixed "supreme value" that can create appropriate flexible organizational forms at all times. Having no counterparts in medieval Christian Europe or in the contemporary conception of nationalism as brought along by the Enlightenment, the Muslim Ummah has a distinctive civilizational character that is not bound by specific historical conditions because its continuity is correlated with the faith it embodies. Therefore, the capital of the Muslim Ummah was not confined to a specific geographical location, because Islam is universal by its very nature, and it goes against centrality and defies the logic of having a fixed capital. Whenever a capital falls, another rises somewhere else; and regardless of whichever organizational forms the revivals take, their frame of reference is the Ummah that continually pursues renewal and change.

What about the Ummah as a level of analysis? What are the implications of the preceding reflections on the methodological foundations of the concept of the Ummah? The preceding methodological foundation has revealed that the religious tie is the basis for the emergence, continuity, and survival of the Ummah. So, the Ummah, in modern political language, represents a civilizational and cultural zone, within which interactions and relations are taking place. These interactions and relations can be studied by reflecting on the impact of the common Islamic tie on them, while taking into consideration the impact of the variations and diversity of material aspects among the different parts of the Ummah, the impact of the developments of events and reality, and the impact of the multiplicity of "Islamic" nation-states within the Ummah.

When tackling the historical experience of the Muslim Ummah, the Project of International Relations in Islam tackled the Muslim Ummah as an international system, and the systemic approach was used to study its changing position within the international system. Later on, collective research efforts have approached the Ummah as a level of analysis, advancing, thereby, the process of constructing an Islamic Civilizational Paradigm.[35] In the meantime, some Western theoretical efforts started to pay attention to the level of the "political Muslim community,"[36] seeking to move beyond the traditional levels of analysis towards more holistic and comprehensive levels, criticizing, thereby, the realist Westphalian model that ignores religion, values, and culture. These efforts include, among others, the diverse efforts of the international society school,[37] world society school,[38] world community school,[39] and neo-constructivist school.[40]

In other words, the rising renewed interest in the cultural-normative aspects to the study of international relations had its impact on the levels of analysis, and it brought along a transition from the level of the nation-state, prevalent under materialist positivism, to the level of the post-nation-state, under revisions of materialist positivism.

In this context, the Islamic Civilizational Paradigm proposes the Ummah as a level of analysis, making, therewith, a contribution to the accumulating research reflecting a renewed interest in values, cultures, and religion in social sciences in general and international relations theory in particular.[41]

Amani Saleh's analysis of the advantages and disadvantages of addressing the Ummah as a level of analysis points to the fact that the Ummah as a level of analysis transcends the mere call for focusing on non-state actors along with states, as the Ummah as a level of analysis is interconnected with all three levels of analysis that have been regularly addressed by dominant Western paradigms (i.e., the individual, the state, and the international levels of analysis).[42] The level of the Ummah provides a credible diagnosis and explanation of international interactions at different stages of the development of international relations, whether stages that witnessed the rise of the nation-state or stages that witnessed the rise of non-state actors. Thus, it attests to the complexity of the aspects and the contents of the international phenomena, where one aspect does not dismiss the importance of others. Same applies to the concept of the Ummah itself. Here, too, no single aspect dismisses the importance of others. Contrary to Western paradigms of international relations, the Ummah is not confined to political, military, economic, or cultural dimensions, singling out a specific dimension; as it accommodates different types of interactions, in which individuals as well as groups are involved, not only decision makers or executors, be they diplomats, military men, or businessmen. In short, the Ummah as a level of analysis, enjoys a degree of lasting credibility in understanding and explaining international relations as it acknowledges the complexity of the international (and in general the human) phenomena and the interconnectedness between its various aspects and variables.

Like the Islamic Civilizational Paradigm in general, the Ummah as a level of analysis receives methodological, theoretical, and epistemological criticisms,[43] the most important of which revolve around the agenda of issues to be studied at this level, the methodology for their study, and the indicators of whether the Ummah exists or not.[44] The relationship between the nation-state, the Islamic state, and the Ummah raises many questions and many epistemological and intellectual aspects of comparison with the different paradigms, especially when the regional and global context of the Muslim Ummah is taken into consideration.[45]

Globalization and the relationship between cultures and civilizations are important areas for implementing and activating the assumptions of the Islamic Civilizational Paradigm in what concerns the study of the position of the Muslim Ummah (the Islamic/Muslim world) within the contemporary international system. Globalization provides the systemic framework for locating the Ummah within the international and global system, while the relationship between cultures and civilizations underlines the type of relations between the Muslim Ummah and other communities and nations. Both areas call upon the Ummah as a level of analysis, depart from a criticism of the realist concept of power, and address the cultural and religious aspects of different issues and tools without dismissing the importance of political, military, and economic aspects.

9.5 INTERNATIONAL PROCESSES, INTERACTIONS, AND TOOLS

From an Islamic perspective, jihad is a multidimensional origin or base. Hence, it is much more than a process, a type of interaction, or a (peaceful or military) tool for conducting international relations. Even processes of international relations, from an Islamic perspective, are wider and more comprehensive than the dichotomies of war/peace and conflict/cooperation prevailing in international studies. Being normative and civilizational in essence, the Islamic Civilizational Paradigm is founded on a humane acquaintance-driven perspective that calls upon different patterns of general or partial processes. Mapping the subsidiaries of these processes could highlight the following: first, divine laws governing international interactions[46] (namely, difference, diversity, heterogeneity, *taʿāruf*, dialogue; civilizational *tadāwul*, civilizational *tadāfuʿ*, civilizational balance, civilizational *shuhūd* (being witnesses to humankind/the opposite of absence); *ibtilā'* of nations (trial), tyranny, and hubris);[47] second, globalization-globalism/universalism[48] and the clash/dialogue of cultures and civilizations;[49] and third, global reform/change, global democracy, human justice, and the message of Islam.[50]

This very broad map of relevant processes, along with the two previously discussed systems, provides for the Islamic Civilizational Paradigm's view of international processes which transcends the traditional dichotomies of dominant paradigms: peace/war, conflict/cooperation, political and military/human. The Islamic perspective challenges civilizational unilateralism and Western civilizational hegemony produced by the ideologies and policies of globalization, embracing, instead, more spacious concepts of universalism, justice, and humanity, even when compared to concepts advocated by critical theorists such as global democracy and global governance.[51] A comparison, involving all the previously discussed systems of concepts, would highlight the distinctions and differences between a critical Islamic Civilizational Paradigm and Western critical approaches in terms of the grounds for change, the purpose of change, its philosophy, objectives, areas, and priorities.

9.6 THE SYSTEM OF INTERRELATED AND CONCERTED ISSUES

This aspect of studying the Islamic Civilizational Paradigm relates to the content of the complex international phenomena and the interrelationship between their different political, military, economic, social, and cultural dimensions. The previous analysis has highlighted the nature of the Islamic Paradigm as a civilizational and normative paradigm and the impact of this nature on the driver of relations, main actors, and processes. This section discusses the paradigm's agenda of issues which necessarily reflects the rising importance of religious, cultural, and civilizational dimensions (which are by their very nature normative) in explaining and analyzing international interactions, alongside other aspects, thus transcending the continuous oscillation of Western paradigms between giving priority to one dimension or another. The kind of interaction taking place between these dimensions determines when and why a dimension is given priority, when priorities alternate, not to mention the levels at which these dimensions exercise their influence (global system, regional systems, and foreign policies), and when they serve as sources of conflict, interdependence, or dependency, or as sources of war or cooperation, etc.

Many studies have compared the approach of the Islamic Civilizational Paradigm to these normative aspects to the approach of other paradigms to them. Of relevance here are studies that reflected on the normative dimension with reference to the sources of Islamic thought and history. These studies address different areas: the explanation of the rise and fall of nations and civilizations as well as the explanation of the systemic development of Islamic history and other histories as well;[52] how modern colonization got hold of the Muslim Ummah and the world in the context of colonial powers' competition over the colonization of the New World and the heart of the Old World;[53] projects of modern and contemporary Arab and Islamic revival;[54] and the nature of globalization, its policies, tools, discourses, and interactions, including the clash or dialogue of religions, cultures, and civilizations.

One telling example of these studies warns against the consequences of considering culture to be the only factor behind the current clash between the West and the Islamic world since 2001.[55] That is because cultural and social change, according to this study, are inseparable from the political change that was imposed from above as a result of the modern colonial push on the Ummah and the world. Cultural and social change was in fact paving the road for that political change and supporting it.. Moreover, this study asserts that the Islamic jurisprudential and intellectual rigidity accompanying the ages of deterioration was an outcome of the economic, political, and social deterioration experienced by the Ummah all together.[56] Although positivists maintain that the relevance of the materialist dimensions always outweighs the relevance of other dimensions, including the cultural one, they attribute the Muslim deterioration to some structural features of Islam itself, rather than to political and social conditions that impact the views and perceptions of different communities.

It is important to note that the system of issues covered by the Islamic Civilizational Paradigm is quite broad, reflecting deep normative and humane considerations. This system of issues is not confined to the issues of elites and rulers, issues related to military leaders, diplomats, or businesspeople, or to those of the nation-state or the traditional international system. Rather, this system of issues addresses the issues of peoples, nations, homelands, communities, and individuals. These four systems of concepts, discussed in the preceding sections, are cumulative and integrated systems that contribute to the construction of an Islamic civilizational perspective that pays due and proper attention to the different dimensions of international relations (i.e., the political, cultural, economic,[57] jurisprudential, normative, material dimensions, etc.), without one dimension receiving the attention at the expense of all the other dimensions. By constructing these systems of concepts and rereading models of Islamic political thought, some accumulation can be achieved, at two levels: the level of studying international relations from a civilizational paradigm, and the level of studying the Islamic heritage of international relations, which was unfortunately usually confined to issues of jihad and from a jurisprudential perspective mainly. A renewed approach to the study of Islamic heritage is much needed to uncover the Islamic civilizational perspective of international relations, its foundations, as well as its contemporary reality. In other words, the concepts directly related to international relations constitute only one branch of a set of umbrella concepts around which revolves the Islamic worldview and its corresponding epistemological, intellectual, and theoretical manifestations, with the external and internal being a continuation of one another from the Islamic perspective.

The construction of these systems of concepts requires attention being paid to the complex relationship between the state of Islamic unity, the Muslim relations with the non-Muslim other, and the Islamic internal model. The study of this tripartite complex relationship constitutes the grounds for examining the trajectory of the development of Islamic thought throughout the phases of strength, conquest, and unity, the phases of deterioration, defense, and plurality, and the phases of weakness, colonization, and fragmentation. The study of this tripartite relationship over the course of time also helps examine the relationship between the external and the internal, between external security and internal reform, and between the homeland and the nation, etc.

In brief, constructing concepts such as jihad, power, the Ummah, and the state from the perspective of an Islamic Civilizational Paradigm and in a way that corresponds to the requirements of the international relations discipline differs from the treatment of these concepts in Islamic Studies in general or the study of Islamic political thought in particular. The construction of these concepts as a part of the theoretical framework for the study of international relations aims to explain the normative dimensions of the Islamic Civilizational Paradigm compared to the materialist dimensions of corresponding concepts of Western paradigms, and to compare normative dimensions of the Islamic Paradigm and Western critical approaches. The Islamic Civilizational Paradigm and these critical approaches respond to the same crisis of the discipline, albeit differently. The plurality and diversity of such responses mitigate the crisis resulting from epistemological unilateralism and fluctuations between binary oppositions. Built upon a constant that manages such diversity, this Islamic paradigm humanizes politics and change for all humanity at both Islamic and global levels, as it founds a relationship between values and existing reality, on the one hand, and values, action, and practice, on the other.

NOTES

1. This part of the study shows, in particular, the map of the comparative studies of this book at the different levels and degrees of comparison, and their objectives and starting points, whether in terms of contribution to building an Islamic paradigm, of its comparison with other paradigms, or of comparison between dominant paradigms or Western critical approaches.
2. See the first part of this book.
3. See the editorial introduction to Nadia M. Mostafa et al., eds., *Al-Qiyam fī al-Ẓāhirah al-Ijtimāʿiyyah* [Norms in Social Phenomena], pp. 14-15.
4. See for example: the publications of the International Institute of Islamic Thought (1985-2015); Nadia M. Mostafa and Saif AbdelFattah, *Dawrat al-Manhājiyyah al-Islāmiyyah fī al-ʿUlūm al-Ijtimāʿiyyah: Ḥaql al-ʿUlūm al-Siyāsiyyah Namūdhajan* [The Role of Islamic Methodology in Social Sciences: The Case of Political Science], especially the proceedings of the three workshops: "Madkhal al-Maqāsid wa al-Madkhal al-Muʿassasī" [The Approach of Objectives and the Institutional Approach], pp. 331-376; "Al-Taḥlīl al-Thaqāfī wa Binā' al-Mafāhīm" [Cultural Analysis and Concept Building], pp. 377-414; "Al-Madkhal al-Sunanī" [The Divine Canons Approach], pp. 415-446. See also the part devoted to research papers entitled "Ḥawl Maʿnā al-Manhājiyyah al-Islāmiyyah wa Ishkāliyyāt al-Taṭbīq fī al-ʿUlūm al-Ijtimāʿiyyah" [On the Meaning of Islamic Methodology and the Problematics of Application in Social Sciences], pp. 25-320. On the fertile contribution of the scholars of the nation to the field of rooting relationships between Muslims and other in terms or either war or peace, see for example: Wahba al-Zuhayli, *Al-ʿAlāqāt al-Dawliyyah fī al-Islām* [International Relations in Islam] (Beirut: Mu'assisat al-Risālah, 1981); Imam Muhammad Abu Zahra, *Al-ʿAlāqāt al-Dawliyyah fī al-Islām* [International Relations in Islam] (Cairo: Dār al-Fikr al-ʿArabī, 1980; Saeed Abdullah Hareb al-Muhairi, *Al-ʿAlāqāt al-Khārijiyyah li al-Dawlah al-Islāmiyyah* [Foreign Relations of the Islamic State: A

Comparative Study] (Beirut: Mu'assisat al-Risālah, 1995); Adnan al-Sayyid Husayn, *Al-ʿAlāqāt al-Dawliyyah fī al-Islām* [International Relations in Islam] (Beirut: Al-Muʾassasah al-Jāmiʿiyyah li al-Dirāsāt wa al-Nashr wa al-Tawzīʿ, 2006); Zafir al-Qassemi, *Al-Jihād wa al-Ḥuqūq al-Dawliyyah al-ʿĀmah fī al-Islām* [Jihad and Public International Rights in Islam] (Beirut: Dār al-ʿIlm li al-Malayīn, 1982); Khadija Abu Atlah, *Al-Islām wa al-ʿAlāqāt al-Dawliyyah fī al-Salām wa al-Ḥarb* [Islam and International Relations at Peace and War] (Cairo: Dār al-Maʿārif, 1983); Jaafar Abdelsalam, *Qawāʿid al-ʿAlāqāt al-Dawliyyah fī al-Qanūn al-Dawlī wa fī al-Sharīʿah al-Islāmiyyah* [Rules of International Relations in International Law and the Shariʿah] (Cairo: Maktabat al-Salām al-Dawliyyah, 1981); Najib al-Armanazi, *Al-Shariʿ al-Dawlī fī al-Islām* [International Law in Islam] (Cairo: Maṭbaʿat Ibn Zaydūn, 1930); Mostafa Kamal Wasfi, *Mudawwanat al-ʿAlāqāt al-Dawliyyah fī al-Islām* [Code of International Relations in Islam] (n.p., n.d.); Ismail Abu Shareeaa, *Naẓariyyat al-Ḥarb fī al-Sharīʿah al-Islāmiyyah* [War Theory in Islamic Law] (Kuwait: n. p., 1981); Muhammad Raafat Osman, *Al-Ḥuqūq wa al-Wājibāt wa al-ʿAlāqāt fī al-Islām* [Rights, Obligations, and Relations in Islam] (Cairo: Dār al-Kitāb al-Jāmiʿī, n. d.); Muhammad Alsadiq Afifi, Al-*Mujtamiʿ al-Islāmī wa al-ʿAlāqāt al-Dawliyyah* [Islamic Society and International Relations] (Cairo: Maktabat al-Khānkhī, n. d.); Muhammad Alsadiq Afifi, *Al-Islām wa al-ʿAlāqāt al-Dawliyyah* [Islam and International Relations] (Beirut: Dār Iqra', 1986).

5. The studies of this book, which are derived from scientific theses and dissertations, are a basic structural unit in these efforts, and they cover the theoretical framework that was developed and published in 2000.
6. Mohammad Hashim Kamali, "Issues in the Understanding of Jihād and Ijtihād," *Islamic Studies* 41, no. 4 (2002): 620.
7. Marcel Boisard, *Insāniyyat al-Islām*, Translated by Afif Dimashqiyyah (Beirut: Manshūrāt Dār al-Ādāb, 1983).
8. Hugh Kennedy, *Al-Futūḥ al-ʿArabiyyah al-Kubrā: Kayfa Athara Intishār al-Islām ʿalā Taghayyur al-ʿĀlam* [The Great Arab Conquests: How the Spread of Islam Changed the World We Live In], Translated by Qasim Abduh Qasim (Cairo: Al-Markaz al-Qawmī, 2007).
9. Bernard Lewis, "Al-Siyāsah wa al-Ḥarb fī al-Islām" [Politics and War in

Islam], in *Turāth al-Islām* [The Legacy of Islam], edited by Joseph Schacht and C.E. Bosworth, Translated by Mohammad Zahir al-Samhuri, Hassan Mu'nis, and Ihsan Sidqi (Kuwait: Al-Majlis al-Waṭanī li al-Thiqāfah wa al-Fanūn wa al-Ādāb, 1998).

10. Nadia Mostafa, "The Missing Logic in the Discourse of Peace and Violence in Islam," in *Contemporary Islam: Dynamic not Static*, edited by Abdul Aziz Said, Mohamed Abu Nimer and Meena Sharify-Funk (New York: Routledge, 2006), pp. 173-189.

11. For a detailed account of this, see: Nadia Mostafa, "Al-ʿAlāqāt al-Dawliyyah fī al-Fikr al-Siyāsī al-Islāmī: al-Ishkāliyyāt al-Manhājiyyah wa Kharīṭah wa al-Namādhij al-Fikriyyah wa Manẓūmat al-Mafāhīm" [International Relations in Islamic Political Thought: Methodological Problematics, Intellectual Models Map, and Conceptual System], pp. 152-167.

12. As shown in the first part of this study.

13. On a classification and definitions of the systems of these concepts, see: Saif AbdelFattah, *Madkhal al-Qiyam: Iṭār Marjaʿī li Dirāsat al-ʿAlaqāt al-Dawliyyah fī al-Islām* [Introduction to Values: A Referential Framework for the Study of International Relations in Islam]; also see: Nadia M. Mostafa, Saif AbdelFattah et al., "Fī Manẓūmat Mafāhīm Naẓm al-Ḥukm wa al-ʿAlāqāt al-Dawliyyah fī al-Islām" [On the System of the Concepts of Regimes and International Relations in Islam], in *Mawsūʿat al-Ḥaḍārah al-Islāmiyyah* [Encyclopedia of Islamic Civilization], ed. Ahmad-Fouad Basha et al. (Cairo: The Supreme Council of Islamic Affairs, 2005), pp. 397-496; On the original Islamic concepts and the concepts comparable with other paradigms, see: Dr. Muhammad Amara, *Maʿrakat al-Muṣṭalaḥāt bayn al-Gharb wa al-Islām* [The War of Concepts between the West and Islam] (Cairo: Nahdat Miṣr for Printing, Publication, and Distribution, 2004); Abdelwahab Elmessiri, *Fiqh of Bias*; also see: "Ta'thīr Ikhtilāf al-Namādhij al-Maʿrifiyyah ʿalā Dirāsat al-Mafāhīm al-Asāsiyyah fī ʿIlm al-Siyāsah" [The Impact of the Difference of Epistemological Models on Studying Key Concepts in Political Science], in *Fī Maṣādir Dirāsat al-Turāth al-Siyāsī al-Islāmī* [On the Sources of Studying Islamic Political Heritage]; Ahmet Davutoğlu, *Political Philosophy*.

14. On the characteristics and dimensions of this worldview, see: AbdulHamid AbuSulayman, *Al-Ru'yah al-Kawniyyah al-Ḥaḍāriyyah*

al-Qur'āniyyah al-Munṭalaq al-Asās li al-Iṣlāḥ al-Insānī [The Quranic, Civilizational Worldview as the Key Starting Point of Human Reform] (Cairo: International Institute of Islamic Thought and Dār al-Salām for Printing, Publication, and Distribution, 2009); See the articles in *Majalat Islāmiyyah al-Maʿrifiyyah* 11, no. 42-43 (2009).

15. Ahmad Abdelwanees, *Al-Uṣūl al-ʿĀmah li al-ʿAlaqāt al-Dawliyyah fī al-Islām fī Waqt al-Silm* [General Foundations of International Relations in Islam in the Time of Peace], pp. 131-222.
16. Saif AbdelFattah, *Madkhal al-Qiyam: Iṭār Marjaʿī li Dirāsat al-ʿAlaqāt al-Dawliyyah fī al-Islām* [Introduction to Values: A Referential Framework for the Study of International Relations in Islam], pp. 349-360.
17. Wadoudah Badran, *Waḍʿ al-Duwal al-Islāmiyyah fī al-Niẓām al-Dawlī fī Aʿqāb Suqūṭ al-Khilāfah* [The Position of Islamic States in the International Order after the Fall of the Caliphate (1924-1991)].
18. On the concept of power in the realist paradigm, see: Ismail S. Maqlad, *Naẓariyyāt al-Siyāsah al-Dawliyyah: Dirāsāh fī al-Uṣūl wa al-Naẓariyyāt* [Theories of International Politics: Fundamentals and Theories], pp. 63-131; Nadia M. Mostafa, "Theory of International Relations between the Realist Paradigm and the Call for a New Paradigm." Op. Cit., pp. 54-82.
19. On the concept of power in the paradigm of pluralism and interdependence, see: Joseph S. Nye, "The Changing Nature of American Power," *American Journal of Political Science*, volume 84, issue 04, 1990; Nadia Mahmoud Mostafa, "Naẓariyat al-ʿAlaqāt al-Dawliyyah: Bayn al-Manẓūr al-Wāqiʿī wa al-Daʿwah ilā Manẓūr Jadīd" [International Relations Theory: Between the Realist Paradigm and the Call for a New One], pp. 54-82.
20. On the changes of the concept at the age of globalization and information, see: Walter B. Wriston, "Bits, Bytes and Diplomacy," *Foreign Affairs* 76, no. 5 (October 1997); David J. Rothkopf, "*Cyberpolitik*: The Changing Nature of Power in the Information Age," *Journal of International Affairs* 51, no. 2 (Spring 1998); Hazem Hosni, "Al-Liqā' bayn Wathār al-Ḥāsib wa al-ʿIlm al-Ijtimāʿī ʿind Multaqā ʿAṣr Qayṣar bi ʿAṣr al-Maʿlūmā" [Computer and Social Science when the Age of Caesar Meets the Age of Information], *Majalet al-Nahḍah*, no. 1 (October 1999).

21. See for instance: Alvin Toffler, *Powershift: Knowledge, Wealth, and Violence at the Edge of the 21st Century* (New York: Bantam Books, 1990); Fred Halliday, "The End of the Cold War and International Relations," pp. 24-27.
22. On the implications of the development of this concept on contemporary international theoretical and applied dimensions, see the studies of Shereen Fahmi and Samah Abdelsabour; also see: Noran Shafiq, *Al-Faḍā al-Iliktrūnī wa Anmāṭ al-Tafāʿalāt al-Dawliyyah: Dirāsah fī Abʿād al-Aman al-Iliktrūnī* [Cyperspace and Types of International Interaction: A Study of the Dimensions of Cybersecurity] (master's thesis, Cairo University, 2014).
23. Saif AbdelFattah, *Madkhal al-Qiyam: Iṭār Marjaʿī li Dirāsat al-ʿAlaqāt al-Dawliyyah fī al-Islām* [Introduction to Values: A Referential Framework for the Study of International Relations in Islam], pp. 416-446.
24. On the concept of power in Islamic, intellectual perspectives, see: Muhammad Hussain FadlAllah, *Al-Islām wa Manṭiq al-Quwah* [Islam and the Logic of Power] (Beirut: Al-Dār Al-Islāmiyyah, 1986).
25. See Kamali, "Issues in the Understanding of Jihād and Ijtihād," p. 619.
26. Ibid.
27. Nadia M. Mostafa, "The Missing Logic in the Discourse of Peace and Violence in Islam," in *Contemporary Islam: Dynamic not Static*, eds. Abdul Aziz Said, Mohamed Abu Nimer and Meena Sharify-Funk (New York: Routledge, 2006), pp. 173-189.
28. On post-behaviorist debate about actors, see: Nadia M. Mostafa, "Naẓariyat al-ʿAlaqāt al-Dawliyyah: Bayn al-Manẓūr al-Wāqiʿī wa al-Daʿwah ilā Manẓūr Jadīd" [International Relations Theory: Between the Realist Paradigm and the Call for a New One].
29. See: Mostafa Manjoud, *Al-Dawlah al-Islāmiyyah Waḥdat al-ʿAlāqāt al-Khārijiyyah fī al-Islām* [The Islamic State as the Unit of Foreign Relations in Islam] (Cairo: Al-Maʿhad al-ʿĀlamī li al-Fikr al-Islāmī, 1996); Hamid Abd al-Majid, *Al-Waẓīfah al-ʿAqīdiyyah li al-Dawlah al-Islāmiyyah* [The Belief Function of the Islamic State].
30. See: Muhammad al-Sayyid Salim, *Al-ʿAlāqāt al-Dawliyyah fī al-Islām* [Islamic International Relations] (Riyadh: King Saud University, 1992).
31. For instance, see: Saif AbdelFattah, "Al-Ummah al-Islāmiyyah wa

ʿAwāqib al-Dawlah al-Qawmiyyah" [The Islamic Nation and the Consequences of the National State], *Majalet Ḥawliyyat Ummatī fī al-ʿĀlam* [Journal of My Nation around the World] (Cairo: Hadara Center for Political Studies, 2000), pp. 41-45.

32. See a critical and comparative review of such studies in Alsayed Omar's "*Ḥawl Mafhūm al-Ummah fī Qarn: Naqd Tarākumī Muqāran*" [On the Concept of the Nation in a Century: A Comparative, Accumulative Critique], *Majalet Ḥawliyyat Ummatī fī al-ʿĀlam* [Journal of My Nation around the World] (Cairo: Hadara Center for Political Studies, 2000), pp. 61-130.

33. Titles of Hamed Rabie's studies in this field include: "Al-Islām wa al-Quwā al-Dawliyyah" [Islam and International Powers] (1981); "Sawfa Aẓal ʿArabī" [I Will Remain an Arab] (13 visions; 1980-1987); "Naḥnu wa al-ʿĀlam" [We and the World]; "Qiyamanā al-Maʿnawiyyah fī al-Tārīkh al-Insānī" [Our Immaterial Norms in Human History]; "Al-Qiyam al-Islāmiyyah wa al-Turāth al-Orūbbī" [Islamic Norms and European Heritage]; "Al-Ḥaḍārah al-Islāmiyyah wa al-Ḥaḍārah al-Orūbbiyyah: Bayn al-Karāhiyyah wa al-Iʿjāb" [Islamic Civilization and European Civilization: Between Hatred and Admiration]; "Ayn Qiyam al-ʿUrūbah wa al-Islām min ʿĀlamnā al-Muʿāṣir" [Where Are the Values of Arabism and Islam in Our Contemporary World?]; "Al-Waẓīfah al-Ḥaḍāriyyah li al-ʿUrūbah al-Islāmiyyah" [The Civilizational Function of Islamic Arabism]; "Al-Dawlah al-ʿĀlamiyyah wa al-ʿUrūbah al-Islāmiyyah" [The Global State and Islamic Arabism]; "Naḥnu wa al-Ḥaḍārah al-Bayḍā': Ilā Ayn al-Ṭarīq?" [We and White Civilization: to Where?]; "Al-Islām fī Luʿbat al-Ummam: al-Ṣaḥwah al-Islāmiyyah Ḥarikat Shuʿūb Tabḥath ʿan Dhātihā wa Laysa Taḥrīkā li Juyūsh Tasʿā ilā al-Qitāl al-Fikr al-Qawmī fī al-ʿĀlam" [Islam in the Game of Nations: Islamic Revival as an Action of Peoples in Quest of Themselves, Not a Mobilization of Armies Seeking War] (1985); "Ḥiwār maʿ Ḥāmid Rabīʿ Ḥawl al-Mashrūʿ al-Ḥaḍārī al-Islāmī: al-Fikr al-Qawmī fī al-ʿĀlam al-ʿArabī ʿAfā ʿalayhi al-Zamān" [An Interview with Hamed Rabie on the Islamic, Civilizational Project: Nationalist Thought in the Arab World Is Outdated] (1988); "ʿAmaliyyat Tawẓīf al-Waraqah al-Islāmiyyah fī Taḥṭīm al-Qudrāt al-Dhātiyyah li al-Waṭan al-ʿArabī: al-Iṭār al-Fikrī li al-Taʿāmul" [Using the Islamic Card in Destroying the Self-Abilities of

the Arab World: The Intellectual Framework of Interaction]; "Al-Islām wa ʿAmaliyyat Takhrīb al-Waṭan al-ʿArabī" [Islam and the Process of Ruining the Arab World]; "Ishkāliyyat al-Turāth wa Tadrīs al-ʿUlūm al-Siyāsiyyah fī al-Jāmiʿāt al-ʿArabī" [The Problematics of Heritage and Teaching Political Science in Arab Universities] (1985); "Istirātījiyyah al-Taʿāmul al-Dawlī fī Taqālīd al-Mumārasah al-Islāmī" [The Strategy of International Treatment in the Traditions of Islamic Practice]; One of his most important books on the nation, *Al-Islām wa al-Quwā al-Dawliyyah fī al-Qarn al-Ḥādī wa al-ʿIshrīn* [Islam and International Powers in the 21st Century], roots the motives and reasons of studying the issues of the nation, the agenda of these issues, the methodology of rooting them, and their influence on the world. On a reading of these works, see: Nadia M. Mostafa, "Qirā'ah fī Aʿmāl Ḥāmid Rabīʿ ʿan al-ʿAlāqāt al-Dawliyyah wa al-Siyāsiyyah al-Khārijiyyah" [Reading of the Works of Hamed Rabie on Foreign Political and International Relations], in *Aʿmāl Nadwah Qirā'ah fī Turāth Ḥāmid Rabīʿ* [Proceedings of the Forum on the Legacy of Hamed Rabie], ed. Amr Hamzawi (Cairo: Cairo University Department of Political Science, 2004).

34. Mona Abul-Fadl, *Al-Ummah al-Quṭb: Naḥū Ta'ṣīl Minhājī li Mafhūm al-Ummah fī al-Islām* [The Nation as the Pole: Towards a Methodological Rooting of the Concept of the Nation in Islam] (Cairo: Maktabat al-Shurūq al-Dawliyyah, 2005). On a reading of the most important aspects of this rooting, see: Nadia M. Mostafa and Saif AbdelFattah, the introduction to the second issue of *Ḥawliyyat Ummatī fī al-ʿĀlam* [Journal of My Nation in the World] (Hadara Center for Political Studies, 2000).

35. Amani Saleh, "Tawẓīf al-Mafāhīm al-Ḥaḍāriyyah fī al-Taḥlīl al-Siyāsī: al-Ummah ka Mustawā li al-Taḥlīl fī al-ʿAlāqāt al-Dawliyyah" [Employing Civilizational Concepts in Political Analysis: The Nation as a Level of Analysis in International Relations], in *Al-Ta'ṣīl al-Naẓrī li al-Dirāsāt al-Ḥaḍāriyyah* [Theoretical Rooting of Civilizational Studies] Nadia M. Mostafa and Mona Abul-Fadl, 5:29-80.

36. Peter Mandeville, *Transnational Muslim Politics* (London: Routledge, 2001).

37. Robert Jackson, "The Political Theory of International Society," in *International Relations Theory Today*, eds. Ken Booth and Steve Smith;

Martin Shaw, "Global Society and Global Responsibility: The Theoretical, Historical and Political Limits of 'International Society'," in *International Society after Cold War*, eds. Rick Fawn and Jeremy Herkins (Great Britain: Macmillan Press LTD, 1996), pp. 47- 60.

38. John Burton, "World Society," in *International Relations Theory*, eds. Paul R. Vioti and Mark V. Kauppi (New York: Macmillan Publishing Company, 1972), pp. 375-384.
39. Chris Brown, "International Political Theory and the Idea of World Community," in *International Relations Theory Today*, eds. Ken Booth and Steve Smith.
40. Alexander Wendt, *The Social Theory of International Relations* (Cambridge, UK: Cambridge University Press, 1999); Peter Mandeville, *Transnational Muslim Politics*.
41. See: Nesma Sherif Sharara, *Al-Fikr al-Istirātījī al-Amrīkī Tajāhu al-ʿĀlam al-Islāmī: Dirāsah baʿḍ Marākiz al-Fikr al-Istirātījī* [American Strategic Thinking towards the Islamic World: A Study of Some Strategic Thinking Centers] (master's thesis, Cairo University, 2009).
42. Amani Saleh, "Tawẓīf al-Mafāhīm al-Ḥaḍāriyyah fī al-Taḥlīl al-Siyāsī: al-Ummah ka Mustawā li al-Taḥlīl fī al-ʿAlāqāt al-Dawliyyah" [Employing Civilizational Concepts in Political Analysis: The Nation as a Level of Analysis in International Relations], pp. 54-68.
43. On such critiques, see: Nadia M. Mostafa and Saif AbdelFattah, "Muqadimmah" [Introduction], *Ḥawliyyat Ummatī fī al-ʿĀlam* [Journal of My Nation in the World], no. 2 (Cairo: Hadara Center for Political Studies, 2000): pp. 11-36.
44. See Tariq al-Bishri's introductions to the twelve issues of *Ḥawliyyat Ummatī fī al-ʿĀlam* [Journal of My Nation in the World] (Cairo: Hadara Center for Political Studies and Dār al-Bashīr for Culture and Sciences, 2014).
45. Magda Ibrahim, et al., "Al-Ummah wa al-ʿĀlam al-Islāmī wa al-Dawlah al-Islāmiyyah: Ishkāliyyat al-ʿAlāqah bayn al-Mafāhīm" [The Nation, the Islamic World, and the Islamic State: Problematics of the Relationships between Concepts], *Majalet al-Muslim al-Muʿāṣir* [Journal of the Contemporary Muslim], no. 137-138 (October 2010): pp. 75-95.
46. See: Muhammad Amara, *Maqāl fī ʿIlm al-Sunan al-Ilahiyyah al-Kawniyyah wa al-Ijtimāʿiyyah* [An Essay on the Discipline of Universal

and Social Divine Canons] (Cairo: Dār al-Salām, 2009). On samples of such concepts, see: Nadia M. Mostafa, et al., "Fī Manẓūmat Mafāhīm Naẓm al-Ḥukm wa al-ʿAlāqāt al-Dawliyyah fī al-Islām" [On the System of the Concepts of Regimes and International Relations in Islam], pp. 397-496. Also see: Nadia M. Mostafa, "Al-Ru'yah al-Kawniyyah al-Qur'āniyyah: Waḥdat al-Maṣdar wa Waḥdat al-Tanawuʿ" [Quranic Universal Vision: Unity of Source, and Unity of Diversity], a paper delivered at the conference of "Al-Ijmāʿ wa al-Waʿī al-Jamʿī: Fiqhan wa Sulūkan wa Rūḥan wa Thaqāfah" [Consensus and Collective Awareness: Jurisprudence, Conduct, Spirit, and Culture], organized by *Majalet Hirā'* in collaboration with Banī Imīd in Istanbul, May 26-27, 2013. It can be accessed via the following link: http://www.hadara-center.com/index.php?option=com_content&view=article&id=1498:2 ; Saif AbdelFattah and Medhat Maher, eds., *Muʿjam Mafāhīm al-Wasaṭiyyah: Namūdhaj li Binā' al-Mafāhīm al-Asāsiyyah min Manẓūr Ḥaḍārī* [Dictionary of Moderation Concepts: A Model of Building Key Concepts from a Civilizational Perspective] (Cairo: Hadara Center for Political Studies; Sudan: Forum of Revival and Civilizational Communication, 2008-2009).

47. For a detailed explanation, see: Nadia Mahmoud Mostafa, *Al-ʿAdālah wa al-Dīmuqrāṭiyyah: al-Taghiyīr al-ʿĀlamī min Manẓūr Naqdī Ḥaḍārī Islāmī* [Justice and Democracy: Global Change from an Islamic, Civilizational, Critical Perspective], *Justice and Democracy: Global Change from an Islamic, Critical, Civilizational Perspective*. Op. Cit., pp. 233-260.

48. For instance, see: Ali Mazrui, "Globalization, Homogenization or Hegemonization," *American Journal of Islamic Social Sciences (AJISS)* (Fall 1998): p. 115; Ali Mazrui, "Al-ʿAwlamah wa al-Islām: Ṣadīq am ʿAdū?" [Globalization and Islam: Friends or Foes?] in *Mashrūʿ al-ʿAlaqāt al-Dawliyyah fī al-Islām: Bayn al-Uṣūl al-Islāmiyyah wa Khibrat al-Tārīkh al-Islāmī* [The Project of International Relations in Islam: Between Islamic Fundamentals and Historic Experience], eds. Nadia M. Mostafa and Saif AbdelFattah, pp. 925-929; Ibrahim Abu Rabie, "Al-ʿAwlamah: Hal min Radd Islāmī Muʿāṣir?" [Globalization: Is There a Contemporary Islamic Response?], *Majalet Islāmiyyah al-Maʿrifah* 6, no. 21 (July 2000): pp. 9-44; Saif AbdelFattah, "Al-ʿAwlamah wa al-Islām Ru'yatān li al-ʿĀlam: Qirā'ah Maʿrifiyyah

wa Manhajiyyah" [Globalization and Islam as Worldviews: An Epistemological and Methodological Reading], *Majalet al-Ḥikmah* 11, no. 42 (2004); Nadia M. Mostafa, "Taḥaddiyāt al-ʿAwlamah wa al-Abʿād al-Thaqāfiyyah: Ru'yah Islāmiyyah" [Challenges of Globalization and Cultural Dimensions: An Islamic View], in *The Future of Islam* (Damascus: Dār al-Fikr al-ʿArabī, 2004); Ali Alshami, *Al-Ḥaḍārah wa al-Niẓām al-ʿĀlamī: Uṣūl al-ʿĀlamiyyah fī Ḥaḍāratay al-Islām wa al-Gharb* [Civilization and World Order: Global Origins in Islamic and Western Civilizations] (Beirut: Dār al-Insāniyyah, 1995); Asma Barlas, "Revising Islamic Universalism," in *Contemporary Islam: Dynamic Not Static*, eds. Abdul Aziz Said, Mohammed Abu-Nimer and Meena Sharify-Funk (London; New York: Routledge, 2006).

49. For instance, see: Ahmad Arafat Alqadi, "Al-Ḥaḍārāt, Ḥiwār am Ṣirāʿ: Ru'yah Islāmiyyah" [Civilizations, Dialogue or Clash: An Islamic View], *Majalat al-Islām al-Yawm* [Journal of Islam Today], no. 19 (2002); Zaki Milad, *Taʿāruf al-Ḥaḍārāt* [Interactions of Civilizations] (Damascus: Dār al-Fikr al-ʿArabī, 2006); Issa Barhouma, "Ḥiwār Ḥaḍārāt am Ṣirāʿ?: Nahū Ru'yah Mutawāzinah li al-Taʿāyush" [A Dialogue or Clash of Civilizations? Towards a Balanced Vision of Coexistence], *Majalat al-Islāmiyyah al-Maʿrifah* 12, no. 46-47 (January 2007); Nadia M. Mostafa, "Ishkāliyyat al-ʿAlāqah bayn al-Ḥaḍārāt: Qirā'ah fī Khiṭābāt ʿArabiyyah wa Islāmiyyah" [The Problematics of Relations between Civilizations: A Reading of Arab and Islamic Discourses], *Majalat al-Siyāsah al-Dawliyyah* [International Politics Journal] (April 2007); also see the list of publications of the Center of Civilizational Studies and Dialogue of Culture, Faculty of Economics and Political Science, Cairo University, in the Handbook of the center activities; Ejaz Akram, "Religion as the Source of Reconciliations among Civilizations," *American Journal of Islamic Social Sciences (AJISS)* 19, no. 2 (Spring 2001).

50. Nadia M. Mostafa, *Al-ʿAdālah wa al-Dīmuqrāṭiyyah: al-Taghiyīr al-ʿĀlamī min Manẓūr Naqdī Ḥaḍārī Islāmī* [Justice and Democracy: Global Change from an Islamic, Civilizational, Critical Perspective], pp. 183-269; Saif AbdelFattah, "Al-Muqadimmah al-Taḥrīriyyah" [Editorial Introduction], *Ḥawliyyat Ummatī fī al-ʿĀlam* [Journal of My Nation in the World], no. 6 (Cairo: Hadara Center for Political Studies, 2006): pp. 7-40; Ibrahim al-Bayoumi Ghanem, "Taqrīr Khitāmī: Itijāhāt

Qaḍāyā Munāqashah" [A Closing Report: Approaches and Discussion Issues], in *Ḥālat Tajdīd al-Khiṭāb al-Dīnī fī Miṣr* [The State of the Renewal of Religious Discourse in Egypt] eds. Nadia M. Mostafa and Ibrahim al-Bayoumi Ghanem (Cairo: Center of Political Research and Studies, 2006), pp. 799-828; Nadia M. Mostafa, Ibrahim al-Bayoumi, and Pakinam al-Sharqawi, eds., *Mustaqbal al-Iṣlāḥ fī al-ʿĀlam al-Islāmī: Khibrāt Maqāranah maʿ Ḥarikat Fatḥ Allāh Kūlīn* [Future of Reform in the Islamic World: Experiences Compared to Fethullah Gülen Movement], *Majalet Hirā'* (Cairo: Markaz al-Dirāsāt al-Ḥaḍāriyyah, 2011); Farish A. Noor, "What is the Victory of Islam? Towards a Different Understanding of the Umma and Political Success in the Contemporary World," in *Progressive Muslims*, ed. Omid Safi (Oxford: Oneworld, 2003); Nasser Ahmed al-Braik, *Islam and World Order: Foundations and Values* (PhD diss., American University, 1986); Mona Abul Fadel, "Islamization as a Force of Global Renewal," *American Journal of Islamic Social Sciences* 5, no. 2 (Spring 1988); Khurshid Ahmed, "Introduction," in *Muslim Civilization: The Causes of Decline and the Need for Reform*, M. Umer Chapra (Leicestershire, UK: The Islamic Foundation, 2008), p. ix; Ismail al-Faruqi, "Introduction," in *Towards an Islamic Theory of International Relations: New Directions for Methodology and Thought*, Translation, revision, and commentary by Nasser Al-Breik (Herndon, VA: International Institute of Islamic Thought, 1992), pp. 25-53; Ahmet Davutoğlu, *The Islamic World in the Wind of Global Transformation*, Trans. Ibrahim al-Bayoumi (Cairo: Maktabat al-Shurūq al-Dawliyyah, 2006); Nadia M. Mostafa, "Madhā Yuqadim al-Islām li al-ʿĀlam al-Ḥadīth?" [What Does Islam Present to the Modern World?] (A paper delivered at the conference of "Al-Islām wa Al-ʿAlmāniyyah wa Al-Ḥadāthah" [Islam, Secularism, and Modernity] in Cairo organized by Al-Ahram Center of Political and Strategic Studies in collaboration with the Abant Platform (Turkey), February 2007.

51. On this critical comparison, see: Nadia M. Mostafa, *Al-ʿAdālah wa al-Dīmuqrāṭiyyah: al-Taghiyīr al-ʿĀlamī min Manẓūr Naqdī Ḥaḍārī Islāmī* [Justice and Democracy: Global Change from an Islamic, Civilizational, Critical Perspective], especially the analysis of the level of debates about global democracy, the level of the philosophy, and goals of global democracy, pp. 86-126, and the analysis of the ways of contributing to

the debate about Islam and democracy, pp. 171-179.

52. See: Nadia M. Mostafa, *Al-ʿAlāqāt al-Dawliyyah fī Tarīkh al-Islāmī Manẓūr Ḥaḍārī Muqāran* [International Relations in Islamic History: A Comparative Civilizational Perspective], especially the first study entitled "Al-Tārīkh wa Dirāsat al-Niẓām al-Dawlī: Ru'ā Naẓariyyah wa Minhājiyyah Maqāranah" [History and the Study of International System: Comparative Theoretical and Methodological Views], pp. 37-68, and the fourth study entitled "Al-Naẓmī li al-Tārīkh al-Islāmī wa Dirāsat al-ʿAlāqāt al-Dawliyyah: al-Anmāṭ al-Tārīkhiyyah wa Qawāʿid al-Tafsīr" [Systemic Analysis of Islamic History and the Study of International Relations: Historical Patterns and Rules of Explanation], pp. 350-420. Also, see: M. Umer Chapra, *Muslim Civilization: The Causes of Decline and the Need for Reform*, Markfield: Kube Publishing, 2015.

53. See: Tariq al-Bishri's books in *Silsilat al-Masa'lah al-Islāmiyyah al-Muʿāṣirah* [Contemporary Islamic Questions Series]: *Al-Ḥiwār al-Islāmī-al-ʿAlmānī* [Islamic-Secular Dialogue] (Cairo: Dār al-Shurūq, 1996); *Al-Waḍʿ al-Qānūnī al-Muʿāṣir bayn al-Sharīʿah al-Islāmiyyah wa al-Qanūn al-Waḍʿī* [Contemporary Legal Situation between Islamic Law and Positivist Law] (Cairo: Dār al-Shurūq, 1996); *Al-Malāmiḥ al-ʿĀmah li al-Fikr al-Siyāsī al-Islāmī fī al-Tārīkh al-Muʿāṣir* [General Features of Islamic Political Thought in Contemporary History] (Cairo: Maktabat al-Shurūq al-Dawliyyah, 1996); *Bayn al-Islām wa al-ʿUrūbah* [Between Islam and Arabism] (Cairo: Dār al-Shurūq, 1996). On a critique of the literature of revival and reform in Islamic thought, see: Nadia M. Mostafa, "Al-ʿAlāqāt al-Dawliyyah fī al-Fikr al-Siyāsī al-Islāmī: al-Ishkāliyyāt al-Manhājiyyah wa Kharīṭah wa al-Namādhij al-Fikriyyah wa Manẓūmat al-Mafāhīm" [International Relations in Islamic Political Thought: Methodological Problematics, Intellectual Models Map, and Conceptual System], pp. 123-160.

54. Nadia M. Mostafa, "Naḥū Binā' Mashrūʿ Istirātījī li Nuhūḍ Ḥaḍārī Wasṭī: Dirāsah Istikshāfiyyah fī Mashrūʿāt Nahḍat al-Ummah" [Towards Building a Strategic Project of a Moderate Civilizational Revival: An Exploratory Study of the Projects of the Nation's Revival], in *Mashrūʿ al-Nuhūḍ al-Ḥaḍārī wa Namādhijahu al-Taṭbīqiyyah* [The Project of Civilizational Revival and Its Applied Models], eds. Nadia M.

Mostafa and Heba Raouf Ezzat (Cairo: Hadara Center for Political Studies; Khartoum: Forum of Revival and Civilizational Communication, 2011).

55. See Tariq al-Bishri's introductions to the twelve issues of *Ḥawliyyat Ummatī fī al-ʿĀlam* [Journal of My Nation in the World] (Cairo: Hadara Center for Political Studies and Dār al-Bashīr for Culture and Sciences, 2014), especially "Al-Ummah fī ʿĀm al-Sanah" [The Nation in the Year of Barrenness], pp. 32-47, and "Ayn al-Miḥnah al-Latī Tawājuh al-Ummah" [Where is the Plight that Confront the Nation?], pp. 48-69.

56. Tariq al-Bishri, *Al-Tajadud al-Ḥaḍārī: Dirāsāt fī Tadākhul al-Mafāhīm al-Muʿāṣirah maʿ al-Marjiʿiyyāt al-Mawrithah* [Civilizational Renewal: Studies in the Convergence of Contemporary Concepts with Inherited Authorities] (Beirut: Arab Network of Research and Publication, 2015).

57. In the systems of issues in the Islamic civilizational paradigm, the economic dimension has not received due attention, unlike the religious-cultural dimension in its interaction with the political-military one, at the levels of theorization or contemporary global issues.

10
APPLYING THE ISLAMIC PERSPECTIVE TO CONTEMPORARY INTERNATIONAL RELATIONS ISSUES: MOTIVES AND CRITICISM

Foundation, activation, and application are parallel and interactive processes essential for the construction and utilization of any academic paradigm in a specific discipline. Application means providing guidelines and practical suggestions that fix and guide behavior or performance towards uprightness, efficiency, and effectiveness (as understood by the paradigm in light of its own foundations and principles and its open and interactive nature). The relevance of the paradigm becomes only visible once a map reflecting on its application to the study of "present reality" is drawn. This map is also essential for contrasting the motives behind the construction of the Islamic Paradigm against the criticism it receives. Whereas the main positivist criticism of Western critical theorizing revolves around the absence of a clear agenda and the lack of impact on reality (esp. the interactions between states), the main criticism addressed to the Islamic Civilizational Paradigm revolves around the extent of its credibility in the study of global conditions in general and solving the problems of the Islamic world in particular, in addition to epistemological and methodological criticisms, as will be further elaborated on. Therefore, reflecting, from within the school of the Islamic Civilizational Paradigm itself, on the possible areas of its application, is of utmost importance, especially considering the absence of the consistent cumulative critical revisions of academic production amongst our civilizational circles and considering the absence of tools and methods for academic fertilization and interaction that enrich the academic production (academic ties, academic schools, periodicals, etc.). This is why it is essential to address the following questions: Why is there a need for the application of the

Islamic Civilizational Paradigm? What are the possible areas of its application? What are the most important criticisms directed at the application of the paradigm?

The motives and goals behind the application of the Islamic Civilizational Paradigm converge with the motives and goals behind its construction. In addition to epistemological and theoretical motives, the construction of this paradigm aims to guide action and practice.[1] The development and debates of the dominant paradigms in the discipline interacted with major developments in international relations in a way that revealed a continuous relationship between power and knowledge since the inception of the discipline of IR (as has already been discussed). Besides, the South in general and the Islamic world in particular do not occupy any distinct position in the dominant paradigms and their theories. By contrast, the interests of the great powers dominate international studies.[2] Since the 1970s and 1980s, critiques of the discipline have shown that the theories of development, the theories of foreign policy, and other Western theories are not adequate for studying the conditions of the Third World.[3] At the same time, these critiques were accompanied by changes in the conditions of the Third World and its position within the international system. These critiques were also accompanied by changes that led to the growing importance of the Marxist contribution to the discipline of international relations during the last three decades of the 20th century. The rise of these critiques reflected the correlation between theoretical revisions and practical necessities, leading, thereby, to the criticism of Western political, theoretical, and intellectual centrism, though from within Western circles (as has also already been discussed). Especially since the end of the Cold War, Western critical approaches have provided evidence and justifications for the necessity of non-Western contributions to international theorizing. In addition to that, evidence and justifications for the necessity of an Islamic Civilizational Paradigm have been advanced from within the Muslim civilizational circle itself.

The conditions of the Muslim Ummah and its position within the international system, especially throughout the past three decades, provide enough justification for the need for an Islamic paradigm that offers theoretical insights into the problems of the Ummah and the world, not for the sake of theorizing per se but for the sake of guiding actions and proposing solutions. Many Muslim scholars, who reflected on the need for "new" Islamic theoretical contributions to address the reality and needs of the Islamic Ummah, have explored the possibility (even the necessity) of an Islamic contribution to "global reform." Their writings tackle two interrelated problematics: (1) the world needs an Islamic model that contributes to global societal and intellectual renewal; and (2) intellectual and epistemological innovation at the level of the Ummah, one that is based on its civilizational foundations, is a necessary condition for reinvigorating its powers and for contributing to world stability and security. These problematics show that an Islamic perspective, although capable of contributing to the solution of global problems, should give priority to solving the problems of the Muslim Ummah.

In the context of an Islamic paradigm of International Relations Islam plays a unique role. Straddling an intermediate position in the field it not only draws upon a rich history embodying varying stages of strength and weakness, but more importantly a vision (as part of its universal message to humanity) inseparable from what it can present to Muslims and what it can present to the world. This is evident in the works of scholars such as Hamed Rabie, Mona Abul-Fadl, and Ahmet Davutoğlu which need to be considered.[4]

In *Islam and International Powers: Towards the Revolution of the 21st Century* (1981), Hamed Rabie asks, "Does contemporary international reality allow Islam to perform its mission?" That is because, according to him, making sense of the position of Islam as an international power requires full knowledge of the features of international development. Rabie appreciates the importance of the international dimension in the contemporary stage of Muslim peoples' lives. However, the reasons that led him to raise this question were not limited to the pressures and restrictions imposed on Muslims, externally, but also reflect the opportunities and possibilities that he identified within the Ummah, internally. He argues that Islam can resist neocolonialism and its different mechanisms that try to weaken the Muslim civilizational self-confidence.[5]

In her study "Islamization as a Force of Global Cultural Renewal,"

Mona Abul-Fadl connects the Ummah's need for renewing its thought with Islam's ability to contribute to the renewal of global thought. In the context of global change, Islamic revival is a means for restoring the vitality of the intellectual and cultural heritage of the Islamic Ummah, because reviving the awareness of the Ummah's Islamic cultural identity is a key component of such a revival. The persistent cultural chaos of our world is a force that oppresses contemporary civilizations. Islam has been a source of cultural and civilizational renewal throughout history in different areas of the world (Arabs before and after Islam, the Berber, the Turks, the Mongols, the Persians, the Indians, the kingdoms of East and West Africa, the Christian Mediterranean cities). Bridging the current gap between cultures is a necessity for the cultural renewal of the Ummah itself, to renew its identity and to solve its problems. This process is part of the global cultural renewal that all cultures in the world need and in which all dominant and subordinate cultures can participate. Mona Abul-Fadl regards the Islamic paradigm as a "vocational ideal," not merely an academic profession.[6]

For Ahmet Davutoğlu, the Muslim civilization has a responsibility to offer solutions for the world's contemporary problems. The current civilizational crisis of the international system is neither the first, nor will it be the last one. Previous civilizational crises were overcome by opening to new ethical foundations and standards from other civilizations. However, the distinctive feature of the current crisis is that it does not allow original cultures to coexist or to participate. Most of these cultures suffer under the hegemony of the modernization of the Western civilization as it marginalizes deep-rooted cultures and homogenizes ideas and styles of life across the world, thereby, deeply threatening the historical plurality of human cultures. To overcome the current crisis of the international system, Davutoğlu proposes an Islamic perspective that depends on four premises. First, the Muslim individual becomes aware of the self, whereas the Western individual experiences alienation. Second, in the Islamic episteme, all sources of knowledge, regardless of how diverse, remain consistent and compatible with the supreme principle, *tawḥīd*. Third, a system of values guides and directs social life. Fourth, Muslims' conception of society and history provides them with psychological and social motives to maintain the authentic features of their civilization, despite the harshness of the means of oppression produced by the modern version of the Western civilization. These premises lead Davutoğlu to devise a project for reforming the international system in which solving the Islamic intellectual, economic, political, and security crisis is a first step. The early signs of a way out of this complex crisis can be seen in the escalating crisis of the world, the aggravated dilemma confronting Westernized intellectual tendencies within the Ummah, and an emerging civilizational shift in the Islamic world, which draws anew on the Islamic frame of reference and guides a new generation of active and enlightened Muslims.[7]

These and similar contributions do not draw on utopian perceptions, blinded to the actual problems of the contemporary Muslim world. Rather, they argue that the way to solve the problems of the Muslim world is not to address them domestically only, but to address them globally through a serious participation in solving global problems that have their consequences on the Muslim world. These global problems include those of the structure of the global system and its non-pluralistic or non-democratic character. In other words, these contributions, inter alia, consider the Islamic project of reform and revival while reflecting on its global, holistic context, that is because such a project cannot be achieved in a hostile environment that reinforces, in collaboration with domestic despotic regimes, domestic retardation and tyranny.

In addition, practical necessities led some scholars from outside the circle of the Islamic Civilizational Paradigm to recognize the importance of developing an Islamic civilizational perspective of International Relations. However, some of them correlate these necessities with the need for studying and understanding the implications of the Islamic phenomenon, which they call "religious fundamentalism," on the post-Cold-War international system, wherein the cultural dimensions of international politics come to the fore because of globalization, fragmentation, and a permanent state of flux.[8] Other scholars argue that the study of the problems and concerns of one fifth of the world population, those problems and concerns that happen to evoke current global interest also, require a paradigm that grasps their particularity, and demonstrates the extent to which Islam can play a role, when it comes to specifying their causes, motives, and possible solutions.[9]

The international interactions of the post-Cold-War era deeply involved the world of Islam and Muslims. However, this involvement escalated in the aftermath of the events of September 11. Multiple approaches to the study of the position of the Islamic world within the international system and as a target of the foreign policies of the great powers were introduced. These approaches were mainly products of the dominant paradigms of IR, and have led, therefore, to calls, from within the West as well as from within the Islamic world, for a comparative paradigm and an alternative perspective to the one dominated by materialist and conflictual power politics.[10] Therefore, the efforts of the Egyptian School of an Islamic Civilizational Paradigm caught the attention of some prominent scholars, including Bahgat Korany, as a school that shares, along with the critical approaches in the discipline, interest in values, thought, history, and a new agenda of issues.[11] Throughout the first decade of the 21st century, a growing Western interest in the study of the conditions of the Islamic World was accompanied by a growing Western interest in the Islamic perspective on international relations; an interest that is though quite distinct from the traditional Orientalist interest.[12]

10.1 AREAS AND OBJECTIVES OF APPLICATION

The areas of application relate to the position of the Muslim Ummah within the global system and its relations with the West. From a comparative perspective, the debates between the different discourses on the relations between Islam and the West need to be located on the map of the development of international Islamic thought. Worth emphasizing are elements of continuity versus elements of change and the factors shaping and influencing these debates: Has the West been so weighty in the thought of Muslims throughout their history? It is also worth noting that the grave challenges that beset the Muslim Ummah are manifested in conceptual chaos and the crisis of Islamic thought. For example, occupation has turned into just war and a war of liberation, self-defense and resistance into aggression and terrorism, secularization of Islam into a renewal of religious discourse, civil education into non-violence, tolerance, and peace (for the West, not for the Arab and Muslim world), and rational government into pragmatism, etc.[13]

With the rising attack on "Islam," not only on Muslims' thought and practices, Muslims' self-flagellation increases and is even accompanied by numerous clashing views on how to get out of this crisis. Although the crisis of the Ummah is originally a crisis of thought and the crisis of the thought a mere reflection of the crisis of the Ummah, reading the international thought of the Ummah and its development helps us examine the stages of the rise and fall of the Ummah and the causes of its strength and weakness, compared to other nations. It also helps us understand the questions and details of the major issues that have developed throughout Muslim history, especially in terms of the relationship between the religious, cultural, and political and between reform, unity of the Ummah, and its independence.

In order to confront self-flagellation, conceptual chaos, and the war of ideas that the West has waged against Muslims in the age of globalization, after having waged it against the elite during and after colonialism, intellectual renewal and intellectual counter-war are much needed as ends in themselves and as means to guide a reform movement and a rational *tadafu*ᶜ process, because the crisis of the Muslim Ummah is an intellectual crisis, not just a materialist one. That is why the following question is raised: Were the absence of the effective action techniques and the need for moving from theory to specifying strategies for action and to forging development plans the reason behind the failure of numerous reform programs over the last three centuries?

To sum up, the questions of the international (external) relations of the Muslim Ummah and the world at large are not confined to the questions of war and peace. According to the Qur'anic perspective, these relations also include other questions related to the human civilizational field at large, necessitating a perspective that reflects on the change in human conditions and how to manage them. Such a perspective requires a deep understanding of reality in light of the holistic Islamic perspective, not only for the purpose of reaching new jurisprudential rulings on specific issues, but also for the purpose of providing a holistic intellectual perspective on these conditions from external, internal, and intermediary approaches.

The state of the crisis of contemporary Islamic thought is characterized by the polarization between the so-called traditional approaches that refuse to take Western influences into their consideration and reject them and the modern approaches that succumb to the pressures of reality and produce apologetic discourses. Overcoming this acute state of polarization requires a constructional response that transcends these two kinds of approaches. This response should consider reality first, try to understand it, and then change it according to the rules, foundations, and principles of the Islamic perspective and its general judgements, not according to the dictates of the dominating West, which sometimes carry misleading labels such as the need for a new and contemporary *ijtihād* that responds to the challenges of reality. This desired constructional response does not take place in a vacuum and is not the mere product of the current moment. Rather, it should deeply reflect on the development of the civilizational approach of the Islamic thought. The civilizational thought goes far beyond the jurisprudential thought. It broadens the scope of Shariʿah to include more than jurisprudential rulings; that is, to also include thought that embodies the Islamic worldview, reflects the features of the Islamic culture and civilization, or represents the different schools of the Islamic interpretation of history, next to civilizational as well as jurisprudential thought. The jurisprudential rulings and the vast heritage related to them should be tackled tactfully to avoid committing the mistake of rejecting them as mere history, or falling into a chaos of interpretations or rather into rigidity out of fear of exceeding the limits for acceptable interpretation.

By closely examining the development of Islamic civilizational thought, a contemporary Islamic humane discourse can be formulated; one that bridges the gap between the discourse of conflict and division (which is a mere contemporary literal repetition of the discourse of the "abode of peace" and the "abode of war") and the discourse of surrender and submission (upholding the culture of peace and tolerance, while taking the form of apology and defense).

Understanding the development of international civilizational thought also helps us understand the causes of this bi-polarization and the means to overcome and interrupt their negative rumination and produce a contemporary Islamic human discourse. This new discourse is to be upheld by the dominant main currents of various national communities across the whole Ummah. It must be activated and applied as a constructive way to bring domestic change and confront external and foreign aggression and attack, and as an effective response to confronting the challenges of current reality, whether these challenges relate to structural conditions or to the cultural environment, since these types of challenges cannot be addressed as separate when designing this constructive response. For example, the external dimensions of extremism or the so-called foreign extensions of *jihādī* movements, or what is termed global terrorism, cannot be explained – not justified – neither by cultural causes alone (related to the attitude of Islam towards non-Muslims), nor by structural causes alone (related to the conditions of domestic and foreign tyranny and injustice against Muslims religiously, normatively, systemically, and historically). Simply, the two sets of causes are interrelated and reinforce each other. Various intellectual and historical models throughout the trajectory of the civilizational thought of states must prove this connection and its impact on the types of jurisprudential, intellectual, and political discourses across different temporal stages.

Therefore, reflecting on the foundational perspective of international relations in Islam and relations with the other must respond, according to the rules of *ijtihād* and renewal, to the foreign challenges and threats that beset the contemporary reality of Muslims in a way that fulfills the purposes of Shariʿah. Moreover, this renewed perspective should not remain confined to thought, for although thought entails necessarily a sort of activation, such a perspective needs to move beyond activation to application.

Reflecting on the foundational and constructional sources of the Islamic Civilizational Paradigm and its characteristics is not a goal in itself, rather it is a means to explore global conditions and to provide an Islamic perspective (or perspectives) on the causes of these conditions and the way to manage and change them. Global conditions have their strong influence on Muslims. Whereas public policies in the Muslim world have acquired obvious international dimensions, they are also connected with contemporary global issues that are closely related to the domestic conditions of the Islamic world.

Therefore, this application moves our interest from the intellectual, theoretical, and epistemological level to the practical level in more than one sense. Public policies serve as a link between the jurisprudential foundation, the civilizational foundation, and the intellectual projects, on the one hand, and their application in reality, on the other. Therefore, mapping global issues related to Islamic states is a strategic step that follows the stage of foundation.

These global issues can be divided into the following categories: issues of reform, change and the building of human security; issues of development and the building of economic power and security; issues related to the building of military power and security; issues related to the Islamic circle in the foreign policy of Muslim states or non-Muslim great powers; issues related to Islamic and trans-civilizational interrelationships; issues related to regional and transregional conflicts in the Muslim world; issues related to Muslims in the West; issues related to civilizational dialogue and *taʿāruf*; and issues related to the reformation of the global system, seeking to make it more democratic and just. These issues cover the three major categories: the internal, the external, and the intermediate. And they combine the worlds of events, ideas, institutions, and symbols.

Each item on this map includes a network of issues. For example, the issues of reform and change include the renewal of religious discourse and education, women rights, human rights, civil education, globalization and education, the activation of civil society, citizenship, the relationship between religion and *daʿwah*, and between politics and political parties, circles of belonging, reform and renewal, and the state of Islamic culture, all being issues related to democracy and governance. Although these issues seem domestic, cultural, and social, they lie at the heart of contemporary international and global interactions, and of the balances and policies of domestic, regional, and global powers.[14]

In other words, the discussion of globalization from an Islamic perspective in order to explain the problematic relationship between the internal and the external aspects, the cultural and the political aspects, and between individuals, groups, states, and the global system, in an attempt to elucidate the features of a perspective or a discourse on a global human society, raises four main issues.

First, there are questions and discourses related to war and peace that are relevant to a critical discussion of the uses of military power in Muslim majority countries, whether domestically, regionally, or trans-regionally. That discussion is essential for the introduction of an alternative discourse on power, where power serves justice and protects rights. That is a discourse that overcomes polarization and avoids falling into a spiral of defenses and apologies and avoids equating legitimate with illegitimate uses of power.

Second, there is the question of the relations between civilizations needed to confront the polarized discourses that classify these relations as either relations of conflict or relations of dialogue. In fact, Muslims are obliged to introduce a human discourse of *taʿāruf* that determines when and how relations turn into conflict or cooperation and how dialogue is only one tool of *taʿāruf* that is based on plurality and diversity.

Third, there is the question of Muslim political movements and the process of reform within the Ummah, which is a process with internal as well as external aspects. The diversity of the subsidiaries, tools, and objectives of these movements cause their confrontation with regimes and secular movements, whether those who rule or those in opposition. Foreign pressures affect this confrontation. It is argued that these (Muslim political) movements, especially those having foreign extensions, threaten global stability, security, and peace. This has given rise to intellectual and political debates about other sources of threat to global peace, especially from global dominant powers. Therefore, the question of reform within Muslim majority states is torn between domestic struggle against despotism and the struggle against the foreign hegemony that is allied with domestic despotism.

Fourth, there is the question of reforming the global system and how Muslims, whether living in Muslim states or in the West, can take part in this reform. This participation requires Muslims to manage two main perceptions related to their relations with non-Muslims: Muslims are an integral part of the world and have a great responsibility towards not only Muslims, but also humankind at large, this responsibility obliges them first to reform the conditions of Muslims.[15]

The early years of the second decade of the third millennium, marked by the outbreak of Arab revolutions and uprisings, counterrevolutions, and coups, whether reflected upon from within their regional or their global systemic contexts, further supported the need for an Islamic perspective on international relations, even on political systems, and other political fields.[16] They also highlighted the necessity for an academic and organized study of such a perspective that serves practical as well as theoretical purposes and avoids biased ideologization and politicization by those interested in an Islamic paradigm or perspective of international relations or those who refute it, at the levels of both theory and practice.[17]

10.2 THE ISLAMIC CIVILIZATIONAL PARADIGM QUESTIONED, REFUTED, AND CRITICIZED

So far, as far as this author knows, there is no direct methodological or theoretical debate or dialogue between dominant or critical Western paradigms and nascent non-Western schools, perspectives, or paradigms, comparable to the three great debates, the following inter-paradigm debates, or the great fourth debate. This study has attempted to take charge of this demanding task. It seems valid to conclude that the epistemological debates between opposite epistemes that have been taking place at the levels of the philosophy of science and sociology of knowledge still have not produced comparative studies from different Western and non-Western civilizational circles (i.e., they still have not reflected themselves on the paradigm debates of the discipline of IR).

In general, many international and political studies in Western and non-Western academic circles have dealt with the relationship between Islam and many contemporary global issues and questions, producing, thereby, a plethora of contrasting and opposite views about the influence of Islam and Muslims on the international system after the Cold War and globalization. However, these studies usually do not go beyond the criticism of policies and political positions, even if taking religious and epistemological dimensions into consideration. Missing is still a holistic approach to epistemological diversity in the form of "a contribution to the production of science in the discipline on the grounds of a comparative episteme."[18]

Western critical studies, as highlighted earlier, have generally surveyed the features of non-Western perspectives, including the "Islamic perspective," without conducting any comparisons and without engaging in any epistemological or political dialogue with them. There are many reasons that could possibly explain this condition, including the absence of direct contact in global or regional academic forums and the fact that non-Western academic production is rarely published in English. It is also worth noting that the calls for non-Western contributions to the discipline of international relations were initiated by secular Western critical approaches, not by secular Arab approaches (whether traditional realist or postmodern critical). In fact, the latter have been rather hostile to epistemological plurality due to political or epistemological biases, borne out of a stance against the relationship between Islam and science or between Islam and politics.

Without going into too much detail, this next section emphasises major features of the encounter between the arguments put forward by the Islamic Civilizational Paradigm and that of those who adopt other paradigms in the Department of Political Science at Cairo University.[19] This "encounter" or "engagement," note rather than debate or dialogue, has taken place during many forums and various academic occasions held by the Department of Political Science over two decades (1996-2016) since the inauguration of the works of the Project of International Relations in Islam during an international academic conference at the Faculty of Economics and Political Science.[20] Criticisms of the notion of the Islamization of knowledge, which had been adopted by the International Institute of Islamic Thought since 1981, preceded and accompanied this encounter. Although the Project of International Relations in Islam was originally influenced by this notion, the Egyptian School of the Islamic Civilizational Paradigm has contributed to the criticism and revision of the notion of the Islamization of knowledge throughout three decades,[21] producing, in the process, the concept of the "Islamic Civilizational Paradigm," whose foundations were laid by Mona Abul-Fadl, as has been previously elaborated on.

The features of this encounter or engagement have varied widely, resulting in questions seeking clarification or expressing astonishment;

rejection and refutation; conditional acceptance; a search for credibility; or the activation in research and political analysis.

Graduate students have been the key source of both inquisitive questions as well as questions seeking clarification and elaboration, or expressing astonishment. Throughout the years from 1997 to 2002, answers to the following questions were recorded: What is an Islamic Civilizational Paradigm of International Relations? What is its relevance for the study of the paradigms of international relations theory? Where is it located on the map of IR theories? In a later stage, from 2002 to 2006, students were asked to classify their answers and to think about the reasons that led them and their previous colleagues to give these responses.

Their answers can be summarized as follows:

1. A paradigm is a scientific approach that is not supposed to be biased in favor of an Islamic or a non-Islamic point of view.
2. Western academic production in the field of international relations in general is sufficient to serve the goals of international study. Moreover, this production engages in a continuous process of self-reflection with the purpose of achieving more internal cohesion. Therefore, we can depend on it confidently without the need for adopting a new paradigm.
3. Western scholars do not confine themselves to narrow theoretical frameworks, and they show an obvious degree of flexibility as they exchange their concepts with and borrow them from different intellectual schools, so why should we, instead, limit ourselves to a single secluded paradigm?
4. In contrast to the Islamic Civilizational Paradigm, most Western thought revolves around reality. Shouldn't that characteristic be regarded as one advantage of Western paradigms? Moreover, any paradigm aims to understand reality, and, therefore, the strong connection between Western paradigms and reality should not become a subject of criticism, especially because reality in the Western environment is a reality of strength, upon which a whole academic discipline could be founded, rather than a reality of weakness as is the case with the contemporary Muslim reality.

5. If the Islamic Civilizational Paradigm is not expected to provide except wishful thinking that does not help much in understanding reality, is this the right time for holding onto ideological statements and slogans that are void of any analytical capacity?
6. If the Islamic Paradigm is driven by the goal of crystallizing a civilizational identity with integrated dimensions, then why isn't the question of identity translated into an Arab paradigm of international relations, rather than an Islamic one?
7. Western theorizing was born of a desire to explain reality, and when reality changes, theorizing does too. Therefore, the strength of Western theorizing derives from its being explanatory. By contrast, the Islamic Civilizational Paradigm is proposed now at the time of the civilizational crisis of the Ummah. Can the theorizing drawn from the paradigm serve as a means to get out of this crisis? Does the far-fetched idealistic image that this paradigm is propagating suggest a route to its own application in reality? Or is it limited to specifying the ought-to-be image of reality? Hence, the challenge that faces the Islamic Civilizational Paradigm lies in its ability to explain reality and to be activated for the purpose of changing that reality.
8. The Islamic Civilizational Paradigm as such has existed for fourteen centuries, so what are the conditions and causes that have led to reintroducing it now as if it were something new?
9. Why wasn't the Islamic Civilizational Paradigm of IR introduced to students at earlier stages of education? Why is it introduced to them all of a sudden after four years of undergraduate study?
10. Why is the Islamic Civilizational Paradigm studied in comparison with the Western paradigms of the discipline? Why is the study of the Islamic Paradigm linked to the modern discipline of international relations? Is the West interested in studying the Islamic Civilizational Paradigm as an academic tradition?
11. Compared to already existing Islamic studies that are interested in international interactions and relations, what is the value added of the Islamic Civilizational Paradigm?
12. How can real politics that does not abide by values and ethics be

linked to this paradigm that is based on religious sources with a fundamental normative content?

13. Is interest in motives and justifications intentional and deliberate just to confer legitimacy on the new paradigm within Western academic circles or does the paradigm derive its legitimacy from other sources?
14. What is the meaning of a paradigm, a frame of reference, and episteme? Is jurisprudence the only ground for the Islamic Civilizational Paradigm? What is the Islamic methodology?
15. What are the conditions under which an Islamic Civilizational Paradigm could grow and develop? How can it be accepted and acknowledged regionally and globally? Does the material weakness of the Ummah impede the development of this paradigm and its acceptance within the academic circles of the discipline? Are the efforts of developing the paradigm mere reactions to this weakness of the Ummah and an expression of the need for self-assertion, even if at the intellectual level alone?
16. Proposing an Islamic Civilizational Paradigm paves the way for proposing other religious paradigms; is there a Jewish or Christian paradigm? Is the Islamic Civilizational Paradigm the last among the religious paradigms?
17. When studying international relations, how can the Islamic sources be consulted? Is not this task particularly difficult in the absence of specialization in religious studies, especially that the books of jurisprudence, exegesis, and Sunnah are difficult and ambiguous?
18. Speaking about an Islamic Civilizational Paradigm makes us feel distanced from reality, because it presents an ideal model very distant from reality. Therefore, the paradigm lacks the credibility driven from its being applicable. It is inapplicable because there are no links between contemporary reality and the teachings of religion.
19. How can we speak about a Civilizational Civilizational Paradigm revolving around the external relations of the Muslim Ummah, whereas this Ummah does not exist because Muslims have been experiencing internal wars since the Great Sedition (or *Fitnah*)?

Moreover, are there any Islamic states for us to speak about an Islamic Paradigm of their international relations?

20. Does not interest in introducing an Islamic Civilizational Paradigm imply cutting ties with non-Muslims, rejecting the idea of citizenship, and portraying Christians as non-believers?
21. What is the relationship between the Islamic Civilizational Paradigm and other paradigms of international relations? Is it a relationship of detachment, seclusion, and superiority? Is it, rather, a relationship of mutual critique and comparison so that intellectual fertilization and epistemological communication can take place? Is this latter kind of relationship possible between a religiously rooted paradigm and secular ones?
22. Are there any specific Islamic methods and tools for the study of the international phenomena, or is the Islamic Civilizational Paradigm confined to a frame of reference and rules for viewing the world, not for analyzing or studying it? Will we engage in criticizing Western research methods and methodology, without specifying an Islamic alternative?
23. The Western discipline of international relations analyzes and explains all types of relations among all types of actors, so will the Islamic Paradigm be confined to relations between Muslims and non-Muslims or relations among Muslims alone?
24. How can the Islamic Civilizational Paradigm – or any other paradigm – be acquired? Does it have a cultural character, or is it a learning process with organized foundations?

In addition to these critiques and questions, a few students supported the Islamic Paradigm and expressed enthusiasm about it for different reasons, and in at least three different ways: (1) without being grounded in any organized or academic justifications; (2) based on an understanding of the evidence and justifications driven from prior acquaintance with and adoption of the Islamic frame of reference; or (3) on the basis of a distinction between Islam as a religion and faith and Islam as a cultural and civilizational context or worldview that allows us to speak about an Islamic Paradigm of the International Relations. These categories and answers provide important indicators about the problematics of epistemological and political biases in a way that enables us to locate the opposite biases in these categories. They can be attributed to tensions that students feel in dominant dichotomies and binary oppositions, including, to name but a few, reality/theorization, self/other, materialist/normative, religious/scientific, objectivity/bias, traditional/innovative, power/science, power/problem solving, and Western/global. Moreover, these views and categories can be divided into three general issues: the need for the paradigm (birth), form (content and method), and efficiency and interaction (the paradigm in contemporary reality).

10.3 THE ISLAMIC CIVILIZATIONAL PARADIGM: ACADEMIC REACTIONS

These reactions, coming basically from specialists, are ranged from refutation and rejection of the notion and the project as such to cautiously inquiring about the credibility of the paradigm, its feasibility, and the challenges it should confront. A first set of arguments refuted and rejected the Islamic Civilizational Paradigm. The justifications and evidence of refutation and rejection, which were synchronous with the inauguration of the project, can be summarized as follows:[22]

First, rejecting the replacement of Euro-centrism or Western-centrism by Islamic-centrism. To them, the Islamic Civilizational Paradigm is merely providing a mirror image of the Western paradigm and, hence, it is just re-asserting the traditional dichotomy of the West and Islam. The only difference is that the Islamic Civilizational Paradigm views this dichotomy this time from the position of Muslims, whereas it has already rejected this dichotomy in the literature of Western-centrism.

Second, refusing to acknowledge that the critique of Euro-centrism came from outside the Western academic circle. Here it is emphasized that the methodological and epistemological critique of the foundations of knowledge came from Western scholars themselves, and that Western materialism (i.e., liberalism and Marxism) was subjected to internal self-reflection, in contrast to the dominant Islamic intellectual and mental state that has never undergone such a process of self-reflection.

Third, refusing the implications of the Islamic Civilizational Paradigm's being described as a "religious" paradigm. That confers on the paradigm unwarranted sanctity, correctness, and comprehensiveness in a way that makes it immune against criticism, whereas the scientific pursuit depends on doubt and critique. The paradigm should not be laden with any religious or doctrinal attributes to save the necessary demarcation line between the religious and the political, or the divine and the human.

Fourth, criticizing the distinction between Western research methods and tools of analysis, such as systemic analysis, and the need for explanation and analysis from an Islamic perspective. However, this distinction is based on a symmetrical and projective mental state, where the Islamic researcher uses the accoutrements of Western critique and the developments of non-Islamic knowledge and methods and attributes them to the Islamic Paradigm, even claiming this paradigm to be the root and foundation of this critique.

These statements and criticisms are in fact laden with epistemological biases, maintaining that the "religious" is the opposite of the "scientific," and that research tools and methods have universal applicability. Besides, they reject the notion that Islam can produce knowledge and science because they view it as a mere religion.

As for the second set of arguments, either reflecting a supportive position or expressing reservations, they can be summarized as follows.[23] First, the field of Islamic Studies does not look the same in different social sciences in Egyptian universities. Islamic Studies have made a remarkable contribution to the disciplines of law, history, and philosophy, where schools and generations of researchers for at least a quarter of a century have been highlighting the contribution of Muslim thinkers to these fields as a part of human history in different fields. As for sociology, this epistemological communication did not take place; there are only some readings of Ibn Khaldūn's theoretical contributions. In less fortunate disciplines, such as political science and economics, there are only disparate individual efforts that cannot be compared to the contributions of Islamic Studies to law, history, philosophy, or even sociology. Therefore, academics interested in examining political and economic phenomena in Egypt and the Arab world should bear the responsibility to address this shortage.

Second, social sciences, especially political science and economics, are influenced by the civilizational, cultural, social, and ethical climate in their countries. These sciences are determined culturally, civilizationally, and socially, and when we consider the origins of some major ideas, we discover that they are connected with specific cultural, historical, and civilizational contexts. In other words, we should not shy away from exploring Islamic sources or contributions of Muslim thinkers in order to uncover their contributions to the fields of political science and economics.

Third, in order for this endeavor to remain academic and objective, it should be characterized by some attributes. It should detach itself from specific political developments, as it should be an ongoing pursuit, irrespective of emergent political events that may, or may not, serve this kind of academic activity. This endeavor should be characterized by continuity, because what we do not know about the Islamic contribution to the fields of political science and economics far outweighs what we know about it. The mission should involve covering, documenting, examining, analyzing, and studying the different manuscripts and sources. If researchers undertake such a study with apologetic attitudes or with preconceptions about the superiority of Islamic contributions, their work will neither be scientific nor useful for an objective and academic understanding of our history and thought. The claim that the contributions of Muslim thinkers are inherently superior to the contributions of other thinkers, from India, China, Europe, or the United States, cannot be grounded. Muslims are humans, and the eternal divine laws governing all human nature are applicable to Muslims and non-Muslims as well. Muslims have their particularity as much as others have their particularities, that end up all contributing to the history and development of humankind. The real value added of this endeavor is not to prove that Muslims have been an exception in history, but rather that Muslims have contributed thought, theory, and findings that served humanity and have contributed to the civilizational development of humankind; that they have been one rich and fertile subsidiary of humanity. What is good for Muslim communities can be good for other communities because it has some human and universal aspects that address humankind across time and space.

A third set of arguments and positions has crystallized during the scientific conferences and seminars that have been held by the Department of Political Science over the past two decades. Here, supporting, though challenging, positions raise questions of the credibility and the competitiveness of this paradigm at many levels. First, is there any Islamic theory of international relations? What are its research methods and tools? How does the renewed interest in values and culture justify proposing the Islamic Paradigm? What are the contributions of this paradigm?[24] Second, there are efforts to develop an Islamic Civilizational Paradigm, but they are neither visible nor sufficient, and they require the efforts of whole institutions, not merely those of one research group.[25] Third, the development of the Islamic Civilizational Paradigm of International Relations at the Faculty of Economics and Political Science is one of the most important theoretical innovations of the Faculty, although this paradigm is primarily normative and does not address contemporary world problems, especially those of the Islamic World.[26] Fourth, many important questions raised epistemological and theoretical concerns, drawing attention to the problematic relationship between Islamic Studies and political science in general and international relations in particular, and to the implications of the comparative teaching of political science courses.[27] Finally, a few professors of international relations, especially Bahgat Korany, have approached the Islamic Civilizational Paradigm of International Relations with reference to the rising critical approaches in the discipline of international relations.

Bahgat Korany argues that the Egyptian School of an Islamic Civilizational Paradigm engages and interacts with the recent developments in the discipline and the ongoing criticism that has led to a renewed interest in the normative, religious, and cultural dimensions as a part of the criticism directed at positivism. His opinion highlights the importance of the epistemological dimensions as the primary foundations of the discipline, followed by theory and method, and he argues that our understanding of the relationship between reality and theorizing should not be confined to the empiricists' understanding, where reality precedes theorizing, because in fact researchers never approach any research domain without some sort of prior theorizing.[28]

He raises a twofold question: What can Islam possibly contribute to science? How can it engage in a debate with the theory of international relations? He argues that Islam, which focuses on the Ummah as a level of analysis, and on values, provides an alternative contribution to the positivist realist contribution, which confines itself to the nation-state and empiricism.

However, Bahgat Korany's view sets some conditions for an Islamic Paradigm to be able to contribute to the theory of international relations and become an integral part of the discipline. He thinks these conditions are already fulfilled by the Egyptian School's Islamic Paradigm: First, the Islamic cultural religious approach should not proceed in isolation from what is taking place in the discipline, rather, it should interact with the theories of the discipline, departing, therein, from a deep critical knowledge of the state of the discipline and of what has already been accomplished by others. Second, that approach should pay special attention to the unit and level of analysis, especially what the level of the Ummah can contribute to the field of IR in comparison to the prevailing levels of analysis. Third, that approach should focus on the concepts related to the management of the relationship between Muslims and the world, such as the credibility of concepts like "the abode of war," "the abode of peace," "the abode of treaty," "the abode of jihad," and "the abode of neutrality," in comparison to concepts such as transnationalism and global systems.

Bahgat Korany argues that the interest in an Islamic civilizational paradigm generally falls within the scope of the interests of critical theories, which direct criticism at the realist, positivist American school of IR and refuse to acknowledge its universality. Korany highlights that the Islamic Civilizational Paradigm moves beyond the fragmentation of the field, as it engages with literature from different strands of international relations theory. Moreover, the paradigm transcends the debate between international relations theory and history, on the one hand, and values, on the other. He describes the paradigm as a critical and scientific effort that convinces the researcher to reconsider their intellectual perspectives. The paradigm, according to him, does not sanctify its own intellectual construct, but rather highlights the diversity and plurality of opinions and reasonings. The discipline of international relations is, therefore, in need of this project in its pursuit of diversity and globalization.[29] Bahgat Korany also reflects on the questions of engagement with other approaches, the units of analysis, and research agenda as challenges that confront the project of the Islamic Civilizational Paradigm of International Relations[30] and how it can survive by developing a research program that can guarantee and support its continuity.[31]

It is worth noting that throughout two decades the Islamic Paradigm has been put on academic "trial," rather than debated or subjected to epistemological or theoretical academic discussion in a manner known to Western academic circles, between dominant and emerging paradigms or theories. Different sets of arguments, raising various concerns and questions, have been predominantly dealing with the paradigm as a deviation from the norms of science, as if the "dominant secular Western discourse" was the only discourse allowed to set the definition of science.

The aforementioned stances and positions, which continued to exist throughout the last decade, still interrogate and question the very notion and conception of an Islamic Paradigm, instead of discussing or engaging with the outcomes of the processes of construction and activation that ensued the inauguration of the Project of International Relations in Islam in 1997, although many of the paradigm's assumptions have been elaborated on over more than two decades and at more than one level.

Few scholars, like Bahgat Korany, have managed to approach the map of the Islamic Civilizational Paradigm and fit it into the map of the critical theoretical approaches in the discipline. These scholars called attention to the challenges that face the paradigm such as the absence of direct contact or interaction with corresponding academic circles abroad, the construction of comparative concepts, and the drawing of a map of research agenda. These challenges remind us of the positivists' critiques of Western critical approaches (as has been previously discussed).

The Islamic Paradigm has regularly engaged with Western theoretical production and addressed its different criticisms, whether through direct, published or unpublished dialogue. Meanwhile, teaching graduate students about an Islamic Civilizational Paradigm has paid almost equal attention to introducing the foundations, criticisms, and the substance of the paradigm.[32]

NOTES

1. See: Nadia M. Mostafa, "Al-Dawāfiʿ, al-Ahdāf, al-Munṭaliqāt" [Motives, Goals, and Precepts], in *Al-Muqadimmah al-ʿĀmah li Mashrūʿ al-ʿAlāqāt al-Dawliyyah fī al-Islām* [The General Introduction to the Project of International Relations in Islam], ed. Nadia M. Mostafa (Cairo: International Institute of Islamic Thought, 1996), pp. 54-64; Nadia M. Mostafa, "Ishkāliyyāt al-Baḥth wa al-Tadrīs fī ʿIlm al-ʿAlaqāt al-Dawliyyah min Manẓūr Ḥaḍārī Muqāran" [Problematics of Research and Teaching International Relations from a Comparative Civilizational Paradigm], pp. 833-840.
2. Caroline Thomas and Peter Wilkin, "Still Waiting after all These Years: The Third World on the Periphery of International Relations," *Political Studies Association* 6, no. 2 (May 2004): pp. 241-258.
3. See: Bahgat Korany and Ali el Din Hilal Dessouki, eds., *The Foreign Policies of Arab States*, Trans. Jabir Saeed Awad, 2nd ed. (Cairo University: Center of Political Research and Studies at the Faculty of Economics and Political Science, 2002); Nasr Arif, *Naẓriyyāt al-Siyāsah al-Maqāranah wa Minhājiyyat Dirāsat al-Naẓm al-Siyāsiyyah al-ʿArabiyyah: Maqārabah Ibstimūlūjiyyah* [Theories of Comparative Politics and the Methodology of Studying Arab Political Systems: An Epistemological Comparison] (Virginia: School of Islamic and Social Sciences, 1998); Pakinam al-Sharqawi, "Itijāhāt Ḥadīthah fī Dirāsat al-Naẓm al-Maqāranah bi al-Tarkīz ʿalā al-Janūb" [Modern Approaches to the Study of Comparative Systems, With a Focus on the South], in *ʿIlm al-Siyāsah: Murājaʿāt Naẓriyyah wa Manhājiyyah* [Political Science: Theoretical and Methodological Revisions] ed. Nadia M. Mostafa, pp. 193-348.
4. On a comparison of with contributions with other contributions, see: Nadia M. Mostafa, "Mādhā Yuqadim al-Islām li al-ʿĀlam al-Ḥadīth" [What Can Islam Present to the Modern World], a paper delivered at the conference of "Al-Islām wa Al-ʿAlmāniyyah wa Al-Ḥadāthah" [Islam,

Secularism, and Modernity] organized by Al-Ahram Center of Strategic and Political Studies in collaboration with Abant Platform (Turkey) (Cairo: Al-Ahram Center of Strategic and Political Studies, 2007).

5. Hamed Rabie, *Al-Islām wa al-Quwā al-Dawliyyah: Naḥū Thawrah al-Qarn al-Ḥādī wa al-ʿIshrīn* [Islam and International Powers: Towards the Revolution of the 21st Century] (Cairo: Dār al-Mawqif al-ʿArabī, 1981).
6. Mona Abul-Fadl, "Islamization as a Force of Global Renewal."
7. Ahmet Davutoğlu, *Civilizational Transformation and the Muslim World* (Kuala Lumpur: Mahir Publications, 1994).
8. Bassam Tibi, *The Challenge of Fundamentalism, Political Islam and the New World Order* (Berkeley: University of California Press, 1998).
9. Bahgat Korany in unpublished forum on discussing the first issue of *Majalet Ḥawliyyat Ummatī fī al-ʿĀlam* [Journal of My Nation around the World] Hadara Center for Political Studies in collaboration with the Center of Political Research and Studies, Cairo University, Faculty of Economics and Political Science, May 1999.
10. For instance, see: Nadia M. Mostafa, "Ūlā Ḥurūb al-Qarn al-Ḥādī wa al-ʿIshrīn wa Waḍʿ al-Ummah al-Islāmiyyah: Ṣuʿūd al-Taḥadiyyāt al-Ḥaḍāriyyah al-Thaqāfiyyah wa Shurūṭ Istimrār Ḥiwār al-Ḥaḍārāt" [The First War of the Twenty-First Century and the Position of the Islamic Nation: The Rise of Civilizational and Cultural Challenges and the Conditions of Continuing the Dialogue of Civilizations], in *Aʿmāl Mu'tamar: Kayfa Tawāṣul Ḥiwār al-Ḥaḍārāt* [Proceeding of the Conference on How to Continue the Dialogue of Civilizations] (Damascus: Center of Arab-Iranian Relations, 2002); Akbar Ahmed, "Ibn Khaldūn's Understanding of Civilizations and the Dilemmas of Islam and the West Today," *Middle East Journal* 56, no. 1 (January 2002); Shireen T. Hunter, *The Future of Islam and the West: Clash of Civilizations or Peaceful Coexistence?* (Westport: Praeger, 1998); Fawaz Gerges, *America and Political Islam: Clash of Cultures or Clash of Interests* (Cambridge, UK: Cambridge University Press, 1999).
11. Bahgat Korany, "Taʿqīb ʿalā Baḥth ʿAbd al-Khabīr ʿAṭā ʿan al-Buʿd al-Dīnī fī Dirāsat al-ʿAlāqāt al-Dawliyyah" [Comment on Abdelkhabir Atta's Paper on the Religious Dimension of the Study of International Relations], in *Madākhil al-Taḥlīl al-Thaqāfī lī Dirāsat al-Ẓawāhir al-Siyāsiyyah wa al-Ijtimāʿiyyah: al-Munṭaliqāt wa al-Mafāhīm fī al-ʿUlūm*

al-Ijtimāʿiyyah wa al-Siyāsiyyah [The Cultural Analysis Approach to the Study of Political and Social Phenomena: Origins, Fields, and Concepts in Social and Political Sciences], eds. Nadia M. Mostafa and Amira Abou Samra, pp. 239-244.

12. For instance, see: Richard Falk, "False Universalism and the Geopolitics of Exclusion: The Case of Islam"; Ralph Pettman, *Reasons, Culture, Religion: the Metaphysics of World Politics*; Jonathon W. Moses, "The Umma of Democracy"; Giorgio Shani, "Provincializing Critical Theory: Islam, Sikhism and International Relations Theory."
13. Nadia M. Mostafa, Al-ʿAlāqāt al-Dawliyyah fī al-Fikr al-Islāmī" [International Relations in Islamic Thought], in *Al-Manẓūr al-Baynī wa al-ʿAlāqāt al-Bayniyyah fi al-ʿUlūm al-Siyāsiyyah: Iʿādat Naẓr wa Qirā'ah Jadīdah* [Interdisciplinary Perspective and Interdisciplinary Relationships in Political Science: Re-View and a New Reading], Omaima Abboud ed., pp. 105-109.
14. For a list of the studies on the Islamic paradigm's activation of these questions and issues from a comparative perspective, see: Nadia M. Mostafa, "Muqadimah Taḥrīriyyah: al-ʿAlaqāt al-Dawliyyah fī al-Islām" [Editorial Introduction: International Relations in Islam], a special issue of *Majalet al-Muslim al-Muʿāṣir* [Journal of the Contemporary Muslim], no. 137-138 (October 2010); also see: Nadia M. Mostafa and Saif AbdelFattah, *Fī Tajdīd al-ʿUlūm al-Ijtimāʿiyyah: Binā' Manẓūr Maʿrifī Ḥaḍārī (Al-Khibrah wa al-Fikrah)* [On Renewing the Social Sciences: Constructing a Civilizational Epistemological Paradigm (Idea and Experience)], pp. 521-632.
15. Nadia M. Mostafa, "Al-ʿAlāqāt al-Dawliyyah fī al-Islām: Naḥū Ta'ṣīl min Manẓūr al-Fiqh al-Ḥaḍārī" [International Relations in Islam: Towards a Rooting from the Perspective of Civilizational Jurisprudence], pp. 172-175.
16. Nadia M. Mostafa, *Al-ʿAdālah wa al-Dīmuqrāṭiyyah* [Justice and Democracy], pp. 271-298.
17. Here lies the importance of such comprehensive and evaluative scientific projects as the project of "Al-Abʿād al-Islāmiyyah fī al-Rasā'il al-ʿIlmiyyah" [Islamic Dimensions in Academic Theses and Dissertations]. The map of topics tackled in these theses and dissertations, in the fields of thought, theory, regimes, or international relations, shows that rooting, comparative contemporary and historical experiences, and the

development of intellectual approaches are necessary givens for uncovering the intentional negative confusion of the relationship between Islam and politics domestically and abroad. See: Horeyya Mujahed, ed., *Taḥlīl al-Abʿād al-Islāmiyyah fī al-Rasā'il al-ʿIlmiyyah* [Analysis of Islamic Dimensions in Academic Theses and Dissertations] (Cairo: Cairo University and UNESCO, 2016).

18. See for example: Nadia M. Mostafa, *Al-ʿAdālah wa al-Dīmuqrāṭiyyah* [Justice and Democracy], pp. 127-181.
19. On other fields of contact outside the department and with foreign scientific circles, see: Nadia M. Mostafa's comment on Abdullahi An-Na'im's "Religion and Global Civil Society" (a study prepared for publication in the Arabic version of the 2002 report of global civil society as a critique of, and comment on, the English version of the report and its studies). Available at: Abdullahi An-Na'im, "Religion and Global Civil Society: Inherent Incompatibility or Synergy and Interdependence?" in *Global Civil Society Report*, eds., G. Marlies, M. Kaldor and H. Anheier (Oxford: Oxford University, 2002), pp. 55-74; Nadia M. Mostafa, "The Missing Logic in the Discourse of Peace and Violence in Islam," pp. 173-189; Nadia M. Mostafa, "Beyond Western Paradigms of International Relations: Towards an Islamic Perspective on Global Democracy," a paper presented to the International Workshop on "Building Global Democracy," held in Cairo, December 6-8, 2009, available at: ; See Nadia M. Mostafa's comment in the international conference on "Are Islam and Democracy Compatible?" organized by American Studies Center at the American University in Cairo in November 2007. Available at: See the consultative forum on "Democracy in the Arab World" organized by the Secretariat of the Arab League in collaboration with the Swedish IDEA organization in April 2009. It preceded Sweden's chairmanship of European Union in June 2009. See the website of this Swedish organization: ; Louay M. Safi, "The Intellectual Challenge Facing Contemporary Islamic Scholarship," *American Journal of Islamic Social Sciences (AJISS)* 19, no. 2 (Spring 2002); Louay M. Safi, "Overcoming the Cultural Divide," *American Journal of Islamic Social Sciences (AJISS)* 19, no. 1 (Winter 2002); Louay M. Safi, "Muslim Renaissance: Challenges in the Twenty-First Century," *American Journal of Islamic Social Sciences (AJISS)* 20, no. 1 (Winter 2003); Heba Raouf Ezzat, "Glocalized Democracy and the Challenge of

Comprehensive Security," December 29, 2005, available at: ; Heba Raouf Ezzat and Mary Kaldor, "Not Even a Tree: Delegitimizing Violence and the Prospects for Pre-emptive Civility," in *Global Civil Society Yearbook*, eds., G. Marlies, M. Kaldor and H. Anheier (London: Sage, 2007), pp. 18-38.

20. See the proceedings of the forum in Nadia M. Mostafa and Saif AbdelFattah, eds., *Mashrūʿ al-ʿAlaqāt al-Dawliyyah fī al-Islām: Bayn al-Uṣūl al-Islāmiyyah wa Khibrat al-Tārīkh al-Islāmī* [The Project of International Relations in Islam: Between Islamic Fundamentals and Historic Experience].

21. On a survey and analysis of these critiques and an evaluation of the Islamization of Knowledge Project, see the following studies in the proceedings of the research project "Taqwīm Islāmiyyah al-Maʿrifah baʿd Rubuʿ Qarn" [Evaluation of the Islamization of Knowledge after a Quarter of a Century]: Samer Rashwan, "Qirā'ah fī Dirāsāt Naqdiyyah li Khiṭāb Islāmiyyah al-Maʿrifah: Madkhal Ibstimūlūjiyyah" [A Reading of Critical Studies of Islamization of Knowledge Discourse: An Epistemological Approach], in *Fī Tajdīd al-ʿUlūm al-Ijtimāʿiyyah: Binā' Manẓūr Maʿrifī Ḥaḍārī (Al-Khibrah wa al-Fikrah)* [On Renewing the Social Sciences: Constructing a Civilizational Epistemological Paradigm (Idea and Experience)], Nadia M. Mostafa and Saif AbdelFattah, pp. 147-182; Amani Saleh, "Qirā'ah fī Mafhūm Islāmiyyah al-Maʿrifah Dākhil al-Tayyār al-Asāsī li al-Maʿhad" [A Reading of the Concept of Islamization of Knowledge in the Mainstream of the Institute], in *Fī Tajdīd al-ʿUlūm al-Ijtimāʿiyyah: Binā' Manẓūr Maʿrifī Ḥaḍārī (Al-Khibrah wa al-Fikrah)* [On Renewing the Social Sciences: Constructing a Civilizational Epistemological Paradigm (Idea and Experience)], pp. 95-146; Nadia M. Mostafa, "Minhājiyyah Islāmiyyah al-Maʿrifah: Min al-Manẓūr wa al-Ta'ṣīl al-ʿĀm ilā Khibrat al-Taṭbiqāt" [Methodology of the Islamization of Knowledge: From the Paradigm and General Rooting to Applied Experience], in *Fī Tajdīd al-ʿUlūm al-Ijtimāʿiyyah: Binā' Manẓūr Maʿrifī Ḥaḍārī (Al-Khibrah wa al-Fikrah)* [On Renewing the Social Sciences: Constructing a Civilizational Epistemological Paradigm (Idea and Experience)], pp. 185-416; Also see: Mona Abaza, *Debates on Islam and Knowledge in Malaysia and Egypt: Shifting Worlds* (London: Routledge Curzon, 2002).

22. For instance, the vision of Wajih Kawtharani, which he delivered in the conference on the works of the project of international relations, in his comment on the seventh part of the project. He later published it in: Wajih Kawtharani, *Al-Dhākirah wa al-Tārīkh fī al-Qarn al-ʿIshrīn al-Ṭawīl* [Memory and History in the Twentieth Century] (Beirut: Dār al-Ṭalīʿah, 2000), in chapter eight, "Fī al-Baḥth ʿan Khibrat al-Tārīkh al-Islāmī li Dirāsat al-ʿAlāqāt al-Dawliyyah: Naqd li al-Manhaj al-Islāmī aw al-Manẓūr al-Islāmī" [Search for the Experience of Islamic History in Studying International Relations: A Critique of the Islamic Method or Paradigm].
23. On these arguments, see: Nadia M. Mostafa and Saif AbdelFattah, eds., *Mashrūʿ al-ʿAlaqāt al-Dawliyyah fī al-Islām: Bayn al-Uṣūl al-Islāmiy-yah wa Khibrat al-Tārīkh al-Islāmī* [The Project of International Relations in Islam: Between Islamic Fundamentals and Historic Experience], 1:17-19. The same conservative view is still based on non-superiority, non-closure, non-politicization. This was elucidated by the pivotal comment of Ali al-Din Hilal in a session of the monthly scientific seminar of the Department of Political Science (May 2015) where Amira Abou Samra surveyed her achievement in her doctoral dissertation. Bahgat Korany gave the final comment (unpublished).
24. For instance, see the comments of Kamal Almonoufi and Mostafa Kamel Alsayed in *ʿIlm al-Siyāsah: Murājaʿāt Naẓriyyah wa Manhājiyyah* [Political Science: Theoretical and Methodological Revisions], pp. 440-446; also see the comments of Kamal Almonoufi on Abdel-Khabeer Atta's paper in *Madākhil al-Taḥlīl al-Thaqāfī lī Dirāsat al-Ẓawāhir al-Siyāsiyyah wa al-Ijtimāʿiyyah* [The Cultural Analysis Approach to the Study of Political and Social Phenomena], eds. Nadia M. Mostafa and Amira Abou Samra, pp. 250-251.
25. For instance, see: Mostafa Elwi, "Al-Ḥarb ʿalā al-ʿIrāq wa Azmat al-Tanẓīr fī al-ʿAlaqāt al-Dawliyyah" [The War on Iraq and the Crisis of Theorizing in International Relations], pp. 316-329.
26. Muhammad al-Sayyid Salim, "Ishāmāt Kuliyyat al-Iqtiṣād wa al-ʿUlūm al-Siyāsiyyah fī Ta'ṣīl ʿIlm al-ʿAlāqāt al-Dawliyyah" [Contributions of the Faculty of Economics and Political Science to Rooting the Discipline of International Relations].
27. See the comments of Ahmad Alrasheedi, Muhammad Hussain, Abdelghaffar Rashad, Ibrahim Shalabi, Mostafa Manjoud, Horeyya

Mugahed, Mostafa Kamel Alsayed, Muhammad Shawki, Hassan Nafi'ah, and Nadia M. Mostafa on Abdel Khabeer Ata's paper in: *Namādhhij ʿĀlamiyah fī Tadrīs al-ʿUlūm al-Siyāsiyyah: Aʿmāl al-Mu'tamar al-ʿIlmī li Qism al-ʿUlūm al-Siyāsiyyah* [Global Models of Teaching Political Science: Proceedings of the Scientific Conference of the Department of Political Science], ed. Mostafa Manjoud (Cairo: Cairo University Faculty of Economics and Political Science, 2002), pp. 208-239.

28. See his comment on Abdel Khabeer Ata's paper in *Madākhil al-Taḥlīl al-Thaqāfī lī Dirāsat al-Ẓawāhir al-Siyāsiyyah wa al-Ijtimāʿiyyah* [The Cultural Analysis Approach to the Study of Political and Social Phenomena], eds. Nadia M. Mostafa and Amira Abou Samra, pp. 239-244.

29. See his speech in the ceremony of the achievements of Professor Nadia M. Mostafa on April 13, 2013, at the Faculty of Economics and Political Science, Cairo University "Lifetime Achievement Award" of 2012. The Association of Muslim Social Scientists (UK) gives this award to scholars in recognition of their contributions to their fields of study in terms of social homogeneity, dialogue of religions, and Islamic thought. This speech is available via the following link: https://www.hadaracenter.com/index.php?option=com_content&view=article&id=1500.

30. Unpublished comment on Amira Abou Samra's review of the problematics of her doctoral dissertation in the scientific seminar of the Department of Political Science, at the Faculty of Economics and Political Science, Cairo University, in May 2015.

31. See Ayat Mohamed, *The Sacred Cow and the New Comer: A Comparative Study of Nation State and Umma* (master's thesis, American University of Cairo, 2014).

32. See the proceedings of the scientific seminars and conferences of the Department of Political Science: *Aʿmāl Mu'tamar al-Namādhij al-ʿĀlamiyyah li Tadrīs al-ʿUlūm al-Siyāsiyyah* [Proceedings of the Conference on Global Models of Teaching Political Science]; *ʿIlm al-Siyāsiyyah: Murājiʿāt Naẓriyyah wa Minhājiyyah* [Political Science: Theoretical and Methodological Critiques]; *Madākhil al-Taḥlīl al-Thaqāfī* [Cultural Analysis Approaches]; and *Al-Bayniyyah fī al-ʿUlūm al-Siyāsiyyah* [Interdisciplinarity in Political Science].

CONCLUSION

To conclude this extensive and interrelated study, I assert that science is an ongoing process that does not have finite borders or limits. Scientific schools cannot be perceived as secluded islands, whether in the West or the East. Regardless of how diverse the civilizational circles might be, they must meet in a certain locus, as Mona Abul-Fadl asserts in her early study *Where East Meets West.*[1] Critical revisions of schools and paradigms from within their circles, from the heart of their centers, as well as from outside, constitute a scientific, epistemological, and even human necessity, especially when these schools and paradigms transcend their domains and extend to those of their counterparts through methodological, theoretical, and epistemological dialogue.[2] The importance of this revision rises especially in the aftermath of periods in which a paradigm dominates the academic scene, raising claims of universality.

Despite the difficulties facing epistemological, theoretical, and methodological dialogue between Western and non-Western paradigms,[3] and those facing non-Western paradigms when introducing themselves to global circles and even to their own civilizational circles, the world still searches for new creative and innovative perspectives that can effect global change for the sake of a freer, more just and more humane world.

The Islamic Paradigm is not a utopian endeavor or an academic luxury, but a normative realist perspective maintaining that there is no reality without values, no right without might, no power without ethics, no science without action, and no thought without change. This perspective rejects conflictual dichotomies and believes in the impossibility of separating the components of binaries such as the religious/the political, the normative/the material, etc., since this perspective is based on political and epistemological integration and multiplicity.

The course of the development of the discipline of international relations, as well as the course of the development of international relations for about a century, has produced a variety of comparative civilizational theoretical perspectives and paradigms. Yet, the following questions still need to be addressed: What is the next step after the crystallization of these perspectives and conceptions? What about the programs, plans, and tools that can translate these ideas into action for the sake of reforming the world? This study has drawn attention to the importance of theoretical diversity, multiplicity, and accumulation as a way to address the problems of our contemporary world.

Praise be to Allah, the Lord of all worlds.

NOTES

1. Mona Abul-Fadl, *Where East Meets West.*
2. This was, for instance, presented in the conference on "Dialogue of Civilizations and the Various Paths of Knowledge" (February 2007) under the coordination of Abdelwahab Elmessiri, Cairo University: Program of Civilizational Studies and the Dialogue of Cultures at the Faculty of Economics and Political Science. Some of its proceedings were published in *Fiqh al-Taḥayuz: Ru'yah Maʿrifiyyah wa Daʿwah li al-Ijtihād* [Fiqh of Bias: An Epistemological Perspective and a Call for Ijtihād].
3. Nadia M. Mostafa, *Al-ʿAdālah wa al-Dīmuqrāṭiyyah* [Justice and Democracy], pp. 260-269.

BIBLIOGRAPHY

Abaza, Mona. *Debates on Islam and Knowledge in Malaysia and Egypt: Shifting Worlds*. London: Routledge Curzon, 2002.

Abboud, Omaima, ed. *Al-Manẓūr al-Baynī wa al-ʿAlāqāt al-Bayniyyah fi al-ʿUlūm al-Siyāsiyyah: Iʿādat Naẓr wa Qirā'ah Jadīdah* [Interdisciplinary Perspective and Interdisciplinary Relationships in Political Science: Re-View and a New Reading]. Cairo: Cairo University Faculty of Economics and Political Science, 2012.

Abd al-Majid, Hamid. *Al-Waẓīfah al-ʿAqīdiyyah li al-Dawlah al-Islāmiyyah* [The Religious Function of Islamic State]. Cairo: Dār Al-Tawzīʿ Al-Islāmiyyah, 1993.

AbdelFattah, Saif. "Al-ʿAwlamah wa al-Islām Ru'yatān li al-ʿĀlam: Qirā'ah Maʿrifiyyah wa Manhajiyyah" [Globalization and Islam as Worldviews: An Epistemological and Methodological Reading]. *Majalet al-Ḥikmah* 11, no. 42 (2004).

—. "Binā' ʿIlm Siyāsah Islāmī" [Constructing an Islamic Political Science]. In *Silsilat Buḥūth Siyāsiyyah* [Political Research Series]. Cairo University: Centre for Political Research and Studies, 1988.

—. *Dawrat al-Manhājiyyah al-Islāmiyyah fī al-ʿUlūm al-Ijtimāʿiyyah: Ḥaql al-ʿUlūm al-Siyāsiyyah Namūdhajan* [The Role of Islamic Methodology in Social Sciences: The Case of Political Science]. Cairo: Hadara Center for Political Studies and International Institute of Islamic Thought, 2002.

—. "Ishkāliyyāt wa Maqārabāt fī Mafhūm al-Ḥaḍārī, al-ʿUdwān wa al-Maqāwamah al-Ḥaḍāriyyah fī Ḥarb Lubnān: Al-Dalālāt wa al-Mālāt" [Problematics and Approaches in the Concepts of the Civilizational, Transgression, and Civilizational Resistance in the Lebanese War: Implications and Consequences]. In *Al-ʿUdwān wa al-Muqāwamah al-Ḥaḍāriah fī Ḥarb Lubnān: al-Dalālāt wa al-Mālāt* [Transgression and the Civilizational Resistance in the Lebanese War: Implications and Consequences], edited by Nadia M. Mostafa, Saif AbdelFattah, Amani Ghanim and Medhat Maher, pp. 239-249. Cairo: Cairo University Program of Civilizational Studies and Dialogue of Cultures at the Faculty of Economics and Political Science, 2007.

—. *Madkhal al-Qiyam Iṭār Marjaʿī li Dirāsat al-ʿAlaqāt al-Dawliyyah fī al-Islām* [Introduction to Values: A Referential Framework for the Study of International Relations in Islam]. Vol. 2. Cairo: International Institute of Islamic Thought, 1996.

—. "Al-Muqadimmah al-Taḥrīriyyah" [Editorial Introduction]. *Ḥawliyyat Ummatī fī al-ʿĀlam* [Journal of My Nation in the World], no. 6 (Cairo: Hadara Center for Political Studies, 2006): pp. 7-40.

—. "Qiyam al-Wāqiʿ wa Wāqiʿ al-Qiyam: Mā al-Maʿnā al-ʿIlmī li al-Qiyam?" [The Norms of Reality, the Reality of Norms: What is the Scientific Meaning of Norms?]. In *Al-Qiyam fī al-Ẓāhirah al-Ijtimāʿiyyah* [Norms in the Social Phenomenon], edited by Nadia Mahmoud Mostafa et al., pp. 43-65. Cairo: Cairo University Center for Civilizational Studies and Dialogue of Cultures and Hadara Center for Political Studies, 2012.

—. "Turāth al-ʿAlāqāt al-Dawliyyah fī al-Islām" [Heritage of International Relations in Islam]. In *Nadwat Turāth al-ʿArab* [Arabs' Political Heritage], edited Faisal Alhafyan. Cairo: Institute of Arabic Manuscripts, 2002.

—. "Al-Ummah al-Islāmiyyah wa ʿAwāqib al-Dawlah al-Qawmiyyah" [The Islamic Nation and the Consequences of the National State]. *Majalet Ḥawliyyat Ummatī fī al-ʿĀlam* [Journal of My Nation around the World]. Cairo: Hadara Center for Political Studies, 2000.

AbdelFattah, Saif and Medhat Maher, eds. *Muʿjam Mafāhīm al-Wasaṭiyyah: Namūdhaj li Binā' al-Mafāhīm al-Asāsiyyah min Manẓūr Ḥaḍārī* [Dictionary of Moderation Concepts: A Model of Building Key Concepts from a Civilizational Perspective]. Cairo: Hadara Center for Political Studies; Sudan: Forum of Revival and Civilizational Communication, 2008-2009.

Abdelmajeed, Waheed. "Azmat al-Niẓām al-ʿĀlamī wa Aghrab Ḥurūb al-Tārīkh: Iftitāḥiyyah al-ʿAdad" [The Crisis of World Order and the Strangest Wars in History: Editorial Introduction]. *Majalat al-Siyāsiyyah al-Dawliyyah* [Journal of International Politics], no. 199 (January 2015).

—. "Dawr al-Quwah al-Dawliyyah al-Kubrā fī Tanāmī al-Irhāb: Iftitāḥiyyah al-ʿAdad" [The Role of International Great Powers in the Growth of Terrorism: Editorial Introduction]. *Majalat al-Siyāsiyyah al-Dawliyyah* [Journal of International Politics], no. 203 (January 2016).

—. "Mādhā Yabqā min Qawāʿid al-Niẓām al-ʿĀlamī: al-Iftitāḥiyyah al-ʿAdad" [What Remains out of the Rules of World Order: Editorial Introduction]. *Majalat al-Siyāsiyyah al-Dawliyyah* [Journal of International Politics], no. 198 (October 2014).

—. "Naḥū Tafsīr Jadīd li al-Taghiyīr fī al-ʿĀlam: Iftitāḥiyyah al-ʿAdad" [Towards a New Explanation of Change in the World: Editorial Introduction], *Majalat al-Siyāsiyyah al-Dawliyyah* [Journal of International Politics], no. 200 (April 2015).

—. "Tawāzun al-Ḍuʿf fī al-Niẓām al-ʿĀlamī: Iftitāḥiyyah al-ʿAdad" [Balance of Weakness in World Order: Editorial Introduction]. *Majalat al-Siyāsiyyah al-Dawliyyah* [Journal of International Politics], no. 201 (July 2015).

Abdel-Sabour, Samah. "Smart Power in Foreign Policy: Theory and Practice." In *Al-ʿAlāqāt al-Dawliyyah fī ʿĀlim Mutaghayyir: Manẓūrāt wa Madākhil Muqāranah* [International Relations in a Changing World: Comparative Paradigms and Approaches], edited by Nadia Mostafa, pp. 264-331. Cairo: Hadara Center for Political Studies, 2016.

Abdelsalam, Jaafar. *Qawāʿid al-ʿAlāqāt al-Dawliyyah fī al-Qanūn al-Dawlī wa fī al-Sharīʿah al-Islāmiyyah* [Rules of International Relations in International Law and the Shariʿah]. Cairo: Maktabat al-Salām al-Dawliyyah, 1981.

Abdelshafi, Essam. *Al-Siyāsah al-Amrīkiyyah Tujāha al-Mamlakah al-ʿArabiyyah al-Saʿūdiyyah: Dirāsah fī Ta'thīr al-Buʿd al-Dīnī* [American Politics Toward the Kingdom of Saudi Arabia: A Study of the Effect of the Religious Dimension 2000-2005]. PhD diss., Cairo University, 2009.

Abdelwanees, Ahmad. "Al-Asās al-Sharʿī wa al-Mabādi' al-Ḥākimah li al-ʿAlāqāt al-Khārijiyyah li al-Dawlah al-Islāmiyyah" [The Religiously Legal Foundation and the Principles Governing Foreign Relations of the Islamic State]. In *Mashrūʿ al-ʿAlaqāt al-Dawliyyah fī al-Islām*, ed. Nadia M. Mostafa, 1:131-222. Cairo: Cairo University Center of Political Research and Studies, 2000.

Abdelwanees, Ahmad et al. *Al-Madākhil al-Manhājiyyah li al-Baḥth fī al-ʿAlaqāt al-Dawliyyah fī al-Islām* [Methodological Introductions for the Study of International Relations in Islam]. Vol. 3. Cairo: International Institute of Islamic Thought, 1996.

—. *Al-Uṣūl al-ʿĀmah li al-ʿAlaqāt al-Dawliyyah fī al-Islām fī Waqt al-Silm* [General Foundations of International Relations in Islam in the Time of Peace]. Vol. 5. Cairo: International Institute of Islamic Thought, 1996.

Abdulrahman, Shareef. *Naẓariyat al-Niẓām wa Dirāsat al-Taghiyīr al-Dawlī* [Systems Theory and the Study of International Change]. Master's thesis, Cairo University, 2003.

Abou Samra, Amira. *Al-Buʿd al-Miʿyārī li Istikhdām al-Quwah al-ʿAskariyyah: Dirāsah Muqāranah fī Ishāmāt Naẓriyyah Naqdiyyah* [The Standard Dimension of the Use of Military Force: A Comparative Study of the Contributions of a Critical Theory]. In *Al-ʿAlāqāt al-Dawliyyah fī ʿĀlim Mutaghayyir: Manẓūrāt wa Madākhil Muqāranah* [International Relations in a Changing World: Comparative Paradigms and Approaches], edited by Nadia Mostafa, pp. 1628-1734. Cairo: Hadara Center for Political Studies, 2016.

—. *Madākhil al-Taḥlīl al-Thaqāfī lī Dirāsat al-Ẓawāhir al-Siyāsiyyah wa al-Ijtimāʿiyyah: al-Munṭaliqāt wa al-Mafāhīm fī al-ʿUlūm al-Ijtimāʿiyyah wa al-Siyāsiyyah* [The Cultural Analysis Approach to the Study of Political and Social Phenomena: Origins, Fields, and Concepts in Social and Political Sciences]. Cairo: Cairo University Faculty of Economics and Political Science, 2011.

—. *Mafhūm al-ʿĀlamiyyah fī al-ʿAlaqāt al-Dawliyyah: Dirāsah Muqāranah Ishāmāt Naẓriyyah* [The Concept of Universality in International Relations: A Comparative Study of the Contributions of a Critical Theory]. PhD diss., Cairo University, 2014.

Abou-Zeid, Fatema. "Al-ʿAmaliyāt al-Dawliyyah min Manẓūrāt Muqāranah" [International Processes in Comparative Paradigms]. In *Al-ʿAlāqāt al-Dawliyyah fī ʿĀlim Mutaghayyir: Manẓūrāt wa Madākhil Muqāranah* [International Relations in a Changing World: Comparative Paradigms and Approaches], edited by Nadia Mostafa, pp. 1104-1202. Cairo: Hadara Center for Political Studies, 2016.

Abou-Zeid, Ola. *Al-Dawlah al-ʿAbāsiyyah: Min al-Takhallī ʿan Siyāsāt al-Fatḥ ilā al-Suqūṭ* [The Abbasid Caliphate: From Abandoning Policies of Conquest to its Downfall (750-1258 CE)]. Vol. 9. Cairo: International Institute of Islamic Thought, 1996.

—. *Al-Dawlah al-Umawiyyah: Dawlat al-Futūḥāt* [The Umayyad Caliphate: The Age of Conquest (661-750 CE)]. Vol. 8. Cairo: International Institute of Islamic Thought, 1996.

Abu Atlah, Khadija. *Al-Islām wa al-ʿAlāqāt al-Dawliyyah fī al-Salām wa al-Ḥarb* [Islam and International Relations at Peace and War]. Cairo: Dār al-Maʿārif, 1983.

Abu Rabie, Ibrahim. "Al-ʿAwlamah: Hal min Radd Islāmī Muʿāṣir?" [Globalization: Is There a Contemporary Islamic Response?]. *Majalet Islāmiyyah al-Maʿrifah* 6, no. 21 (July 2000): pp. 9-44.

Abu Shareeaa, Ismail. *Naẓariyyat al-Ḥarb fī al-Sharīʿah al-Islāmiyyah* [War Theory in Islamic Law]. Kuwait: n. p., 1981.

AbuSulayman, AbdulHamid. *Al-Ru'yah al-Kawniyyah al-Ḥaḍāriyyah al-Qur'āniyyah al-Munṭalaq al-Asās li al-Iṣlāḥ al-Insānī* [The Quranic, Civilizational Worldview as the Key Starting Point of Human Reform]. Cairo: International Institute of Islamic Thought and Dār al-Salām for Printing, Publication, and Distribution, 2009.

—. *Towards an Islamic Theory of International Relations: New Directions for Methodology and Thought.* Translated by Nasser Albreik. Herndon, VA: International Institute of Islamic Thought, 1992.

Abu Talib, Hassan. "Naḥū ʿĀlam bidūn Haymanah Gharbiyyah" [Towards a World without Western Hegemony]. *Majalat al-Siyāsiyyah al-Dawliyyah* [Journal of International Politics], no. 202 (December 2015).

Abu Zahra, Imam Muhammad. *Al-ʿAlāqāt al-Dawliyyah fī al-Islām* [International Relations in Islam]. Cairo: Dār al-Fikr al-ʿArabī, 1980.

Abul-Fadl, Mona. "Contemporary Social Theory: Towards Tawḥīdī Projections in the Principles of Theorization and the Need for an Alternative." *Islamiyyat Al-Maʿrifah* 2, no. 6 (September 1996): pp. 69-109.

—. "Islamization as a Force of Global Cultural Renewal: Relevance of *Tawḥīdī* Episteme to Modernity." *The American Journal of Islamic Social Sciences* 5, no. 2 (December 1988): p. 163.

—. "Islamization as a Force of Global Renewal." *American Journal of Islamic Social Sciences* 5, no. 2 (Spring 1988).

—. "Naḥū Manhājiyyah li al-Taʿāmul maʿ Maṣādir al-Tanẓīr al-Islāmī: Bayn al-Muqadimāt wa al-Muqawanāt" [Towards an Islamic Methodology of Dealing with Sources of Islamic Theorizing: Between Introductions and Capabilities]. In *Al-Manhājiyyah al-Islāmiyyah*, no. 13. Cairo: International Institute of Islamic Thought, 1996.

—. "Paradigms in Political Science Revisited." *The American Journal of Islamic Social Sciences* 6, no. 1 (September 1989): pp. 1-15.

—. *Al-Ummah al-Quṭb: Naḥū Ta'ṣīl Minhājī li Mafhūm al-Ummah fī al-Islām* [The Nation as the Pole: Towards a Methodological Rooting of the Concept of the Nation in Islam]. Cairo: Maktabat al-Shurūq al-Dawliyyah, 2005.

—. *Where East Meets West: The West on the Agenda of the Islamic Revival.* Herndon, VA: International Institute of Islamic Thought, 1992.

Abul-Fadl, Mona and Nadia Mahmoud Mostafa, eds. *Al-Ta'ṣīl al-Naẓrī li al-Dirāsāt al-Ḥaḍāriyyah: al-ʿAlāqāt bayn al-Ḥaḍārah wa al-Thaqāfah wa al-Dīn* [Theoretical Rooting of Civilizational Studies: Relationships among Civilization, Culture, and Religion]. Vol. 4. Cairo: Cairo University Program of Civilizational Studies and the Dialogue of Cultures; Damascus: Dār al-Fikr, 2008.

Acharya, Amitav and Barry Buzan. *Non-Western International Relations Theory: Perspectives on and beyond Asia.* London; New York: Routledge, 2010.

—. *The Making of Global International Relations: Origins and Evolution of IR at its Centenary.* Cambridge: Cambridge University Press, 2019.

Adams, Robert. "A New Age in International Relations." *International Relations* 67, no. 3, (July 1991).

Afifi, Muhammad Alsadiq. *Al-Islām wa al-ʿAlāqāt al-Dawliyyah* [Islam and International Relations]. Beirut: Dār Iqra', 1986.

—. *Al-Mujtamiʿ al-Islāmī wa al-ʿAlāqāt al-Dawliyyah* [Islamic Society and International Relations]. Cairo: Maktabat al-Khānkhī, n. d.

Ahmad, Ahmad Youssef, ed. *Al-Waṭan al-ʿArabī wa al-Taghayyirāt al-ʿĀlamiyyah* [The Arab World and Global Changes]. Cairo: Institute of Arab Research and Studies, 1991.

Ahmed, Akbar. "Ibn Khaldūn's Understanding of Civilizations and the Dilemmas of Islam and the West Today." *Middle East Journal* 56, no. 1 (January 2002).

Ahmed, Khurshid. "Introduction." In *Muslim Civilization: The Causes of Decline and the Need for Reform*, M. Umer Chapra. Leicestershire, UK: The Islamic Foundation, 2008.

Akram, Ejaz. "Religion as the Source of Reconciliations among Civilizations." *American Journal of Islamic Social Sciences (AJISS)* 19, no. 2 (Spring 2001).

Ali, Khalid Hanafi. "Ayy Dawr li al-Shabakāt fi Taghiyīr ʿĀlamanā" [What is the Role of Networks in Changing Our World?]. *Ittijāhāt Naẓariyyah* [Theoretical Approaches], no. 203 (October 2016).

Aljandali, Abdulnasser. "Al-Manẓūmah al-Qiyamiyyah li al-Niẓām al-Dawlī baʿd al-Ḥarb al-Bāridah" [The Normative System of World Order after the Cold War]. *Majalat al-Siyāsiyyah al-Dawliyyah* [Journal of International Politics], no. 200 (April 2015).

Almutadayyin, Abdellatif. *Imārat al-Taghallub fī al-Fikr al-Siyāsī al-Islāmī* [Emirate of the Conqueror in Islamic Political Thought]. Master's thesis, Cairo University, 1998.

Alqadi, Ahmad Arafat. "Al-Ḥaḍārāt, Ḥiwār am Ṣirāʿ: Ru'yah Islāmiyyah" [Civilizations, Dialogue or Clash: An Islamic View]. *Majalat al-Islām al-Yawm* [Journal of Islam Today], no. 19 (2002).

Alshami, Ali. *Al-Ḥaḍārah wa al-Niẓām al-ʿĀlamī: Uṣūl al-ʿĀlamiyyah fī Ḥaḍāratay al-Islām wa al-Gharb* [Civilization and World Order: Global Origins in Islamic and Western Civilizations]. Beirut: Dār al-Insāniyyah, 1995.

al-Alwani, Taha Jabir. "Al-Qiyam bayn al-Ru'yah al-Islāmiyyah wa al-Ru'yah al-Gharbiyyah fī Manhaj al-Maʿrifī al-Qur'ānī" [Norms between the Islamic Vision and the Western Vision in the Quranic Epistemological Method]. In *Al-Qiyam fī al-Ẓāhirah al-Ijtimāʿiyyah* [Norms in the Social Phenomenon], edited by Nadia Mahmoud Mostafa et al., pp. 103-147. Cairo: Cairo University Center for Civilizational Studies and Dialogue of Cultures and Hadara Center for Political Studies, 2012.

Amara, Muhammad. "ʿIlm al-Sunan al-Ilāhiyyah ʿind al-Imām Muḥammad ʿAbduh" [The Discipline of Divine Canons According to Imam Muhammad Abduh]. In *Mafhūm al-Sunan al-Rabāniyyah: Min al-Fihm ilā al-Taskhīr—Dirāsah fī Ḍaw` al-Qur'ān al-Karīm* [The Concept of Divine Canons: From Understanding to Predestination—A Study in the Light of the Holy Quran]. Cairo: Maktaba al-Shurūq al-Dawliyyah, 2006.

—. *Maʿrakat al-Muṣṭalaḥāt bayn al-Gharb wa al-Islām* [The War of Concepts between the West and Islam]. Cairo: Nahdat Miṣr for Printing, Publication, and Distribution, 2004.

—. *Maqāl fī ʿIlm al-Sunan al-Ilahiyyah al-Kawniyyah wa al-Ijtimāʿiyyah* [An Essay on the Discipline of Universal and Social Divine Canons]. Cairo: Dār al-Salām, 2009.

Amezian, Mohammed. *Al-Manhaj al-Ijtimāʿī: Bayn al-Waḍʿiyyah wa al-Miʿyāriyyah* [Social Methods: Between Positivism and Normativism]. Herndon, VA: International Institute of Islamic Thought, 1981.

An-Na'im, Abdullahi. "Religion and Global Civil Society: Inherent Incompatibility or Synergy and Interdependence?" In *Global Civil Society Report*, edited by G. Marlies, M. Kaldor and H. Anheier, pp. 55-74. Oxford: Oxford University, 2002.

Arif, Nasr. *Fī Maṣādir Dirāsat al-Turāth al-Siyāsī al-Islāmī* [On the Sources of Studying Islamic Political Heritage]. Herndon, VA: International Institute of Islamic Thought, 1993.

—. "Muqadimah" [Introduction]. In *Qaḍāyā al-Manhājiyyah fī al-ʿUlūm al-Islāmiyyah wa al-Ijtimāʿiyyah* [Issues of Methodology in Islamic and Social Sciences], edited by Nasr Arif, pp. 7-15. Cairo: International Institute of Islamic Thought, 1996.

—. *Naẓriyyāt al-Siyāsah al-Maqāranah wa Minhājiyyat Dirāsat al-Naẓm al-Siyāsiyyah al-ʿArabiyyah: Maqārabah Ibstimūlūjiyyah* [Theories of Comparative Politics and the Methodology of Studying Arab Political Systems: An Epistemological Comparison]. Virginia: School of Islamic and Social Sciences, 1998.

al-Armanazi, Najib. *Al-Shariʿ al-Dawlī fī al-Islām* [International Law in Islam]. Cairo: Maṭbaʿat Ibn Zaydūn, 1930.

Arnold, Thomas. *The Preaching of Islam: A History of the Propagation of the Muslim Faith*. Cairo: Maktabat al-Nahḍah al-Miṣriyyah, 1970.

Ata, Abdel Khabeer. "Al-Buʿd al-Dīnī fī Dirāsat al-ʿAlāqāt al-Dawliyyah (Dirāsat fī Taṭawur al-Ḥaql): ʿAmaliyat al-Ta'ṣīl al-Ḥaḍārī li Dawr al-Buʿd al-Dīnī fī Dirāsat al-ʿAlāqāt al-Dawliyyah" [The Religious Dimension in Studying International Relations (A Study in the

Development of the Field): The Process of the Civilizational Rooting of the Role of the Religious Dimension in Studying International Relations]. In *Madākhil al-Taḥlīl al-Thaqāfī lī Dirāsat al-Ẓawāhir al-Siyāsiyyah wa al-Ijtimāʿiyyah: al-Munṭaliqāt wa al-Mafāhīm fī al-ʿUlūm al-Ijtimāʿiyyah wa al-Siyāsiyyah* [The Cultural Analysis Approach to the Study of Political and Social Phenomena: Origins, Fields, and Concepts in Social and Political Sciences], edited by Nadia M. Mostafa and Amira Abou Samra, pp. 201-238. Cairo: Cairo University, Faculty of Economics and Political Science, Department of Political Science, 2011.

—. "Tajribat al-Jāmiʿah al-Islāmiyyah fī Mālīziyā fī Tadrīs al-ʿUlūm al-Siyāsiyyah min Manẓūr al-Takāmul bayn al-Ijtimāʿiyyah wa bayn al-ʿUlūm al-Sharʿiyyah" [The Experience of the Islamic University in Malaysia in Teaching Political Science from the Perspective of the Integration between Social Sciences and Religious Studies]. In *Namādhij ʿĀlamiyyah fī Tadrīs al-ʿUlūm al-Siyāsiyyah* [Global Examples in Teaching Political Science], edited by Mostafa Manjoud, pp. 171-207. Cairo: Cairo University, 2002.

Awni, Malik et al. *Al-Aman al-Iqlīmī: al-Muʿādalāt al-Mutaghayyirah li al-Taʿāwun al-Amnī wa Mustaqbal al-Niẓām al-Dawlī* [Regional Security: Changing Equations of Security Cooperation and the Future of World Order]. "Taḥawalāt al-Istirātījiyyah" [Strategic Transformations], no. 205 (Jul 2016).

—. "Intiṣār al-Wāqiʿiyyah: Asāṭīr al-Taʿāwun al-Dawlī fī Idārat al-Taghiyīr al-ʿĀlamī" [The Triumph of Realism: Myths of International Cooperation in Managing Global Change]. *Majalat al-Siyāsah al-Dawliyyah* (June 2015).

—. "Mā baʿd al-Tafakkuk: Hal Intahat Ṣalāḥiyat al-Sharq al-Awsaṭ?" [Post-Deconstruction: Has the Middle East Expired?]. In *Taḥawalāt al-Istirātījiyyah* [Strategic Transformations], no. 203, (January 2016).

Badr-Eddin, Ikram, Nadia M. Mostafa and Amal Hamada, eds. *Al-Thawrah al-Miṣriyyah wa Dirāsat al-ʿUlūm al-Siyāsiyyah* [Egyptian Revolution and the Study of Political Science]. Cairo: Cairo University Faculty of Economics and Political Science and the Arab Center for Political Research and Policy Study, 2011.

Badran, Wadoudah. "Dirāsat al-ʿAlāqāt al-Dawliyyah fī al-Adabiyyāt al-Gharbiyyah wa Baḥth al-ʿAlāqāt al-Dawliyyah fī al-Islām" [Study of International Relations in Western Literature and the Project of International Relations in Islam]. In *Al-Muqadimmah al-ʿĀmah li Mashrūʿ al-ʿAlāqāt al-Dawliyyah fī al-Islām* [General Introduction to the Project of International Relations in Islam]. Vol. 1, edited by Nadia

M. Mostafa, pp. 79-131. Cairo: International Institute of Islamic Thought, 1996.

—. "Al-Ruʿā al-Mukhtalifah li al-Niẓām al-ʿĀlimī al-Jadīd" [Different Perspectives on the World Order]. In *Al-Niẓām al-Dawlī al-Jadīd* [The New International Order], edited by Mohammed Elsayed Selim. Cairo: Cairo University Center for Political Research and Studies, 1994.

—. *Waḍʿ al-Duwal al-Islāmiyyah fī al-Niẓām al-Dawlī fī Aʿqāb Suqūṭ al-Khilāfah* [The Position of Islamic States in the International Order after the Fall of the Caliphate (1924-1991)]. Vol. 12. Cairo: International Institute of Islamic Thought, 1996.

Barhouma, Issa. "Ḥiwār Ḥaḍārāt am Ṣirāʿ?: Nahū Ru'yah Mutawāzinah li al-Taʿāyush" [A Dialogue or Clash of Civilizations? Towards a Balanced Vision of Coexistence]. *Majalat al-Islāmiyyah al -Maʿrifah* 12, no. 46-47 (January 2007).

Barlas, Asma. "Revising Islamic Universalism." In *Contemporary Islam: Dynamic Not Static*, edited by Abdul Aziz Said, Mohammed Abu-Nimer and Meena Sharify-Funk. London; New York: Routledge, 2006.

Basha, Ahmad-Fouad et al. *Al-Manhājiyyah al-Islāmiyyah* [The Islamic Methodology]. Cairo: Markaz al-Dirāsāt al-Maʿrifiyyah wa Dār al-Islām, 2010.

Basheer, Muhammad Si. "Naḥū Inshā' Madrasah ʿArabiyyah fī al-ʿUlūm al-Siyāsiyyah" [Towards the Foundation of an Arabic School of Political Science]. *Majalat al-Dīmuqrāṭīyah* [Journal of Democracy], no. 51 (July 2013).

Basic, Nedzad S. and Anwar Hussain Siddiqui, eds. *Rethinking Global Terrorism*. Islamabad: International Islamic University in Islamabad, 2009.

Behera, Navnita Chadha. "Re-imagining International Relations in India." In *Non-Western International Relations Theory: Perspectives On and Beyond Asia*, edited by Barry Buzan and Amitav Acharya, pp. 92-116. New York: Routledge, 2010.

Beitz, Charles R. "Recent International Thought." *International Journal* 43, No. 2, *Ethics in World Politics* (Spring 1988): pp. 183-204.

Berger, Peter L. ed. *The Desecularization of the World: Resurgent Religion and World Politics*. Washington D.C.: W.B. Eerdmans, 1999.

al-Bishri, Tariq. *Bayn al-Islām wa al-ʿUrūbah* [Between Islam and Arabism]. Cairo: Dār al-Shurūq, 1996.

—. *Al-Malāmiḥ al-ʿĀmah li al-Fikr al-Siyāsī al-Islāmī fī al-Tārīkh al-Muʿāṣir* [General Features of Islamic Political Thought in Contemporary History]. Cairo: Maktabat al-Shurūq al-Dawliyyah, 1996.

—. *Al-Malāmiḥ al-ʿĀmah li al-Fikr al-Siyāsī al-Islāmī fī al-Tārīkh al-Muʿāṣir* [General Features of Islamic Political Thought in Contemporary History]. Cairo: Maktabat al-Shurūq al-Dawliyyah, 1996.

—. *Silsilat al-Masa'lah al-Islāmiyyah al-Muʿāṣirah* [Contemporary Islamic Questions Series]. Cairo: Dār al-Shurūq, 1996.

—. *Al-Tajadud al-Ḥaḍārī: Dirāsāt fī Tadākhul al-Mafāhīm al-Muʿāṣirah maʿ al-Marjiʿiyyāt al-Mawrithah* [Civilizational Renewal: Studies in the Convergence of Contemporary Concepts with Inherited Authorities]. Beirut: Arab Network of Research and Publication, 2015.

—. *Al-Waḍʿ al-Qānūnī al-Muʿāṣir bayn al-Sharīʿah al-Islāmiyyah wa al-Qanūn al-Waḍʿī* [Contemporary Legal Situation between Islamic Law and Positivist Law]. Cairo: Dār al-Shurūq, 1996.

Boisard, Marcel. *Insāniyyat al-Islām* [Humanism in Islam]. Translated by Afif Dimashqiyyah. Beirut: Dār al-Ādāb, 1983.

—. *Jihad: A Commitment to Universal Peace.* Indianapolis: American Trust Publications, 1988.

Booth, Ken. "Security in Anarchy: Utopian Realism in Theory and Practice." *International Affairs* 67, no.3 (July 1991): pp. 527-545.

Bowden, Brett. "Politics in a World of Civilizations: Long-term Perspectives on Relations between Peoples." *Human Figurations: Long-term Perspectives on the Human Condition* 1, no. 2 (July 2012), http://hdl.handle.net/2027/spo.11217607.0001.204.

al-Braik, Nasser Ahmed. *Islam and World Order: Foundations and Values.* PhD diss., American University, 1986.

Braillard, Philippe. *Theories de Relations Internationales.* Paris: Presses Universitaires de France, 1977.

Brown, Chris. "International Political Theory and the Idea of World Community." In *International Relation Theory Today*, edited by Ken Booth and Steve Smith. University Park: Pennsylvania State University Press, 1995.

Brown, Chris, Terry Nardin, and Nicholas Rengger, *International Relations in Political Thought.* Cambridge: Cambridge University Press, 2002.

Brown, Seymon. *International Relations in a Changing Global System: Toward a Theory of the World Polity.* Boulder, CO: Westview Press, 1992.

—. "The Changing Essence of Power." *Foreign Affairs* 51, no. 2 (January 1973), p. 286.

Brummer, Klaus and Valerie M. Hudson. *Foreign Policy Analysis Beyond North America.* Boulder, CO: L. Rienner Publishers, 2015.

Brzeziński, Zbigniew. *Out of Control: Global Turmoil on the Eve of the*

21st Century. Translated by Malek Fadel. Beirut: Lebanese Company for Print and Publication, 1998.

Bucaille, Maurice. *La Bible, le Coran et la science*. Paris: Seghers, 1976.

Buck-Morss, Susan. *Thinking Past Terror: Islamism and Critical Theory on the Left*. London and New York: Verso Press, 2003.

al-Bukhārī, Muḥammad ibn Ismāʿīl. "Sahih Al-Bukhari." June 2, 2020. Sunna.com. https://sunnah.com/bukhari/81/1.

Bull, Hedley. "New Directions in the Theory of International Relations," *International Studies* 14, no. 2 (1975): pp. 286-287.

—. "Traditionalism Versus Behavioralism." In *Contending Approaches of International Relations*, edited by Klauss Knorr and James Rosenau. Princeton: Princeton University Press, 1969.

Burchill, Scott and Andrew Linklater, eds. "Introduction." In *Theories of International Relations*. Translated by Mohammed Soffar, pp. 7-50. Cairo: National Center for Translation, 2014.

—. *Theories of International Relations*. 5th ed. New York: Palgrave MacMillan, 2013.

Burchill, Scott et al. *Theories of International Relations*. 3rd ed. Hampshire: Palgrave MacMillan, 2005.

Burton, John. "World Society." In *International Relations Theory*, edited by Paul R. Vioti and Mark V. Kauppi, pp. 375-384. New York: Macmillan Publishing Company, 1972.

Carlsnaes, Walter, Thomas Risse, and Beth A. Simmons. *Handbook of International Relations*. Thousand Oaks: SAGE, 2012.

Carlson, John D. and Erik C. Owen. *The Sacred and the Sovereign: Religion and International Politics*. Washington D.C.: Georgetown University Press, 2003.

Cerny, Philip. "Globalization and Other Stories: The Search for a New Paradigm for International Relations." *International Journal* 51, no. 4 (December 1996): pp. 616-637.

Chapra, M. Umer. *Muslim Civilization*. Markfield: Kube Publishing, 2015.

Cox, Robert W. *Production, Power, and World Order: Social Forces in the Making of History*. New York: Columbia University Press, 1987.

—. *Universal Foreigner: The Individual and the World*. Toh Tuck Link: World Scientific, 2013.

Cox, Robert W. and Timothy J. Sinclair. *Approaches to World Order*. Cambridge: Cambridge University Press, 1996.

Crawford, Robert M.A. and Darryl Jarvis, *International Relations- Still an American Social Science?: Toward Diversity in International Thought*. Albany: State University of New York Press, 2001.

Dark, Ken. "Defending Global Change." In *The Ethical Dimensions of Global Change*, edited by Barry Holden, pp. 7-17. UK: Palgrave Macmillan, 1996.

Davuto lu, Ahmet. "Al-Falsafah al-Siyāsiyyah" [Political Philosophy]. In *Hadhā Huwa al-Islām* [This is Islam]. Translated by Ibrahim al-Bayoumi Ghanem. Cairo: Maktabat al-Shurūq al-Dawliyyah, 2006.

—. "Al-Namādhaj al-Maʿrifiyyah al-Islāmiyyah wa al-Gharbiyyah: Taḥlīl Muqāran" [Islamic and Western Paradigms: A Comparative Analysis]. *Islamiyyat al-Maʿrifah* 6, no. 22 (October 2000): pp. 11-34.

—. *Alternative Paradigms: The Impact of Islamic and Western Weltanschauungs on Political Theory*. Lanham, MD: University Press of America, 1994.

—. *Civilizational Transformation and the Muslim World*. Kuala Lumpur: Mahir Publications, 1994.

—. *The Islamic World in the Wind of Global Transformation*. Translated by Ibrahim al-Bayoumi. Cairo: Maktabat al-Shurūq al-Dawliyyah, 2006.

Dougherty, J. and R. Pfaltzgraff. *Contending Theories of International Relations*. 5th ed. New York: Longman, 2001.

—. *Contending Theories of International Relations*. New York: Longman, 1997.

Dunne, Tim, Milja Kurki, and Steve Smith, eds. *International Relations Theory: Discipline and Diversity*. 3rd ed. Oxford: Oxford University Press, 2013.

El-Kholy, Yomna T. *Falsafat al-ʿIlm fī al-Qarn al-ʿIshrīn: al-Uṣūl, al-Ḥaṣād, al-Afāq* [Philosophy of Science in the Twentieth Century: Origins, Harvest, and Future Horizons]. Kuwait: ʿĀlam al-Maʿrifah, 2000.

Elmessiri, Abdelwahab. "Fiqh al-Taḥayuz" [The Fiqh of Bias]. In *Ishkāliyyāt al-Taḥayuz* [The Problematic of Bias], edited by Abdelwahab Elmessiri. Vol. 1. Cairo: International Institute of Islamic Thought, 1995.

—. "Al-Namādhaj al-Maʿrifiyyah al-Idrākiyyah wa al-Taḥlīliyyah" [Cognitive and Analytical Paradigms]. In *Al-Manhājiyyah al-Islāmiyyah* [Islamic Methodology], edited by Ahmad-Fouad Basha et al. Vol. 2, pp. 795-816. Cairo: Markaz al-Dirāsāt al-Maʿrifiyyah wa Dār al-Islām, 2010.

Elshtain, Jean Bethke. "International Politics and Political Theory." In, *International Relation Theory Today*, edited by Ken Booth and Steve Smith, pp. 263 -279. University Park: Pennsylvania State University Press, 1995.

Elwi, Mostafa. "Al-Ḥarb ʿalā al-ʿIrāq wa Azmat al-Tanẓīr fī al-ʿAlaqāt al-Dawliyyah" [The War on Iraq and the Crisis of Theorizing in International Relations]. In *ʿIlm al-Siyāsah: Murājaʿāt Naẓriyyah wa Manhājiyyah* [Political Science: Theoretical and Methodological Revisions], edited by Nadia Mostafa. Cairo University: Department of Political Science, 2004.

Esposito, John. *Unholy War: Terror in the Name of Islam*. Oxford: Oxford University Press, 2002.

Ezzat, Heba Raouf. "Glocalized Democracy and the Challenge of Comprehensive Security." December 29, 2005. http://www.islamonline.net/servlet/Satellite?c=Article_C&cid=1162385920367&pagename=Zone-English-Euro_Muslims%2FEMELayout.

—. "Iʿādat Taʿrīf al-Siyāsī fī al-ʿAlāqāt al-Dawliyyah: Ru'yah min Dākhil Ḥaql al-ʿAlāqāt al-Dawliyyah" [Redefining the Political in International Relations: A View from within the Field of International Relations]. In *ʿIlm al-Siyāsah: Murājaʿāt Naẓriyyah wa Manhājiyyah* [Political Science: Theoretical and Methodological Revisions], edited by Nadia Mostafa. Cairo University: Department of Political Science, 2004.

Ezzat, Heba Raouf and Mary Kaldor. "Not Even a Tree: Delegitimizing Violence and the Prospects for Pre-emptive Civility." In *Global Civil Society Yearbook*, edited by G. Marlies, M. Kaldor and H. Anheier, pp. 18-38. London: Sage, 2007.

FadlAllah, Muhammad Hussain. *Al-Islām wa Manṭiq al-Quwah* [Islam and the Logic of Power]. Beirut: Al-Dār Al-Islāmiyyah, 1986.

Falk, Richard. "False Universalism and the Geopolitics of Exclusion: The Case of Islam." *Third World Quarterly* 18, no. 1 (March 1997).

al-Faruqi, Ismail. "Introduction." In *Towards an Islamic Theory of International Relations: New Directions for Methodology and Thought*. Translated by Nasser al-Braik, Herndon, VA: International Institute of Islamic Thought, 1992.

Ferguson, R. James. "The Contested Role of Culture in International Relations." http://www.international-relations.com.

Fikry, Marwa. *Athīr al-Taghayyurāt al-ʿĀlamiyyah ʿalā al-Dawlah al-Qawmiyyah Khilāl al-Tisʿīnīyāt: Dirāsah Naẓariyyah* [The Impact of Global Changes upon the National State in the 1990s: A Theoretical Study]. Master's thesis, Cairo University, 2006.

—. "Global Transformations and the Nation-State: A Theoretical Study." In *Al-ʿAlāqāt al-Dawliyyah fī ʿĀlim Mutaghayyir: Manẓūrāt wa Madākhil Muqāranah* [International Relations in a Changing World: Comparative Paradigms and Approaches], edited by Nadia Mostafa, pp. 460-545. Cairo: Hadara Center for Political Studies, 2016.

Finnemore, Martha. "Norms, Culture and World Politics: Insights from Sociology's Institutionalism." *International Organization* 50, no. 2, (Spring 1996): pp. 325- 345.

Fox, Jonathan and Shmuel Sandler. *Bringing Religion into International Relations*. New York: Palgrave Macmillan, 2004.

Fry, Greg and Jacinta O'Hagan, eds. *Contending Images of World Politics*. London: Macmillan International, 2000.

Gaddis, John Lewis. "International Relations Theory and the End of the Cold War." *International Security* 17, no. 3, (Winter 1992): pp. 29-53.

George, Jim. *Discourses of Global Politics: A Critical (Re) Introduction to International Relations*. Boulder, CO: Lynne Rienner Publishers, 1994.

Gerges, Fawaz, *America and Political Islam: Clash of Cultures or Clash of Interests*. Cambridge, UK: Cambridge University Press, 1999.

Ghanem, Amany. "Al-Abʿād al-Thaqāfiyyah wa al-ʿAlāqāt al-Dawliyyah: Dirāsah fī Khaṭāb Ṣadām al-Ḥaḍārāt" [Cultural Aspects in International Relations: A Study of the Clash of Civilizations Discourse]. In *Al-ʿAlāqāt al-Dawliyyah fī ʿĀlim Mutaghayyir: Manẓūrāt wa Madākhil Muqāranah* [International Relations in a Changing World: Comparative Paradigms and Approaches], edited by Nadia M. Mostafa, pp. 1509-1627. Cairo: Hadara Center for Political Studies, 2016.

Ghanem, Amany and Amira Abou Samra. "Al-Thawrah wa Naẓariyyat al-ʿAlāqāt al-Dawliyyah" [The Revolution and International Relations Theory]. In *Al-ʿAlāqāt al-Dawliyyah fī ʿĀlim Mutaghayyir: Manẓūrāt wa Madākhil Muqāranah* [International Relations in a Changing World: Comparative Paradigms and Approaches], edited by Nadia Mostafa, pp. 1891-1944. Cairo: Hadara Center for Political Studies, 2016.

Ghanem, Ibrahim al-Bayoumi. "Al-ʿĀmah li al-Naẓariyyah al-Islāmiyyah fī al-ʿAlāqāt al-Dawliyyah" [General Principles of the Islamic Theory of International Relations]. *Majalet al-Muslim al-Muʿāṣir* [Journal of the Contemporary Muslim], no. 100 (July 2001).

—. "Taqrīr Khitāmī: Itijāhāt Qaḍāyā Munāqashah" [A Closing Report: Approaches and Discussion Issues]. In *Ḥālat Tajdīd al-Khiṭāb al-Dīnī fī Miṣr* [The State of the Renewal of Religious Discourse in Egypt], edited by Nadia M. Mostafa and Ibrahim al-Bayoumi Ghanem, pp. 799-828. Cairo: Center of Political Research and Studies, 2006.

Ghanem, Ibrahim al-Bayoumi et al. *Binā' al-Mafāhīm: Dirāsah Maʿrifiyyah wa Namādhij Taṭbīqiyyah* [*Construction of Concepts: An Epistemological Study and Applied Examples*]. Cairo: International Institute of Islamic Thought, 1998.

Grosser, Pierre. *Les Temps de la Guerre froide:* Réflexions *Sur l'histoire de la Guerre Froide et Sur les Causes de Sa Fin.* Bruxelles: Editions Comlexe, 1995.

Halliday, Fred. "Culture and International Relations: A New Reductionism?." In *Confronting the Political in International Relations*, edited by M. Ebata and B. Neufeld, pp. 47-71. UK: Basingstoke, Macmillan, 2000.

—. *Islam and the Myth of Confrontation: Religion and Politics in the Middle East.* Cairo: Madbouli Bookshop, 1996.

—. "The End of the Cold War and International Relations." In *International Relations Theory Today*, edited by Ken Booth and Steve Smith, pp. 39-61. University Park: Pennsylvania State University Press, 1995.

—. "The Future of International Relations: Fears and Hopes." In *International Theory: Positivism and Beyond.* Cambridge, UK: Cambridge University Press, 1996.

Hanafi, Khalid et al. *Al-Lājiʾūn: al-Ikhtibār al-Kāshif li al-Dawlah wa al-Iqlīm wa al-ʿĀlam* [Refugees: The Test Revealing the State, the Region, and the World]. "Ittijāhāt Naẓariyyah" [Theoretical Approaches], no. 205 (April 2016).

Hanrieder, Wolfram F. "Dissolving International Politics: Reflections on the Nation State." *American Political Science Review*, no. 4 (1978).

Harrod, Jeffrey. "Transitional Power." *Yearbook of World Affairs* (1976): pp. 102-105.

Hatzopoulos, Paylos and Fabio Petito, eds. *Religion in International Relations: The Return from Exile.* London: Palgrave Macmillan, 2003.

Haynes, Jeff. "Religion." In *Issues in World Politics*, edited by Brian White, Richard Little and Michael Smith, pp. 153-170. 2nd ed. London: Palgrave, 2001.

—. *Religion in the Third World Politics.* Boulder, CO: Lynne Rienner Publishers, 1994.

Hilal, Aliyyedin. "Tajadud al-Ahammiyyah: Fī Naqd Uṭrūḥat Tarājuʿ al-Sharq al-Awsaṭ" [Renewal of Importance: On the Critique of the Argument of the Regression of the Middle East]. In "Taḥawalāt al-Istirātījiyyah" [Strategic Transformations], no. 203, (January 2016).

Hirst, Paul. "Global Economy: Myths and Realities." *International Affairs* 73, no. 3 (1997): pp. 409-425

Hoffmann, Stanley, ed. *Contemporary Theory in International Relations.* Englewood Cliffs, N.J., Prentice-Hall, 1960.

—. "Obstinate or Obsolete? The Fate of the Nation-State and the Case of Western Europe." *Tradition and Change* 95, no. 3 (Summer 1966), pp. 862-915.

Holsti, K. J. "A Long Road to International Theory," *International Journal* 39, no. 2 (1984): pp. 337-365.

Holsti, Ole R., Randolph M. Siverson, and Alexander L. George, eds. *Change in International System*. Boulder, CO: Westview Press, 1980.

Hosni, Hazem. "Al-Liqā' bayn Wathār al-Ḥāsib wa al-ʿIlm al-Ijtimāʿī ʿind Multaqā ʿAṣr Qayṣar bi ʿAṣr al-Maʿlūmā" [Computer and Social Science when the Age of Caesar Meets the Age of Information]. *Majalet al-Nahḍah*, no. 1 (October 1999).

Hudson, Valerie M., ed. *Culture and Foreign Policy*. London: Lynne Rienner Publishers, 1997.

Hughes, Barry B. *Continuity and Change in World Politics: The Clash of Perspectives*. Englewood Cliffs, NJ: Prentice Hall, 1991.

Hunter, Shireen T. *The Future of Islam and the West: Clash of Civilizations or Peaceful Coexistence?* Westport: Praeger, 1998.

Hurd, Elizabeth Shakman. "The Political Authority of Secularism in International Relations." *European Journal of International Relations* 10, no. 2, (June 2004): pp. 235-262.

Husayn, Adnan al-Sayyid. *Al-ʿAlāqāt al-Dawliyyah fī al-Islām* [International Relations in Islam]. Beirut: Al-Muʾassasah al-Jāmiʿiyyah li al-Dirāsāt wa al-Nashr wa al-Tawzīʿ, 2006.

Ibrahim, Magda. "Al-Ummah wa al-ʿĀlam al-Islāmī wa al-Dawlah al-Islāmiyyah: Ishkāliyyat al-ʿAlāqah bayn al-Mafāhīm" [The Nation, the Islamic World, and the Islamic State: Problematics of the Relationships between Concepts], *Majalet al-Muslim al-Muʿāṣir* [Journal of the Contemporary Muslim], no. 137-138 (October 2010): pp. 75-95.

Inayatullah, Naeem and David L. Blaney. *International Relations and the Problem of Difference*. New York: Routledge, 2004.

Jackson, Robert. "Is There a Classical International Theory." In *International Relations Theory Today*, edited by Ken Booth and Steve Smith, pp. 16-71. University Park: Pennsylvania State University Press, 1995.

—. "The Political Theory of International Society." In *International Relations Theory Today*, edited by Ken Booth and Steve Smith. University Park: Pennsylvania State University Press, 1995.

Jørgensen, Knud Eric. "Towards a Six-Continents Social Science: International Relations." In *Journal of International Relations and Development* 6, no. 4 (December 2003), pp. 330-343.

Kamali, Mohammad Hashim. "Issues in the Understanding of Jihād and Ijtihād." *Islamic Studies* 41, no. 4 (2002): 617–34.

Khafaja, Rania. "Al-Shabakāt wa Taghiyīr Mafhūm: al-Quwah fī al-ʿAlāqāt al-Dawliyyah" [Networks and Concept Change: Power in International Relations]. *Ittijāhāt Naẓariyyah* [Theoretical Approaches], no. 203 (October 2016).

Kahler, Miles. "Rationality in International Relations." International Organizations 52, no. 4, (Autumn 1998).

Katzenstein, Peter J., ed. *Civilizations in World Politics: Plural and Pluralistic Perspectives.* Translated by Fadel Jaktar. Kuwait: National Council for Culture, Arts and Letters, 2012.

Kawtharani, Wajih. *Al-Dhākirah wa al-Tārīkh fī al-Qarn al-ʿIshrīn al- awīl* [Memory and History in the Twentieth Century]. Beirut: Dār al- alīʿah, 2000.

Kegley Jr., Charles W., ed. *Controversies in International Relations Theory: Realism and the Neoliberal Challenge.* New York: Palgrave Macmillan, 1995.

Kegley Jr., Charles W. and Eugene Wittkopf. *World Politics: Trend and Transformations.* New York: St. Martin's Press, 1983.

Kennedy, Hugh. *Al-Futūḥ al-ʿArabiyyah al-Kubrā: Kayfa Athara Intishār al-Islām ʿalā Taghayyur al-ʿĀlam* [The Great Arab Conquests: How the Spread of Islam Changed the World We Live In]. Translated by Qasim Abduh Qasim. Cairo: Al-Markaz al-Qawmī, 2007.

Kennedy, Paul. *The Rise and Fall of the Great Powers.* New York: Vintage Books, 1987.

Keohan, Robert O. and Joseph S. Nye. *Power and Interdependence: World Politics in Transition.* Boston: Little Brown Co, 1977.

Khadduri, Majid. *War and Peace in the Law of Islam.* Baltimore: Johns Hopkins Press, 1955.

Khalil, Fawzi and Fouad Alsaid. "Al-Thaqāfah wa al-Ḥaḍārah: Maqārabah bayn al-Fikrayn al-Gharbī wal al-Islām" [Culture and Civilization: A Comparison of Western and Islamic Modes of Thought]. In *Al-Ta'ṣīl al-Naẓrī li al-Dirāsāt al-Ḥaḍāriyyah: al-ʿAlāqāt bayn al-Ḥaḍārah wa al-Thaqāfah wa al-Dīn* [Theoretical Rooting of Civilizational Studies: Relationships among Civilization, Culture, and Religion], edited by Mona Abul-Fadl and Nadia M. Mostafa. Vol. 4. Cairo: Cairo University Program of Civilizational Studies and the Dialogue of Cultures; Damascus: Dār al-Fikr, 2008.

Korany, Bahgat. "A Universal International Relations Discipline?" Speech, Distinguished Global South Award, International Studies Association Convention, New Orleans, LA, 2015.

—. *Al-ʿAlāqāt al-Dawliyyah ʿalā Mushārif al-Qarn al-Ḥādī wa al-ʿIshrīn* [International Relations at the Threshold of the Twenty-First Century]. Cairo: Cairo University Center for Political Research and Studies, 1996.

—. "Taʿqīb ʿalā Baḥth ʿAbd al-Khabīr ʿAṭā ʿan al-Buʿd al-Dīnī fī Dirāsat al-ʿAlāqāt al-Dawliyyah" [Comment on Abdelkhabir Atta's Paper on the Religious Dimension of the Study of International Relations]. In *Madākhil al-Taḥlīl al-Thaqāfī lī Dirāsat al-Ẓawāhir al-Siyāsiyyah wa al-Ijtimāʿiyyah: al-Munṭaliqāt wa al-Mafāhīm fī al-ʿUlūm al-Ijtimāʿiyyah wa al-Siyāsiyyah* [The Cultural Analysis Approach to the Study of Political and Social Phenomena: Origins, Fields, and Concepts in Social and Political Sciences], edited by Nadia M. Mostafa and Amira Abou Samra, pp. 239-244. Cairo: Cairo University Faculty of Economics and Political Science, 2011.

Korany, Bahgat and Ali El Deen Hilal Dessouki, eds. *The Foreign Policies of Arab States*. Translated by Jabir Saeed Awad. 2nd ed. Cairo University: Center of Political Research and Studies at the Faculty of Economics and Political Science, 2002.

Krause, Keith and Michael C. Williams. *Critical Security Studies: Concepts and Cases*. London: UCL Press, 1997.

Kurki, Milja and Colin Wight. "International Relations and Social Sciences." In *International Relations Theories: Discipline and Diversity*, edited by Tim Dunne, Milja Kurki, and Steve Smith, pp. 14-35. 3rd ed. Oxford: Oxford University Press, 2013.

Lapid, Youssef, ed. *The Return of Culture and Identity in International Relations Theory*. London: Lynne Rienner Publishers, 1996.

Lewis, Bernard. "Al-Siyāsah wa al-Ḥarb fī al-Islām" [Politics and War in Islam]. In *Turāth al-Islām* [The Legacy of Islam], edited by Joseph Schacht and C.E. Bosworth. Translated by Mohammad Zahir al-Samhuri, Hassan Mu'nis, and Ihsan Sidqi. Kuwait: Al-Majlis al-Waṭanī li al-Thiqāfah wa al-Fanūn wa al-Ādāb, 1998.

Maghroori, Ray. "Major Debates in International Relations." In *Globalism Versus Realism: International Third Debate*, edited by Ray Maghroori and Bennett Ramberg, pp. 9-22. Boulder: Westview Press, 1982.

Maghroori, Ray and Bennett Ramberg, eds. *Globalism versus Realism: International Third Debate*. Boulder: Westview Press, 1982.

Maher, Medhat. *Fiqh al-Wāqiʿ fī al-Turāth al-Siyāsī al-Islāmī: Namādhij Fiqhiyyah wa Falsafiyyah wa Ijtimāʿiyyah* [Jurisprudence of Reality in Islamic, Political Heritage: Jurisprudential, Philosophical, and Social Models]. Beirut: Arab Network for Research and Publication, 2015.

Malkawi, Fathi, ed. *Naḥū Niẓām Maʿrifī Islāmī* [Towards and Islamic Episteme]. Amman: International Institute of Islamic Thought, 2000.

Mandeville, Peter. *Transnational Muslim Politics*. London: Routledge, 2001.

Manjoud, Mostafa. *Al-Dawlah al-Islāmiyyah Waḥdat al-ʿAlāqāt al-Khārijiyyah fī al-Islām* [The Islamic State as the Unit of Foreign Relations in Islam]. Cairo: Al-Maʿhad al-ʿĀlamī li al-Fikr al-Islāmī, 1996.

—. *Al-Dawlah fī al-Islām: Waḥdat al-Taʿāmul al-Khārijī* [The State in Islam: The Unity of Foreign Action]. Vol. 4. Cairo: International Institute of Islamic Thought, 1996.

—. *Namādhbij ʿĀlamiyah fī Tadrīs al-ʿUlūm al-Siyāsiyyah: Aʿmāl al-Mu'tamar al-ʿIlmī li Qism al-ʿUlūm al-Siyāsiyyah* [Global Models of Teaching Political Science: Proceedings of the Scientific Conference of the Department of Political Science]. Cairo: Cairo University Faculty of Economics and Political Science, 2002.

Maqlad, Ismail S. *Naẓariyyāt al-Siyāsah al-Dawliyyah: Dirāsāh fī al-Uṣūl wa al-Naẓariyyāt* [Theories of International Politics: Fundamentals and Theories]. Cairo: Al-Maktabah Al-Akadimiyyah, 1991.

Martin, Hans-Peter and Harald Schumann, *The Global Trap: Globalization and the Assault on Prosperity and Democracy*. Translated by Adnan Abbas Ali. Kuwait: ʿĀlam al-Maʿrifa, 1998.

Mazrui, Ali. "Al-ʿAwlamah wa al-Islām: Ṣadīq am ʿAdū?" [Globalization and Islam: Friends or Foes?]. In *Mashrūʿ al-ʿAlaqāt al-Dawliyyah fī al-Islām: Bayn al-Uṣūl al-Islāmiyyah wa Khibrat al-Tārīkh al-Islāmī* [The Project of International Relations in Islam: Between Islamic Fundamentals and Historic Experience], edited by Nadia M. Mostafa and Saif AbdelFattah, pp. 925-929. Cairo: Cairo University Center of Political Research and Studies, 2000.

—. *Culture Forces in World Politics*. London: James Currey; Portsmouth, NH and Nairobi: Heinemann, 1999.

—. "Globalization, Homogenization or Hegemonization." *American Journal of Islamic Social Sciences (AJISS)* (Fall 1998): p. 115.

Mazrui, Ali et al. "Globalization." *Special Issue of the American Journal of Islamic Social Sciences* 15, no. 3 (1998).

Michalak, Stanley J. "Theoretical Perspectives for Understanding International Interdependence." *World Politics* 32, no. 1 (October 1979): pp. 136-150.

Michális, Michael and Fabio Petito, eds. *Civilizational Dialogue and World Order: The Other Politics of Cultures, Religion and Civilizations in International Relations*. New York: Palgrave Macmillan, 2009.

Milad, Zaki. *Taʿāruf al-Ḥaḍārāt* [Interactions of Civilizations]. Damascus: Dār al-Fikr al-ʿArabī, 2006.

Mohamed, Ayat. *The Sacred Cow and the New Comer: A Comparative Study of Nation State and Umma*. Master's thesis, American University of Cairo, 2014.

Moore, Candice. "Multiple Perspectives on Hierarchy." *International Studies Association Convention*. San Francisco, 2008.

Moses, Jonathon W. "The Umma of Democracy." *Security Dialogue* 37, no. 4 (2006).

Mostafa, Nadia Mahmoud. *Al-ʿAdālah wa al-Dīmuqrāṭiyyah: al-Taghiyīr al-ʿĀlamī min Manẓūr Naqdī Ḥaḍārī Islāmī* [Justice and Democracy: Global Change from an Islamic, Civilizational, Critical Perspective]. Cairo: Arab Network for Research and Publication, 2005.

—. *Al-ʿAlāqāt al-Dawliyyah fī ʿĀlim Mutaghayyir: Manẓūrāt wa Madākhil Muqāranah* [International Relations in a Changing World: Comparative Paradigms and Approaches], edited by Nadia Mahmoud Mostafa. Cairo: Hadara Center for Political Studies, 2016.

—. "Al-ʿAlāqāt al-Dawliyyah fī al-Fikr al-Siyāsī al-Islāmī: al-Ishkāliyyāt al-Manhājiyyah wa Kharīṭah wa al-Namādhij al-Fikriyyah wa Manẓūmat al-Mafāhīm" [International Relations in Islamic Political Thought: Methodological Problematics, Intellectual Models Map, and Conceptual System]. Cairo: Hadara Center for Political Studies and Dar Al-Salam for Printing, Publication, and Distribution, 2013.

—. "Al-ʿAlāqāt al-Dawliyyah fī al-Islām: Min Khibrah Jamāʿah ʿIlmiyyah ilā Maʿālim Manẓūr" [International Relations in Islam: From the Experience of a Scientific Group to the Aspects of a New Civilizational Paradigm]. *Majalat al-Muslim al-Muʿāṣir* [Journal of the Contemporary Muslim], no 133/134 (2009), pp. 5-56.

—. "Al-ʿAlāqāt al-Dawliyyah fī al-Islām: Naḥū Ta'ṣīl min Manẓūr al-Fiqh al-Ḥaḍārī" [International Relations in Islam: Towards a Rooting from the Perspective of Civilizational Jurisprudence]. *Majelat al-Muslim al-Muʿāṣir* [Journal of the Contemporary Muslim], no. 133/134 (2009), pp. 121-190.

—. *Al-ʿAlāqāt al-Dawliyyah fī Tarīkh al-Islāmī Manẓūr Ḥaḍārī Muqāran* [International Relations in Islamic History: A Comparative Civilizational Perspective]. Cairo: Civilization Center for Political Studies and Dār al-Bashīr for Culture and Sciences, 2015.

—. "ʿAmaliyat Binā' Manẓūr Islāmī li Dirāsat al-ʿAlaqāt al-Dawliyyah: Ishkāliyyāt Khibrat al-Baḥth wa al-Tadrīs" [The Process of Building an Islamic Paradigm for the Study of International Relations: Problems of Research and Teaching Experience]. In *Al-Manhājiyyah al-Islāmiyyah fī al-ʿUlūm: Ḥaql al-ʿUlūm al-Siyāsiyyah Namūdhaj* [Islamic Methodology in the Social Sciences: The Case of Political Science], edited by Nadia M. Mostafa and Saif AbdelFattah. Cairo: Al-Hadara Center for Studies and Research and the International Institute of Islamic Thought, 2002.

—. "Arabic Islamic Debates on Dialogue and Conflict between Cultures." In *Human Values and Global Governance: Studies in Development, Security and Culture*, edited by Bjorn Hettne, pp. 96-191. Vol. 2. New York: Palgrave MacMillan, 2008.

—. "Āsiyā al-Wusṭā wa al-Qawqāz bayn al-Quwā al-Islāmiyyah al-Kubrā wa al-Rūsiyā: Anmāṭ wa Muḥadadāt al-Taṭawur al-Tārīkhī li al-Tafāᶜalāt al-Dawliyyah: Iṭār Muqtaraḥ li al-Taḥlīl al-Siyāsī li al-Tārīkh al-Islāmī" [Central Asia and Caucasia between Great Islamic Powers and Russia: Types and Determinants of the Historical Developments of International Interactions: A Proposed Framework of the Political Analysis of Islamic History]. In *Al-Waṭan al-ᶜArabī wa Kūmanwalth al-Duwal al-Mustaqillah* [The Arab World and the Commonwealth of Independent States], ed. Mostafa Elwi. Cairo: Institute of Arab Research and Studies, 1994.

—. *Al-ᶜAṣr al-Mamlūkī: Min Taṣfiyat al-Wujūd al-Ṣalībī ilā Bidāyat al-Hajmah al-Awrūbiyyah al-Thāniyyah* [The Age of the Mamelukes: From the End of the Crusaders Presence to the Beginning of the Second European Assault (1258-1517 CE). Vol. 10. Cairo: International Institute of Islamic Thought, 1996.

—. *Al-ᶜAṣr al-ᶜUthmānī: Min al-Quwah wa al-Haymanah ilā Bidāyat al-Mas'alah al-Sharqiyyah* [The Ottoman Caliphate: From Power and Dominance to the Start of the Eastern Question]. Vol.11. Cairo: International Institute of Islamic Thought, 1996.

—. Al-ᶜAwlamah wa Ḥaql al-ᶜAlāqāt" [Globalization and the Discipline of International Relations]. In *Al-ᶜAwlamah wa al-ᶜUlūm al-Siyāsiyyah* [Globalization and Political Science], edited by Saif Abdel-Fattah and Hassan Nafaa. Cairo: Cairo University Faculty of Economics and Political Science, 2000.

—. "Azmat al-Khalīj al-Thāniyyah wa al-Niẓam al-Dawlī al-Jadīd" [The Second Gulf Crisis and the New International Order]. In *Azmat al-Khalīj wa al-Abᶜād al-Dawliyyah wa al-Iqlimiyyah* [The Gulf Crisis and the International and Regional Aspects], edited by Ahmad Rashidy. Cairo: Cairo University Center for Political Research and Studies, 1991.

—. "Beyond Western Paradigms of International Relations: Towards an Islamic Perspective on Global Democracy." Paper presented to the International Workshop on "Building Global Democracy," Cairo, Egypt, December 6-8, 2009.

http://buildingglobaldemocracy.org/content/beyond-western-paradigms-international-relations-towards-islamic-perspective-global-democracy.

—. "Binā' al-Manẓūr al-Ḥaḍārī fī al-ʿUlūm al-Ijtimāʿiyyah wa al-Insāniyyah" [Constructing a Civilizational Paradigm in the Social Sciences and Humanities]. In *Al-Taḥawwūl al-Maʿrifī wa al-Taghiyīr al-Ḥaḍārī: Qirā'ah fī Manẓūmat Fikr Munā Abū al-Faḍl* [Epistemological Transformation and Civilizational Change: A Perusal of Mona Abul-Fadl's Thought], edited by Nadia Mostafa et al., pp. 21-77. Cairo: Civilization Center for Political Studies, 2011.

—. "Al-Būsnah wa al-Harsak: Min Iʿlān al-Istiqlāl wa Ḥattā Farḍ al-Taqsīm: Najāḥ al-ʿUdwān al-Musliḥ fī Farḍ al-Amr al-Wāqiʿ Amām al-Niẓār wa al-Niẓām al-ʿĀlamī al-Jadīd" [Bosnia and Herzegovina from Declaration of Independence to Forced Division (March 1992 – July 1993): A De Facto Situation Imposed Successfully by Armed Aggression in Front of the New World Order]. Cairo: Center for Civilization Studies, 1994.

—. "Al-Dawāfiʿ, al-Ahdāf, al-Munṭaliqāt" [Motives, Goals, and Precepts]. In *Al-Muqadimmah al-ʿĀmah li Mashrūʿ al-ʿAlāqāt al-Dawliyyah fī al-Islām* [The General Introduction to the Project of International Relations in Islam], edited by Nadia M. Mostafa. Cairo: International Institute of Islamic Thought, 1996.

—. "Daʿwah li al-Tafkīr al-ʿIlmī: al-Gharb wa al-ʿĀlim wa al-ʿAlāqah bayn al-Sulṭah wa al-Maʿrifah" [A Call for Scientific Thinking: The West and the World and the Relationship between Power and Knowledge]. In *Ḥalaqāt Tajadud al-Ihtimām bi al-Qiyam wa al-Abʿād al-Ḥaḍāriyyah fī al-Dirāsāt al-Siyāsiyyah al-Dawliyyah: Kayf? wa li-Mādhā?* [Series of the Renewal of Interest in Norms and Civilizational Dimension in International Political Studies: How? Why?], Hadara Center for Political Studies], http://www.hadaracenter.com/index.php?option=com_content&view=article&id=1047:2.

—. *Al-Dīmuqrāṭīyah al-ʿĀlamiyyah min Manẓūrāt Gharbiyyah wa Naḥū Manẓūr Islāmi fī ʿIlm al-ʿAlāqāt al-Dawliyyah* [World Democracy from Western Perspectives and Towards an Islamic Perspective in the Discipline of International Relations]. *Silsilah al-Waʿī al-Ḥaḍārī* [Civilizational Awareness Series]. Cairo: Civilization Center for Political Studies, 2011.

—. "Dirāsat al-ʿAlāqāt al-Dawliyyah fī al-Fikr al-Siyāsī al-Islāmī" [The Study of International Relations in Islamic Political Thought]. In *Al-Manẓūr al-Baynī wa al-ʿAlāqāt al-Bayniyyah fi al-ʿUlūm al-Siyāsiyyah:*

Iʿādat Naẓr wa Qirā'ah Jadīdah [Interdisciplinary Perspective and Interdisciplinary Relationships in Political Science: Re-View and a New Reading], edited by Omaima Abboud, pp. 86-100. Cairo: Cairo University Faculty of Economics and Political Science, 2012.

—. *Fī Tajdīd al-ʿUlūm al-Ijtimāʿiyyah: Binā' Manẓūr Maʿrifī Ḥaḍārī* [On the Renewal of Social Sciences: Building an Epistemological and Civilizational Paradigm]. Cairo: Dār al-Bashīr li al-Thaqāfah wa al-ʿUlūm, 2016.

—. "Ḥawl Tajadud al-Ihtimām bi al-Iqtiṣād al-Siyāsī al-Dawlī" [On the Renewed Interest in International Political Economy]. *Majalat al-ʿUlūm al-Ijtimāʿiyyah* 14, no. 3 (1986): pp. 15-42.

—. "Iʿādat Taʿrīf al-Siyāsī: Ru'yah min Dākhil Ḥaql al-ʿAlāqāt al-Dawliyyah" [Redefining the Political in IR: A Vision from within the Discipline]. In *ʿIlm al-Siyāsah: Murājaʿāt Naẓriyyah wa Manhājiyyah* [Political Science: Theoretical and Methodological Revisions], edited by Nadia M. Mostafa, pp. 423-434. Cairo University: Department of Political Science, 2004.

—. *ʿIlm al-Siyāsah: Murājaʿāt Naẓriyyah wa Manhājiyyah* [Political Science: Theoretical and Methodological Revisions]. Cairo University: Department of Political Science, 2004.

—. "Ishkāliyyat al-ʿAlāqah bayn al-Ḥaḍārāt: Qirā'ah fī Khiṭābāt ʿArabiyyah wa Islāmiyyah" [The Problematics of Relations between Civilizations: A Reading of Arab and Islamic Discourses]. *Majalat al-Siyāsah al-Dawliyyah* [International Politics Journal] (April 2007).

—. "Ishkāliyyāt al-Baḥth wa al-Tadrīs fī ʿIlm al-ʿAlaqāt al-Dawliyyah min Mandhūr Ḥaḍārī Muqāran" [The Problems of Research and Teaching International Relations from a Comparative Civilizational Paradigm]. In *Fiqh al-Taḥayuz: Ru'yah Maʿrifiyyah wa Daʿwah li al-Ijtihād* [Fiqh of Bias: An Epistemological Perspective and a Call for Ijtihād], pp. 319-394. Cairo: International Institute of Islamic Thought and Dar Al-Salam, 2016.

—. "Ishkāliyyāt al-Baḥth wa al-Tadrīs fī ʿIlm al-ʿAlaqāt al-Dawliyyah min Manẓūr Ḥaḍārī Muqāran" [Problematics of Research and Teaching International Relations from a Comparative Civilizational Paradigm], in *Al-Manhajiyyah al-Islāmiyyah* [Islamic Methodology], edited by Ahmad-Fouad Basha et al., pp. 817-914. Cairo: Markaz al-Dirāsāt al-Maʿrifiyyah wa Dār al-Islām, 2010.

—. "Jadālāt Ḥiwār/Ṣirāʿ al-Ḥaḍārāt: Ishkāliyyat al-ʿAlāqah bayn al-Siyāsī—al-Thaqāfī fī Khiṭābāt ʿArabiyyah wa Islāmiyyah" [Debates of the Dialogue/Clash of Civilizations: The Problematics of the Cultural-Political Relationship in Arab and Islamic Discourses]. *Majalat al-Siyāsah al-Dawliyyah* [Journal of International Politics], no. 168 (April 2007).

—. "Madhā Yuqadim al-Islām li al-ʿĀlam al-Ḥadīth?" [What Does Islam Present to the Modern World?]. Paper delivered at the conference of "Al-Islām wa Al-ʿAlmāniyyah wa Al-Ḥadāthah" [Islam, Secularism, and Modernity] in Cairo organized by Al-Ahram Center of Political and Strategic Studies in collaboration with the Abant Platform (Turkey), February 2007.

—. *Madkhal Minhājī li Dirāsat Taṭawur Waḍʿ wa Dawr al-ʿĀlim al-Islāmī fī al-Niẓām al-Dawlī* [Methodological Introduction for the Study of the Position and Role of the Islamic World in the World Order]. Vol. 7. Cairo: International Institute of Islamic Thought, 1996.

—. "Al-Manṭiqah al-ʿArabiyyah wa al-Niẓām al-Dawlī al-Jadīd" [The Arab Region and the New International Order]. In *Taqrīr al-Ummah fī ʿĀm* [The Ummah Over a Year]. Cairo: Center for Civilizational Studies, 1993.

—. "Manẓūmat al-Daʿwah, al-Quwah, al-Jihād: Min Mafāhīm al-ʿAlāqāt al-Dawliyyah fī al-Islām" [The System of *Daʿwah*, Power, and Jihad: Among the Concepts of International Relations in Islam]. *Majelat al-Muslim al-Muʿāṣir* [Journal of the Contemporary Muslim], no. 137/138 (October 2010), pp. 95-104.

—. "Min Kibrah Jamāʿah ʿIlmiyyah ilā Maʿālim Manẓūr Ḥaḍārī" [From a Collective Scientific Experience to the Characteristics of a New Civilizational Paradigm]. *Majalat al-Muslim al-Muʿāṣir* [Journal of the Contemporary Muslim], no. 137/138 (2010), pp. 5-56.

—. "Minhājiyyah Islāmiyyah al-Maʿrifah: Min al-Manẓūr wa al-Ta'ṣīl al-ʿĀm ilā Khibrat al-Taṭbiqāt" [Methodology of the Islamization of Knowledge: From the Paradigm and General Rooting to Applied Experience]. In *Fī Tajdīd al-ʿUlūm al-Ijtimāʿiyyah: Binā' Manẓūr Maʿrifī Ḥaḍārī (Al-Khibrah wa al-Fikrah)* [On Renewing the Social Sciences: Constructing a Civilizational Epistemological Paradigm (Idea and Experience)], edited by Nadia M. Mostafa et al., pp. 185-416. Cairo: Civilization Center for Political Studies, 2016.

—. *Al-Muqadimah al-ʿĀmah li al-Mashrūʿ* [An Introduction to the Project on International Relations in Islam], vol. 1. Cairo: International Institute of Islamic Thought, 1996.

—. "Muqadimah fī Dirāsat al-ʿAlaqāt al-Dawliyyah" [An Introduction to the Study of International Relations]. Unpublished manuscript, 1981.

—. "Muqadimah fī Naẓariyat al-ʿAlaqāt al-Dawliyyah" [An Introduction on International Relation's Theory]. Unpublished manuscript, 1992.

—. "Muqadimah Taḥrīriyyah: al-ʿAlaqāt al-Dawliyyah fī al-Islām" [Editorial Introduction: International Relations in Islam]. *Majalet al-Muslim al-Muʿāṣir* [Journal of the Contemporary Muslim], no. 137-138 (October 2010).

—. "Naḥū Binā' Mashrūʿ Istirātījī li Nuhūḍ Ḥaḍārī Wasṭī: Dirāsah Istikshāfiyyah fī Mashrūʿāt Nahḍat al-Ummah" [Towards Building a Strategic Project of a Moderate Civilizational Revival: An Exploratory Study of the Projects of the Nation's Revival]. In *Mashrūʿ al-Nuhūḍ al-Ḥaḍārī wa Namādhijahu al-Taṭbīqiyyah* [The Project of Civilizational Revival and Its Applied Models], edited by Nadia M. Mostafa and Heba Raouf Ezzat. Cairo: Hadara Center for Political Studies; Khartoum: Forum of Revival and Civilizational Communication, 2011.

—. "Nāqashāt: Li-Mādhā Inhār al-Ittiḥād al-Sūfiyitī" [Discussions: Why did the Soviet Union Collapse?]. In *Inhiyār al-Ittiḥād al-Sūfīyitī wa Ta'thīrātuhu ʿalā al-Waṭan al-ʿArabī* [The Collapse of the Soviet Union and its Impact on the Arab World], edited by Taha Abdel-Aleem, pp. 93-107. Cairo: Al-Ahram Center for Political and Strategic Studies, 1993.

—. "Naẓariyat al-ʿAlaqāt al-Dawliyyah: Bayn al-Manẓūr al-Wāqiʿī wa al-Daʿwah ilā Manẓūr Jadīd" [International Relations Theory: Between the Realist Paradigm and the Call for a New One]. *Al-Siyāsah Al-Dawliyyah*, no. 82 (1985): pp. 54-82.

—. "Naẓariyat al-Naẓm wa Dirāsat al-ʿAlaqāt al-Dawliyyah" [Systems Theory and the Study of International Relations]. Unpublished manuscript, 1983.

—. "Qirā'ah fī Aʿmāl Ḥāmid Rabīʿ ʿan al-ʿAlāqāt al-Dawliyyah wa al-Siyāsiyyah al-Khārijiyyah" [Reading of the Works of Hamed Rabie on Foreign Political and International Relations]. In *Aʿmāl Nadwah Qirā'ah fī Turāth Ḥāmid Rabīʿ* [Proceedings of the Forum on the Legacy of Hamed Rabie], edited by Amr Hamzawi. Cairo: Cairo University Department of Political Science, 2004.

—. *Qirā'āt fī Fikr Aʿlām al-'Ummah* [Readings in the Thought of the Public Figures of the Nation]. Cairo: Hadara Center for Political Studied and Dār al-Bashīr for Culture and Sciences, 2014.

—. "Al-Quwā al-Thanawiyyah wa al-Niẓām al-Dawlī" [Secondary Powers and World Order]. Cairo: Center for Civilizational Studies, 1993.

—. "Al-Quwatān al-Aʿẓam wa al-ʿĀlam al-Thālith min al-Ḥarb al-Bāridah ilā al-Ḥarb al-Bāridah al-Jadīdah" [The Two Greatest Powers and the Third World: From the Cold War to the New Cold War]. *Majalat al-Fikr al-Istirātījī al-ʿArabī* [Journal of Strategic Arab Thought] (October 1986).

—. "Review of 'Les temps de la guerre froide' by Pierre Grosser." *Al-Mustaqbal Al-Arabi*. Vol. 8, 1999.

—. "Al-Ru'yah al-Kawniyyah al-Qur'āniyyah: Waḥdat al-Maṣdar wa Waḥdat al-Tanawuᶜ" [Quranic Universal Vision: Unity of Source, and Unity of Diversity]. Paper delivered at the conference of "Al-Ijmāᶜ wa al-Waᶜī al-Jamᶜī: Fiqhan wa Sulūkan wa Rūḥan wa Thaqāfah" [Consensus and Collective Awareness: Jurisprudence, Conduct, Spirit, and Culture], organized by *Majalet Hirā'* in collaboration with Banī Imīd in Istanbul, May 26-27, 2013. http://www.hadaracenter.com/index.php?option=com_content&view=article&id=1498:2.

—. "Al-Siyāsah al-Khārijiyyah li-Charles De Gaulle fī dhul al-Jumhūriyyah al-Khāmisah" [The Foreign Policy of Charles De Gaulle During the Fifth Republic]. Master's thesis, Cairo University, 1976.

—. "Siyāsah Faransiyyah Tijāha Azmat al-Sharq al-Awsaṭ (1967-1977)" [French Policy Towards the Middle East Crisis (1967-1977)]. PhD diss., Cairo University, 1981.

—. "Taḥaddiyāt al-ᶜAwlamah wa al-Abᶜād al-Thaqāfiyyah al-Ḥaḍāriyyah wa al-Qiyamiyyah: Ru'yah Islāmiyyah" [Challenges of Globalization and the Cultural and Civilizational Alternative Aspects: An Islamic Perspective]. In *Mustaqbal al-Islām* [The Future of Islam]. Damascus: Dar al-Fikr al-Arabī, 2004.

—. "Al-Taḥaddiyāt al-Siyāsiyyah al-Khārijiyyah li al-ᶜĀlam al-Islāmī" [External Political Challenges to the Muslim World]. In *Aᶜmāl Mashrūᶜ al-Taḥaddiyāt al-Lati Tuwājih al-ᶜĀlim al-Islāmī* [Proceedings of the Project on Challenges that Face the Muslim World]. pp. 27-77. Cairo: League of Islamic Universities, 1999.

—. "Al-Taḥaddiyāt al-Siyāsiyyah al-Khārijiyyah li al-ᶜĀlam al-Islāmī" [External Political Challenges to the Muslim World]. In *Al-Ummah fī Qarn* [The Nation in a Century], edited by Nadia M. Mostafa and Saif AbdelFattah. Cairo: Hadara Center for Political Studies and International Shorouq Publishing House, 2002.

—. "Al-Taḥlīl al-Naẓmī li al-Tārīkh al-Islāmī wa Dirāsat al-ᶜAlāqāt al-Dawliyyah: al-Anmāṭ al-Tārīkhiyyah wa Qawāᶜid al-Tafsīr" [Systemic Analysis of Islamic History and the Study of International Relations: Historical Types and the Rules of Explanation]. In *Al-Tārīkh al-Islāmī wa Binā' Manẓūr Ḥaḍārī li al-ᶜAlāqāt al-Dawliyyah* [Islamic History and Building a Civilizational Paradigm of International Relations], pp. 350-420. Cairo: Hadara Center for Political Studies and Dar Al- Bashir for Culture and Science, 2015.

—. "The First War in the 21st Century: A Preliminary View." *Journal of International Politics*, 2003.

—. "The Missing Logic in the Discourse of Peace and Violence in Islam." In *Contemporary Islam: Dynamic not Static*, edited by Abdul Aziz Said, Mohamed Abu Nimer and Meena Sharify-Funk, pp. 173-189. New York: Routledge, 2006.

—. " lā Ḥurūb al-Qarn al-Ḥādī wa al-ʿIshrīn wa Waḍʿ al-Ummah al-Islāmiyyah: Ṣuʿūd al-Taḥadiyyāt al-Ḥaḍāriyyah al-Thaqāfiyyah wa Shurūṭ Istimrār Ḥiwār al-Ḥaḍārāt" [The First War of the Twenty-First Century and the Position of the Islamic Nation: The Rise of Civilizational and Cultural Challenges and the Conditions of Continuing the Dialogue of Civilizations]. In *Aʿmāl Mu'tamar: Kayfa Tawāṣul Ḥiwār al-Ḥaḍārāt* [Proceeding of the Conference on How to Continue the Dialogue of Civilizations]. Damascus: Center of Arab-Iranian Relations, 2002.

Mostafa, Nadia Mahmoud et al. *ʿAmāl Mashrūʿ al-ʿAlaqāt al-Dawliyyah* [The Project on International Relations in Islam]. Cairo: International Institute of Islamic Thought, 1996.

—. "Fī Manẓūmat Mafāhīm Naẓm al-Ḥukm wa al-ʿAlāqāt al-Dawliyyah fī al-Islām" [On the System of the Concepts of Regimes and International Relations in Islam]. In *Mawsūʿat al-Ḥaḍārah al-Islāmiyyah* [Encyclopedia of Islamic Civilization], edited by Ahmad-Fouad Basha et al. pp. 397-496. Cairo: The Supreme Council of Islamic Affairs, 2005.

—. *Fī Tajdīd al-ʿUlūm al-Ijtimāʿiyyah: Binā' Manẓūr Maʿrifī Ḥaḍārī (Al-Khibrah wa al-Fikrah)* [On Renewing the Social Sciences: Constructing a Civilizational Epistemological Paradigm (Idea and Experience)]. Cairo: Civilization Center for Political Studies, 2016.

Mostafa, Nadia Mahmoud and Hassan Nafaa, eds. *Kharīṭat Azmah wa Mustaqbal Ummah* [Transgression on Iraq: A Map of Crisis and the Future of a Nation]. Cairo: Center for Research and Political Studies & Department of Political Science at the Faculty of Economics and Political Science, 2003.

Mostafa, Nadia Mahmoud, Ibrahim al-Bayoumi, and Pakinam al-Sharqawi, eds. *Mustaqbal al-Iṣlāḥ fī al-ʿĀlam al-Islāmī: Khibrāt Maqāranah maʿ Ḥarikat Fatḥ Allāh Kūlīn* [Future of Reform in the Islamic World: Experiences Compared to Fethullah Gülen Movement]. *Majalet Hirā'*. Cairo: Markaz al-Dirāsāt al-Ḥaḍāriyyah, 2011.

Mostafa, Nadia Mahmoud and Saif AbdelFattah, eds. "Ghazzah bayn al-Ḥiṣār wa al-ʿUdwān" [Gaza between Besiege and Transgression], *Ḥawlīyat Ummatī fī al-ʿĀlam* [Journal of My Nation in the World] (2010).

—. *Ḥawlīyat Ummatī fī al-ʿĀlam* [Journal of My Nation in the World], no 1 (Cairo: Hadara Center for Political Studies, 1999).

—. *Ḥawlīyat Ummatī fī al-ʿĀlam* [Journal of My Nation in the World], no. 2 (Cairo: Hadara Center for Political Studies, 2000): pp. 11-36.

—. *Mashrūʿ al-ʿAlaqāt al-Dawliyyah fī al-Islām: Bayn al-Uṣūl al-Islāmiyyah wa Khibrat al-Tārīkh al-Islāmī* [The Project of International Relations in Islam: Between Islamic Fundamentals and Historic Experience]. Cairo: Cairo University Center of Political Research and Studies, 2000.

—. "Tadāʿiyāt al-Ḥādī ʿAshar min Sibtambir ʿalā Ummat al-Islām" [The Consequences of September 11 on the Nation of Islam]. *Ḥawlīyat Ummatī fī al-ʿĀlam* [Journal of My Nation in the World], no. 5 (2004).

—. "Al-ʿUdwān ʿalā al-ʿIrāq" [Transgression on Iraq]. *Ḥawlīyat Ummatī fī al-ʿĀlam* [Journal of My Nation in the World], no. 6 (2005).

—. *Al-ʿUmmah wa Mashrūʿ al-Nuhūḍ al-Ḥaḍārī: Ḥāl al-Ummah* [The Nation and the Project of Civilizational Renaissance: The State of the Nation]. *Ḥawlīyat Ummatī fī al-ʿĀlam* [Journal of My Nation in the World], no. 8 (2009).

Mostafa, Nadia M., Saif AbdelFattah, Amani Ghanim and Medhat Maher. *Al-ʿUdwān wa al-Muqāwamah al-Ḥaḍāriah fī Ḥarb Lubnān: al-Dalālāt wa al-Mālāt* [Transgression and the Civilizational Resistance in the Lebanese War: Implications and Consequences]. Cairo: Cairo University Program of Civilizational Studies and Dialogue of Cultures at the Faculty of Economics and Political Science, 2007.

Muhammad, Fatma Mahmoud Ahmad. *Anmāṭ al-ʿAmaliyāt al-Dawliyyah: al-Mandhūrāt wa al-Namādhij Dirāsah Maqārinah* [Types of International Relations: Paradigms and Models: A Comparative Study]. PhD diss., Cairo University, 2017.

al-Muhairi, Saeed Abdullah Hareb. *Al-ʿAlāqāt al-Khārijiyyah li al-Dawlah al-Islāmiyyah* [Foreign Relations of the Islamic State: A Comparative Study]. Beirut: Mu'assisat al-Risālah, 1995.

Mujahed, Horeyya, ed. *Taḥlīl al-Abʿād al-Islāmiyyah fī al-Rasā'il al-ʿIlmiyyah* [Analysis of Islamic Dimensions in Academic Theses and Dissertations]. Cairo: Cairo University and UNESCO, 2016.

Murden, Simon. "Culture and World Politics." In *Globalization and World Politics*, edited by Steve Smith and Ken Booth. Oxford: Oxford University Press, 1997.

Noor, Farish A. "What is the Victory of Islam? Towards a Different Understanding of the Umma and Political Success in the Contemporary World." In *Progressive Muslims*, edited by Omid Safi. Oxford: Oneworld, 2003.

Nye, Joseph S. "The Changing Nature of American Power." *American Journal of Political Science*. Volume 84, Issue 04, 1990.

O'Leary, James. "Envisioning Interdependence: Perspectives on Future World Orders." *Orbis* 22 (October 1978): pp. 503-537.

Omar, Alsayed. "*Ḥawl Mafhūm al-Ummah fī Qarn: Naqd Tarākumī Muqāran*" [On the Concept of the Nation in a Century: A Comparative, Accumulative Critique]. *Majalet Ḥawliyyat Ummatī fī al-ʿĀlam* [Journal of My Nation around the World], pp. 61-130. Cairo: Hadara Center for Political Studies, 2000.

Osman, Muhammad Raafat. *Al-Ḥuqūq wa al-Wājibāt wa al-ʿAlāqāt fī al-Islām* [Rights, Obligations, and Relations in Islam]. Cairo: Dār al-Kitāb al-Jāmiʿī, n. d.

Pasha, Mustapha Kamal. "Islam as International Relations." Paper presented at The Annual Meeting of the International Studies Association, Montreal, Canada, 2006. www.allacademic.com.

Peters, Rudolph F. *Islam and Colonialism: The Doctrine of Jihad in Modern History*. New York: Mouton, 1979.

Petito, Fabio. "Dialogue of Civilizations as an Alternative Model for World Order." In *Civilizational Dialogue and World Order: The Other Politics of Cultures, Religion and Civilizations in International Relations*, edited by Michael Michális and Fabio Petito, pp. 47-67. New York: Palgrave Macmillan, 2009.

Pettman, Ralph. *Reason, Culture, Religion: The Metaphysics of World Politics*. New York: Palgrave MacMillan, 2004.

Pinder, John. "Globalisation vs. Sovereignty? The European Response: The 1997 Rede Lecture and Related Speeches, by Sir Leon Brittan QC." European Foreign Affairs Review 6, no. 1 (2001): pp. 143-144.

Pipes, Daniel. *In the Path of God: Islam and Political Power*. New York: Basic Books, 1983.

Piscatori, James. *Islam in a World of Nation-States*. New York: Cambridge University Press, 1991.

—. *Islam in a World of Nation-States*. Cambridge, UK: Cambridge University Press, 1988.

Proctor, Harris, ed. *Islam and International Relations*. London: Pall Mall Press, 1963.

al-Qassemi, Zafir. *Al-Jihād wa al-Ḥuqūq al-Dawliyyah al-ʿĀmah fī al-Islām* [Jihad and Public International Rights in Islam. Beirut: Dār al-ʿIlm li al-Malayīn, 1982.

Rabie, Hamed. *Al-Islām wa al-Quwā al-Dawliyyah: Naḥū Thawrah al-Qarn al-Ḥādī wa al-ʿIshrīn* [Islam and International Powers: Towards the Revolution of the 21st Century]. Cairo: Dār al-Mawqif al-ʿArabī, 1981.

Rashed, Bassem. "The World according to Kissinger: How to Defend Global Order?" *Majalat al-Siyāsiyyah al-Dawliyyah* [Journal of International Politics], no. 199 (January 2015).

Rashwan, Samer. "Qirā'ah fī Dirāsāt Naqdiyyah li Khiṭāb Islāmiyyah al-Maʿrifah: Madkhal Ibstimūlūjiyyah" [A Reading of Critical Studies of Islamization of Knowledge Discourse: An Epistemological Approach]. In *Fī Tajdīd al-ʿUlūm al-Ijtimāʿiyyah: Binā' Manẓūr Maʿrifī Ḥaḍārī (Al-Khibrah wa al-Fikrah)* [On Renewing the Social Sciences: Constructing a Civilizational Epistemological Paradigm (Idea and Experience)], edited by Nadia M. Mostafa et al., pp. 147-182. Cairo: Civilization Center for Political Studies, 2016.

Reus-Smit, Christian and Duncan Snidal. "Reuniting Ethics and Social Sciences." *The Oxford Handbook of International Relations* 22, no. 3 (Fall 2008).

—. *The Oxford Handbook of International Relations*. New York: Oxford University Press, 2010.

Rosenau, James. "The Dynamics of Globalization: Toward an Operational Formulation." *Security Dialogue* 26, no. 3 (1996): pp. 247-262.

—. *Linkage Politics: Essays on the Convergence of National and International System*. New York: Free Press, 1969.

—. "Order and Disorder in the Study of World Politics: Ten Essays in Search of Perspective." In *Globalism Versus Realism*, edited by R. Maghroori and B. Ramurg, pp. 9-22. Boulder, CO: Westview Press, 1982.

—. "The Need of Theory." In *Thinking Theory Thoroughly: Coherent Approaches to an Incoherent World*, edited by James Rosenau and Mary Durfee. New York: West View Press, 1997.

Rosenau, James and Mary Durfee, eds. *Thinking Theory Thoroughly*. 2nd ed. Boulder: Taylor and Francis Group, 1999.

Rothkopf, David J. "*Cyberpolitik*: The Changing Nature of Power in the Information Age." Journal of International Affairs 51, no. 2 (Spring 1998).

Rubin, Barry. "Religion and International Affairs." *The Washington Quarterly* (Spring 1990).

Saadeddin, Nadia. "Al-Irtibāk al-Istirātījī: Iqtirābāt al-Qawī al-Kubrī fī Manṭiqat al-Sharq al-Awsaṭ" [Strategic Confusion: Approaches of Great Powers in the Middle East]. In *Taḥawalāt al-Istirātījiyyah* [Strategic Transformations], no. 203, (January 2016).

Sabet, Amr. "The Islamic Paradigm of Nations: Toward a Neo-classical Approach." *Peace and Conflict Studies* 8, no. 2 (November 2001).

Sadeq, Ahmad Nabeel. *Ishām Ibn Khaldūn fī al-Naẓariyyah al-Dawliyyah bayn al-Fikr wa al-Ḥarakah* [Ibn Khaldūn's Contribution to International Theory between Thought and Action]. Master's thesis, Cairo University, 2011.

Safi, Louay. "Muslim Renaissance: Challenges in the Twenty-First Century." *American Journal of Islamic Social Sciences (AJISS)* 20, no. 1 (Winter 2003).

—. "Overcoming the Cultural Divide." *American Journal of Islamic Social Sciences (AJISS)* 19, no. 1 (Winter 2002).

—. *The Foundation of Knowledge: A Comparative Study in Islamic and Western Methods of Inquiry*. Malaysia: International Islamic University and International Institute of Islamic Thought, 1996.

—. "The Intellectual Challenge Facing Contemporary Islamic Scholarship." *American Journal of Islamic Social Sciences (AJISS)* 19, no. 2 (Spring 2002).

Said, Edward W. *Orientalism*. New York: Pantheon Books, 1978.

Sakr, A. *Al-ʿAlaqāt al-Dawliyyah fī al-Islām fī Waqt al-Ḥarb: Dirāsat li al-Qawāʿid al-Munaẓamah li Sīr al-Qitāl* [International Relations in Islam in the Time of War: A Study of Rules of Engagement]. Vol. 6. Cairo: International Institute of Islamic Thought, 1996.

Saleh, Amani. "Qirā'ah fī Mafhūm Islāmiyyah al-Maʿrifah Dākhil al-Tayyār al-Asāsī li al-Maʿhad" [A Reading of the Concept of Islamization of Knowledge in the Mainstream of the Institute]. In *Fī Tajdīd al-ʿUlūm al-Ijtimāʿiyyah: Binā' Manẓūr Maʿrifī Ḥaḍārī (Al-Khibrah wa al-Fikrah)* [On Renewing the Social Sciences: Constructing a Civilizational Epistemological Paradigm (Idea and Experience)], edited by Nadia M. Mostafa et al., pp. 95-146. Cairo: Civilization Center for Political Studies, 2016.

—. "Tawẓīf al-Mafāhīm al-Ḥaḍāriyyah fī al-Taḥlīl al-Siyāsī: al-Ummah ka Mustawā li al-Taḥlīl fī al-ʿAlāqāt al-Dawliyyah" [Employing Civilizational Concepts in Political Analysis: The Nation as a Level of Analysis in International Relations]. In *Al-Ta'ṣīl al-Naẓrī li al-Dirāsāt al-Ḥaḍāriyyah: al-ʿAlāqāt bayn al-Ḥaḍārah wa al-Thaqāfah wa al-Dīn* [Theoretical Rooting of Civilizational Studies: Relationships among Civilization, Culture, and Religion], edited by Nadia M. Mostafa and Mona Abul-Fadl, 5:29-80. Vol. 4. Cairo: Cairo University Program of Civilizational Studies and the Dialogue of Cultures; Damascus: Dār al-Fikr, 2008.

Salim, Muhammad al-Sayyid. *Al-ʿAlāqāt al-Dawliyyah fī al-Islām* [Islamic International Relations]. Riyadh: King Saud University, 1992.

—. "Ishāmāt Kuliyyat al-Iqtiṣād wa al-ʿUlūm al-Siyāsiyyah fī Ta'ṣīl ʿIlm al-ʿAlāqāt al-Dawliyyah" [Contributions of the Faculty of Economics and Political Science to Rooting the Discipline of International Relations], *Majalat al-Siyāsah al-Dawliyyah* [Journal of International Politics], http://digital.ahram.org.eg/articles.aspx?Serial=145990&eid=306.

—. "Taṭawur al-Iṭār al-Naẓrī li ʿIlm al-Siyāsah al-Dawliyyah" [The Development of the Theoretical Framework of the Discipline of International Politics]. *Majalat al-Siyāsah al-Dawliyyah* [Journal of International Politics], no. 161 (July 2006): pp. 46-51.

Sampson, Martin W. "Culture Influences on Foreign Policy." In *New Directions in the Study of Foreign Policy*, edited by Charles F. Hermann, Charles W. Kegley, James N. Roseneau. London: HarperCollins, 1987.

Saunders, Harold H. *Politics is about Relationship: A Blueprint for the Citizens' Century*. New York: Palgrave MacMillan, 2005.

Scholte, Jan Aart. "Global Capitalism and the State." *International Affairs* 73, no. 3 (1997): pp. 427-440.

Selim, Mohammed. "Al-Taḥawalāt al-ʿĀlamiyyah wa Athāruhā ʿalā al-ʿĀlim al-Islāmī" [Global Transformations and their Impacts on the Muslim World]. In *Qaḍāyā Islāmiyyah Muʿāṣirah* [Contemporary Islamic Issues], edited by Hassan El-Alkeem. Cairo: Cairo University Center for Asian Studies, 1997.

Shafiq, Noran. *Al-Faḍā al-Iliktrūnī wa Anmāṭ al-Tafāʿalāt al-Dawliyyah: Dirāsah fī Abʿād al-Aman al-Iliktrūnī* [Cyperspace and Types of International Interaction: A Study of the Dimensions of Cybersecurity]. Master's thesis, Cairo University, 2014.

Shani, Giorgio. "Provincializing Critical Theory: Islam, Sikhism and International Relations Theory." *Cambridge Review of International Affairs* 20, no. 3 (September 2007).

Sharara, Nesma Sherif. *Al-Fikr al-Istirātījī al-Amrīkī Tajāhu al-ʿĀlam al-Islāmī: Dirāsah baʿḍ Marākiz al-Fikr al-Istirātījī* [American Strategic Thinking towards the Islamic World: A Study of Some Strategic Thinking Centers]. Master's thesis, Cairo University, 2009.

al-Sharqawi, Pakinam. "Itijāhāt Ḥadīthah fī Dirāsat al-Naẓm al-Maqāranah bi al-Tarkīz ʿalā al-Janūb" [Modern Approaches to the Study of Comparative Systems, With a Focus on the South]. In *ʿIlm al-Siyāsah: Murājaʿāt Naẓriyyah wa Manhājiyyah* [Political Science: Theoretical and Methodological Revisions] edited by Nadia M.

Mostafa, pp. 193-348. Cairo University: Department of Political Science, 2004.

Shaw, Martin. "Global Society and Global Responsibility: The Theoretical, Historical and Political Limits of 'International Society'." In *International Society after Cold War*, edited by Rick Fawn and Jeremy Herkins, pp. 47-60. Great Britain: Macmillan Press LTD, 1996.

Shawky, Ahmed. "Al-Iqtiṣād al-Siyāsī al-Dawlī: Bayn al-Iqtirāb al-Naẓmī wa al-Siyāsah al-Khārijiyyah wa al-Taghayyir al-ʿĀlamī" [International Political Economy: Systems Approach, Foreign Policy and Global Change]. In *Al-ʿAlāqāt al-Dawliyyah fī ʿĀlim Mutaghayyir: Manẓūrāt wa Madākhil Muqāranah* [International Relations in a Changing World: Comparative Paradigms and Approaches], edited by Nadia Mostafa, pp. 1204-1283. Cairo: Hadara Center for Political Studies, 2016.

Shaybānī, Muḥammad Ibn Al-Ḥasan and Majid Khadduri, *The Islamic Law of Nations: Shaybānī's Siyar*. Beirut: Al-Dār al-Mutaḥidah li al-Nashr, 1975.

Sjolander, Claire Turenne. "The Rhetoric of Globalization: What's in a World?" *International Journal* 51, no. 4 (December 1996): pp. 603-615.

Smith, M. et al., eds. *Perspectives on World Politics*. London: Croom Helm, 1981.

Smith, Steve. "Introduction: Diversity and Disciplinarity in International Relations Theories." In *International Relations Theories: Discipline and Diversity*, edited by Timothy Dunne et al. Oxford: Oxford University Press, 2007.

—. "Singing Our World into Existence: International Relations Theory and September 11." *International Studies Quarterly* 48, no. 3 (September 2004): pp. 499-515.

—. "Ten Self-Images of a Discipline: A Genealogy of International Relations Theory." In *International Relations Theory Today*, edited by Ken Booth and Steve Smith, pp. 16-71. University Park: Pennsylvania State University Press, 1995.

—. "The Discipline of International Relations: Still an American Social Science?" *British Journal of Politics and International Relations* 2, no. 3 (2000): pp. 374-402.

Smith, Steve and Ken Booth, eds. *Globalization and World Politics*. Oxford: Oxford University Press, 1997.

Smith, Steve, Ken Booth, Marysia Zalewski, eds. *International Theory: Positivism and Beyond*. New York: Cambridge University Press, 1996.

Smith, S., P. Owens and J. Baylis, *The Globalization of World Politics: An Introduction to International Relations*. Oxford: Oxford University Press, 1997.

Snyder, Jack. "One World, Rival Theories." In *Foreign Policy* (November/December 2004).

Soffar, Muhammad Basheer. "Al-Sharq fī Qalb al-Gharb: al-Badīl al-Thālith" [The East at the Heart of the West: The Third Alternative]. In *Al-Taḥawwūl al-Maʿrifī wa al-Taghiyīr al-Ḥaḍārī: Qirā'ah fī Manẓūmat Fikr Munā Abū al-Faḍl* [Epistemological Transformation and Civilizational Change: A Perusal of Mona Abul-Fadl's Thought], edited by Nadia Mostafa et al., pp. 361-395. Cairo: Civilization Center for Political Studies, 2011.

Tadjbakhsh, Shahbranou "International Relations Theory and the Islamic World View." In *Non-Western International Relations Theory*, edited by Amitav Acharya and Barry Buzan, pp. 174-196. London; New York: Routledge, 2010.

al-Taweel, Muhammad. "ʿIlm Siyāsiyyah min Wajhat Naẓr ʿArabiyyah/Islāmiyyah: Fī al-Hājah ilā Ta'sīs Maʿrifī Mutaḥayuz" [Political Science from an Arabic/Islamic Perspective: On the Need for a Biased Epistemological Foundation] (May 2014), http://massaealjiha.com/index.php/plus/opinion/104744-56-08-08-05-2014.

Tawfik, Hassanein. *Al-Niẓām al-Dawlī al-Jadīd* [The New International Order]. Cairo: Egyptian General Book Authority, 1992.

Thomas, Caroline and Peter Wilkin. "Still Waiting after all These Years: The Third World on the Periphery of International Relations." *Political Studies Association* 6, no. 2 (May 2004): pp. 241-258.

Tibi, Bassam. *The Challenge of Fundamentalism, Political Islam and the New World Order*. Berkeley: University of California Press, 1998.

Toffler, Alvin. *Powershift: Knowledge, Wealth, and Violence at the Edge of the 21st Century*. New York: Bantam Books, 1990.

—. *Transformation of Authority Between Violence, Wealth and Knowledge*. Benghazi: Al-Dār al-Jumāʿīriyyah, 1992.

United Nations. "Al-ʿAwlamah: Umum Faqīrah wa Qawm Fuqarā'" [Globalization: Poor Nations and Poor People]. *Al-ijtihād* 38 (Winter 1998), pp. 65-100.

—. "G-7 Summit Economic Communique." *Presidents and Prime Ministers* 5, no. 4 (1996): p. 12.

Viotti, Paul R. and Mark V. Kauppi. *International Relations Theory*. 5th ed. Boston: Longman, 2012.

—. *International Relations Theory: Realism, Pluralism, Globalism and Beyond*. 2nd ed. USA Upper Saddle River: Prentice-Hall, 1998.

Wæver, Ole. "Still a Discipline after All These Debates?" In *International Relations Theory: Discipline and Diversity*, edited by Dunne, Kurk and Smith, pp. 288-308. Oxford: Oxford University Press, 2013.

—. "The Rise and Fall of Inter-Paradigm Debate." In *International Theory: Positivism and Beyond*, edited by Steve Smith, Ken Booth and Marsia Zalewski, pp. 149-185. Cambridge: Cambridge University Press, 1996.

—. "The Sociology of Not So International Discipline: American and European Developments in International Relations." *International Organization* 52, no. 4 (1998): pp. 687-727.

Wagner, R. H. "Dissolving the State: Three Recent Perspectives on International Relations." *International Organization* 28, no. 3 (July 1974): pp. 435-466.

Walt, Steve. "IR: One World, Many Theories." In *Foreign Policy* (Spring 1998).

WaqieAllah, Muhammad. "Madākhil Dirāsat al-ᶜAlāqāt al-Siyāsiyyah al-Dawliyyah" [Approaches of Studying International Political Relations]. *Majalet al-Islāmiyyah al-Maᶜrifah* 4, no. 14 (October 1998).

Warleigh-Lack, Alex and Cini Michelle. "Interdisciplinarity and the Study of Politics." *European Political Science* 8, no. 1 (March 2009), pp. 4-15.

Wasfi, Mostafa Kamal. *Mudawwanat al-ᶜAlāqāt al-Dawliyyah fī al-Islām* [Code of International Relations in Islam]. n.p., n.d.

Weigel, Georges. "Religion and Peace: An Argument Complexified." In *Order and Disorder after the Cold War*, edited by Brad Roberts. Cambridge: MIT Press, 1996.

Wendt, Alexander. *The Social Theory of International Relations*. Cambridge, UK: Cambridge University Press, 1999.

Widgery, Alban Gregory. *Interpretations of History*. Translated by Abdelaziz Tawfiq Jaweed. Cairo: General Egyptian Book Organization, 1996.

Wriston, Walter B. "Bits, Bytes and Diplomacy." *Foreign Affairs* 76, no. 5 (October 1997).

Zalewski, Marysia and Cynthia Enloe. "Questions about Identity on International Relations." In *International Relations Theory Today*, edited by Ken Booth and Steve Smith, pp. 279-305. University Park: Pennsylvania State University Press, 1995.

al-Zuhayli, Wahba. *Al-ᶜAlāqāt al-Dawliyyah fī al-Islām* [International Relations in Islam]. Beirut: Mu'assisat al-Risālah, 1981.

ABOUT THE AUTHOR

Nadia Mahmoud Mostafa
Emeritus Professor of International Relations
Faculty of Economics and Political Science, Cairo University

Professor Dr. Nadia Mahmoud Mostafa was born on August 14th, 1951. She earned her Bachelor, Master's and PhD degrees in political science from the Faculty of Economics and Political Science, Cairo University.

She has held several academic and administrative positions including:

- Chair of the Center for Political Studies and Research at the Faculty of Economics and Political Science (2002-2006)
- Founder and Chair of the Center for Civilizational Studies and Inter-cultural Dialogue) at the Faculty of Economics and Political Science (2002-2008)
- Chair of the Civilization Center for Studies and Research (established in 1997)
- Chair of the political science department at the Faculty of Economics and Political Science, Cairo University (March 2010-August 2011)

She has held membership of some distinguished academic committees inside and outside Egypt. She has also been seconded to a number of Arab universities.

She has delivered lectures at several academic and intellectual institutions across the world, and has been invited to inter-civilizational, interfaith and inter-cultural dialogue conferences inside and outside Egypt (2002-2012).

Research and publication interests cover a wide range of areas including: International relations theory and the field's theoretical debates, critical approaches to the study of international relations, contemporary global issues, regional relations and policies, the religious, intellectual and cultural dimensions of contemporary international conflicts, South and North relations, global justice and democracy, global politics of change, international political economy. In addition, she has been predominantly interested in the foundation and development of an Islamic Civilizational Paradigm in International Relations throughout four decades, something that has had an impact on most of her published works during that period of time.

Since 1981, she has edited and co-edited more than 40 books. Moreover, she is the author of 17 books. She also published around 55 papers in Arab and international journals and presented about 111 papers at academic conferences and seminars, many of which are published in edited volumes in Arabic and English. She has supervised more than 40 Master's and PhD theses. She has been nominated for several awards including Cairo University's Appreciation Award (2012), and been presented with a number of awards, including the AMSS (UK) Lifetime Achievement Award in 2012 from the Association of Muslim Social Scientists in recognition of her achievements in her field of expertise.